COLLEGE MYSTERY NOVELS

GARLAND REFERENCE LIBRARY
OF THE HUMANITIES
(VOL. 360)

COLLEGE MYSTERY NOVELS
An Annotated Bibliography,
Including a Guide to
Professorial Series-Character Sleuths

John E. Kramer, Jr.
John E. Kramer, III

GARLAND PUBLISHING, INC. • NEW YORK & LONDON
1983

Library of Congress Cataloging in Publication Data

Kramer, John E., 1935-
  College mystery novels.

  (Garland reference library of the humanities ; v. 360)
  Includes indexes.
    1. Detective and mystery stories, American—
Bibliography.   2. Detective and mystery stories, English
—Bibliography.   3. College stories, American—
Bibliography.   4. College stories, English—Bibliography.
  5. College teachers in literature—Bibliography.
  6. Education, Higher, in literature—Bibliography.
  7. Bibliography—Books issued in series.   I. Kramer,
John E.   II. Title.   III. Series.
  Z1231.F4K73   1983   016.813′0872   82-48291
  [PS374.D4]
  ISBN 0-8240-9237-6

Printed on acid-free, 250-year-life paper
Manufactured in the United States of America

CONTENTS

v

ACKNOWLEDGMENTS

During the two years in which this bibliography was created, we were aided by many willing and helpful people. Ralph Carlson, Paul Curran, Colleen Donaldson, Allen J. Hubin, Joan Kramer, John Kramer, Sr., Richard Newman, Brenda Peake, and Earl M. Rogers all made important research and/or editorial contributions. Charlene Van Dyke was especially helpful during the indexing phase of the project. Gloria Condoluci typed and pasted together our various drafts, and she once again demonstrated both her secretarial skills and her patience. The bibliography could not have been begun, let alone completed, without the cooperation of the staff of the Drake Memorial Library at the State University of New York College at Brockport. George Cornell, the library's director, deserves our thanks, not only for his work specifically on our behalf, but for running a first-class library operation as well. And Norma Lawrence and Robert Gilliam of Drake's staff merit special praise. We cannot possibly thank them adequately for all of their efforts. However, we at least have the satisfaction of knowing that their work for us has now made them leading experts in the art of finding, obtaining, and processing obscure mystery novels from far "out there" in America's vast inter-library loan network.

INTRODUCTION

This annotated bibliography is intended for three audiences. First, it is aimed at individuals who find leisure-time pleasure in reading mystery novels which have plots, settings, and/or characters drawn from the world of higher education. We hope that the bibliography will direct members of this group—most of whom probably have their own real-life connections with academe—to stories of academic murder, mayhem, and detection which they have not previously encountered.[1] Second, the bibliography is designed for serious students of mystery fiction who might wish to conduct investigations of the "academic" branch of the genre.[2] And, third, it is offered as a sourcebook for scholars interested in the images of higher education which are projected through literature.[3] For the members of these latter two groups, we hope that the bibliography will lead them to mysteries which will serve their particular needs.

The bibliography has two sections. The entries in Section One describe fifty-one "professorial series-character sleuths" and cite the books in which these long-running professorial detectives appear. For purposes of this bibliography, a professorial series-character sleuth is a fictional detective who has (or who once had) faculty status at an institution of higher learning and whose detection career spans two or more novels or two or more short stories of his or her exploits collected in an anthology.[4] Section Two of the bibliography cites and describes 308 "college mystery novels" which are not graced by the presence of professorial series-character sleuths. A college mystery novel, as we defined it, is a full-length work of mystery or suspense fiction which is set at an institution of higher education and/or has as a principal character a student, a faculty member, or an administrator at a college or university. During the remainder of this bibliography, we refer to the mysteries in Section Two as "free-standing" novels, in order to indicate that the sleuthing which is conducted on their pages is not carried out by professorial series-character detectives.

As every aficionado of mystery fiction knows, the field lacks clearly demarked boundaries. When, for example, is a "thriller" or a "crime novel" a "mystery"? In constructing this bibliography we first excluded from consideration science-fiction epics, "horror" tales which stress the supernatural, and mysteries intended expressly for juveniles. Then we built the bibliography around a core of conventionally structured "detective mysteries." Thriller and crime novels were included when they had academic protagonists (students, faculty members, or administrators at colleges or universities), but only when the behavior of these protagonists was clearly influenced by the opportunities, constraints, and experiences of academic life.[5]

In order to make the bibliography as complete as possible, we included (to the extent to which we could identify them) books issued in paperback as well as in hard cover. We made no quality distinctions. Hence, the bibliography incorporates classic mysteries and (we suspect) some of the worst mysteries ever published. We also extended the scope of the bibliography across the entire lifetime of mystery fiction. The first mystery cited in the bibliography bears an 1882 date of issue. The most recent were published in 1982.[6] And we set our bibliographic net to capture all relevant mysteries originally published in the English language. The bibliography includes books by British as well as American authors, and it includes a scattering of mysteries by writers from other English-speaking nations as well.

There is no central source through which aspiring bibliographers might easily ascertain the plots, the settings, and the identities of the central characters in the thousands upon thousands of full-length mysteries published since mystery fiction's inception. Thus, the preparation of this bibliography required us to engage in several long and laborious research tasks. The first was to identify series-character sleuths and free-standing mystery novels which were likely to "fit" within our overarching definitions and subsidiary criteria. We identified "likely" professorial series-character sleuths and free-standing college mystery novels by scouring the scholarly literature about mystery fiction, by reading reviews of mystery novels in back runs of magazines and newspapers, by consulting friends and acquaintances for suggestions, and in some instances by conducting book-by-book shelf searches in libraries with large mystery collections. During the identification process we made extensive use, too, of several general bibliographies of mystery fiction. These general bibliographies did not ordinarily offer plot information or data about the occupational characteristics of series-character sleuths, but they did provide us with hundreds of titles which were suggestive of college-related plots.[7] Once we had identified prospective professorial series-character sleuths and free-standing college mystery novels, we acquired as many of the books in question as it was possible for us to obtain.[8] Then we examined them to verify that they (or the series-character detectives within them) were admissible to the bibliography. If the books passed our tests, they were read in detail for purposes of annotation. Some books were acquired from local libraries. Others were obtained from general-pupose secondhand book dealers and from bookshops specializing in mystery fiction. Some were contributed by friends and acquaintances. Those books which could not be obtained through any other means were requisitioned through inter-library loan.

Most of the entries in the bibliography include author information. The gathering of this material was made difficult both by the fact that some of the mysteries cited in the bibliography are extremely obscure (and their authors long forgotten) and by the tendency of authors of mystery novels to employ pseudonyms. In our quest for author data, we consulted the specialized reference works about mystery fiction, biographic compendia dealing with literary figures, general collections of biographic sketches, obituary columns, and an array of other sources. In some cases, authors, authors' agents, and publishers responded to direct requests for biographic materials.

The two sections of this bibliography differ significantly in format. Section One is organized into a series of fifty-one essays, each of which describes a single professorial series-character sleuth. The books in which each sleuth does his or her detection are cited, without annotation, after each essay.[9] Section Two has a more standard bibliographic structure. In this section, annotations follow the citations for each of the 308 free-standing college mystery novels.

The essays in Section One emphasize the professorial series-character sleuths' academic backgrounds, their detection methods, their eccentricities and mannerisms, and their most noteworthy cases. Many professorial series-character sleuths do most or all of their detection away from college or university settings. Special care was taken in the writing of the essays in Section One to describe any on-campus mysteries in the sleuths' rosters of published adventures.

The annotations in Section Two stress the premises and themes of each novel, and in some annotations we point out special features of the books which are likely to be of interest to the bibliography's users. During the writing of these annotations, we often had to decide which plot particulars to include and which to omit. On the one hand, we wanted to offer a sufficient level of detail. On the other, we did not want to "reveal" the solutions to the mysteries. In all of the annotations in Section Two, we freely discuss victims and detectives, and we record the books' academic settings (if any). We also note the affiliations and disciplines of the novels' major academic characters. Only in rare instance in Section Two, however, do we reveal the identity of the guilty party or parties.

The professorial series-character sleuths in Section One are listed in chronological sequence, according to the year in which the sleuths first appeared in book-length publications. The free-standing college novels in Section Two are also arranged in chronological sequence, by order of their first dates of issue. In part, we decided to organize both sections of the bibliography chronologically because no other scheme seemed taxonomically satisfactory.[10] Furthermore, chronological ordering provides an optimum arrangement for users who desire to employ the entries to observe the development of college mystery fiction over time. Users whose needs include alphabetical listings are also accommodated. The bibliography concludes with three indices. The first provides an alphabetical locator-listing of the fifty-one professorial series-character sleuths described in Section One. The second and third indices, respectively, offer alphabetized locator-listings for authors and titles. The author and title indices integrate the entries from both sections of the bibliography.

Although casual readers of mystery fiction sometimes fall prey to the assumption that college mysteries are "all the same," the entries in this bibliography indicate that the sub-genre has an immense diversity. As literary character-types, the professorial series-character sleuths surveyed in Section One are obviously descended from that illustrious non-academic detective, Sherlock Holmes. But while most professorial series-character sleuths, like Holmes, display prodigious powers of deduction, some are bumblers who resolve mysteries more through luck than through skill. Moreover, professorial series-character sleuths display a great range of personality characteristics. Some resemble Holmes in their cerebral moodiness and their often-acerbic personal conduct. But others are garrulous and acquire important clues through casual socializing. Furthermore, the professorial series-character sleuths arrayed in Section One include females as well as males in their number, represent disciplines from across the full spectrum of academic subject-areas, are old, middle-aged, and young, and come in a variety of physical shapes and sizes.

Nor are the free-standing college mysteries in Section Two all cut from the same literary cloth. Writers of general works about mystery fiction often confine their discussions of college mystery novels to the witty, reticular Oxbridge stories of the 1930s, 1940s, and 1950s. Section Two of the bibliography includes these exemplars of British mystery literature, but it also encompasses a variegated assortment of other college-mystery forms. The section contains police procedurals with academic settings, private-eye-on-the-campus sagas, professor-on-sabbatical novels, and a host of other sub-species of college-related mystery fiction. Some of the novels brought to light in Section Two blend two or more mystery modes before reaching their conclusions. Anyone who surveys the entire universe of college-related mystery fiction, as we have done, must come to the conclusion that the few existing assessments of the field do not do it justice.

An appendix, which lists fifty-five "outstanding" college mystery novels, can be found just prior to the indices. Each of the fifty-five novels listed in the appendix is marked with an asterisk at the point of its citation in the body of the bibliography. Twelve of the novels which we deemed worthy of including in the appendix have professorial series-character sleuths as their detective-protagonists. The remaining forty-three are free-standing mysteries. The appendix is intended principally as a starter-syllabus for individuals who have not yet read widely among the 632 college mysteries cited in the bibliography as a whole. All of the novels which appear in the appendix challenge their readers with especially puzzling mysteries. All have particularly well-etched academic characters, and most are set on well-limned college or university campuses. Users of the bibliography are warned, however, that the appendix necessarily reflects our own reading tastes and our own skills in making literary judgments. The appendix should not be interpreted as either a definitive or a widely agreed-upon list of "best" college mysteries.

Finally, some brief notes are in order about the creators of the bibliography. John E. Kramer, Jr., is a professor of sociology at the State University College of New York at Brockport. His professional interests lie generally in the sociology of literature, and he is currently engaged in a long-term research undertaking which is focusing upon the images of higher education which emanate from popular fiction. This bibliography is the second to emerge from his project. The first, *The American College Novel*, cites and describes 425 "mainstream" (non-mystery) novels which deal in one way or another with American college or university life.[11] John E. Kramer III is an undergraduate at Dartmouth College. His qualifications for sharing the labors on a bibliography about tales of academic lethality include both a keen interest in mystery fiction and a pressing need to employ whatever royalties accrue from his efforts as protection against the murderous fiscal perils of his own college career.

Notes

1. For an article which probes the fascination which mystery fiction in general holds for academics, see Marjorie Nicholson, "The Professor and the Detective," *Atlantic Monthly* (Vol. 143, 1929, pp. 483-493).

2. Two pioneering efforts to explore the dimensions of college mystery fiction are Agate Nesaule Krause and Margot Peters, "Murder in Academe," *Southwest Review* (Vol. 62, 1977, pp. 371-378) and Jane Gottschalk, "Mystery, Murder, and Academe," *The Armchair Detective* (Vol. 11, 1978, pp. 159-169).

3. Mainstream novels have been examined by several writers for the images of higher education which they project. See, for example, John O. Lyons, *The College Novel in America* (Carbondale, Illinois: Southern Illinois University Press, 1962); John E. Kramer, Jr., "Images of Sociology and Sociologists in Fiction," *Contemporary Sociology* (Vol. 8, 1979, pp. 356-362); and John E. Kramer, Jr., "College and University Presidents in Fiction," *The Journal of Higher Education* (Vol. 52, 1981, pp. 81-95). No one has yet had the temerity, however, to assess mystery fiction for the messages (often unflattering) which it sends forth about the world of higher learning.

4. No attempt was made to include professorial series-character sleuths whose literary exploits are confined only to uncollected short stories. Nor was any attempt made to locate and to include in the bibliography any professorial series-character villains. Nonetheless, in the course of our research we encountered three professorial series-character evildoers. One of these academic nasties, of course, was Sherlock Holmes' archenemy, Professor James Moriarty. The others were Professors Anselm Krueutzemark and Elihu Blinkwell. Professor Krueutzemark, a German chemist with an adumbrative academic history, is the inventor of "Yellow Cross gas," a terrifying compound which wreaked havoc upon British troops during World War I. After the armistice, Krueutzemark places himself in the service of various international conspirators. His creators were John Leslie Palmer (1885-1944) and Hilary Aidan St. George Saunders (1898-1951), who wrote under the joint pseudonym Francis Beeding. The professor appears in at least two novels: *The Seven Sleepers* (London: Hutchinson and Co., 1925; Boston: Little, Brown, 1925) and *The Hidden Kingdom* (London: Hodder and Stoughton, 1927; Boston: Little, Brown, 1927). Professor Elihu Blinkwell, whose academic background is also ambiguous, serves as technical advisor to Vantoms, Ltd., a London filmmaking firm. Professor Blinkwell's creator was Sydney Fowler Wright (1874-1965), who wrote under the alias Sydney Fowler. Professor Blinkwell does his dirty work in at least three novels: *The Bell Street Murders* (London: G.G. Harrop, 1931; New York: The Macauley Co., 1931); *The Secret of the Screen* (London: Jarrolds, 1933); and *Who Murdered Reynard?* (London: Jarrolds, 1947).

5. Especially vexing in this regard were "archeological dig" mysteries. These epics sometimes contain students and/or faculty members from college or universities, but the "academic" aspects of the stories are often submerged under the weight of exotic settings, elements of the supernatural, and/or considerations of ancient legends. Moreover, in some archeological dig sagas the academic affiliations of the participants are imprecise. In general, we did not include archeological dig mysteries in the bibliography.

6. Editorial work on the bibliography was completed in May of 1982, and we halted our systematic search for relevant mysteries with works published in 1981. However, in the interests of thoroughness, we included four novels published early in 1982 in the professorial series-character sleuth section.

7. Before we launched this bibliography, our own familiarities with college mystery novels were reasonably well-developed (from casual reading) but certainly not encyclopedic. It would be both impractical and impossible for us to list all of the many sources which we employed in our search for "likely" professorial series-character sleuths and free-standing college mysteries. The most useful back runs of book reviews were found in *The Armchair Detective, the [London] Times Literary Supplement,* and *The New York Times.* The most useful general bibliographies of mystery fiction were: Jacques Barzun and Wendell Hertig Taylor, *A Catalog of Crime* (New York: Harper and Row, 1971); Allen J. Hubin, *The Bibliography of Crime Fiction; 1749-1975* (Del Mar, California: Publisher's Inc. and the University of California, San Diego, 1979); and John M. Reilly, *Twentieth-Century Crime and Mystery Writers* (New York: St. Martin's Press, 1980; London: Macmillan, 1980). Despite the elaborateness of our literary detective work, we are well aware that it is unlikely that we uncovered all of those mystery novels ever published which fall within the bibliography's boundaries. Hence, while we can claim that our research procedure exhausted all of the resources at our command, we cannot claim that the bibliography itself is exhaustive.

8. In the case of professorial series-character sleuths with approximately ten or fewer novel-length appearances, we attempted to obtain all of the works in which these detectives appear. Where professorial series-character sleuths appear in more than ten novels, we attempted to obtain a suitable sample of their exploits. When we limited our acquisitions to samples, we made special efforts to obtain any novels set on college or university campuses. Insofar as free-standing college mysteries were concerned, we tried to obtain all of the novels which we had identified as "likely." Of the more

than four hundred free-standing novels which we sought, we were eventually able to acquire all but thirty-four. For the most part, the books we found impossible to obtain are older British mysteries. Because we could not verify that these thirty-four elusive free-standing mysteries fall within our definitions and our subsidiary boundaries (and because in the absence of in-hand examinations we would be able to offer no more than cursory annotations based on time-of-publication reviews), we did not accord these works entries in the bibliography.

9. In both sections of the bibliography we offer American and British first-edition citations. In the many instances where novels were published in both the United States and in Great Britain in the same year, publication data from the author's nation of origin is placed first. The citations contain, where appropriate, British and American titles, and we included in the citations any additional titles under which books were subsequently published.

10. We experimented with several systems of sub-dividing the free-standing mysteries in Section Two, and we rejected all of them. A categorization scheme involving on-campus as opposed to off-campus mysteries proved to be unworkable because so many of the novels in Section Two show their characters in both academic and non-academic settings. Two schemes to array British college mysteries separately from their American counterparts also proved to be inadequate. An attempt to segregate British works from American ones in terms of the nationalities of their protagonists turned out to be relatively meaningless because many American protagonists in college mystery novels are depicted in British locales. An attempt to set works by British authors apart from those of American writers also failed. This plan was not adopted because we could not identify the nationalities of all of the authors represented in Section Two and because some of the authors whose biographies we did obtain have lived and worked in both Great Britain and the United States.

11. John E. Kramer, Jr., *The American College Novel* (New York and London: Garland Publishing, 1981).

I.
Professorial
Series-Character Sleuths

AUGUSTUS S.F.X. VAN DUSEN (1906)

Creator: Futrelle, Jacques (1875-1912)

Augustus S.F.X. Van Dusen is a research professor at a world-famous (but unspecified) university in the Boston area. He does not have any particular disciplinary affiliation. Rather, he is a master of all known sciences, a physician, and a prodigious logician. Van Dusen is known as "The Thinking Machine." He received this very fitting title from Tschaikowsky, the great Russian chess champion. Van Dusen once defeated Tschaikowsky in a challenge match. Van Dusen had never before played chess, and in a burst of both admiration and frustration Tschaikowsky exclaimed: "You are not a man; you are a brain—a machine—a thinking machine."

In his academic role, Van Dusen is something of a maverick. He delights in proving false the orthodox theories which are accepted as gospel by the leading scientific figures of his day. Indeed, Van Dusen was once dismissed by "Hale University" for propounding new and unconventional theories of his own. Hale has now seen the error of its ways, however. It has awarded Van Dusen an honorary LL.D., a degree which the professor can add to the Ph.D., the F.R.S., the M.D., and the M.D.S. which he already possesses.

Van Dusen lives in a modest apartment on Beacon Hill. A middle-aged bachelor, he is short and stooped, almost dwarf-like in appearance. Because of his over-developed brain, he has a huge head and must wear a size-eight hat. He has a streak of bright yellow hair and peers out at the world through thick spectacles. Since his blue eyes are compressed into a perpetual squint, many of those with whom he comes into contact believe that he has a cold and forbidding disposition. In reality, Van Dusen has a puckish, professorial sense of humor. While he does not suffer fools gladly and is capable of delivering devastating verbal insults, he enjoys perpetuating practical jokes. Moreover, he likes to tease those unfortunate individuals who believe that they can successfully engage him in intellectual competition.

As a sleuth, Van Dusen employs his voluminous knowledge and his infallible logic to solve "impossible" puzzles. Most of his cases are brought to him by Hutchinson Hatch, an ener-

getic young newspaperman. Van Dusen is only marginally interested in the moral or human ramifications of crime. His
chief concern is with the mental tests which "insoluble"
mysteries present him. In fact, Van Dusen's most famous
published exploit--"The Problem of Cell 13"--a story which
can be found in *The Thinking Machine* (2) as well as in many
multi-detective anthologies of Edwardian mystery fiction, involves neither crime nor classical detection. Responding to
a dare made by several highly placed acquaintances, the professor offers to escape within a week from tightly guarded
"Chisholm Prison." His acquaintances arrange for him to be
placed in a sealed death cell, and they inform the warden
that his unusual prisoner will be attempting to extricate
himself from confinement. True to his word, Van Dusen escapes from the prison before his deadline and reinforces his
image as the world's most intelligent human being.

      Jacques Futrelle was born in Pike County, Georgia. He
began his working life as a theatrical manager but soon switched
to journalism and became an editorial writer and reporter for
The Boston American. Professor Van Dusen made his literary
debut in the final chapters of a novel entitled *The Chase of
the Golden Plate* (1), but thereafter Futrelle employed him
only in novelette and short story format. Before they were
collected in book form, most of the Van Dusen stories first
appeared in popular American magazines and/or in newspapers.
Van Dusen was seen by literary critics of the day as a worthy
cerebral successor to Sherlock Holmes, although some thought
that Futrelle had modeled the professor less on Sherlock than
upon his more sedentary and aloof brother, Mycroft. Augustus
S.F.X. Van Dusen's role in the emerging, turn-of-the-century
literary image of professors has never been systematically examined, but virtually all current-day historians of mystery
fiction recognize him as a major figure in the early development
of the series-character sleuth. Unfortunately, Professor Van
Dusen's career was cut short when Futrelle perished in the
sinking of the *Titanic*.

Augustus S.F.X. Van Dusen Bibliography

1. *The Chase of the Golden Plate*. New York: Dodd, Mead
       Co., 1906.

2. *The Thinking Machine*. New York: Dodd, Mead and Co., 1907;
       London: Chapman and Hall, 1907. Also published as *The
       Problem of Cell 13*. New York: Dodd, Mead and Co., 1917.
       (Short Stories.)
3. *The Thinking Machine on the Case*. New York: D. Appleton

and Co., 1908. Also published as *The Professor on the
Case*. New York and London: Thomas Nelson and Sons,
1909. (Short Stories.)

4. *The Diamond Master*. Indianapolis: Bobbs Merrill, 1909;
London: Holden and Hardingham, 1912. (Contains novelette about Van Dusen.)

5. *Best Thinking Machine Detective Stories*. New York:
Dover, 1973. (Contains twelve stories, ten from *The
Thinking Machine* and *The Thinking Machine on the Case*
and two previously uncollected.)

6. *Great Cases of the Thinking Machine*. New York: Dover,
1978. (Contains thirteen stories, all of them previously uncollected.)

CRAIG KENNEDY (1912)

Creator: Reeve, Arthur Benjamin (1880-1936)

Craig Kennedy is a professor of chemistry at a New York
City university which bears an exceedingly strong resemblance
to Columbia. Like Professor Augustus S.F.X. Van Dusen (1-6),
his immediate professorial predecessor in the ranks of fictional sleuths, Kennedy fights crime by applying logic and by
drawing upon his immense storehouse of scientific information.
But Kennedy's real strength as a detective lies in gadgetry
and from his laboratory in the university's Chemistry Building
he brings forth such before-their-time "marvels" as lie detec-
tors, portable seismographs, and voiceprint machines. Although
the Kennedy tales ignore the vexing question of whether the
university or Kennedy owns the patent rights to these instru-
ments (most of which the professor has either invented or perfected using university facilities), the fact remains that in
Kennedy's hands the devices prove of inestimable value in
filling America's prisons with captured criminals.
Known to his friends, his foes, and his readers alike as
"The American Sherlock Holmes," Professor Kennedy lives in an
apartment on Riverside Drive with Walter Jameson, a newspaper
reporter. Jameson, who narrates most of the Kennedy exploits,
acts as the professor's Watson. And, in Holmesian fashion,
Kennedy is propelled into most of his adventures by strangers
in trouble who visit his rooms asking for assistance. Furthermore, Kennedy styles himself a "consulting detective," and, as

Holmes before him, he sometimes takes money for his services.
But whereas Sherlock Holmes was capable of articulate dialogue,
Kennedy lacks a flair for verbal expression. Best described
as strong and silent, except when explaining the intricacies
of a new crime-fighting machine, Kennedy is seldom witty, seems
to possess only a rudimentary vocabulary, and generally speaks
in stilted, melodramatic prose.

Handsome, athletic, and thirtyish (he does not age during
his long literary lifetime), Kennedy frequently engages in
derring-do adventure and often survives extreme physical peril.
Many of his criminal adversaries are archvillains who are not
beyond employing killer robots, vicious dogs, invisible death
rays, poison gases, and other hideous evils against him. In
his battles against such blackguards, Kennedy cooperates on
occasion with Inspector Barney O'Connor of the New York Police.
And, though Walter Jameson's constant presence in the Riverside Drive apartment acts to impede his relationships with
women, in some of his cases the professor gains emotional
support from Elaine Dodge, a lovely young lady with whom he
has a sporadic romance.

Arthur Benjamin Reeve was born in Patchogue, Long Island,
New York. He graduated from Princeton in 1903 and then attended New York Law School. Instead of entering the field of
law, however, Reeve became a journalist, and during his first
years in the work world he was a staff writer and editor for
a number of popular American magazines. Craig Kennedy made
his first appearance as the protagonist of a 1910 *Cosmopolitan
Magazine* story and became an immediate favorite with the reading public. With the publication of *The Silent Bullet* (8), a
collection of Kennedy stories, Reeve suddenly found himself
one of America's most commercially successful authors. Over
the next decade the various Kennedy books which Reeve produced
sold more than two million copies in the United States and in
Great Britain, and Professor Kennedy became the hero of several
silent film serials. Kennedy's appeal began to fade in the
1920s, as more realistic fictional detectives came into vogue.
Reeve continued to turn out Kennedy sagas, but as the sales of
these epics slowed, he also wrote non-Kennedy mystery stories,
filmscripts, and non-fiction articles for magazines and newspapers. Reeve died in 1936, but Craig Kennedy did not die
with him. In 1952 the professor was the subject of a half-hour
syndicated television series starring Donald Woods.

Craig Kennedy Bibliography

7. *The Poisoned Pen.* New York: Harper and Brothers, 1911;
    London: Hodder and Stoughton, 1916.

8. *The Silent Bullet: Adventures of Craig Kennedy, Scientific Detective.* New York: Dodd, Mead and Co., 1912 Published in Great Britain as *The Black Hand.* London Eveleigh Nash, 1912. (Short Stories.)

9. *The Dream Doctor.* New York: Hearst's International Library, 1914; London: Hodder and Stoughton, 1916. (Short stories.)

10. *The Exploits of Elaine.* New York: Hearst's International Library, 1915; London: Hodder and Stoughton, 1915.

11. *The Gold of the Gods.* New York: Hearst's International Library, 1915; London: Hodder and Stoughton, 1916.

12. *The War Terror.* New York: Hearst's International Library, 1915. Published in Great Britain as *Craig Kennedy, Detective.* London: Simpkin and Co., 1916. (Short Stories.)

13. *The Ear in the Wall.* New York: Hearst's International Library, 1916; London: Hodder and Stoughton, 1917.

14. *The Romance of Elaine.* New York: Hearst's International Library, 1916; London: Hodder and Stoughton, 1916.

15. *The Social Gangster.* New York: Hearst's International Library, 1916. Published in Great Britain as *The Diamond Queen.* London: Hodder and Stoughton, 1917. (Short Stories.)

16. *The Triumph of Elaine.* London: Hodder and Stoughton, 1916.

17. *The Adventuress.* New York: Harper and Brothers, 1917; London: William Collins Sons, 1918.

18. *The Treasure Train.* New York: Harper and Brothers, 1917; London: William Collins Sons, 1920. (Short Stories.)

19. *The Panama Plot.* New York: Harper and Brothers, 1918; London: William Collins Sons, 1920. (Short Stories.)

20. *The Soul Scar.* New York: Harper and Brothers, 1919.

21. *The Film Mystery.* New York: Harper and Brothers, 1921; London: Hodder and Stoughton, 1922.

22. *Craig Kennedy Listens In.* New York: Harper and Brothers, 1923; London: Hodder and Stoughton, 1924.

23. *Atavar.* New York: Harper and Brothers, 1924.

24. *The Boy Scouts' Craig Kennedy.* New York: Harper and Brothers, 1925. (Short Stories.)

25. *Craig Kennedy on the Farm.* New York: Harper and Brothers, 1925. (Short Stories.)

26. *The Fourteen Points: Tales of Craig Kennedy, Master Detective.* New York: Harper and Brothers, 1925. (Short Stories.)

27. *Pandora.* New York: Harper and Brothers, 1926.

28. *The Kidnap Club.* New York: Macauley, 1932.

29. *The Clutching Hand.* Chicago: Reilly and Lee, 1934.

30. *Enter Craig Kennedy.* New York: Macauley, 1935. (Four Novelettes.)

31. *The Stars Scream Murder.* New York: D. Appleton-Century, 1936.

HUMPHREY CHALLONER (1914)

Creator: Freeman, R(ichard) Austin (1862-1943)

Whereas many professorial sleuths fight crime because of the intellectual stimulation which detection offers, Humphrey Challoner hunts down criminals for revenge. Challoner's beloved wife Kate is murdered by a burglar in their home, and for the next twenty years the British professor of anthropology stalks and traps the thieves of London. He does not involve the police in his work. Indeed, he keeps his activities a secret from the law. Why does he operate in isolation? Because he kills his captives, shrinks their skulls, and stores his collection of "doll-like heads" in a private museum which he maintains in his residence in the Bloomsbury section of London.

Considering Challoner's rather macabre pursuits, one might
expect him to be personally unpleasant, even sinister in demeanor. In fact, he is a friendly, almost garrulous man,
though an occasional "horrible grin" warns those with whom he
associates that he is, perhaps, not the simple, humble scholar
he pretends to be. Because his wife left him a large legacy,
Challoner has been able to retire from academe. When not
snaring new exhibits, he studies criminology and anatomy textbooks, learns boxing skills under Mr. "Slimy" Cohen (a famous
London prizefighter now turned instructor in the art of pugil-
ism), and writes narrative accounts ("museum archives") about
the conditions under which each of his specimens has been
acquired.

As a "sleuth," Challoner does not practice especially
subtle methods. Early in his crook-hunting career, he deliberately hires dishonest servants, who then invite their
friends to the Challoner abode for nighttime robberies. Lured
into the professor's trap, the unfortunate housebreakers are
soon incorporated into his grisly exhibition. Later in his
crusade against the underworld, Challoner sets up shop as a
barber in London's East End. Hoodlums and thugs are frequent
customers, and many eventually become his victims. After two
decades of his unique crime-fighting, Challoner contracts terminal cancer and dies after leaving his museum to the care of
Dr. Wharton, his physician. As Dr. Wharton discovers while
inventorying the horrifying cache, Challoner has gone to his
well-earned rest with a full sense of accomplishment. The
twenty-fifth, and last, skull in the professor's collection
is that of the very burglar who murdered Mrs. Challoner.

Richard Austin Freeman was born in London, studied medicine at Middlesex Hospital, and qualified as a physician and
surgeon in 1887. His first medical post was as an assistant
colonial surgeon on the Gold Coast of Africa. Invalided out
of colonial service in 1891, he returned to Great Britain and
combined private practice with medical service to various institutions in the London area. In 1900 he was an assistant
medical officer at Holloway Prison. Dr. Freeman began his
writing career with travel books based on his African experiences, but in the early 1900s he branched into mystery fiction.
Humphrey Challoner, who first appeared as a character in a
continuing series of stories published in *Pearson's Magazine*
in 1913, is considered a professorial series-character sleuth
for purposes of this bibliography because *The Uttermost Farthing* (32) consists of a linked collection of the *Pearson's
Magazine* stories. As every devotee of mystery literature
knows, Richard Austin Freeman's most celebrated series-character was Dr. John Evelyn Thorndike, a painstakingly precise

physician-attorney, whose twenty-one novel-length exploits
(and many story-length adventures) entertained untold millions
of readers during the first half of this century.

Humphrey Challoner Bibliography

32. *The Uttermost Farthing: A Savant's Vendetta.* Philadel-
    phia: John C. Winston, 1914. Published in Great Brit-
    ain as *A Savant's Vendetta.* London: C.A. Pearson,
    1920.

CHRISTOPHER QUARLES (1914)

Creator: Brebner, Percy James (1864-1922)

An elderly but vigorous British professor of philosophy,
Christopher Quarles is a member of the faculty at an unidentified institution of higher learning in London. Quarles'
professional interests lie in the nature of human motive, and
in the course of his research he often employs some of the
theories and methodologies which, today, are more commonly
associated with psychology. Sleuthing is Quarles' hobby. Although he uses generalized deduction in some of his crime-
fighting endeavors, his ability to gauge suspects' motivations
leads him to the solutions of his most difficult cases.
     Professor Quarles' on-campus academic duties seem to re-
quire very, very little of his attention. He spends most of
his time in his residence--a house in London's fashionable
Chelsea section--where he lives with his attractive granddaughter, Zena. All but one of the rooms of the house are
luxuriously furnished. The exception is Quarles' study. This
facility is barren except for a "cheap" writing desk. It is
in this room that the professor does his heavy ratiocination,
and it is his strong belief that pictures, books, or other
paraphernalia would only distract him from his thinking.
     Like so many other early professorial series-character
sleuths, Professor Quarles bears a significant resemblance to
Sherlock Holmes. He is an assiduous reader of newspapers, an
expert in disguises, and the possessor of a tumid ego. His
Watson is Murray Wigan, a young Scotland Yard inspector. Wigan is a frequent visitor to the Quarles household, largely
because he pays perpetual court to Zena. The inspector records
the professor's adventures and also enlists his aid in solving
those mysteries with which the Yard is incapable of dealing.
Often brusque, Quarles considers Wigan and all other "police-

men" to be his intellectual inferiors. When asked about his own immense detection powers, Quarles refers cryptically to his many years as a philosopher ("philosophy is mysterious"), and he claims immodestly to have an imagination which allows him "to bridge the interval between facts."

Percy James Brebner was a popular turn-of-the-century novelist and a frequent contributor of stories to the popular magazines of his day. Professor Quarles appeared only in story-length format. *Christopher Quarles: College Professor and Master Detective* (33) contains sixteen separate Quarles exploits. *The Master Detective* (34) continues Quarles' detection adventures through fourteen further cases. Brebner sometimes employed the pseudonym Christopher Lys. One of his Lys novels barely escaped being included in the second section of this bibliography. First published in Great Britain as *The Gate of Temptation* (London: John Long, 1920), the book was subsequently issued in the United States as *The Ivory Disc* (New York: Duffield and Co., 1920). In this sinister saga a professor named Bocara meets an ugly fate after putting his wife and her brain-surgeon paramour under a hypnotic spell. The novel is not included in this bibliography because it downplays detection in favor of explorations into the supernatural.

Christopher Quarles Bibliography

33. *Christopher Quarles: College Professor and Master Detective.* New York: E.P. Dutton, 1914; London: Holden and Hardingham, 1921. (Short Stories.)

34. *The Master Detective: Being Some Further Investigations of Christopher Quarles.* New York: E.P. Dutton, 1916; London: Holden and Hardingham, 1922 (Short Stories.)

LANCELOT PRIESTLEY (1925)

Creator: Rhode, John [Street, Cecil John Charles (1884-1965)]

Although he uses the title "Professor" without any noticeable self-consciousness, Lancelot Priestley is, in fact, a defrocked academic. A mathematician, Priestley once held a professorship at one of Great Britain's leading universities. He had a bitter (but unspecified) quarrel with the university's

authorities, however, and was dismissed from his post. A man
of independent means, Priestley now lives in a house on West-
bourne Terrace in London's Bayswater section. There, still
nursing his grudges against academe, he does research, writes
weighty, argumentative books, and like Augustus S.F.X. Van
Dusen (1-6) before him, he takes relish in demolishing the
pet theories of the world's foremost scientists.

Professor Priestley engages in detection for the amusement
which it offers his "restless brain." Again in the manner of
Professor Van Dusen, Priestley is relatively unconcerned with
the human aspects of crime. His interests lie in solving the
puzzles which especially vexing crimes present, and he attacks
these problems by "building elaborate edifices of unshakable
truth from loose bricks of fact which to others are merely a
profitless rubbish heap." Because Priestley seldom leaves his
home (except in some of his early adventures), the facts with
which he constructs his truths are brought to him by Inspectors Hanslet and Waghorn of Scotland Yard and by Harold Merefield, his son-in-law and private secretary. Merefield, who is
married to Priestley's daughter April, also performs a Watsonian
function by narrating most of the Priestley cases. The professor supplements the data delivered to him by Merefield and
the police by careful reading of London newspapers. But, because
of a slight deafness in his right ear, he will not use a telephone.

A widower, in his late middle-age, Lancelot Priestley is
one of the least personable of all professorial series-
character sleuths. He lacks patience for small talk, possesses
little or no sense of humor, and has a habit of terminating
discussions by exclaiming that his listeners are unable to
grasp the subtleties of his own trains of thought. Nevertheless, because of his great reputation both as a mathematician
and as a detective, Priestley has many prominent visitors. He
often entertains his guests at dinner, after which (over brandy) he provides them with monologues about his talents, his
theories, and his accomplishments.

A one-time British Army career officer who attained the
rank of major, Cecil John Charles Street wrote nearly 150
mystery novels during his lifetime. After publishing several
moderately successful, non-Priestley mysteries, Street launched
what was to become an immensely popular, seventy-one volume
Lancelot Priestley series in 1925 with *The Paddington Mystery*
(35). Using the pseudonym John Rhode on his Priestley stories,
Street produced the professor's adventures at a rate of two
or three per year until 1961. Under the pseudonym Miles Bur-
ton, Street also wrote more than sixty mystery novels with
Inspector Arnold and Desmond Merrion as a team of series-
character detectives, but the Arnold-Merrion stories never rivaled the Priestley books in sales. Under his own name Street

wrote thirteen non-fiction works, including a biography of President Thomas Masaryk of Czechoslovakia, a study of the situation in post-World War I Ireland, and a history of printing.

Lancelot Priestley Bibliography

35. _The Paddington Mystery._ London: Geoffrey Bles, 1925.

36. _Dr. Priestley's Quest._ London: Geoffrey Bles, 1926.

37. _The Ellerby Case._ London: Geoffrey Bles, 1926; New York: Dodd, Mead and Co., 1927.

38. _The Murder in Praed Street._ London: Geoffrey Bles, 1928; New York: Dodd, Mead and Co., 1928.

39. _Tragedy at the Unicorn._ London: Geoffrey Bles, 1928; New York: Dodd, Mead and Co., 1928.

40. _The Davidson Case._ London: Geoffrey Bles, 1929. Published in the United States as _Murder at Bratton Grange._ New York: Dodd, Mead and Co., 1929.

41. _The House on Tollard Ridge._ London: Geoffrey Bles, 1929; New York: Dodd, Mead and Co., 1929.

42. _The Peril at Cranbury Hall._ London: Geoffrey Bles, 1930; New York: Dodd, Mead and Co., 1930.

43. _Pinehurst._ London: Geoffrey Bles, 1930. Published in the United States as _Dr. Priestley Investigates._ New York: Dodd, Mead and Co., 1930.

44. _The Hanging Woman._ London: William Collins Sons, 1931; New York: Dodd, Mead and Co., 1931.

45. _Tragedy on the Line._ London: William Collins Sons, 1931; New York: Dodd, Mead and Co., 1931.

46. _Dead Men at the Folly._ London: William Collins Sons, 1932; New York: Dodd, Mead and Co., 1932.

47. _Mystery at Greycombe Farm._ London: William Collins Sons, 1932. Published in the United States as _The Fire at Greycombe Farm._ New York: Dodd, Mead and Co., 1933.

48. *The Claverton Mystery.* London: William Collins Sons,
    1933. Published in the United States as *The Claver-
    ton Affair.* New York: Dodd, Mead and Co., 1933.

49. *The Motor Rally Mystery.* London: Williams Collins Sons,
    1933. Published in the United States as *Dr. Priestley
    Lays a Trap.* New York: Dodd, Mead and Co., 1933.

50. *The Venner Crime.* London: Odhasm Press, 1933; New York:
    Dodd, Mead and Co., 1934.

51. *Poison for One.* London: William Collins Sons, 1934;
    New York: Dodd, Mead and Co., 1934.

52. *The Robthorne Mystery.* London: William Collins Sons,
    1934; New York: Dodd, Mead and Co., 1934.

53. *Shot at Dawn.* London: William Collins Sons, 1934; New
    York: Dodd, Mead and Co., 1934.

54. *The Corpse in the Car.* London: William Collins Sons,
    1935; New York: Dodd, Mead and Co., 1935.

55. *Hendon's First Case.* London: William Collins Sons,
    1935; New York: Dodd, Mead and Co,, 1935.

56. *Mystery at Olympia.* London: William Collins Sons,
    1935. Published in the United States as *Murder at
    the Murder Show.* New York: Dodd, Mead and Co., 1936.

57. *Death at Breakfast.* London: William Collins Sons, 1936;
    New York: Dodd, Mead and Co., 1936.

58. *In Face of the Verdict.* London: William Collins Sons,
    1936. Published in the United States as *In the Face
    of the Verdict.* New York: Dodd, Mead and Co., 1940.

59. *Death in the Hop Fields.* London: William Collins Sons,
    1937. Published in the United States as *The Harvest
    Murder.* New York: Dodd, Mead and Co., 1937.

60. *Death on the Board.* London: William Collins Sons, 1937.
    Published in the United States as *Death Sits on the
    Board.* New York: Dodd, Mead and Co., 1937.

61. *Proceed with Caution.* London: William Collins Sons,
    1937. Published in the United States as *Body Un-
    identified.* New York; Dodd, Mead and Co., 1938.

62. *The Bloody Tower.* London: William Collins Sons, 1938.
     Published in the United States as *The Tower of Evil.*
     New York: Dodd, Mead and Co., 1938.

63. *Invisible Weapons.* London: William Collins Sons, 1938;
     New York: Dodd, Mead and Co., 1938.

64. *Death on Sunday.* London: William Collins Sons, 1939.
     Published in the United States as *The Elm Tree Mur-
     der.* New York: Dodd, Mead and Co., 1939.

65. *Death Pays a Dividend.* London: William Collins Sons,
     1939; New York: Dodd, Mead and Co., 1939.

66. *Death on the Boat-Train.* William Collins Sons, 1940;
     New York: Dodd, Mead and Co., 1940.

67. *Murder at Lilac Cottage.* London: William Collins Sons,
     1940; New York: Dodd, Mead and Co., 1940.

68. *Death at the Helm.* London: William Collins Sons, 1941;
     New York: Dodd, Mead and Co., 1941.

69. *They Watched by Night.* London: William Collins Sons,
     1941. Published in the United States as *Signal for
     Death.* New York: Dodd, Mead and Co., 1941.

70. *The Fourth Bomb.* London: William Collins Sons, 1942;
     New York: Dodd, Mead and Co., 1942.

71. *Dead on the Track.* London: William Collins Sons, 1943;
     New York: Dodd, Mead and Co., 1943.

72. *Men Die at Cyprus Lodge.* London: William Collins Sons,
     1943; New York: Dodd, Mead and Co., 1944.

73. *Death Invades the Meeting.* London: William Collins
     Sons, 1944; New York: Dodd, Mead and Co., 1944.

74. *The Bricklayer's Arms.* London: William Collins Sons,
     1945. Published in the United States as *Shadow of a
     Crime.* New York: Dodd, Mead and Co., 1945.

75. *Death in Harley Street.* London: Geoffrey Bles, 1946;
     New York: Dodd, Mead and Co., 1946.

76. *The Lake House.* London: Geoffrey Bles, 1946. Published
     in the United States as *The Secret of the Lake House.*

New York: Dodd, Mead and Co., 1946.

77. *Death of an Author.* London: Geoffrey Bles, 1947; New
York: Dodd, Mead and Co., 1948.

78. *Nothing But the Truth.* London: Geoffrey Bles, 1947.
Published in the United States as *Experiment in
Crime.* New York: Dodd, Mead and Co., 1947.

79. *The Paper Bag.* London: Geoffrey Bles, 1948. Published
in the United States as *The Links in the Chain.* New
York: Dodd, Mead and Co., 1948.

80. *The Telephone Call.* London: Geoffrey Bles, 1948.
Published in the United States as *Shadow of an Alibi.*
New York: Dodd, Mead and Co., 1949.

81. *Blackthorn House.* London: Geoffrey Bles, 1949; New
York: Dodd, Mead and Co., 1949.

82. *Up the Garden Path.* London: Geoffrey Bles, 1949. Published in the United States as *The Fatal Garden.*
New York: Dodd, Mead and Co., 1949.

83. *Family Affairs.* London: Geoffrey Bles, 1950. Published
in the United States as *The Last Suspect.* New York:
Dodd, Mead and Co., 1951.

84. *The Two Graphs.* London: Geoffrey Bles, 1950. Published
in the United States as *Double Identities.* New York:
Dodd, Mead and Co., 1950.

85. *Dr. Goodwood's Locum.* London: Geoffrey Bles, 1951.
Published in the United States as *The Affair of the
Substitute Doctor.* New York: Dodd, Mead and Co.,
1951.

86. *The Secret Meeting.* London: Geoffrey Bles, 1951;
New York: Dodd, Mead and Co., 1951.

87. *Death at the Dance.* London: Geoffrey Bles, 1952; New
York: Dodd, Mead and Co., 1953.

88. *Death in Wellington Road.* London: Geoffrey Bles, 1952;
New York: Dodd, Mead and Co., 1952.

89. *By Registered Post.* London: Geoffrey Bles, 1953. Published in the United States as *The Mysterious Suspect.*

New York: Dodd, Mead and Co., 1953.

90. *Death at the Inn*. London: Geoffrey Bles, 1953. Published in the United States as *The Case of the Forty Thieves*. New York: Dodd, Mead and Co., 1954.

91. *Death on the Lawn*. London: Geoffrey Bles, 1954; New York: Dodd, Mead and Co., 1955.

92. *The Dovebury Murders*. London: Geoffrey Bles, 1954; New York: Dodd, Mead and Co., 1954.

93. *Death of a Godmother*. London: Geoffrey Bles, 1955. Published in the United States as *Delayed Payment*. New York: Dodd, Mead and Co., 1956.

94. *The Domestic Agency*. London: Geoffrey Bles, 1955. Published in the United States as *Grave Matters*. New York: Dodd, Mead and Co., 1955.

95. *An Artist Dies*. London: Geoffrey Bles, 1955. Published in the United States as *Death of an Artist*. New York: Dodd, Mead and Co., 1956.

96. *Open Verdict*. London: Geoffrey Bles; 1956; New York: Dodd, Mead and Co., 1957.

97. *Death of a Bridegroom*. London: Geoffrey Bles, 1957; New York: Dodd, Mead and Co., 1958.

98. *Robbery with Violence*. London: Geoffrey Bles, 1957; New York: Dodd, Mead and Co., 1957.

99. *Death Takes a Partner*. London: Geoffrey Bles, 1958; New York: Dodd, Mead and Co., 1959.

100. *Licensed for Murder*. London: Geoffrey Bles, 1958: New York: Dodd, Mead and Co., 1959.

101. *Murder at Derivale*. London: Geoffrey Bles, 1958; New York: Dodd, Mead and Co., 1958.

102. *Three Cousins Die*. London: Geoffrey Bles, 1959; New York: Dodd, Mead and Co., 1960.

103. *The Fatal Pool*. London: Geoffrey Bles, 1960; New York: Dodd, Mead and Co., 1961.

104. *Twice Dead*. London: Geoffrey Bles, 1960; New York: Dodd,
      Mead and Co., 1960.

105. *The Vanishing Diary*. London: Geoffrey Bles, 1961; New
      York: Dodd, Mead and Co., 1961.

PROFESSOR WELLS (1926)

Creator: Grierson, Francis Durham (1888-1972)

A resident of London's picturesque Russell Square, Professor Wells is a combination medical doctor, chemist, and
amateur criminologist. Thanks to a "timely legacy," he has
retired both from his medical practice and from his teaching
post at a London university. He now devotes himself to
scientific research and to the solving of crime-related mysteries.

Professor Wells (whose full name is never revealed) is
middle-aged, broad-shouldered, and slightly stooped. Gray-
bearded, he wears gold-rimmed spectacles. Though he often
speaks with "portentous gravity," he is not beyond modest,
intellectual witticisms which, on occasion, confuse his less-
cerebral listeners. Wells is constantly wreathed in a cloud
of pipe smoke, and he enjoys a convivial glass of sherry. A
bachelor, without any reported romantic life, he nonetheless
displays a surprisingly well-developed knowledge of women's
fashions and hairstyles.

Wells undertakes his cases at the request of Sir Charles
Merivale, the head of the Criminal Investigation Department
of New Scotland Yard. Wells and Merivale were schoolmates.
The professor's closest crime-fighting relationship, however,
is with Superintendent Sims, Sir Charles' most trusted officer.
Sims and Wells form what both call "a mutual admiration society." Sims contributes his brawn and the resources of the Yard,
while Wells provides the resources of his home laboratory and
his "constructive reasoning" to their mutual endeavors.

Since New Scotland Yard is quite capable of handling pede-
strian crimes on its own, Professor Wells is consulted only when
the Yard finds itself up against especially baffling cases.
In *The Limping Man* (106), for instance, Wells' extensive
knowledge of poisons enables him to solve the mysterious murder of a wealthy aristocrat. In *The Zoo Murder* (110), Wells
and Sims successfully cope with the matter of a small woman
found dead inside the carcass of a deceased lion at the London Zoo. And in *Murder in Black* (118), Wells uses his well-

honed powers of deduction to assist Superintendent Sims in apprehending a dark-skinned, one-man London crime wave. Professor Wells prefers to receive information from Sims, and then to weigh facts and clues in the comfort of his home. But he often finds it necessary to venture forth from Russell Square in order to visit crime scenes and to conduct his own inquiries. The professor prefers to keep his sleuthing activities out of the newspapers. Publicity as a master detective, he feels, would limit his ability to gain information from witnesses and suspects. As a result of his properly professorial distaste for public acclaim, the credit for most of his peerless detection goes to Superintendent Sims and, to an even greater extent, to Sir Charles Merivale. In fact, the few individuals who know of Professor Wells' invaluable work for New Scotland Yard suspect that Merivale owes his knighthood to the unsung ratiocination which the professor performs on his behalf.

British-born, Francis Durham Grierson was educated at St. Dunstan's College. A journalist, as well as a prodigious writer of mystery novels, Grierson was at one point in his career the editor of *Lloyds Magazine*. He published fifty mysteries between 1924 and 1960 and, in addition to Professor Wells and Inspector Sims, he created Superintendent Andrew Ash, Inspector George Muir, Richard Fulring, and Commissaire Patras as series-character sleuths. In a BBC-Radio interview, published in *Meet the Detective* (London: Allen and Unwin, 1935; New York: The Telegraph Press, 1935), Grierson claimed that Professor Wells was modeled after a real-life London scientist whom he declined to identify. Furthermore, Grierson asserted that he created Wells with the intention of representing him as a "human being" and not as a "demi-god of criminology."

Professor Wells Bibliography

106. *The Limping Man*. London: Hodder and Stoughton, 1924; New York: Edward J. Clode, 1926.

107. *The Double Thumb*. London: Hodder and Stoughton, 1925. (Short Stories.)

108. *The Lost Pearl*. London: Hodder and Stoughton, 1925; New York: Edward J. Clode, 1926.

109. *Secret Judges*. London: Hodder and Stoughton, 1925.

110. *The Zoo Murder*. London: Geoffrey Bles, 1926. Published in the United States as *The Murder in the Garden*.

New York: Edward J. Clode, 1927.

111. *The Smiling Death*. London: Geoffrey Bles, 1927; New
      York: Edward J. Clode, 1927.

112. *The Blue Bucket Mystery*. London: Geoffrey Bles, 1929;
      New York: Edward J. Clode, 1930.

113. *The White Camellia*. London: Geoffrey Bles, 1929; New
      York: Edward J. Clode, 1929.

114. *The Yellow Rat*. London: William Collins Sons, 1929.
      Also published as *Murder at the Wedding*. London:
      William Collins Sons, 1932.

115. *The Mysterious Mademoiselle*. London: William Collins
      Sons, 1930.

116. *Murder at Lancaster Gate*. London: Thornton Butterworth,
      1934.

117. *Death on Deposit*. London: Thornton Butterworth, 1935.

118. *Murder in Black*. London: Thornton Butterworth, 1935;
      New York: D. Appleton-Century, 1935.

LUTHER BASTION (1928)

Creator: Holt, Gavin [Rodda, Percival Charles (1891-)]

     Luther Bastion, O.B.E., D.Sc., F.R.S., F.A.S.L., is a
professor of anthropology and archeology at an unidentified
university in London. Small, bald, and in his late middle
age, he has an enormous fund of nervous energy. A roll-your-
own cigarette smoker, Bastion's hobbies are attending ballet
and the theater, tramping through the English countryside
looking for Roman artifacts, and sleuthing. Well-dressed for
the most part, the professor destroys his sartorial image out-
of-doors by wearing a large, ill-fitting raincoat "with
capacious pockets."
     A bachelor, Professor Bastion lives in a flat near the
Charing Cross Bridge, from which (if he leans far out of the
window) he can see the dome of St. Paul's Cathedral. His
flatmate and constant companion is Major Kettering-Bevis, a
retired British Army officer. Major Kettering-Bevis is tall,

lanky, and wears a glass eye. Badly wounded at the Somme,
Kettering-Bevis has now recovered to the point where he is
trying valiantly to read through the entire output of Anthony
Trollope. He also accompanies Bastion on all of his cases and
attempts, when appropriate, to restrain the exuberant professor
from placing himself in unneeded personal peril.

Professor Bastion has an "infernal instinct" for detective
work. Naturally inquisitive, and restless unless he is occupied by a challenging mental problem, Bastion jumps enthusi-
astically into any mystery about which he hears. Some of his
cases are brought to him by Inspector Burchell of Scotland
Yard, a man who admires the professor's skills. Bastion's
talents as a sleuth include a phenomenal memory for small details, an ability to deduce a man's moral character by "reading" his face, and a disciplined mind which will not permit
him to leap precipitously at conclusions. An expert in examining physical evidence, Bastion often studies material clues
under a microscope which he keeps in his rooms. A theoreti-
cian as well as a practitioner of criminology, he has written
a classic textbook titled "Anthropology and the Criminal."
This work, which disputes the theories of Lombroso and Ber-
tillion, should be consulted for a more thorough explication
of the professor's detection strategies.

Although Bastion frequently delivers anthropological papers
(often on Maya civilization) to learned London societies, he
seems to pay almost no attention to his academic duties. Most
of his exploits take place in England, but he and Major
Kettering-Bevis can pack their bags and travel to Continental
Europe when the sleuthing situation demands. In *Green Talons*
(121), for example, Professor Bastion and the Major are found
in Paris and in various cities on the Mediterranean. Bastion
has an archenemy, "The Hawk," a master criminal who delivers
a small disc etched with a hawkprint to those whom he is about
to kill. This nasty individual appears in several early Bastion stories, but his reign of terror is ended in *Death Takes
the Stage* (130). Professor Bastion does recurrent battle,
too, with Jammy Varehov, a Bolshevik secret agent who was born
of Russian parents, was raised in the United States, "speaks
American like a native," and takes his orders from Moscow.
In *Six Minutes Past Twelve* (119), for instance, Varehov proves
to be responsible for what at first glance seems to be the
apolitical murder of Samuel Dubeyne, the squire of stately
Pembridge Hall in rural southern England. Considering the
fiendish nature of the villains with whom he so often deals,
it is little wonder that the Professor feels compelled to
drape himself in his baggy raincoat. This garment allows
him to conceal a large, sometimes life-saving, revolver for

use in emergencies.

Percival Charles Rodda was born in Port Augusta, South Australia. After working on various Australian newspapers Rodda migrated to New York in 1919 where he became a music critic. In the late 1920s he migrated again, this time to England, and by 1939 he was settled in Cornwall, where he devoted his full talents to creative writing. In addition to his Professor Bastion epics, Rodda's publishing credits include many other mystery novels, short stories, plays, mainstream novels, television scripts, and libretto of an opera, "Marriage of Aude," which was performed in Rochester, New York, in 1931. Rodda used the pseudonyms Gavin Holt and Gardner Low for his mystery fiction.

Luther Bastion Bibliography

119. *Six Minutes Past Twelve*. London: Hodder and Stoughton, 1928.

120. *The White-Faced Man*. London: Hodder and Stoughton, 1929. Published in the United States as *The Praying Monkey*. New York: Dial Press, 1930.

121. *Green Talons*. London: Hodder and Stoughton, 1930; Indianapolis: Bobbs-Merrill, 1931.

122. *The Garden of Silent Beasts*. London: Hodder and Stoughton, 1931.

123. *Murder at Marble Arch*. London: Hodder and Stoughton, 1931.

124. *Trail of the Skull*. London, Hodder and Stoughton, 1931.

125. *Drums Beat at Night*. London: Hodder and Stoughton, 1932.

126. *Red Eagle*. London: Hodder and Stoughton, 1932.

127. *Dark Lady*. London: Hodder and Stoughton, 1933.

128. *The Golden Witch*. London: Hodder and Stoughton, 1933.

129. *Mark of the Paw*. London: Hodder and Stoughton, 1933.

130. *Death Takes the Stage*. London: Hodder and Stoughton, 1934; Boston: Little, Brown and Co., 1934.

131. *Trafalgar Square*. London: Hodder and Stoughton, 1934.

132. *Black Bullets*. London: Hodder and Stoughton, 1935.

133. *The Emerald Spider*. London: Hodder and Stoughton, 1935.

134. *Steel Shutters*. London: Hodder and Stoughton, 1935.

HERMAN BRIERLY (1929)

Creator: Levinrew, Will [Levine, William (1881-)]

Professor Herman Brierly is one of the United States' most eminent chemists. He is also one of the nation's most distinguished physicists, anatomists, physiologists, and bacteriologists as well. Thus it is little wonder that many of the world's premier men of science beat a path to his door for help with their research. Various other people ask the professor for assistance, too, especially when they are involved in murder cases in which exotic poisons have been employed. A very busy man, Brierly takes on sleuthing chores only when the problem in question seems to pose a significant scientific challenge and/or when the welfare of mankind is at stake. In *The Poison Plague* (135), for example, the professor successfully copes with a potential mass murderer whose lethal brew consists of an unusually deadly mixture of silver cyanide, zinc cyanide, mercuric cyanide, copper cyanide, and prussic acid. Considering the gravity of the crimes with which Brierly deals, it is perhaps fortunate for the world of higher learning that he is never called upon to exercise his sleuthing talents in an academic setting.

Well over seventy years old, and retired from teaching at a university in the American city of "Masonville," Professor Brierly watches his diet, exercises, and is in exceedingly fine physical condition. Barely five feet tall, he resembles "an Apollo in miniature." He is a health food addict, with skin and snow-white hair glowing with the lustre "that is sometimes found in very old men who are clean and healthy physically and mentally." Between his work and his zealous care for his body, Brierly has little time for the usual human frivolities. He has almost no knowledge of the mundane matters of everyday life, and his conversations, particularly when he is engaged in crime fighting, tend to consist of impatient mini-lectures in which he informs his listeners of their intellectual shortcomings. The professor's only hobby is driving fast cars. Although he employs a chauffeur named Henry to transport him through normal traffic, Brierly owns a "stripped racecar...with a two-speed transmission," which he keeps at a local speedway. When faced with a knotty sleuthing problem, he stimulates his thought processes by navigating his machine at top speeds around the empty oval.

Brierly is a life-long bachelor, but he lives with John Matthews, his adopted son. A former student of the professor, John almost had to abort his undergraduate education because of the deaths of his parents. Brierly took John into his home, paid his university tuition, and eventually legalized their father-son relationship. Now in his twenties, John is six feet tall, a teacher of chemistry at the "Masonville Dental College," and a talented amateur boxer. He serves as the professor's legman during criminological investigations, and when the situation arises he employs his pugilistic skills to protect his adoptive father's welfare.

Professor Brierly Bibliography

135. *The Poison Plague*. New York: Robert M. McBride, 1929;
      London: Cassell and Co., 1930.

136. *Murder from the Grave*. New York: Robert M. McBride,
      1930; London: Cassell and Co., 1931.

137. *Murder on the Palisades*. New York: Robert M. McBride,
      1930; London: Victor Gollancz, 1930. Also published
      as *The Wheelchair Corpse*. New York: Bart House,
      1945.

138. *Death Points a Finger*. New York and London: Mystery
      League, Inc., 1933.

HARLEY MANNERS (1929)

Creator: Dutton, Charles Judson (1888-1964)

A professor of abnormal psychology at an unidentified university in the eastern United States, Harley Manners believes that the most efficient way to solve a mystery is to focus upon motives. Not all motives can be deduced, of course, simply by knowing the superficial life histories of victims and likely suspects. Some motives have roots in deep-seated psychologi-

cal aberrations, and it is by employing his vast knowledge of
mental pathology that Manners cuts his way to the heart of
criminological riddles.

Professor Manners is young, tall, well-dressed, a bachelor,
a cigarette and pipe smoker, and a man of great inherited
wealth. He is so wealthy, in fact, that his non-academic
friends constantly wonder why he has chosen to shun the flesh-
pots of the rich in favor of the professorial life. They wonder, too, why he should have chosen abnormal psychology as his
academic field instead of English literature, history, or
another of the more gentlemanly disciplines. But, for Manners,
the teaching and practical application of abnormal psychology
are "experiences," the rewards of which far exceed the dubious
delights of Newport, Park Avenue, or the French Rivera. Moreover, Manner is a man with a strong desire to contribute to
America's social well-being. His particular sleuthing talents
--which put dangerous psychopaths behind bars--help make the
nation safe for decent men and women.

Since Professor Manners is truly dedicated to detection, it
his abilities. He is an avid reader of criminology texts, and
he devours books which deal with the history of crime. He is
also a student of poisons, decoding, footprints, and the meaning of body language. He has even trained a huge brown aire-
dale--named Satin--to attack criminals at his command. Always
seeking to learn, Manners is quick to pick up new investigatory
techniques from his piano-playing friend, George Carter, an
agent with the United States Treasury Department. And he cooperates to the fullest extent possible with John Rogan, the
local, cigar-smoking chief of police, whose own knowledge of
crime fighting stems from his days as a beat patrolman in
New York City. Rogan routinely calls upon Manners for assistance, and the professor inevitably succeeds where Rogan has
failed. But Manners refuses publicity for his efforts. He
prefers, instead, to have Rogan reap all of the glory.

The university at which Manners is employed is unusual
among both real and fictional institutions of higher learning
in the sense that it seems to be populated exclusively by
well-adjusted students, faculty members, and administrators.
Hence the professor must go off-campus to find the kinds of
cases in which he can employ his special knowledge of aberrant
behavior. In *Murder in a Library* (141), for instance, Manners'
professional familiarity with the "strange psychology" of
unmarried adult women allows him to find the killer of a
spinster public librarian. And his expertise in the nature
of inhibitions gives him the basis for resolving the matter
of a murdered clergyman in *The Shadow of Evil* (140). Professor Manners' most vexing exploit is found in *Streaked with
Crimson* (139). In this, his first published case, his know-

ledge of sadism gives him crucial insight into the dark side
of a seemingly innocuous man in whose garage he finds a copy
of a "pornographic" book on flagellation.
Charles Judson Dutton was born in Fall River, Massachusetts. A Unitarian clergyman as well as a mystery writer.
Dutton also wrote a column entitled "The World We Live In,"
for the *Albany* [*N.Y.*] *Telegram* from 1916 until 1928.

Harley Manners Bibliography

139. *Streaked with Crimson.* New York: Dodd, Mead and Co.,
     1929.

140. *The Shadow of Evil.* New York: Dodd, Mead and Co., 1930;
     London: Hurst and Blackett, 1930.

141. *Murder in a Library.* New York: Dodd, Mead and Co.,
     1931; London: Hurst and Blackett, 1931.

142. *Poison Unknown.* New York: Dodd, Mead and Co., 1932.
     Published in Great Britain as *The Vanishing Murderer.*
     London: Hurst and Blackett, 1932.

143. *The Circle of Death.* New York: Dodd, Mead and Co.,
     1933; London: Hurst and Blackett, 1933.

144. *Black Fog.* New York: Dodd, Mead and Co., 1934; London:
     Hurst and Blackett, 1934.

HENRY POGGIOLI (1929)

Creator: Stribling, T(homas) S(igismund) (1881-1965)

     Born in Boston of Italian parentage and the holder of a
Ph.D. from Cornell, Henry Poggioli is a professor of psychology at Ohio State University. He is best known in academic
circles for his studies of the frequencies with which members
of various occupations puff their cigarettes while under
stress. He is also a widely respected consulting detective.
Although he sometimes employs psychological analysis in his
sleuthing, Poggioli relies as well upon astute observation
and upon a dogged determination to think through all possible
explanations for the crimes which he is examining.
     Professor Poggioli is a bachelor. He once studied a
sample of married couples and discovered that husbands and

wives have dramatically opposed goals. After finishing that
research, he vowed to remain single. Short, with dark eyes
and "a certain academic appearance," Poggioli has an uneven
personality. Although he is friendly and even convivial at
times, he can also burst forth with biting sarcasm. He takes
his detection seriously, but he sometimes feels that those
who seek his services expect an impossible level of perfec-
tion. Unlike most professorial series-character sleuths,
Professor Poggioli does not always bring his cases to successful conclusions. Indeed, in "A Passage to Benares," the
fifth and last story in *Clues of the Caribbees* (145), Poggioli's frustrated attempts to identify a murderer in Port of
Spain, Trinidad, bring him dire personal consequences. Falsely
accused of the very killing which he is trying to investigate,
he is tried, convicted, and hanged. How the professor manages
to return to life and resume his career in subsequent exploits
is one of the nagging, unsolved riddles in the annals of
mystery fiction.

Professor Poggioli's adventures appear only in short-story
format. The five stories in *Clues of the Caribbees* were first
published in *Adventure Magazine* in 1925 and 1926, and all are
set in the Caribbean, where Poggioli is spending a sabbatical
leave. The Poggioli in these episodes is in his early middle
age, interested in furthering his knowledge of "racial psychology," and something of an expert in native customs. *Best
Dr. Poggioli Detective Stories* (146) is a collection of fifteen later Poggioli pieces which were published originally in
The Saint Mystery Magazine and in *Ellery Queen's Mystery Magazine* between 1945 and 1957. These stories show an older,
more cantankerous Poggioli traveling from the Ohio State campus into the southern United States and Mexico on various
detection missions. The pieces in *Best Dr. Pogglioli Detective Stories* also feature as narrator an unnamed male Watsonian character who resides with the professor and who apparently makes his living chronicling Pogglioli's cases. This
individual is not present in *Clues of the Caribbees*.

Thomas Sigismund Stribling was born in Clifton, Tennessee.
He attended Forence (Alabama) Normal School and then, in
1904, received an LL.B. degree from the University of Alabama.
Stribling practiced law for only one year before launching a
career as a creative writer. Although he wrote in a number
of genres, he is best remembered as a mainstream novelist.
The Store (Garden City, New York: Doubleday, Doran and Co.,
1932; London: William Heinemann, 1932), a novel about life
in a small southern town, won the 1932 Pulitzer Prize. One
of Stribling's lesser-known novels, *These Bars of Flesh* describes the adventures of an uneducated superintendent of

of schools from rural Georgia who enrolls in a New York City
university and is immediately given a position on the school's
faculty. The Dr. Poggioli stories were Stribling's only ventures into the mystery field. Inventive in their construction
and laced with sardonic wit, they are often rated as "forgotten
treasures" by historians of detective fiction.

Henry Poggioli Bibliography

145. *Clues of the Caribbees. Being Certain Investigations
       of Henry Poggioli.* Garden City, New York: Doubleday,
       Doran and Co., 1929; London: William Heinemann, 1930.

146. *Best Dr. Poggioli Detective Stories.* New York: Dover,
       1975; London: Dover, 1976.

HENRY ARTHUR FIELDING (1930)

Creator: Sharp, David

     The narrator of his own stories, Henry Arthur Fielding is
a British professor of philology. A bachelor, now in his
late middle-age, Fielding taught for a number of years at Manchester University, but he is now a free-floating intellectual
in London. He has written many books and is highly sought
after as a guest lecturer by London's literary clubs and societies. But the modest fees which Fielding receives from his
lecture appearances are not crucial to his economic well-
being. Though the source of his wealth is never made clear,
he is a man of significant independent means.
     Professor Fielding is affable, possessed of a well-
developed sense of humor, and seemingly capable of finding
fun even in the face of extreme adversity. He writes of his
sleuthing exploits, which often lead him to the brink of his
own death, with sardonic detachment. Moreover, his accounts
of these adventures suggest that he conducts his detection
with something less than maximum seriousness. Indeed, most
of the professor's cases are of the bumble-in-and-bumble-out
variety. He tends to encounter crime by virtue of his own
rather bizarre personal deportment. In *I, the Criminal* (150),
for instance, Fielding breaks into a friend's house to borrow
a book, only to become a suspect when his friend is murdered
shortly thereafter. And he tends to solve mysteries by such
less-than-surefire tactics as adopting easily-seen-through
disguises. Attempting to find the killer of a London stock-

broker in *My Particular Murder* (148), for example, the professor removes his false teeth and assumes the role of Mr. Henry Fothergill, a retired Anglo-Indian civil servant from Bombay.

Thanks to his innate pleasantness, Professor Fielding has a great many friends. These individuals (some of whom are as impish as he) often rescue him from danger and/or provide him with critical information. The professor's principal associate in sleuthing is Sheridan Orford, a young-man-about-town whose expertise in ventriloquism often works to Fielding's advantage. Mark Penrigg (a London journalist), Goddard (an attorney), and Dinsmore (the elevator operator in the high-rise apartment building in which the professor lives) play key supporting roles in some of the professor's cases.

Fielding also has an archenemy. This individual, known only as Mr. Mabberly, is the leader of a large gang of London thieves and murderers. Professor Fielding was once instrumental in Mr. Mabberly's capture, conviction, and sentencing to Brixton Prison. In several of the Fielding stories the villain turns out to be Mabberly, who is acting out his in-prison fantasies by attempting to send the professor to his final rest. Mabberly is never successful in eradicating the professor, but he does cause him considerable discomfort. In *My Particular Murder,* Mabberly kidnaps Fielding and subjects him to the ultimate in torture. Holding him in a room which has been redecorated to resemble a Brixton cell, Mabberly takes away the professor's tobacco and refuses to let him smoke his pipe.

Henry Arthur Fielding Bibliography

147. *When No Man Pursueth*. London: Ernest Benn, 1930.

148. *My Particular Murder*. London: Ernest Benn, 1931; Boston: Houghton Mifflin, 1931.

149. *None of My Business*. London: Ernest Benn, 1931. Published in the United States as *The Code-Letter Mystery*. Boston: Houghton Mifflin, 1932.

150. *I, the Criminal*. London: Ernest Benn, 1932; Boston: Houghton Mifflin, 1933.

151. *The Inconvenient Corpse*. London: Ernest Benn, 1933.

152. *Marriage and Murder*. London: Ernest Benn, 1934.

153. *Disputed Quarry.* London: Herbert Jenkins, 1939.

154. *Everybody Suspect.* London: Herbert Jenkins, 1939.

155. *The Frightened Sailor.* London: Herbert Jenkins, 1939.

PETER SHANE (1931)

Creator:　Bonnamy, Francis [Walz, Audrey Boyer]

Highly respected in both academic and law enforcement circles, Peter Shane is head of the criminology department at the
University of Chicago. Tall, middle-aged, and always impec-
cably attired, he resembles "a cross between a successful
broker and an English actor." Professor Shane is sometimes
known as "The Man in Grey" because he is partial to suits of
that color and because his grey wardrobe complements his grey
hair and opaque grey eyes. He lives in a modest bachelor
apartment in a Chicago lakefront hotel, where the doorman
wards off unwanted visitors. Shane has few professorial
eccentricities. For relaxation he enjoys an occasional high-
ball, a game of billiards, and a good book. His particular
literary passion is post-Shakespearean tragedy. Even-tempered,
Shane sometimes appears to be lazy and indifferent. When circumstances warrant, however, he can engage in a chase with as
much verve as any other professorial series-character sleuth.
　　Professor Shane serves as an unpaid consultant to Chief
Hurley of the Chicago police, but the professor is also consulted by the FBI and by the Royal Canadian Mounted Police;
hence most of his exploits are set in non-Chicago locales.
Shane's most scenic adventure occurs in *The Man in the Mist*
(163). In this, the last book in his series, he travels across
most of eastern Canada in search of clues in an espionage case.
At the climax of the story he watches from shore as Canadian
authorities attempt to rescue a former professor (and convicted spy) who has fallen into Niagara Falls. During World
War II Shane serves as a major in United States Military Intelligence. *The King Is Dead on Queen Street* (160) and *Portrait
of the Artist as a Dead Man* (161) are set in and near Washington, D.C., where Shane is stationed. No matter where he travels, Shane disdains obvious hypotheses and preconceived no-
tions. And he refuses to allow himself to be the prisoner of
any single way of approaching criminological problems. "Routine," he argues, "is simply a thought pattern that is set up
for those who are incapable of thinking for themselves."

Shane is assisted in both his academic work and in his
crime fighting by Francis "Frank" Bonnamy, a junior member of
the University of Chicago criminology department. Bonnamy is
a graduate student in the early Shane stories (and a civilian
employee of the Signal Corps while Shane is on military duty),
but by the conclusion of the series he is an associate professor. An energetic young man, Bonnamy narrates all of the
Shane novels and, in fact, appears on their title pages as
author. Witty, whereas Shane is bland in his conversation,
and perceptive about the ironies involved in his relationship
with his mentor, Bonnamy is one of the most likeable Watsons
in mystery fiction. Bonnamy also gives the Shane stories their
only elements of romance. Bonnamy marries a girl named Mavis,
and in *Blood and Thirsty* (162) the honeymooning couple must
ask Shane for help when they become involved in murder on the
rockbound coast of Maine.

Married to Jay Walz, a long-time foreign correspondent for
The New York Times, Audrey Boyer Walz wrote several mainstream
novels and travel books (in collaboration with her husband) in
addition to the Peter Shane series. The Peter Shane novels
were her only works of mystery fiction.

Peter Shane Bibliography

156. *Death by Appointment*. Garden City, New York: Doubleday,
     Doran and Co., 1931.

157. *Death on a Dude Ranch*. Garden City, New York: Double-
     day, Doran and Co., 1937.

158. *Dead Reckoning*. New York: Duell, Sloan and Pearce,
     1943.

159. *A Rope of Sand*. New York: Duell, Sloan and Pearce,
     1944.

160. *The King Is Dead on Queen Street*. New York: Duell,
     Sloan and Pearce, 1945.

161. *Portrait of the Artist as a Dead Man*. New York: Duell,
     Sloan and Pearce, 1947; Published in Great Britain as
     Self-Portrait in Murder. London: John Murray, 1951.

162. *Blood and Thirsty*. New York: Duell, Sloan and Pearce,
     1949; London: John Murray, 1952.

163. *The Man in the Mist*. New York: Duell, Sloan and Pearce,
     1951; London: John Murray, 1952.

IAN CRAIG (1932)

Creator: Hughes, Babette Plechner (1906-)

        Ian Craig is a professor of Oriental philosophy. During
his first published adventure, *Murder in the Zoo* (164), he is
a member of the faculty at "Earl College," a small liberal arts
institution somewhere in the western United States. But Craig
is destined for bigger and better academic worlds. In his
second exploit, *Murder in the Church* (165), Craig has become a
professor at Stanford University.
        Like most other professorial series-character sleuths, Ian
Craig has a keen capacity for observation and logical deduction. However, he also employs his unique knowledge of Oriental teachings in the service of crime fighting. Craig is
the only professorial detective in mystery fiction who uses
Oriental mysticism as a sleuthing device. Well-versed in the
teachings of Buddha, Confucius, Li-Po, and other Eastern philo-
sophers, he has trained his mind to register clues "as a
seismograph registers an earthquake." Thanks to this extreme
cerebral sensitivity, Craig experiences crucial intuitive insights which elude the police and the other participants in
his cases. Very willing to discuss his rare methodology--he
hopes that Oriental philosophy will eventually become a part
of every detective's tool kit--Craig is prone to treat those
with whom he interacts to lengthy expositions about the practical, modern-day uses of ancient Oriental teachings.
        In his late thirties, Professor Craig is tall and blonde.
A bachelor, he is often considered handsome by women, though
he has "diabolical" eyes, topped off by sharply arched brows,
which give him "a sort of Spanish inquisition look." Craig
is generally a pleasant, witty conversationalist, but he can
display flashes of arrogance and irritation, especially when
dealing with policemen. Well-known among orientalists, he
routinely gives invited lectures at such institutions as the
Imperial University of Tokyo and the Sorbonne. A man of considerable (but mysterious) financial means, he has expensive
tastes. While at Earl College, Craig lives in a luxurious
apartment in the Eldorado Arms, where he entertains his male
guests with Manila cigars and Spanish brandy. The apartment
is decorated with an assortment of Oriental artifacts and
artwork. The centerpiece of his collection is a wall-size
tenth-century Cambodian bas-relief of a procession of spear-
carrying warriors and prancing horses. Something of a ladies'
man, Craig finds that the exotic decor of his rooms creates
an effective romantic mood when he entertains female visitors.

Both of the novels in which Professor Craig appears are full-fledged college mysteries. The zoo in the title of *Murder in the Zoo* is the animal laboratory maintained by the psychology department at Earl College, and the murder is the in-the-laboratory shooting of Courtney Brown, an unpleasant and unpopular professor. *Murder in the Zoo* includes a large cast of academic characters, considerable sly humor directed at faculty manners and non-manners, and some sharp literary jabs at behavioristic psychology. *Murder in the Church* takes place at "Western Institute of Technology," a richly endowed university at Pasadena, California. A visiting British physicist, Arthur Quinn, collapses and dies during a church service after sucking on poisoned throat lozenges. Knowing of Ian Craig's reputation as a sleuth, Western Institute's President Radford asks the Stanford professor to investigate. Craig identifies Quinn's murderer after probing deeply into international scientific politics and after uncovering the sordid details of the visiting Englishman's private life.

Babette Plechner Hughes was born in Seattle, Washington. While a sophomore at the University of Washington she married Glenn Hughes, then her instructor of playwriting and later a professor of English and director of the division of drama at the university. In addition to her two Ian Craig books, Babette Hughes wrote several plays and mainstream novels. She also wrote *Last Night When We Were Young* (New York: Rinehart and Co., 1947), an autobiographical account of her tempestuous days as a Washington coed. Much of Babette Hughes' later life was spent in the business world. During the 1940s and 1950s she was the president of Benn Hall Associates, a public relations firm.

Ian Craig Bibliography

*164. *Murder in the Zoo.* New York: D. Appleton-Century, 1932; London: Ernest Benn, 1932.

165. *Murder in the Church.* New York: D. Appleton-Century, 1934.

ROBERT DEANE (1933)

Creator: Vandercook, John W(omack) (1902-1963)

Robert Deane is a medieval historian at Yale. The first two novels in which he appears are set in the 1930s, and in

these stories he holds the rank of instructor. Even at this
early stage of his career, he already has published two
books: *Ostrogothic Spain* and *The Decendants of Attila in
Western Europe*. Deane's last two recorded adventures take
place in the 1950s, and by this time he has attained the rank
of full professor. He now has other (unidentified) professional
publications to his credit, and is listed in *Who's Who*.
    Deane's hobby is historical criminology. He has an ency-
clopedic knowledge of the more "celebrated" crimes of the century. He finds teaching boring, and while grading student papers he often daydreams about being a famous detective. In
order to live out his fantasies, Deane responds eagerly when
his British friend, Bertram Lynch, asks for his assistance.
Lynch lives the exciting life to which Deane secretly aspires.
During the first two volumes of the series, Lynch is a special
investigator for the Permanent Central Board of the League of
Nations, and in this capacity he travels the world rooting out
evil. During the series' two concluding novels, Lynch is a
private detective who specializes in serving extremely wealthy
clients. Although Professor Deane is capable of his own insightful ratiocinations, his role in Lynch's company is usually
that of a perceptive Watson. Lynch does most of the heavy
sleuthing. Deane, in turn, records the cases, offers sage
advice, and sometimes acts as Lynch's eyes and ears.
    A large, fleshy man, Deane stands slightly over six feet
tall and weighs well over two hundred pounds. He is a heavy
cigarette smoker, fond of afternoon naps, and (by his own
admission) is lazy and untidy. A bachelor, he seems to be
well-fixed financially. On at least one occasion--in *Murder
in Fiji* (167)--Deane obtains a leave-without-pay from Yale
in order to accompany Bertram Lynch on a sleuthing mission.
All four of Deane's published cases take place far from New Haven. Indeed, all of them take place in exotic, tropical locales.
Because he is not an anthropologist, and hence is unfamiliar
with the customs of the lands which he visits in the course
of his exploits, Deane feels the need to prepare himself intellectually for his adventures. Before embarking on his
detective travels, he stops off at Yale's Sterling Library to
read about his destinations. And even when he is in the midst
of a case, he can sometimes be found doing further background
research in a local library.
    John Womack Vandercook was born in Great Britain. He came
to the United States at an early age, and his first employment
was in journalism. During the 1920s he served as a reporter
for the *Columbus Citizen* and the *Baltimore Post*, and he later
became an editor for the *New York Graphic*. A frequent world-
traveler, Vandercook wrote travel books and histories of small,
underdeveloped nations in addition to mysteries. In his later

years Vandercook was a well-known NBC radio commentator. *Murder in Trinidad* (166), the first work in his Lynch-Deane series, was adapted for film. The 1934 motion picture starred Nigel Bruce as Bertram Lynch. Bruce, of course, went on to become filmdom's premier Watson, playing opposite Basil Rathbone in twelve Sherlock Holmes films. Ironically, the part of Professor Robert Deane, Lynch's own Watson, was not included in the *Murder in Trinidad* screenplay.

Robert Deane Bibliography

166. *Murder in Trinidad.* Garden City, New York: Doubleday, Doran and Co., 1933; London: William Heinemann, 1936.

167. *Murder in Fiji.* Garden City, New York: Doubleday, Doran and Co., 1936; London: William Heinemann, 1937.

168. *Murder in Haiti.* New York: Macmillan, 1956; London: Eyre and Spottiswoode, 1956. Also published as *Out for a Killing.* New York: Avon Books, 1958.

169. *Murder in New Orleans.* New York: Macmillan, 1959; London: W.H. Allen, 1960.

CHARLES HARDING (1936)

Creator: Stanners, Harold H. (1894-)

Tall, lean, and middle-aged, Charles Harding is a professor of international law at a major university in the New York City area. Well-published, he has a worldwide scholarly reputation. He is especially known for his books advocating brotherhood between nations. Harding was born in Great Britain and educated at Oxford. He spends as much time as possible in his native land. In fact, all three of his recorded detective exploits take place in Great Britain. And all three are "country-house mysteries," in which the professor, a guest in a stately home, investigates murders involving fellow guests, staff and permanent residents, and/or local townspeople.

Conscious of his amateur status as a detective, Harding cooperates fully with the police. Although he occasionally photographs crime scenes with his own camera, he depends upon the authorities to develop forensic data and other material clues. Harding's major contributions to crime fighting lie in his painstaking ratiocination. After gathering all possible information in a case, he writes down the names of likely suspects, their relevant movements, and their motives. Then he examines his notes for logical inconsistencies in the suspects' stories and behavior patterns. And then he cogitates. Eventually, the professor receives an "instantaneous mental flash" which allows him to "link up a series of hitherto unimportant details."

Charles Harding is one of professorial sleuthdom's heaviest smokers. He is seldom without a cigarette, pipe, or cigar. Perhaps because of his addiction to tobacco, he fatigues easily and is subject to headaches. Generally charming and gracious, he can be brusque when someone tries to interrupt his thought processes. Charles is married, but his wife Sylvia always seems to be "traveling" in the United States. With his spouse a continent away, Charles has difficulty sleeping at night. In hopes of inducing slumber, he frequently sips whiskey mixed into hot water before retiring. This potion is not always effective, and the professor often tosses and turns into the small hours of the morning. His insomnia works to his advantage as a sleuth. As he lies awake, Charles sometimes experiences the crucial "mental flashes" which allow him to reach the solutions to mysteries.

No information about Harold H. Stanners is contained in any of the standard sourcebooks. Stanners' three Professor Harding novels were his only contributions to mystery fiction.

Charles Harding Bibliography

170. *Murder at Markendon Court.* London: Eyre and Spottis- woode, 1936.

171. *At the Tenth Clue.* London: Eyre and Spottiswoode, 1937.

172. *The Crowning Murder.* London: Eyre and Spottiswoode, 1938.

EDMUND ("JUNIPER") JONES (1936)

Creator: Fuller, Timothy (1914-1971)

Edmund "Juniper" Jones is first seen, in *Harvard Has a Homicide* (173) as a graduate student in fine arts at Harvard. In his next three adventures he is a junior member of the

Harvard fine arts faculty. Finally, in *Keep Cool, Mr. Jones*
(177), he has left academe. The recipient of a sizeable legacy from his late uncle, Juniper has become at the age of
thirty-five a gentleman-scholar in the small New England town
of "Saxon." There, away from the pressures of Cambridge, he
is writing (without any sense of urgency) a book about the
relationship between art and politics.

Jones is tall and thin, excessively sociable, and given
to being the life of every party. Although he grows somewhat
more sedate as he ages, he is best characterized throughout his
series as brash. Chain-smoking Camel cigarettes, and drinking
large quantities of liquor, he possesses a wisecracking sense
of humor and a definite distaste for authority. He has, in
particular, a low estimation of policemen. When confronted
with murders, Jones prefers to conduct investigations on his
own. He sometimes works independently of the police because
he is a suspect. More often, however, he responds to self-
generated challenges to unravel mysteries before they can
be solved by the authorities. And yet, despite a seeming lack
of commitment, Jones is in his last three exploits a dedicated
family man. His wife, whom he courts in *Harvard Has a Homicide* and marries in *Reunion with Murder* (174), is the former
Betty Mahan, a quick-witted young woman who was once an assistant librarian at the Fogg Museum. By the time Jones leaves
Harvard for a life of leisure in Saxon, he and Betty have
three small children.

Of Jones' five published cases, only two have strong academic flavor. In *Reunion with Murder*, Jones finds the killer
of Sherman North, one of his undergraduate classmates from
Harvard's class of 1931. And in *Harvard Has a Homicide*, he
outraces the Cambridge police to a solution in the murder of
Professor Singer, his graduate school tutor. Whereas *Reunion
with Murder* is set largely at a country club where the unfortunate Mr. North is found dead on the golf course, *Harvard Has
a Homicide* takes place almost entirely on the Harvard campus.
Professor Singer is stabbed dead in his rooms at Holloway
House, and Jones, undertaking his first criminological inquiry,
finds that the case involves the theft of rare paintings from
the Fogg. Jones' knowledge of Italian Renaissance art proves
crucial to his success in this exploit, but so, too, does the
support he receives from Sylvester, his black valet. Sylvester, a dark, middle-aged man with a shiny bald head, polishes
Jones's shoes, runs errands, and lends his employer money in
moments of temporary fiscal embarrassment. Sylvester also
rouses Jones on mornings after especially enervating drinking
bouts, often jolting him awake with garbled quotations from
Shakespeare spoken in a heavy Negro dialect.

Timothy Fuller was born in Norwell, Massachusetts. He
entered Harvard in 1932 but did not graduate. Much of his

post-college life was spent as a copywriter with the Boston
advertising firm of Harold Cabot and Co. Fuller wrote many
short stories and articles for national magazines, but his
five Juniper Jones mysteries were his only full-length works
of fiction.

Edmund ("Juniper") Jones Bibliography

*173. *Harvard Has a Homicide.* Boston: Little, Brown and Co.,
      1936. Published in Great Britain as *J for Juniper.*
      London: William Collins Sons, 1937.

174. *Reunion with Murder.* Boston: Little, Brown and Co.,
     1941; London: William Heinemann, 1947.

175. *Three Thirds of a Ghost.* Boston: Little, Brown and Co.,
     1941; London: William Heinemann, 1947.

176. *This Is Murder, Mr. Jones.* Boston: Little, Brown and Co.,
     Co., 1943; London: William Heinemann, 1944.

177. *Keep Cool, Mr. Jones.* Boston: Little, Brown and Co.,
     1950; London: William Heinemann, 1951.

CLIFFORD WELLS (1936)

Creator: Bortner, Norman Stanley

Clifford Wells is a "dabbler in the realm of scientific
logic, a student in the arts of microphotography and criminal
deduction, and a famous name in police records as a breaker of
alibis." Wells is also a junior instructor of physics at
Johns Hopkins University. Despite his reputation as a detective, he has very little status on the Johns Hopkins campus.
He is routinely assigned undesirable 8:30 A.M. classes, and
his older, wiser colleagues constantly advise him to publish
rather than fight crime.
    Although Wells' cases are non-academic in nature, he some-
times interviews suspects and informants in his office in
Maryland Hall. He also uses the laboratories in the building's
basement for analyses of physical clues. Paul Maccabee, one
of his graduate students, often assists him in conducting
laboratory tests. Wells works closely, too, with Lieutenant
Barney Mattingly of the Baltimore police. Mattingly frequently
asks Wells for assistance, and the lieutenant is the central

police figure in both of Wells' published exploits. In *Bond
Grayson Murdered!* (178) Wells and Mattingly cooperate to save
from the gallows a young man who is falsely convicted of killing his millionaire uncle. And in *Death of a Merchant of
Death* (179) Wells and Mattingly join forces again to identify
the assassin of a munitions tycoon who is shot dead as he
watches an anti-war play in a Baltimore theatre.

Thirty-two-years-old, tall, and extremely lean, Wells is
in superb physical condition. He is not handsome, however.
He has angular facial features, and his hands are abnormally
large. What's more, his "long, strong, and blunt" fingers
are covered with scars, the outcome of burns which Wells routinely incurs as he tries to light his ever-present pipe and
talk at the same time. Despite his anatomical flaws, Wells
is thought attractive by Harriett Fleming, a secretary employed
by a large Baltimore investment firm. He thinks that she is
attractive, too, but his low academic salary prevents him from
proposing marriage. One way out of his penurious condition,
Wells believes, may be to moonlight as a paid consulting detective. Thus, in *Bond Grayson, Murdered!*, when offered a "large"
fiscal reward by the grateful man whom he has freed from death
row, Wells briefly ponders the ethics of whether or not he
should compromise his amateur standing, and then he quickly
accepts the money.

Norman Stanley Bortner seems to have disappeared entirely
from the biographic annals of mystery fiction. *Bond Grayson
Murdered!* and *Death of a Merchant of Death* were his only two
mystery novels.

Clifford Wells Bibliography

178. *Bond Grayson Murdered!* Philadelphia: Macrae-Smith, 1936.

179. *Death of a Merchant of Death.* Philadelphia: Macrae-
      Smith, 1937.

THEOCRITUS LUCIUS WESTBOROUGH (1936)

Creator: Clason, Clyde B.

Professor Theocritus Lucius Westborough is an elderly
classicist and historian. Small, frail, and "owlish" behind
gold-rimmed spectacles, he lives in solitary confinement in
"The Equable," a Chicago residential hotel. The professor
once taught at a leading Chicago university, and he is well-

known in academic circles for his biographies of obscure Roman leaders. His best-respected work is *Heliogabulus, Rome's Most Degenerate Emperor*. Unfortunately, Westborough's monographs are not best-sellers, but he is financially secure nonetheless, thanks to a legacy left him by his brother. An occasional victim of absent-mindedness, Westborough takes his meals at odd hours, and because he likes to escape his small apartment he spends many of his afternoons in motion-picture theatres. Westborough draws his greatest visceral pleasure from smoking. He keeps his tobacco in a yellow, oilskin pouch and, in his only affectation, he puffs an amber-stemmed pipe with a bowl shaped in the form of a skull.

Because Professor Westborough has an abundance of free time, his detection tends to be slowly paced and meticulous in its attention to detail. Furthermore, since the professor finds the social aspects of detection a welcome change from his lonely life at The Equable, he sometimes prolongs his investigations beyond the point where most professorial sleuths would come forth with their denouements. A keen observer and an omnivorous collector of clues, Westborough draws deliberately upon his long years of historical scholarship for his detection methodology. When confronted with an especially knotty problem, he writes down all of the facts of the matter, discards "useless information," and eventually arrives at "the stark truth."

Inspector John Mack of the Chicago police calls regularly upon Professor Westborough for assistance. And so, too, do various friends and former students throughout the United States. In *The Death Angel* (180), for example, the professor travels to "Rumpelstiltizgen," a large estate in Wisconsin, in order to probe the disappearance of the property's owner. In *Blind Drifts* (182) he journeys to Denver in order to investigate evil doings in coal mine. And in *The Whispering Ear* (185) he temporarily becomes a participant in the Hollywood scene, first as an official advisor to "Plutarch Pictures" on a film being made about the life of Cleopatra, and later as an unofficial detective in a murder case. Many of Westborough's exploits involve ancient and exotic artifacts. *Murder Gone Minoan* (187), for instance, takes him to "Isleta del Cinturou de Plata," an island off the Coast of California, where he resolves the sinister matter of Cretian art treasures stolen from the sumptuous home of Alexis Papblagloss, the department-store king of Los Angeles.

Clyde B. Clason does not appear in any of the biographic compendia about literary figures. His contributions to mystery fiction were limited to his ten Professor Westborough novels.

180. *The Death Angel.* Garden City, New York: Doubleday, Doran and Co., 1936; London: William Heinemann, 1937.

181. *The Fifth Tumbler.* Garden City, New York: Doubleday, Doran and Co., 1936; London: William Heinemann, 1937.

182. *Blind Drifts.* Garden City, New York: Doubleday, Doran and Co., 1937.

183. *The Purple Parrot.* Garden City, New York: Doubleday, Doran and Co., 1937; London: William Heinemann, 1937.

184. *The Man From Tibet.* Garden City, New York: Doubleday, Doran and Co., 1938; London: William Heinemann, 1938.

185. *The Whispering Ear.* New York: Doubleday, Doran and Co., 1938; London: William Heinemann, 1939.

186. *Dragon's Cave.* New York: Doubleday, Doran and Co., 1939. London: William Heinemann, 1940.

187. *Murder Gone Minoan.* New York: Doubleday, Doran and Co., 1939. Published in Great Britain as *Clues to the Labrynth.* London: William Heinemann, 1939.

188. *Poison Jasmine.* New York: Doubleday, Doran and Co., 1940.

189. *Green Shiver.* New York: Doubleday, Doran and Co., 1941; London: William Heinemann, 1948.

HUNTOON ROGERS (1937)

Creator: Knight, Clifford (1886-)

Huntoon "Hunt" Rogers is a professor of English at a university in Los Angeles. In his late thirties, he has thinning blonde hair, a large nose, "grim-set" lips, and ears which stick out prominently from his head. Pleasant almost to a fault, he is a self-effacing sleuth. He admits to having "only limited reasoning powers." Rogers' real talent for detection lies in his skepticism. Something of an expert in human psychology, he "looks behind easy answers" to pierce lies and phony alibis. He also possesses coolness under stress. And although he has a "laborious cough" from constant cigarette smoking, he is capable of long, tiring searches for physical evidence.

Rogers seems to lead an ideal professorial existence; he is almost never on the campus of the institution from which he draws his paycheck. Instead, he travels constantly, for reasons which are not always fully explained, and he is usually pictured in exotic locales. In *The Affair of the Scarlet Crab* (190), for instance, he resolves a series of murders on the *Cyrene II*, a luxurious cruise ship which is taking him to the Galapagos Islands as part of a scientific research expedition. In *The Affair of the Ginger Lei* (193) and *The Affair of the Splintered Heart* (201), Rogers stumbles upon homicides in Hawaii. And in *The Affair of the Circus Queen* (197) his travels take him to Manila, where he copes with the unexplained death of the owner of a traveling circus.

The cases which confront Rogers are extremely complex. The texts of many of the novels in which he appears are followed by sealed inserts in which crucial clues are recapitulated for readers whose attentions may have flagged during the main narratives. Because the Rogers stories emphasize cluedropping at the expense of characterization, neither Rogers' social background nor his personality are well delineated. The professor displays few eccentricities, although on occasion he admits to fantasies about being a circus clown, a mystery writer, and a poet. His hobbies include surfing, long walks, and photography. Unlike many professors of English who double as series-character sleuths, Rogers is not prone to offer incessant quotations from great literature. In fact, he does not appear to be a devout reader of the classics. Rogers' favorite author seems to be Edith Mary Merker, a detective-story writer, whose untimely death he investigates in *The Affair of the Heavenly Voice* (191).

Clifford Knight was born in Fulton, Kansas. He attended Washburn College and the University of Michigan, and in 1918-1919 he served as an assistant professor at the U.S. Army Signal Corps Officer Training School at Yale. From 1920 to 1929, Knight was an editor with the *Kansas City Star*. He was a frequent contributor of short stories to popular magazines. Knight's initial Professor Rogers novel, *The Affair of the Scarlet Crab*, won the $2000 first prize in the 1937 Dodd, Mead/Red Badge mystery contest. Many of his subsequent Rogers novels also won acclaim for their intricately plotted stories.

Huntoon Rogers Bibliography

190.   *The Affair of the Scarlet Crab*. New York: Dodd, Mead
         and Co., 1937; Victor Gollancz, 1937.

191. *The Affair of the Heavenly Voice.* New York: Dodd, Mead and Co., 1937; London: Robert Hale, 1938.

192. *The Affair at Palm Springs.* New York: Dodd, Mead and Co., 1938.

193. *The Affair of the Ginger Lei.* New York: Dodd, Mead and Co., 1938.

194. *The Affair of the Black Sombrero.* New York: Dodd, Mead and Co., 1939.

195. *The Affair on the Painted Desert.* New York: Dodd, Mead and Co., 1939.

196. *The Affair in Death Valley.* New York: Dodd, Mead and Co., 1940.

197. *The Affair of the Circus Queen.* New York: Dodd, Mead and Co., 1940.

198. *The Affair of the Crimson Gull.* New York: Dodd, Mead and Co., 1941.

199. *The Affair of the Skiing Clown.* New York: Dodd, Mead and Co., 1941.

200. *The Affair of the Limping Sailor.* New York: Dodd, Mead and Co., 1942.

201. *The Affair of the Splintered Heart.* New York: Dodd, Mead and Co., 1942.

202. *The Affair of the Fainting Butler.* New York: Dodd, Mead and Co., 1943.

203. *The Affair of the Jade Monkey.* New York: Dodd, Mead and Co., 1943.

204. *The Affair of the Dead Stranger.* New York: Dodd, Mead and Co., 1944.

205. *The Affair of the Corpse Escort.* New York: Dodd, Mead and Co., 1946.

206. *The Affair of the Golden Buzzard.* New York: Dodd, Mead and Co., 1946.

207. *The Affair of the Sixth Button.* Philadelphia: David
     McKay, 1947.

CYRUS HATCH (1938)

Creator: Davis, Frederick Clyde (1902-1977)

Cyrus Hatch is a sociologist/criminologist at "Knickerbocker College," a high-status institution in the heart of
New York City. Cyrus also is the son of Mark Hatch, New York's
police commissioner. Six-feet-four-inches tall, handsome, and
with an illustrious father, Cyrus is a media celebrity. The
New York daily newspapers report regularly upon his sleuthing
escapades, and his name appears frequently in Walter Winchell's
syndicated column.
    Although Cyrus happens upon some of his cases by accident,
he frequently involves himself deliberately in particularly
intriguing mysteries. He feels strongly that professors of
criminology should get out of their classrooms and conduct
practical detective work. This view is not shared by stodgy
Professor Gilles, the bearded, pipe-smoking chairperson of
Knickerbocker's sociology department, or by Dr. Grampey, Knickerbocker's president. Indeed, in *Coffins for Three* (208)
Gilles and Grampey unsuccessfully attempt to have Cyrus removed
from the school's faculty because of the "indecorous" publicity he brings to the college. Cyrus retains his post only
after convincing his colleagues at a faculty meeting that his
sleuthing is a worthwhile public service.
    As a detective, Cyrus Hatch is a master of modern crimin-
ological technique. Knowledgeable about ballistics, poisons,
and fingerprints, he often conducts his own laboratory work
independently of the police. He is an astute observer, too,
and he possesses enormous amounts of energy. Because he sometimes competes with the police for clues, Cyrus' relationship
with his father is strained. While Mark Hatch admires Cyrus'
skills and his dedication to crime fighting, he is not above
chastising his son for overzealousness. Cyrus is assisted
in his sleuthing by Danny Delevan, a short and stocky body-
guard, and by Jane Porter, who is the Knickerbocker College
sociology department's secretary at the beginning of the series, but who subsequently becomes Cyrus's wife. Danny is in
the employ of Mark Hatch, who has hired him to protect his son
against kidnapping. Danny often functions as Cyrus's legman.
Jane, a lovely young lady with blonde hair and "sky-blue"

eyes, has an insightful mind and an acid-laden tongue. Perhaps because of her secretarial experiences with Knickerbocker's retinue of sociologists, Jane tries to persuade her husband to leave the academic world. Not content to be the wife of "a mere professor," she wants Cyrus to become a full-time private investigator.

The mysteries which Cyrus Hatch solves are set off-campus and they involve non-academic victims and culprits. Nevertheless, Cyrus is frequently pictured in his Knickerbocker College office and in his lecture halls. His untidy office is littered with books, microscopes, and chemical testing devices. The most noteworthy teaching scene in the series, a vignette which almost certainly will elevate the temperatures of modern-day feminists, occurs in *Coffins for Three*. Expounding on the differences between male and female murderers, Cyrus contends that women who kill are prompted to do so by the "powerful, primitive emotions" released by physical love. "Virgins are not murderers," states Cyrus. "I have searched court records for forty years back and I have not been able to find a single case in which a murder was committed by a virgin."

Frederick Clyde Davis attended Dartmouth College. Early in his writing career he specialized in short detective stories for popular American pulp magazines. He began writing full-length detective fiction with *Coffins for Three*, and by the end of his life he had published fifty mystery novels. Davis sometimes used the pseudonyms Stephen Ransome and Curtis Steel. After ending the Cyrus Hatch series at eight volumes, Davis employed Lee Barcello, Steve Ransome, and James Christopher ("Operator No. 5") as series-character sleuths in some of his subsequent works.

Cyrus Hatch Bibliography

208. *Coffins for Three*. New York: Doubleday, Doran and Co., 1938. Published in Great Britain as *One Murder Too Many*. London: William Heinemann, 1938.

209. *He Wouldn't Stay Dead*. New York: Doubleday, Doran and Co., 1939; London: William Heinemann, 1939.

210. *Poor, Poor Yorick*. New York: Doubleday, Doran and Co., 1939. Published in Great Britain as *Murder Doesn't Always Out*. London: William Heinemann, 1939.

211. *The Graveyard Never Closes*. New York: Doubleday, Doran and Co., 1940.

212. *Let the Skeletons Rattle.* Garden City, New York: Dou-
      bleday, Doran and Co., 1944.

213. *Detour to Oblivion.* Garden City, New York: Doubleday
      and Co., 1947.

214. *Thursday's Blade.* Garden City, New York: Doubleday
      and Co., 1947.

215. *Gone Tomorrow.* Garden City, New York: Doubleday and
      Co., 1948.

CHARLES LATIMER (1939)

Creator: Ambler, Eric (1909-)

At the age of thirty-five, Charles Latimer was a lecturer
in political economy at "a minor English university." However,
after completing his third professional monograph (a study of
the economic policies of the then-fledgling Nazi party in Germany), Latimer fell into a deep depression and turned to the
writing of detective fiction as therapy. The commercial success of his detective novels coupled with a quarrel "over
principles" with his university's administrators, prompted
him to resign his teaching post to become a full-time mystery
writer.
     When readers first encounter Latimer, in *The Mask of
Demetrios* (216), he is in Turkey researching a plot tor a new
detective epic, and he quickly becomes embroiled in a mystery
of his own. The escapade involves the search for a former
Greek fig picker who is now a master international criminal.
After bringing this case to a successful conclusion, Latimer
temporarily retires from sleuthing. He devotes himself entirely to writing, produces a series of best sellers, and
presumably becomes the envy of his former faculty colleagues.
But, alas, after twenty years of the good life, he meets his
demise in *The Intercom Conspiracy* (217), the second and last
book in which he is a participant. Attempting another first-
hand research undertaking, this one concerning corruption in
the Allied intelligence establishment, Latimer disappears
(presumably murdered) somewhere on the French/Swiss border.
     A shadowy figure, whose full range of personal attributes
is never revealed, Latimer is taciturn, a cigarette smoker,
and a man who does not seem well-suited for detective work.
He is slow to appreciate the significance of vital clues,

and he is even slower to understand the dangers he incurs by
putting himself in perilous situations. The keys to Latimer's
character might best be discovered by close scrutiny of his
own published works. The two professional books which he
wrote before producing his study of Nazi fiscal policies were
a study of Proudhon's influence on Italian political thought
and a monograph entitled *The Gotha Programme of 1875*. And
Latimer's first three mystery novels (all published before his
adventures in *The Mask of Dimitrios*) were *A Bloody Shovel,
"I", Said the Fly,* and *Murderer's Arms*.

Eric Ambler was born in London and attended the University
of London as an engineering student from 1924 until 1927. After a brief engineering apprenticeship, and after a short stint
as an advertising copywriter, Ambler devoted his full talents
to the writing of suspenseful mysteries and spy thrillers. He
is now generally regarded as the modern-day maestro of these
genres, and *The Mask of Dimitrios* is usually regarded as one
of his most outstanding works. *The Mask of Dimitrios* was
filmed by Warner Brothers in 1944, although liberties were taken with the character of Charles Latimer. In the motion picture Latimer became "Leyden," a Dutch novelist, played by
Peter Lorre.

Charles Latimer Bibliography

216. *The Mask of Dimitrios*. London: Hodder and Stoughton,
     1939. Published in the United States as *A Coffin for
     Dimitrios*. New York: Alfred A. Knopf, 1939.

217. *The Intercom Conspiracy*. New York. Atheneum, 1969; Lon-
     don: Weidenfeld and Nicholson, 1970.

MACDOUGAL DUFF (1942)

Creator: Armstrong, Charlotte (1905-1969)

Don't say "Lay on, MacDuff!" to MacDougal Duff! If you
do, he will mark you down as deficient in intelligence. It
is Duff's opinion that bright people think of the phrase upon
meeting him, realize that it has been said many, many times
before, and then pass immediately into less hackneyed forms
of discourse.

Duff was once a professor of history at a leading American
university. However, he became "tired of having to pound
dates and data into undergraduates." As a means of extricating

himself from academe, he took up work as a private detective.
Because he now depends upon sleuthing fees for his livelihood,
he prefers to work for wealthy clients. Paid by the case,
rather than by the hour, Duff's usual income is from $5000 to
$10,000 per investigation.

Although Duff is no longer a practicing historian, he puts
his academic background to good use in his detective endeavors.
More than occasionally he sees parallels between the crimes he
is investigating and obscure historical events. In addition,
Duff employs an interrogation technique which once worked well
for him with student plagiarizers. He sometimes gets suspects
to admit their guilt by simply glaring at them in silence.
Through "bland passivity" (as he calls this method) Duff embarrasses guilty parties into admitting their wrong-doing.

Physically, Duff is tall and lean with long, bony fingers.
He has a lined, melancholy face which is "masked with both
wisdom and sadness." Middle-aged, energetic, and free from
the cares of the academic world, he radiates an immense inner
calm.

Duff is a public figure. Newspapers frequently run feature stories about the ex-professor turned sleuth. Part of
Duff's notoriety stems from the bizarre nature of the cases
which he undertakes. In *Lay on, MacDuff* (218) he finds the murderer of a wealthy businessman killed after taking part in a
lethal parchessi game. In *The Case of the Weird Sisters* (219)
he eradicates the source of evil in the household of the Whitlock sisters. One of the Whitlock sisters is blind. One is
deaf. And the third is devoid of an arm. And in *The Innocent
Flower* (220) Duff copes with the six cloyingly sweet Moriarity
children, one of whom, it appears, has a penchant for putting
poison in the wine of family guests.

Charlotte Armstrong was one of America's most critically
celebrated and commercially successful writers of mystery fiction. Born in Vulcan, Michigan, she spent two years at the
University of Wisconsin before earning a B.A. from Barnard
College in 1925. Armstrong's initial ambition was to be a
playwright, but when two of her dramas closed after brief
Broadway runs, she turned to the writing of detective stories.
The three MacDougal Duff novels were her first forays into
the detective genre. After concluding the Duff series, Armstrong began to specialize in moralistic tales of suspense
and terror. In most of her post-Duff writings, detection is
less important than are the efforts of innocent victims of
wickedness to work themselves free from perilous entanglements.
Three of Armstrong's post-Duff novels, *The Better to Eat You*
(446), *A Dram of Poison* (453) and the *Witch's House* (486)
appear in the second section of this bibliography.

MacDougal Duff Bibliography

218. *Lay On, MacDuff.* New York: Coward-McCann, 1942; London:
      John Gifford, 1943.

219. *The Case of the Weird Sisters.* New York: Coward-McCann,
      1943; London: William Collins Sons, 1943.

220. *The Innocent Flower.* New York: Coward-McCann, 1945.
      Published in Great Britain as *Death Filled the Glass.*
      London: Cherry Tree Books, 1945.

PERCY PEACOCK (1942)

Creator: Fitzsimmons, Cortland (1883-1949)

     Percy Peacock is a professor of psychology at a university
located near "Palos Rojas," California. Tall, presentable in
appearance (though not handsome), and in his late thirties,
Peacock is shy and quiet. He embarrasses easily and blushes
frequently. A bachelor, he would like to marry. All of the
women with whom he falls in love, however, see him more as a
friend and a confidant than as a prospective husband. In an
attempt to force himself to be more outgoing and aggressive,
Peacock has taken up amateur acting. Each summer he travels
to "Chatwich," Massachusetts, a town on Cape Cod, where he
performs in summer stock with "The Chatwich Players."
     Percy Peacock's sleuthing is an outgrowth of his psycho-
logical research. Though he seldom publishes any of his findings, he is constantly studying human behavior. Eschewing
laboratory experimentation, the professor prefers to observe
real life. He will, for example, go into a store, linger over
a piece of merchandise, and watch customers interact with
salesclerks. He also eavesdrops on conversations. In the
course of his voyeuristic activities, Peacock happens upon
crimes and clues. Then, employing his keen and "rational"
mind, he meditates and brings forth solutions to mysteries
which have baffled the police. Despite his success as a detective, Peacock is at all times humble. Moreover, he experiences
self-doubts during his ratiocinations. He fears that he might
be responsible for sending an innocent man or woman to prison.
Rather than simply announcing the names of evildoers, he prefers to stage elaborate denouments in which villains trap themselves into admitting their own guilt.

Neither of Professor Peacock's two published adventures takes place on a college or university campus. *Tied for Murder* (222), the second and last book in his series, centers on a murder which occurs at a Palos Rojas high school. The case is complicated by fears of the local residents that the Japanese are about to stage an air raid on the town. *Death Rings a Bell* (221), Peacock's first recorded exploit, provides more detailed insight into the professor's character. The story is set in Chatwich, Massachusetts. A series of murders shake the community, and Stryke Ryder, a leading man with the Chatwich Players, is arrested for the outrages. Peacock identifies the actual murderer, and Ryder is set free. During his sleuthing, Peacock proposes to Libby Powell, a young Chatwich belle. When Ryder is released from jail, he, too, asks Libby to marry him. Apologizing to Peacock, Libby accepts Ryder's offer, and the crestfallen professor learns that detection can have bittersweet consequences.

Cortland Fitzsimmons was born in Richmond Hills, Queens, New York. He attended New York University and City College of New York. Early in his working career he was employed as a salesman in several industries, and from 1929 until 1934 he served as sales manager for The Viking Press. During the last fifteen years of his life, Fitzsimmons operated a bookstore in Los Angeles. A well-respected writer, Fitzsimmons was better known for his inventive plots than for his characterizations. *Death Rings a Bell* and *Tied for Murder* were his last published works. An earlier, non-Percy Peacock mystery by Fitzsimmons, *70,000 Witnesses* (352), appears in the second section of this bibliography.

Percy Peacock Bibliography

221. *Death Rings a Bell*. Philadelphia: J.B. Lippincott, 1942; London: T.V. Boardman, 1943.

222. *Tied for Murder*. Philadelphia: J.B. Lippincott, 1943; London: T.V. Boardman, 1945.

GERVASE FEN (1944)

Creator: Crispin, Edmund [Montgomery, Robert Bruce (1921–1978)]

Professor of English language and literature at "St. Christopher's College," Oxford, Gervase Fen is the quintessential

donnish detective. Absentminded, oftentimes caustic in conversation, and a man whose everyday lifestyle is a composite
of eccentricities, Fen can transform himself when the occasion
warrants into an astute and effective (if not always efficient) sleuth. Fen's detection is improvisational. He fancies himself a brilliant armchair logician, but much of his
mystery-solving comes about as the result of dogged fieldwork,
during which he often uncovers clues through accident or coincidence.

The crimes which Professor Fen investigates are non-academic, but he is frequently pictured in his rooms at St.
Christopher's. Early in his sleuthing career he works in uneasy association with Sir Richard Freeman, Oxford's chief constable, a learned policeman who has published books of literary criticism on Shakespeare, Blake and Chaucer. Fen's collaborations with Freeman involve cases in the city of Oxford.
Later in his series Fen travels to various locales in England,
and in some of these non-Oxford adventures he helps, and is
helped by, Inspector Humbleby of New Scotland Yard.

Now in his mid-forties, Gervase Fen was a student at Magdalen College, Oxford, and a lecturer at the University of
Milan before taking up his post at St. Christopher's. He is
a Shakespearean scholar, a self-styled expert on Tennyson, and
given to salting his speech with literary allusions. Fen is
also something of an academic sham. He is willing to quote
from and to give opinions on all modes and genres of literature, whether or not he has any significant familiarity with
them. And while he anxious to talk at length about books and
articles which he is planning to write, he seldom puts pen to
paper. In the last full-length work of his canon, *The Glimpses
of the Moon* (232), Fen is attempting to compose a monograph
about modern English fiction, but the project is almost certain
to be abandoned because he finds most contemporary authors boring. His real ambition seems to be to write mystery stories.
In *Love Lies Bleeding* (227), he reveals part of the plot of
his first, in-process detective novel, but readers gain the
distinct impression that this work, too, will never be completed.

In contrast to most professorial series-character sleuths,
Gervase Fen is married. His wife, Dolly, is a "plain, spec-
tacled, sensible little woman," who appears only in *The Case
of the Gilded Fly* (223). The Fens reside in North Oxford with
their several children. Dolly knits, makes sage and frequently disrespectful comments about Gervase's labors as a detective, and stoically tolerates her husband's difficult behavior. Extroverted and introverted by turns, Fen tries Dolly's
patience by irascibility, by wearing bizarre, mismatched clo-
thing, by plastering his hair with water, and by driving his

red sports car with little skill but reckless abandon. He
also dabbles in politics. In *Buried for Pleasure* (228) he
stands unsuccessfully for Parliament under the improbable slo-
gan, "Vote for Fen and a Brave New World." Perhaps because of
Dolly's immense capacity for understanding, womanizing is not
among Fen's long list of peccadilloes. Although he meets several nubile young women during his cases, Fen remains stead-
fastly faithful to his wife.

Robert Bruce Montgomery was born in Chesham Bois, Bucking-
hamshire, and received a B.A. from St. John's College, Oxford,
in 1943. After a brief career as a schoolmaster, he became
not only a highly respected writer of detective stories, but
one of Great Britain's leading composers of film music as
well. Along with Michael Innes, Montgomery is universally
acknowledged as one of the two founding fathers of the school
of whimsical yet erudite British academic mystery fiction
which flourished in the 1950s and 1960s. Montgomery took his
pseudonym, Edmund Crispin, and the name of his sleuth, Gervase
Fen, from the names of characters in Michael Innes' *Hamlet,
Revenge!* (378). In addition to creating entertaining characters—each book in the Fen series has a cast of well-etched
and often-addled participants—Montgomery was also a master of
plot construction. Mystery buffs sometimes single out the
premise and execution of *The Moving Toyshop* (225) for particular praise. In this novel Fen deals with the matter of a
toystore which seems to transform itself overnight into a
grocery.

Gervase Fen Bibliography

223. *The Case of the Gilded Fly.* London: Victor Gollancz,
      1944. Published in the United States as *Obsequies at
      Oxford.* Philadelphia: J.B. Lippincott, 1949.

224. *Holy Disorders.* London: Victor Gollancz, 1945; Phila-
      delphia: J.B. Lippincott, 1946.

225. *The Moving Toyshop.* London: Victor Gollancz, 1946;
      Philadelphia: J.B. Lippincott, 1946.

226. *Swan Song.* London: Victor Gollancz, 1947. Published in
      the United States as *Dead and Dumb.* Philadelphia:
      J.B. Lippincott, 1947.

227. *Love Lies Bleeding.* London: Victor Gollancz, 1948;
      Philadelphia: J.B. Lippincott, 1949.

228. *Buried for Pleasure.* London: Victor Gollancz, 1948;

Philadelphia: J.B. Lippincott, 1949.

229. *Frequent Hearses.* London: Victor Gollancz, 1950. Published in the United States as *Sudden Vengeance.* New York: Dodd, Mead and Co., 1950.

230. *The Long Divorce.* London: Victor Gollancz, 1951; New York: Dodd, Mead and Co., 1951.

231. *Beware of the Trains: Sixteen Stories.* London: Victor Gollancz, 1953; New York: Walker and Co., 1962. (Short Stories.)

232. *The Glimpses of the Moon.* London: Victor Gollancz, 1977; New York: Walker and Co., 1977.

233. *Fen Country.* London: Victor Gollancz, 1979; New York: Walker and Co., 1980. (Short Stories.)

PAUL HATFIELD (1944)

Creator: Rogers, Samuel (1904-)

. Middle-aged, "thick-set," and the possessor of sharp features and "birdlike" eyes, Paul Hatfield is a professor of chemistry at "Woodside University" in the American Midwest. Hatfield is happily married, perhaps in part because he spends many weekends alone in a hilltop cabin located in a wilderness area twenty miles from the Woodside campus. His hobbies are ornithology and bicycle riding. He travels to his cabin by bike, and then he leaves the conveyance at the bottom of the hill in an old piano box.

The professor is an unofficial consultant to Inspector Waters of the Woodside police. Though he sometimes analyzes physical materials in his laboratory, Hatfield is more often given to logical deductions based upon psychological evidence. Some of his best ratiocination occurs early in the morning, as he walks through the rising midwestern mist looking for rare species of owls and birds. The professor is courteous but didactic in his conversation. He tends to stop at many points during a case in order to summarize for his listeners the progress which he has made in his detection. He speaks in a voice which is "both impersonal and intimate," and he has the useful ability to gain the confidence of others. A man of great earnestness, he occasionally emits a "dry chuckle," but he lacks a well-developed sense of humor.

All three of Professor Hatfield's published adventures take place at or near Woodside University. *You Leave Me Cold!* (236) focuses upon lethal misdeeds in the home of Dr. Chardwicke, a physician who sometimes cares for Woodside students and faculty members. *You'll Be Sorry!* (235) describes the professor's efforts to assist Kate Archer, a Woodside coed, after she receives threatening notes from an unknown source. Some of the action in *You'll Be Sorry!* takes place in Kate's dormitory, but most of the story unfolds at the sumptuous home (near Professor Hatfield's hilltop retreat) of a local millionaire who invites Kate to act as a companion for his lonely teenage daughter. *Don't Look Behind You!* (234), Professor Hatfield's first published exploit, is the most "academic" mystery of the series. In this story Hatfield identifies a demented sadist who stalks Daphne Gray, the lovely young fiancée of a university instructor. Many of the suspects in this case are teachers at Woodside, and Hatfield has ample opportunity to hone his sleuthing skills against the abrasive personalities of some of his faculty colleagues.

Samuel Rogers was born in Newport, Rhode Island. He received a B.A. from Brown University in 1915 and then did graduate work at the University of Chicago. A mainstream novelist as well as a writer of mysteries, Rogers was a professor of French at the University of Wisconsin when the Professor Hatfield novels were published.

*234. *Don't Look Behind You!* New York: Harper and Brothers, 1944.

235.   *You'll Be Sorry!* New York: Harper and Brothers, 1945. Published in Great Britain as *Murder Is Grim.* London: Hammond, Hammond and Co., 1955.

236.   *You Leave Me Cold!* New York: Harper and Brothers, 1946.

SIR RICHARD CHERRINGTON (1945)

Creator: Rees, Dilwyn [Daniel, Glyn Edmund (1914-)]

Professor of prehistory at "Fisher's College," Cambridge, Sir Richard Cherrington is a distinguished scholar. Known the world over for his archeological research, he is the author of many "dry" monographs. Cherrington is a bachelor and lives in college rooms. A connoisseur of rich foods and rare wines, he compensates for his high-caloric diet by taking long walks and by playing squash. In his sixties, he harbors vague thoughts of marriage because he does not want to die, old and alone, in his college apartment. Cherrington is vice-president of Fisher's College, and a power figure in the institution's administrative structure. He hopes to succeed the aged Dr. Quibell as Fisher's president.

Cherrington's hobby is reading detective novels, and he fancies himself a penetrative amateur sleuth. After interviewing participants in crimes, he spins elegant theoretical explanations. Unfortunately, his explanations are apt to be incorrect. Inspector Wyndham of the Cambridge C.I.D. tolerates Cherrington's detection activities, and on occasion even asks him to interrogate witnesses and suspects in cases which the police find baffling. But not all of Great Britain's law enforcement officers welcome Cherrington's gratuitous help. In *The Cambridge Murders* (237) a New Scotland Yard inspector from London marks him as the likely killer of a college porter. The visiting inspector comes to this conclusion because he is suspicious of Cherrington's unusual level of interest in the murder.

Only two of Sir Richard Cherrington's adventures have been published. The first, *The Cambridge Murders*, is a fully realized academic mystery. Lush with Cantabrigian atmosphere, the story takes Cherrington for a brief time to France, but most of the plot is set within the confines of Fisher's College. In addition to the death (by shooting) of the college porter, *The Cambridge Murders* involves the unexplained disappearance of the college dean. As Cherrington's zealous detection proceeds, readers are given considerable insight into the sordid details of life behind Fisher's College's "aesthetically satisfying exterior." *Welcome Death* (238), published nine years after *The Cambridge Murders*, takes Cherrington to Wales. There, in the village in which his sister resides, the would-be master detective deals with railroad timetables, false confessions, and murderous small-town rivalries.

Glyn Edmund Daniel was born in Lampeter in southern Wales. He received a B.A. from Cambridge in 1935 and a Ph.D. from Cambridge in 1938. After service as an intelligence officer in the Royal Air Force during World War II, he returned to Cambridge in 1945 as a lecturer in archeology. In 1974 he became Disney Professor of Archeology at Cambridge. *The Cambridge Murders* and *Welcome Death* are Daniel's only mystery novels. *The Cambridge Murders* was published under the pseudonym Dilwyn Rees. Daniel used his own name on *Welcome Death*.

Sir Richard Cherrington Bibliography

*237. *The Cambridge Murders* (by Dilwyn Rees). London: Victor
       Gollancz, 1945.

238.   *Welcome Death* (by Glyn Daniel). London: Victor Gol-
       lancz, 1954; New York: Dodd, Mead and Co., 1955.

A. PENNYFEATHER (1945)

Creator: Olsen, D.B. [Hitchens, Delores (1907-1973)]

A. Pennyfeather is a well-liked professor of English at
"Clarendon College," a small, high-quality institution in
southern California. In his late fifties, and a bachelor,
Pennyfeather has been at Clarendon for nearly thirty years.
His previous port of academic call was "City College of Gull-
ville [Oregon]," but he left that institution because the students were not sufficiently deferential. Pennyfeather teaches
lively courses on Chaucer and Milton, but he does not seem to
be engaged in research. He is affable and on easy terms with
everyone in the Clarendon community. His polite Clarendon
students sometimes call him "Doc," not knowing that he failed
to complete his Ph.D., and his colleagues sometimes call him
Adam. But Pennyfeather has never told anyone his actual first
name. And for reasons known only to himself, he is determined
never to do so.

Professor Pennyfeather is an astute observer of human
character, and his genius as a sleuth lies in his ability to
grasp the nuances of speech and behavior. When on a case, he
is (in his own words) "alert as an old fox at the door of a
chicken house." The professor has studied the art of debat-
ing, and this has given him added skills as logician and as an
interrogator. Disdaining armchairs, he does most of his own
fieldwork. Considering his age, Pennyfeather possesses unusual physical stamina. He sometimes overextends himself,
however, and when he does get tired he can become uncharacteristically ill-humored. But Pennyfeather's crankiness does
not last for long. With a good night's sleep, he is ready
once again to resume his cheerful crime fighting.

Pennyfeather engages in detection in part because he is
naturally inquisitive and in part because he is constantly
receiving pleas for help from troubled friends and former
students. Moreover, Pennyfeather cannot tolerate an unsolved

mystery. Most of the professor's sleuthing takes him off campus, to the Southwest and to various exotic California locales. But in the last book of his series, Pennyfeather puts his amateur detective abilities to work on the Clarendon campus. *Enrollment Cancelled* (244) describes Pennyfeather's successful efforts to rid Clarendon of a mad, Jack-the-Ripper multiple-murderer. In this exploit Professor Pennyfeather displays a heretofore-hidden familiarity with the niceties of psychosexual deviation. Thanks to his insights and his labors, the troubling affair is resolved, and Clarendon College is made safe once again for its retinue of pleasant, bookish faculty members and students.

Dolores Hitchens was born in Texas and attended the University of Southern California. She specialized in light, sometimes whimsical murder mysteries. In addition to Professor A. Pennyfeather, Hitchens created several other series-character detectives, the most popular of whom were Rachel and Jennifer Murdock—two elderly spinsters who appear as a detection team in nine Hitchens novels. D.B. Olsen, the name which appears on her A. Pennyfeather stories, was only one of Hitchen's pseudonyms. She employed the aliases Dolan Birkley and Noel Burke on some of her other works.

A. Pennyfeather Bibliography

239. *Bring the Bride a Shroud.* Garden City, New York: Doubleday, Doran and Co., 1945; London: Francis Aldor, 1945.

240. *Gallows for the Groom.* Garden City, New York: Doubleday and Co., 1947.

241. *Devious Designs.* Garden City, New York: Doubleday and Co., 1948.

242. *Something About Midnight.* Garden City, New York: Doubleday and Co., 1950.

243. *Love Me in Death.* Garden City, New York: Doubleday and Co., 1951.

*244. *Enrollment Cancelled.* Garden City, New York: Doubleday and Co., 1952. Also published as *Dead Babes in the Wood.* New York: Dell Publishing Co., 1954.

JOHN STUBBS (1945)

Creator: Campbell, R.T. [Todd, Ruthven (1914-)]

Professor John Stubbs is an internationally famous British botanist. Although he does not seem to hold any permanent institutional post, he lectures regularly at Oxford and Cambridge, and he is accepted as a peer by the great academic plant scientists of the world. In his late fifties, Stubbs ressembles a "short-sighted baby elephant." He is a man of immense bulk and wears thick, steel-rimmed glasses. His pachydermous image is enhanced, too, by his behavior. A bellicose man, Stubbs often raises his voice in real (or mock) anger, and he is fond of hurling devastating insults at those whom he considers fools or charlatans. Moreover, the professor is well-known to his friends and associates as an impulsive automobile driver. The owner of a huge Bentley "of uncertain age," he maneuvers his machine through traffic "like a chess player." His technique is to accelerate the Bentley to top speed and then to apply the brakes "just in time to avoid disaster."

Professor Stubbs engages in sleuthing primarily out of his strong sense of intellectual superiority. When murders take place in his environment, he becomes impatient with the clumsy efforts of the police and steps in to apprehend the criminals before they can escape justice. As an accomplished scientist, Stubbs brings a highly developed knowledge of pharmacology to his cases. However, his major strength as a detective lies in his aptitude for logical deduction. After gathering evidence, he writes down elaborate lists of suspects, their opportunities to commit the crimes in question, and their motives. Then he withdraws to a quiet corner, closes his eyes, puffs on a cigar, and thinks through his data until he arrives at the identity of the guilty parties. But he does not always immediately reveal the fruits of his cogitations. Something of a prankster, Stubbs enjoys toying with the police (and with the readers of his stories) by giving them ample time to follow red herrings to false conclusions. Professor Stubbs' playful, delayed-action approach to detection is no doubt the product of his avocational reading habits. He is a constant consumer of mystery novels, and his favorite author is John Dickson Carr.

All of the above information about Professor Stubbs was drawn from *Unholy Dying* (245), the only one of the professor's seven long-out-of-print and difficult-to-locate adventures which was available for purposes of annotation. *Unholy Dying* takes place at the "University of Gowerburgh" in Great Britain.

Narrated by Andrew Blake, Professor Stubb's young, newspaperman nephew, the novel centers on the deaths by poison of Professors Porter and Swartz, both of whom (along with Stubbs)
are attending a conference of geneticists at the university.
Unholy Dying is noteworthy for the unusual strategy which the
culprit-of-the-piece employs to kill Professor Swartz. The
murderer coats the bowl of the professor's pipe with cyanide,
and the unfortunate victim puffs himself to death.

A celebrated poet, a biographer, an art historian, and an
author of children's books, Ruthven Todd was born in Edinburgh, Scotland. He attended Fettes College and the Edinburgh College of Art. Todd immigrated to the United States
in 1948 and became a naturalized American citizen in 1959.
He taught creative writing at Iowa State University during
the 1950s and was a visiting professor at the State University of New York at Buffalo in 1972. Todd's foray into the
field of mystery fiction began and ended with his Professor
John Stubbs novels. His Professor Stubbs stories were composed during World War II while he served as a civil defense
officer in London.

Professor John Stubbs Bibliography

245. *Unholy Dying.* London: John Westhouse, 1945.

246. *Adventures with a Goat.* London: John Westhouse, 1946.

247. *Bodies in a Bookshop.* London: John Westhouse, 1946.

248. *The Death Cap.* London: John Westhouse, 1946.

249. *Death for Madame.* London: John Westhouse, 1946.

250. *Swing Low, Sweet Death.* London: John Westhouse, 1946.

251. *Take Thee a Sharp Knife.* London: John Westhouse, 1946.

PROFESSOR CALDWELL (1947)

Creator: Ozaki, Milton K. (1913-)

A world-famous professor of psychology at "North University," an institution in a midwestern American city, Professor
Caldwell is short, slight, and rumpled. In his forties, he

has closely cropped brown hair and a pockmarked chin which resembles "a butterscotch sundae sprinkled with crushed nuts." His necktie permanently askew, Caldwell wears shabby brown suits. A bachelor, he is a misogamist. His forthcoming book, tentatively entitled *A Syllabus of Wifery*, will be the definitive work about the perils of marriage.

Professor Caldwell engages in sleuthing because of his curiosity about the human mind. Interested primarily in the nature of criminal behavior, he frequently probes for "homicidal tendencies" in suspects by subjecting them to psychological tests. In *The Cuckoo Clock* (252), for example, Caldwell gathers the likely killers of a beautician and then identifies the murderer after giving his subjects a word-association examination. And in *A Fiend in Need* (253), the professor conducts a conditioning-theory demonstration to trap a villain whose habits include murdering people in self-service elevators. But even though Caldwell's specialty is psychological detection, he has other crime-fighting talents as well. He is an expert in poisons, is knowledgeable about the sociological aspects of evildoing, and is well-versed in criminal law.

Caldwell is assisted in his cases by Lieutenant Phelan of the local police and by "Bendy" Brinks, a North University graduate student who serves as the Professor's Watson. Phelan respects Caldwell's acumen and often asks for the professor's help with especially intricate mysteries which seem beyond the capabilities of the authorities. Bendy Brinks lionizes Caldwell. A twenty-three-year-old bundle of insecurities, Bendy freely admits that his greatest thrill in life is to accompany his mentor and Lieutenant Phelan as they ride to the scene of a murder in a speeding, siren-blaring police car.

The crimes with which Caldwell deals take place off-campus but he and Bendy Brinks are often pictured in the office which they share at North University. Crowded with books and mementoes of cases-past, the office is outfitted with a loudly ticking cuckoo clock and a large orange Buddha atop the professor's desk. The office is so crowded, in fact, that Caldwell is constantly mislaying his tobacco pouch. One of Bendy's principal functions is to search for the missing container so that Professor Caldwell, whose thought processes go faster when he is smoking, can relight his pipe and continue his ratiocination.

The identity of Milton K. Ozaki has eluded those who compile the standard biographic reference works. Jacques Barzun and Wendell Hertig Taylor, in *a Catalogue of Crime* (see footnote 7, Introduction), identify him as graduate of Ripon College, a Chicago tax accountant, and the owner of a beauty salon. In addition to his three Professor Caldwell sagas,

Ozaki published twenty-four other mystery novels between 1946
and 1961. Thirteen of his novels were issued under the pseudonym Robert O. Saber.

Professor Caldwell Bibliography

252. *The Cuckoo Clock*. Chicago: Ziff-Davis, 1946. Also pub-
     lished as *Too Many Women*. Kingston, New York: Handi-
     Books, 1950.

253. *A Fiend in Need*. Chicago: Ziff-Davis, 1947.

254. *The Dummy Murder Case*. Hasbrouhk Heights, N.J.: Graphic
     Publishing Co., 1951.

PROFESSOR MANDRAKE (1949)

Creators: Bonnett, John, and Emery Bonnett [Coulson, John Hubert Arthur (1906-); and Felicity Winifred Carter Coulson
(1907-)]

     Professor Mandrake is a famous British anthropologist. He
is so well-known, in fact, that strangers constantly pester
him for his autograph. Mandrake's fame does not stem from
either his academic work or his detection. Instead, he has
become a late-in-life media celebrity. He appears on a weekly
BBC radio program called *The National Quiz*, and he also hosts
How Does It Tick, a television show for children. On *The
National Quiz*, Mandrake fields questions on a variety of obscure topics, and he debates the answers with a panel of other
experts in the arcane. As host of *How Does It Tick*, he explains the wonders of modern-day technology to an under-twelve
audience. In order to capitalize on his prominence, the professor has allowed (even encouraged) the production of such
items as the Mandrake Tick-Tock Series of Little-Books-on-How
-Things-Work, Mandrake Toothpaste, Mandrake Bath Soap, and the
Mandrake Water Pistol.
     Part of Mandrake's media success stems, curiously enough,
from the fact that he is a fat, "strikingly ugly" man who
"wears his skin like a baggy suit." Beneath his "hideous"
exterior, however, Mandrake is a pleasant individual. His
company is ardently sought by his fellow London intellectuals.
He lives in a London suburb and commutes to the city center by
train. Much of his leisure time is spent in a pub near his
home. There, in "The Sitting Hen," he discourses on matters

sundry and indulges himself in the house specialty, chicken
and mushroom pie. As he stuffs himself with this delicacy, he
also reflects upon the ironies of his career. After thirty
years of serious teaching and research at a university in the
London area, during which he remained an anonymous academic,
his roles on radio and television have now made him one of
the most influential men in Great Britain.

None of Mandrake's detection cases has an academic setting. His sleuthing comes about as a result of his celebrity
status. Murders take place in his vicinity, and other people
who are involved in the homicides expect him to resolve the
attendant mysteries. Mandrake tries manfully to be a master
detective, but he is often more clumsy than masterful. In
No Grave for a Lady (257), for example, his attempts at crime
fighting are eclipsed by those of Benjy, a small boy who uses
his junior detective kit to explain the death of an aging German movie star named Lottie Liselotte. In his most notable
exploit, *Dead Lion* (255), Mandrake tries to find the killer
of one of his fellow National Quiz participants. He narrows
the likely murderers down to six of his associate's former
girl friends and then invites the suspects to a mock seance
in hopes of shocking the guilty party into a confession. Mandrake uses for his voice-from-the-dead a recording of one of
the victim's extended speeches on *The National Quiz*, but his
guests immediately detect the sham and storm angrily out of
the room. One of the women then conducts her own investigation of the murder and eventually unmasks the culprit.

John and Emery Bonnett are the pen names of John Hubert
Arthur Coulson and Felicity Winifred Carter Coulson, a British
husband-and-wife writing team. Long-time residents of Spain,
the Coulsons have produced many radio, television, and film
strips in addition to mystery novels. Their mysteries, some of
which feature Inspector Borges of the Spanish police as a series-
character detective, are generally light-hearted and whimsical.

Professor Mandrake Bibliography

255. *Dead Lion*. London: Michael Joseph, 1949; Garden City,
      New York: Doubleday and Co., 1949.

256. *A Banner for Pegasus*. London: Michael Joseph, 1951.
      Published in the United States as *Not in the Script*.
      Garden City, New York: Doubleday and Co., 1951.

257. *No Grave for a Lady*. Garden City, New York: Doubleday
      and Co., 1959; London: Michael Joseph, 1960.

PROFESSOR DALY (1953)

Creator: Dillon, Eilis (1920-)

Retired from King's University, Dublin, where he taught
English literature and creative writing for nearly forty
years, Professor Daly lives at "Crane's Court," a residential
hotel/nursing home in the Irish town of Galway. He is now
in his mid-seventies. Professor Daly is a witty, garrulous
man who enjoys good conversation. On occasion, however, he
angers his companions by correcting them when they end their
sentences with prepositions. Daly is financially comfortable
thanks to the steady sales of his books. These works are not
scholarly monographs. Rather, they are "purple novels" written under the pseudonym Rosemary Downes.

Daly is a close friend of Mike Kenny, a high-ranking Irish
police official who is many years the professor's junior.
Kenny alerts Daly to interesting cases and then serves as his
partner in sleuthing. Altough Daly is capable of insightful
deductions (and capable of arduous fieldwork as well), his
major contribution to crime fighting is talking with and lis-
tening to witnesses and suspects. He sometimes confuses those
with whom he converses by injecting Latin quotations into his
speech, but he unfailingly manages to unearth important clues
in the course of his interactions. One of Daly's tactics is
to talk at great length about himself. It is his view that
persons who are subjected to his interminable oral autobio-
graphies inevitably try to counter his studied boorishness by
injecting off-guard comments about themselves.

Only two of Professor Daly's light-hearted but puzzle-
filled cases have been recorded for posterity. *Death at
Crane's Court* (258) depicts Daly and Mike Kenny at work investigating the death of a fellow lodger at the professor's
Galway residence. *Death in the Quadrangle* (259), on the
other hand, is a college mystery, and it rates with the best
of the genre. Professor Daly returns to King's University to
offer a series of lectures on "the crafty novelist." He is
not back at his old school very long before the institution's
unpopular president, a man named Bradley, dies of poison.
Daly's sleuthing in this exploit takes him back among his former faculty colleagues, and it provides him with the opportunity to take part in one of the best-written academic dinner
scenes in either mystery or mainstream fiction. Food and its
preparation play a large part in *Death in the Quadrangle*, and
this suits Daly perfectly. The professor's hobby, as revealed
in *Death at Crane's Court*, is reading cookbooks, because "they

show you life in the raw."

Eilis Dillon was born in Galway, Ireland. Married for
thirty years to the late Cormac O'Cuilleanian, a professor
of Irish literature at University College, Cork, Dillon has
produced children's books, mainstream novels, and mysteries.
She writes in both English and Gaelic. Dillon has taught creative writing at Trinity College, Dublin, and has made several
lecture tours of the United States, speaking on Anglo-Irish
literature.

Professor Daly Bibliography

258. *Death at Crane's Court.* London: Faber and Faber, 1953;
       New York: Walker and Co., 1963.

*259. *Death in the Quadrangle.* London: Faber and Faber, 1956;
       New York: Walker and Co., 1968.

AMBROSE USHER (1956)

Creator: Davey, Jocelyn [Rapheal, Chaim (1908-)]

A distinguished philosopher at "St. Mary's College," Oxford, Ambrose Usher is middle-aged, dark-haired, squat, and
"rather untidy." Brought by his Serbian parents to Great Britain at the age of three, he still speaks with traces of a
Serbian accent. Usher is a bachelor, a state of affairs which
allows him to accept--though sometimes with reluctance--spur-
of-the-moment international sleuthing assignments from the
British Government. He is a frequent visitor to America, and
in *The Undoubted Deed* (260) he serves as an attaché in Britain's embassy in Washington.

An immensely civilized man, Usher appreciates fine food,
fine wine, and fine women. Although he is not as witty as
some of the other Oxford dons who double as series-character
sleuths, he nonetheless can be a charming and polished conversationalist. A frequent user of the London Library, he has
eclectic reading tastes and is familiar with many literary
genres. Usher can make large talk and small and is a popular
guest at cocktail parties. At these affairs, which he attends
with some frequency, he can discourse, drink in hand, on subjects as diverse as the comedic talents of S.J. Perelman, the
poetry of Rupert Brooke, and the latest fortunes of the Ar-
senal team in the British Professional Football League.

Usher's success in his sleuthing endeavors is the product
in part, of his ability to draw forth information from his
deep and diverse reservoir of arcane knowledge. However, he
also brings a creative and probing mind to his cases. The
crimes with which he deals are non-academic in nature, but he
is often pictured at Oxford and, in *A Treasury Alarm* (264),
he travels to Harvard to present a series of lectures. A
number of his Harvard faculty hosts play roles in *A Treasury
Alarm,* and some of them become involved as their Oxford visitor matches wits with the mastermind of a well-financed ring
of international art thieves. While at Harvard, Usher also
finds romance in the person of Alyss Summers, a comely American art historian.

Chaim Raphael was born in Middlesborough, Great Britain.
He holds an M.A. (honors) from Oxford. Raphael was a lecturer
in Hebrew at Exeter College, Oxford, from 1932 until 1939.
Following his Oxford stint he held several important posts
with the British Foreign Office and the British Treasury before becoming a fellow in Jewish social history at the University of Sussex in 1970. In addition to his Ambrose Usher
novels, Raphael has written extensively about the history of
the Jewish people. Raphael is generally thought to have
modeled Ambrose Usher on Sir Isaiah Berlin, one of Oxford's
more colorful real-life dons, a noted philosopher, and an
occasional consultant to the British Government.

Ambrose Usher Bibliography

260. *The Undoubted Deed*. London: Chatto and Windus, 1956.
     Published in the United States as *A Capitol Offense*.
     New York: Alfred A. Knopf, 1956.

261. *The Naked Villainy*. London: Chatto and Windus, 1958;
     New York: Alfred A. Knopf, 1958.

262. *A Touch of Stagefright*. London: Chatto and Windus,
     1960.

263. *A Killing in Hats*. London: Chatto and Windus, 1965.

264. *A Treasury Alarm*. London: Chatto and Windus, 1976; New
     York: Walker and Co., 1980.

265. *Murder in Paradise*. New York: Walker and Co., 1982.

RONALD CHALLIS (1957)

Creator: Martin, Shane [Johnston, George Henry (1912-1970)]

Ronald Challis did not originally intend to become either a professor or a series-character sleuth. He attended Harvard College. Then, firmly intending to follow in the legal footsteps of his father, a Justice of the United States Supreme Court, he went on to earn his LL.B. from the Harvard Law School. But one day, just as he was completing his law school studies, a young lady from Vassar failed to keep a date with him at the Metropolitan Museum of Art in New York City. Left with a void in his social calendar, Challis wandered into a lecture room in the museum, heard a presentation on Mycenean excavations, and decided to forsake law for archeology. Now, some forty years later, Challis is a celebrated professor of archeology with honorary degrees from institutions of higher learning throughout the world. For reasons which are not entirely clear, he lives in Great Britain. He resides in a flat in London's St. Georges Square and lectures at an unidentified British university. Small and frail, and with his powers of physical endurance weakened by a lifetime of chainsmoking, Challis can no longer stand the physical strain of archeological digs. Instead, he conducts solitary research in the British Museum and writes scholarly monographs. Still a bachelor, he experiences frequent moments of loneliness. In order to involve himself in human interaction, and to add excitement to his life, he has taken up detection as a hobby.

Professor Challis deliberately injects himself (often without invitation) into the affairs of troubled friends and acquaintances in hopes of finding challenging mysteries to solve. Once he has located a criminological puzzle, he constructs an explanatory hypothesis which he proceeds to embellish by building "the pieces" of the case in question around it. A pleasant, sometimes witty man, Challis acquires much of his crime-solving data by conversing casually with witnesses and subjects. But he also employs a practice which he calls "intrusion." This technique, which other characters in his stories sometimes find offensive, is in fact snooping raised to an art form. Challis hides behind bushes to eavesdrop; he listens in on telephone conversations; he peeks into windows; and he reads letters over other people's shoulders. Challis feels no guilt when engaging in these activities. As he sometimes admits in moments of candor, the concept of privacy no longer holds any meaning for him. After all, most of his life has been spent unearthing the remains of ancient civilizations and prying into the smallest secrets of the people who lived within them.

None of Professor Challis' five published adventures has a college or university setting. Instead, the professor is seen in exotic European locales. *The Saracen Shadow* (266) takes place in a chateau in Southern France. *Twelve Girls in the Garden* (267) begins in London and then propels Challis to a variety of European cities as he searches for man who has disappeared after sculpting twelve mock-classical Greek statues. *The Man Made of Tin* (268) is set in Great Britain's Cornwall region. And *The Myth Is Murder* (269) and *A Wake for Mourning* (270) have Mediterranean backdrops. As he conducts his investigations, Challis drinks great quantities of thick Turkish coffee. He also indulges himself with fine wines and, in rare moments of repose, engages in landscape painting. When faced with an especially difficult sleuthing problem, he consults his thick gold pocket-watch for inspiration. The timepiece, given to him by his late father, is inscribed with the words "Never Take No for an Answer."

George Henry Johnston was born in Australia. During World War II he served as a war correspondent in the South Pacific for several Australian newspapers. After the war he spent much of his time in Europe, working as a reporter for Time-Life, Inc. and writing mainstream novels, books about World War II, and mystery fiction. He employed the pseudonym Shane Martin on his mysteries, but he used his real name on most of his other works. One of Johnston's mainstream novels, *My Brother Jack* (London: William Collins Sons, 1964; New York: William Morrow, 1965), won the Miles Franklin Literary Award in 1964. *My Brother Jack* is a story about Australian family life.

Ronald Challis Bibliography

266. *The Saracen Shadow*. London: William Collins Sons, 1957.

267. *Twelve Girls in the Garden*. London: William Collins Sons, 1957; New York: William Morrow, 1957.

268. *The Man Made of Tin*. London: William Collins Sons, 1958.

269. *The Myth Is Murder*. London: William Collins Sons, 1959. Published in the United States as *The Third Statue*. New York: William Morrow, 1959.

270. *A Wake for Mourning*. London: William Collins Sons, 1962. Published in the United States as *Mourner's Voyage*. Garden City, New York: Doubleday and Co., 1963.

GIDEON MANCIPLE (1957)

Creator: Hopkins, (Hector) Kenneth (1914-)

Nearly eighty years of age, Gideon Manciple is a retired
British professor of numismatics. A bachelor, he lives alone
in a modest London rooming house. Although he is forgetful
and sometimes confuses the past with the present, he continues
to do research. The coinage of Britain during the period of
Edward III is his specialty, and Manciple frequently flies off
to international conferences where he delivers papers.
Although he has been awarded many prizes for his scholarship,
his area of expertise is not one with a great amount of popular or professional appeal. As he sometimes sadly admits,
even his most spectacularly successful conference presenta-
tions absorb the interest of fewer than a dozen listeners.

When he is not studying coins at the British Museum, at
coinshops, or in his apartment, Professor Manciple spends
some of his time at his club in Knightsbridge. There he
smokes his pipe and indulges in tea laced with brandy. He
is also an avid fan of grade-B motion pictures. His two
favorite films are "Dracula" and "Rock and Roll Blues." Despite his many years, he has an eye for women, and he has a
lively fantasy life. When the professor actually converses
with attractive ladies, however, he often turns a bright shade
of pink.

Professor Manciple's sleuthing is always conducted in
the company of Dr. William Blow, a more than eighty-year-old
literary gentleman who lives in the same rooming house. A
fellow bachelor, Blow seems to have spent his entire life
editing the works of semi-obscure British writers. While Manciple and Blow display unusual energy for octogenarians, neither man has much real talent for detection. Manciple and
Blow bicker constantly and, fond of disguises, sometimes wear
ludicrous false mustaches and tinted glasses when in pursuit
of criminals. Moreover, they seldom interpret clues correctly. The London police consider them a nuisance. And yet,
by using their own unorthodox devices and by converting incipient senility from a liability into a detection asset, Manciple and Blow inevitably bumble into the solutions of the
mysteries they have set out to solve.

Hector Kenneth Hopkins was born in Bournemouth, Hampshire,
Great Britain. A prolific professional writer, he has a long
list of publications including works of poetry, mainstream
novels, travel books, and children's stories in addition to
mystery fiction. One of Hopkins's non-Gideon Manciple mystery
novels, *Campus Corpse* (488), is included in the second section

of this bibliography.

Gideon Manciple Bibliography

271. *She Died Because.* London: MacDonald and Co., 1957; New
      York: Holt, Rinehart and Winston, 1964.

272. *Dead Against My Principles.* London: MacDonald and Co.,
      1960; New York: Holt, Rinehart and Winston, 1962.

273. *Body Blow.* London: MacDonald and Co., 1962; New York:
      Holt, Rinehart and Winston, 1962.

ADAM LUDLOW (1962)

Creator: Nash, Simon [Chapman, Raymond (1924-)]

      Adam Ludlow is a senior lecturer in English literature at
"North London College." Approaching middle-age, his career
prospects are dim. Though he enjoys reading "unread books,"
he seldom publishes. Nor is he an inspiring teacher. Bored
with academe, Ludlow prefers to sit and meditate, to visit
secondhand bookshops, or to attend art exhibitions in London
museums. People sometimes address him as "Professor," a
rank which he is never likely to attain. These salutations
send him into bouts of introspective self-criticism.
      Ludlow is tall and gaunt with "a long, anxious face." A
bachelor, he is a private man who lives in an untidy but comfortable flat well across London from the college at which he
is employed. He walks with his eyes fixed on the ground, can
be caustic when engaged in conversation, and does not make
friends easily. A pipe-smoker, he is aggressively British.
Ludlow wears tweed suits, even on holiday in the Mediterranean, and one of his major peeves is American-style popular
culture. He especially dislikes the American custom of drinking ice water at meals. But Ludlow can find fault with British customs as well. He is not fond of tea, for example.
His taste in liquid refreshment runs more to beverages with
alcoholic content.
      Ludlow's first detection case, *Dead of a Counterplot* (274),
is set at North London College. A young lady is found dead
in the rooms of one of his best students, and in conjunction
with Inspector Herbert Montero of New Scotland Yard, Ludlow
locates the girl's killer. Inspector Montero and Ludlow main-
tain an uneasy synergistic relationship throughout the series,

but after *Dead of a Counterplot* the pair operates in non-academic settings. Montero considers Ludlow a meddling amateur whose donnish tendency to see simple matters as complex introduces needless inefficiencies into crime fighting. Montero admits, however, that Ludlow inevitably gets "to the center" of mysteries.

As a sleuth, Ludlow is best characterized as determined. Because detection is more interesting to him than are his academic labors, Ludlow pursues seemingly dead-end cases far beyond the points at which most real-life detectives would throw up their hands in surrender. He does considerable fieldwork (while ungraded student essays pile up in his office), and he traverses London by underground in search of witnesses and suspects to interview. Ludlow has a useful knowledge of Freudian psychology, which he occasionally brings to bear, but he more often depends on his sharp observational abilities and upon his skill at logical deduction. At the end of his cases he is prone to offer tutorial-like denouements which are interspersed with references to great and not-so-great works of English literature.

Raymond Chapman was born in Cardiff, Wales. He received a B.A. in 1945 from Jesus College, Oxford and M.A. degrees from Oxford and Kings College, University of London. In 1948 Chapman became a lecturer in English at the London School of Economics, a post he continued to hold during the publication of the Adam Ludlow series. In addition to his Adam Ludlow stories, Chapman has written books and articles on Victorian literature and on religious drama.

Adam Ludlow Bibliography

274. *Dead of a Counterplot*. London: Geoffrey Bles, 1962.

275. *Killed by Scandal*. London: Geoffrey Bles, 1962; New York: Roy Publishers, 1964.

276. *Death Over Deep Water*. London: Geoffrey Bles, 1963: New York: Roy Publishers, 1965.

277. *Dead Woman's Ditch*. London: Geoffrey Bles, 1964; New York: Roy Publishers, 1966.

278. *Unhallowed Murder*. London: Geoffrey Bles, 1966; New York: Roy Publishers, 1966.

KATE FANSLER (1964)

Creator: Cross, Amanda [Heilbrun, Carolyn Gold (1926-)]

    Kate Fansler is the most thoroughly professorial of all
the series-character sleuths reported upon in this bibliography. A professor of English literature at a New York City
university which very much resembles Columbia, Fansler is constantly involved in teaching, researching, consulting, and
committee work. Tall, "willowy," and in her early forties,
she frequently spices her conversation with literary allusions, and, as the product of a wealthy, cultured family, she
tends to employ an archly polysyllabic vocabulary. An expert
in Victorian literature, she most often teaches graduate students. Sometimes outspoken in faculty meetings, Fansler has
both friends and enemies in her department. She is an ardent
feminist. On a visit to Oxford in *The Question of Max* (283),
she finds it utterly distasteful that some of the university's
colleges still bar women from their hallowed dining halls.
And in *Death in a Tenured Position* (284), she journeys to Harvard to lend support to Janet Mandelbaum, Harvard's first female professor of English (and a non-feminist), whose life is
being made miserable both by her male-chauvinist colleagues
and by various women's groups on and near the Harvard campus.
    Kate Fansler does not seek mysteries to solve. Nor does
she especially enjoy her participation in the mysteries in
which she finds herself. In each of her adventures, readers
gain the distinct impression that Fansler would prefer to be
attending to the piles of unanswered professional correspon-
dence and to the unfinished manuscripts which clutter her
office. But once into her detection exploits, Fansler
applies the same precise reasoning skills which have made her
one of America's foremost literary scholars. To these skills
she adds considerable imagination and, in several instances, a
dash of intuition. Fansler gains much of her information
through conversations with key informants (though some of
these conversations are chance affairs, not pre-planned as
part of any grand sleuthing strategy), and she will do fieldwork when the situation demands. Fansler marries Reed Am-
hearst, an assistant New York City district attorney, in *The
Question of Max,* and her husband sometimes provides her with
advice. But because Fansler is an independent woman who travels, vacations, and sleuths alone, the Amhearsts are not a
conventional husband-wife detective team.
    In all six of Kate Fansler's published cases, she is
depicted to a greater or lesser degree in the performance of

her academic duties. Two of her stories, however, are pure
academic mysteries in the sense that they are set almost
totally on university campuses and have large rosters of academic characters. *Poetic Justice* (281) takes place at Fansler's home university. It centers on the death of Dr. Jeremiah Cudlipp, a professor of English, who is one of the major
participants in a campus political embroglio which surrounds
the fate of the school's adult education division. *Death in
a Tenured Position* combines wrongdoing and detection with an
angry exposé of sexism at Harvard. Criticized by some unchar-
itable reviewers (both male and female) for emphasizing its
feminist message at the expense of its mystery components,
Death in a Tenured Position deals at length with the difficulties faced by women scholars who attempt to penetrate into
the upper echelons of Harvard's faculty.

Born in East Orange, New Jersey, Carolyn Gold Heilbrun
received a B.A. in 1947 from Wellesley, an M.A. in 1951 from
Columbia University, and a Ph.D. in 1953 from Columbia. She
joined the Columbia faculty in 1960 and since 1972 has been
a professor of English. The recipient of Guggenheim, Rocke-
feller, and Radcliffe Institute Fellowships, Heilbrun has published several well-received professional monographs in addition to her Kate Fansler series.

Kate Fansler Bibliography

279. *In the Final Analysis*. New York: Macmillan, 1964; Lon-
      don: Victor Gollancz, 1964.

280. *The James Joyce Murder*. New York: Macmillan, 1967; Lon-
      don: Victor Gollancz, 1967.

*281. *Poetic Justice*. New York: Alfred A. Knopf, 1967; Lon-
      don: Victor Gollancz, 1970.

282. *The Theban Mysteries*. New York: Alfred A. Knopf, 1971;
      London: Victor Gollancz, 1972.

283. *The Question of Max*. New York: Alfred A. Knopf, 1976;
      London: Victor Gollancz, 1976.

*284. *Death in a Tenured Position*. New York: E.P. Dutton,
      1981. Published in Great Britain as *A Death in the
      Faculty*. London: Victor Gollancz, 1981.

NATALIE KEITH (1964)

Creator: Langley, Lee [Langley, Sarah (1927-)]

An attractive, middle-aged professor of archeology and
anthropology, Natalie Keith teaches at an unidentified uni-
ersity in the eastern United States. Much to the conster-
nation of its president, Dr. Ulysses Potter, the institution
at which Professor Keith is employed seems to have a faculty
which is dominated by neurotics, psychotics, and/or individuals with homicidal tendencies. As a result, murder is not
an unusual occurrence on the campus, and both of Keith's published cases are set within the university milieu. Her primary assets as a sleuth are her general familiarity with academic customs and her specific knowledge of the troubled personalities of her colleagues.

Keith works closely with Chris Jensen, a young detective
lieutenant with the local police. She does on-campus investigations for Jensen, provides him with crucial information
about faculty (and student) rivalries, and sometimes offers
theoretical explanations for the crimes in question. Because
of her invaluable assistance to Jensen, Keith has been given
a police badge. Thus she is only professorial series-character sleuth in this bibliography with official (albeit unpaid) status as a law-enforcement officer.

Nicknamed "Digs" for her frequent work at an archeological
site near the university, Natalie Keith can be both tough and
tender. Students dislike her demanding classes and her frequent surprise quizzes. And faculty members who offend her
often find themselves recipients of sharp rebukes. In *Osiris
Died in Autumn* (285), for instance, Keith sends one vulgar
male associate off in a sulk by telling him: "You're a
second-rate scholar with a gutter mind and a tongue that
should be boiled." On the other hand, the professor can display sympathy toward the victims of crimes and, on occasion,
she can even feel compassion for murderers. Moreover, her
relationship with Lieutenant Chris Jensen is similar to that
between a mother and a son. She worries constantly about
Jensen's well-being. In turn, he keeps a vigilant watch upon
her welfare.

Natalie Keith's complex character is attributable to her
bizarre and tragic life history. A pilot in the United States
Air Force Transport Command during World War II, she flew many
perilous missions for the Allied cause. Even while she was
serving so heroically, however, her husband Ben was killed in
combat in another theatre of the war. Keith remained loveless
until the early 1960s, when she became engaged to Wilson

Athelslan Gregg, a wealthy professor of geology. But Professor Gregg is murdered in *Osiris Died in Autumn*, and it is
only by turning to detection (and by finding Gregg's killer)
that Keith can overcome the second major sorrow in her life.
In *Dead Center* (286), she encounters romance once again, this
time with Geoffrey Lackland, a visiting professor of music.
Lackland becomes a suspect in this case, which involves the
murder of the university's star basketball player, and Keith
finds herself embroiled in an investigation which might send
her third great love to the electric chair. Fortunately,
Geoffrey Lackland does not prove to be the villain in *Dead
Center*. As the book ends, it appears as though he and Natalie
Keith will soon be married.
       Sarah Langley earned a B.A. in journalism and then trained
as an occupational therapist. At the time her Natalie Keith
books were published, she was employed at Bellevue Hospital in
New York City and was taking graduate courses in cultural
anthropology and archeology at a New York university.

Natalie Keith Bibliography

285.   *Osiris Died in Autumn*. Garden City, New York: Doubleday
        and Co., 1964. Published in Great Britain as *Twilight
        of Death*. London: Robert Hale, 1965.

286.   *Dead Center*. Garden City, New York: Doubleday and Co.,
        1968. Published in Great Britain as *Dead Centre*.
        London: Robert Hale, 1969.

DR. R.V. DAVIE (1967)

Creator: Clinton-Baddeley, V(ictor) C(linton) (1900-1970)

       Dr. R.V. Davie is a wise, wry, septuagenarian fellow of
"St. Nicholas's College," Cambridge. One of the wittiest and
most congenial of all professorial series-character sleuths,
he can be humorous or serious as the situation demands. Davie
is a classicist, but his knowledge extends to many other
fields as well. In particular, he is an expert in opera. And
he knows a great deal about both the past and present of St.
Nicholas's College. A bachelor, Davie occupies first floor
rooms looking onto the College Close, and he monitors the
comings and goings of college personnel. His vantage point
also allows him to eavesdrop on the conversations of passers-

by. When not observing from his window or conversing before
dinner in the Combination Room, Davie strolls in the Fellows'
Garden, takes naps, sips port, collects paperweights and other
bric-a-brac, and contemplates the advantages and disadvantages
of the past as compared with those of the present. During his
musings he often reviews his pet likes and dislikes. Among
the former are roast beef and lemon meringue pie, exotic teas,
and detective novels. Among the latter are most forms of
modern technology and current women's fashions. He refuses to
drive an automobile, and his considered assessment of women in
trousers is that they all should be forced to see themselves
walking away so that they might "be regaled by the sight of
their own behinds."

Dr. Davie is put into the role of sleuth through his natural inquisitiveness. Crimes occur; the police are baffled;
and Dr. Davie steps forward to resolve matters. He is more
interested in satisfying his own curiosity than in catching
criminals. His greatest assets as an amateur detective are
his blotting-paper mind and his ability to draw critical information from witnesses and suspects through disarming conversations. A student of meteorology, Davie frequently opens
his conversational investigations by talking in detail about
the weather. He is adept at sorting real clues from false
ones, and he has the additional facility of turning red herrings into profit. Bogus clues, as Dr. Davie treats them,
are simply "real clues pointing in an opposite direction."

Death's Bright Dart (287), Dr. Davie's first published
case, is set entirely at Cambridge and is academic mystery
fiction in its purest form. The story has Dr. Davie searching
out the culprit who murders a distinguished speaker at an
international science symposium being held at St. Nicholas's
College. The plot incorporates a collection of Cambridge dons,
several prominent visiting scientists, a clutch of naughty
children, and a series of inventive premises. During his subsequent escapades, Dr. Davie's detection takes him away from
the Cambridge scene. In *My Foe Outstretch'd Beneath the Tree*
(288) he spends much of his time at his London Club--"The
Chesterfield"--while he deals with the murders of a former
police officer and a struggling young actor. *Only a Matter of
Time* (289) carries him to a deadly music festival in the South
of England. In *No Case for the Police* (290) Davie returns to
his boyhood home in the West Country to act as the executor of
a will, and he finds himself, engaged in detection instead.
And in *To Study a Long Silence* (291) he copes with the criminal goings on at a London dramatic school.

Victor Clinton Clinton-Baddeley was born in Budleigh Sal-
terton, Devon, and received an M.A. from Jesus College, Cambridge. During his long and varied career he was an actor,

a playwright, a modern history editor for the *Encyclopedia Britannica*, a writer of historical monographs about the English stage, and a director of Juniper Records, a firm which specialized in recording poetry. The Dr. Davie novels were his only excursions into the field of mystery fiction.

Dr. R.V. Davie Bibliography

*287. *Death's Bright Dart*. London: Victor Gollancz, 1967; New York: William Morrow, 1970.

288. *My Foe Outstretch'd Beneath the Tree*. London: Victor Gollancz, 1968; New York: William Morrow, 1968.

289. *Only a Matter of Time*. London: Victor Gollancz, 1969; New York: William Morrow, 1970.

290. *No Case for the Police*. London: Victor Gollancz, 1970; New York: William Morrow, 1970.

291. *To Study a Long Silence*. London: Victor Gollancz, 1972.

NICHOLAS "NICKY" WELT (1967)

Creator: Kemelman, Harry (1908-)

Nicholas "Nicky" Welt is Snowden Professor of English Language and Literature at a university in the New England community of "Fairfield." In his forties, Professor Welt has white hair, a "lined gnomelike face," and a very high opinion of his own intellect. He is an aloof man, frequently sarcastic, and while he has many acquaintances on the faculty of the school at which he teaches, he has few, if any, real friends. Professor Welt's hobbies are chess and golf. A bachelor, he resides in a roominghouse which is a brisk, fifteen-minute walk from the university. He lives at this distance from the campus in order to minimize visits from his colleagues and students.

Professor Welt is an armchair detective. He seldom goes to crime scenes. He works primarily with secondary information brought him by the police or by the local county attorney, an individual (whose name is never given) who acts as his Watson. Welt's special talent as a sleuth lies in his flair for inferential reasoning. Much of his ratiocination is done in the Common Room of the Faculty Club, where he

astounds his colleagues by threading together the few clues
at his disposal to bring forth swift solutions to mysteries.

The Nine Mile Walk (292), the only book in which Professor
Welt appears, is a collection of eight stories, all of which
were published originally in *Ellery Queen's Mystery Magazine*.
Several of the pieces deal with crimes involving Professor
Welt's fellow faculty members. "The Ten O'Clock Scholar,"
the third episode in the collection, is an exemplar of story-
length college mystery fiction. The case centers on the murder of Claude Bennett, a graduate student, who is killed just
before he is scheduled to take his Ph.D. oral examination. The
suspects in the affair include George Korngold and Emmett Hawthorne, two feuding professors of English who have quarreled
over Mr. Bennett's competence. Using photographs of the hotel
room in which the luckless Mr. Bennett was slain (and employing his knowledge of the rivalries in the English department),
Welt identifies the culprit without interviewing a single witness or suspect.

Harry Kemelman was born in Boston, Massachusetts. He
received an A.B. from Boston University in 1930 and an M.A.
from Harvard in 1931. After teaching English at various Boston area secondary schools and at the Franklin Technical Institute, Kemelman joined the English department of Boston
State College in 1964. His Nicholas Welt stories are generally acknowledged to be masterpieces of "fair play" plotting
and many connoisseurs of mystery fiction now rate them among
the finest pieces of fictional detection ever published in
story form. Toward the end of Kemelman's experiences with
Nicholas Welt, he created another series-character sleuth,
Rabbi David Small, and Kemelman is best-known among casual
readers of mysteries for his best-selling Rabbi Small novels.
One of Kemelman's Rabbi Small works, *Tuesday the Rabbi Saw
Red* (553), carries its protagonist into the world of academe;
the book appears in the second section of this bibliography.

Nicholas Welt Bibliography

292. *The Nine Mile Walk.* New York: G.P. Putnam's Sons, 1967;
        London: Hutchinson Publishing Group, 1968. (Short
        Stories.)

DR. GRACE SEVERANCE (1968)

Creator: Scherf, Margaret (Louise) (1908-)

In her mid-seventies, Grace Severance (M.D.) is a retired

professor of pathology and anatomy. She taught for thirty-
five years at a university medical school in Chicago. Unmarried, Dr. Severance how travels the United States. She
stays with friends and relatives and occasionaly visits former students. Because Dr. Severance still possesses enormous
energy and because she has a restless mind, she finds retirement a bore. One of her diversions is to find fault with her
well-meaning hosts. Another is detection.

Dr. Severance's success as a sleuth is in part the result
of her medical expertise. But she also brings to her cases
the insights and the intuitions of an elderly spinster. A
perpetual skeptic, Dr. Severance tends to suspect the worst
in people. Therefore, she is able to see through false plea-
santries thrown up by the murderers whom she encounters. As
to her own demeanor, Dr. Severance can feign sociability, but
even while she is pretending to be interested in the conversations and activities in which she is engaged, she is silently
castigating the people around her. She particularly dislikes
tea parties (she would prefer to be alone with a large glass of
whiskey), and she recoils in silent revulsion when her hostesses
serve her liver for dinner. Dr. Severance also harbors a strong
distaste for government intervention. A life-long cigarette
smoker ("I'm not afraid to die"), she has recently accelerated
her tobacco habit as a reaction to anti-smoking warnings on
cigarette packages. In moments of extreme frustration, Dr.
Severance is inclined to use very direct language. "Horse-
feathers" is one of her favorite exclamations. Through frequent use of this word, the former professor likes to recall,
she both frightened and offended most of her colleagues at the
university, and thus she managed to be excluded from service
on faculty committees.

None of Dr. Severance's three cases takes place on a college or university campus. *The Banker's Bones* (293) is set
in Arizona, where the former professor is staying with her
niece Myrtle. Fleeing from Myrtle's constant nagging ("Aunt
Grace, drink your orange juice, it's good for you."), Dr.
Severance involves herself in the matter of a California bank
vice-president who disappears in the desert near Myrtle's
home. *The Beautiful Birthday Cake* (294) has rural Montana as
its locale. In this story Dr. Severance probes the mysterious
deaths of several local residents who expire after attending
a birthday party given in her honor by Laura and Elliot Lind-
say, two vacationing Hollywood actors. Although *The Beautiful
Birthday Cake* is not a college mystery, it does have in a
crucial role one Althea Doran, a faculty member at a Montana
University. A fellow spinster, Miss Doran befriends Dr. Severance, and during most of the novel she helps the peripa-
tetic pathologist with her investigations. *To Cache a Mil-*

lionaire (295), the final book in her series, has Dr. Severance in Las Vegas with her twenty-two-year-old nephew Clarence. There she bluffs her way into a meeting with Arthur
Acuff, a multi-millionaire who bears a striking resemblance
to the late Howard Hughes, and she involves herself in some
high-stakes (and deadly) gambling involving the ownership of
an Acuff corporation in which she owns one hundred shares.

   Margaret Scherf was born in Fairmont, West Virginia. She
attended Antioch College. A one-time employee of Robert M.
McBride, a New York publishing firm, she became a professional
writer in 1939. A resident of Montana, Scherf has served in
the Montana State Legislature. In addition to more than twenty
adult mystery novels, she has written several mysteries for
juveniles.

Dr. Grace Severance Bibliography

293. *The Banker's Bones.* Garden City, New York: Doubleday
        and Co., 1968; London: Robert Hale, 1969.

294. *The Beautiful Birthday Cake.* Garden City, New York:
        Doubleday and Co., 1971.

295. *To Cache A Millionaire.* Garden City, New York: Double-
        day and Co., 1972.

PATRICK GRANT (1970)

Creator: Yorke, Margaret [Nicholson, Margaret Bede (1924-)]

   Fortyish, nattily attired, highly cultivated, and handsome, Patrick Grant is a fellow of "St. Mark's College," Oxford. His field of study is English literature, but he is
also knowledgeable about art, the theatre, ancient Greek
architecture, and music. A bachelor, Grant has sporadic romantic relationships with several women during the course of
his series. His closest female associate, however, is his
sister, Jane Conway. Jane, whom Grant unflatteringly describes as "cow-like," sometimes offers critical detection advice. She also worries constantly about her brother's failure
to marry, but she is resigned to his staying single. Jane
realizes that life within the walls of St. Mark's--with its
first-class conversation, its good food and wine, and its
leisurely schedule of activities--is "too comfortable" for

Grant to desert in favor of a wife.

Because Jane nags him incessantly about his lazy, elegant
lifestyle, Grant frequently leaves Oxford for excursions to
London and for continental vacations. It is during these
trips away from St. Mark's (and away from Jane) that he comes
across and resolves mysteries. In *Silent Witness* (297), for
instance, he deals with a murder which takes place on a chair-
lift at an Alpine ski resort. *Grave Matters* (298) begins with
Grant witnessing the fatal fall of a fellow tourist down the
steps of an ancient Greek temple. And *Mortal Remains* (299)
involves him in the mysterious death of Felix Lomax, a fellow
in Roman history at St. Mark's College, whose body is found
on a beach on the Island of Crete.

Thanks to the assistance which he has rendered the authorities of various nations, Grant has several friends in the top
echelons of both the British and the Continental European police forces. Detective-Inspector Colin Smithers of New Scotland Yard admires Grant's easy, suave manner. And Dimitris
Manolakis, Inspector of Police for Crete, has great respect
for the Oxford don's erudition. Smithers and Manolakis also
appreciate Grant's unique ability to acquire great amounts of
crucial information simply by asking disarming questions of
witnesses and suspects. On the other hand, both policemen
feel that Grant sometimes takes too many risks. Not always
content to limit himself to interrogations, Grant sometimes
chases evildoers, occasionally placing himself in physical
peril. In *Cast for Death* (300), for example, Grant is almost
killed by an actor-murderer whom he confronts in the dressing
rooms of the National Theatre in London. Grant survives this
harrowing experience, but just barely, and Inspectors Smithers
and Manolakis (who both appear in the story) breathe respec-
tive sighs of relief.

Margaret Bede Nicholson was born in Compton, Surrey. After
a divorce from her husband of twelve years, she joined the
workforce in 1959 as an assistant librarian at St. Hilda's
College, Oxford. She began her writing career in the late
1950s as well, with several "family problems" novels. Nicholson entered the mystery field in 1970 with *Dead in the Morning* (296), her first Patrick Grant story. *Dead in the Morning*, as well as subsequent Patrick Grant novels, were generally received by literary critics as competent, but Grant was
thought by some reviewers to be too derivative of other Oxbridge professorial series-character sleuths. During the late
1970s Nicholson published several highly praised non-Grant
mysteries, and in 1979 she served as chairperson of the British Crime Writers Association.

Patrick Grant Bibliography

296. *Dead in the Morning*. London: Geoffrey Bles, 1970.

297. *Silent Witness*. London: Geoffrey Bles, 1972; New York:
       Walker and Co., 1975.

298. *Grave Matters*. London: Geoffrey Bles, 1973.

299. *Mortal Remains*. London: Geoffrey Bles, 1974.

300. *Cast for Death*. London: Hutchinson Publishing Group,
       1976; New York: Walker and Co., 1976.

JONATHAN HEMLOCK (1972)

Creator: Trevanian [Whitaker, Rodney (1925-)]

The most violence-prone and the least-cerebral professorial
series-character sleuth reported upon in this bibliography,
Jonathan Hemlock is a James Bondish professor of art history
at a leading university in New York City. Poorly paid for his
academic work, yet a man of expensive tastes in art, housing,
and women, Hemlock moonlights as a by-the-job investigator-
assassin for the Search and Sanction Division of CII, an American intelligence agency. An expert in firearms, physical
combat, and mountain climbing, Hemlock is in his late thirties.
He is a bachelor and lives in a converted church on Long Island in which he maintains a collection of illegally acquired
Impressionist paintings. Thin, energetic, and decidedly
heterosexual, Hemlock entertains a succession of luscious
young women during his adventures. Although he has many outstanding physical endowments, when he and his lady friends have
exhausted themselves with sex, his partners inevitably want to
spend the afterplay period discussing the professor's "tragi-
comic" eyes.

Hemlock's perilous work for CII (and for LOO, the British
government's counterpart agency), forces him into a modest
amount of on-the-spot ratiocination in order to survive. But
his special talent lies in cold, calculating direct action,
which most often takes the form of killing-for-a-good-cause.
In *The Eiger Sanction* (301) he joins a team climbing the previously unassaulted North Wall of the Eiger Mountain in the
Swiss Alps. His mission is to identify and "sanction" the
member of the group who once killed another CII agent. In

The Loo Sanction (302) Hemlock undertakes the job of sanc-
tioning a diabolical villain who plans to overthrow the British Empire by employing films which show top British political figures in sexually compromising situations. The Jonathan Hemlock in *The Eiger Sanction* is anxious to take on his
assignment, because he wants the $20,000 fee in order to pur-
chase a Pissaro painting. The Hemlock in *The Loo Sanction* is
reluctant to become involved, however, because he has gone
into "retirement." His co-operation must be gained through
blackmail on the part of the authorities.

Professor Hemlock is seldom seen on the campus of the university which pays him his meager academic salary. But early
in *The Eiger Sanction* readers can learn that the Professor is
a curricular traditionalist (who opposes courses in "Black
Art," "Pop Art," and the like), that he refuses to serve on
committees, and that he shuns any physical contact with coeds.
During the second chapter of *The Eiger Sanction*, a female student in one of his classes seductively offers "to do anything
at all" to get an A. "Do you have anything planned for to-
night?" Hemlock asks. When the girl answers in the negative,
Hemlock replies: "Then I suggest you break out the books and
study your ass off."

Rodney Whitaker was born in Tokyo, Japan. A one-time professor of communications at the University of Texas, Whitaker
was able to take premature retirement from academe thanks to
the vast commercial success of his Jonathan Hemlock novels.
Since writing *The Loo Sanction*, Whitaker has published several
non-Hemlock mysteries (under his Trevanian pseudonym). *The
Eiger Sanction* was transformed into a 1975 motion picture
which starred Clint Eastwood as Whitaker's emotionless, sometimes sullen, but always entertaining professorial creation.

Jonathan Hemlock Bibliography

301. *The Eiger Sanction*. New York: Crown Publishers, 1972;
      London: William Heinemann, 1973.

302. *The Loo Sanction*. New York: Crown Publishers, 1973;
      London: William Heinemann, 1973.

VICKY BLISS (1973)

Creator: Peters, Elizabeth [Mertz, Barbara Gross (1927-)]

Six-feet-three-inches-tall, blonde, beautiful, and brilliant, Vicky Bliss is a fast-talking and frequently cynical young lady who has a Ph.D. in history. During her first adventure, *Borrower of the Night* (303), she is an instructor of history at an unidentified college in the American Midwest. Bliss' academic specialty is medieval Europe, and in her second exploit, *Street of the Five Moons* (304), she has taken leave from her teaching post to work in a history museum in Munich, Germany.

Vicky Bliss' sleuthing is an outgrowth of her professional activities. While doing research she finds that the ancient artifacts in which she is interested are the centerpieces of modern-day crimes. In *Borrower of the Night* she seeks out a historically noteworthy collection of jewels which has been lost for four centuries somewhere within the walls of a German castle. The gems, she finds, are now the subject of intense, murderous relationships among the castle's current residents. In *Street of the Five Moons* Bliss sets out in search of a priceless Charlemagne talisman. This exercise takes her from Munich to Rome on the trail of a gang of forgers.

Although Vicky Bliss' success as an amateur detective stems principally from her familiarity with arcane historical objects, it is the product, too, of her enormous fund of energy. An indefatigable traveler, she is ready with virtually no notice for international trips in pursuit of clues. Furthermore, she is in extraordinarily fine physical condition, and her strength and agility allow her to escape life-threatening perils. In *Borrower of the Night*, for example, she is trapped with two men in a sealed underground tunnel. While her male companions give themselves up for dead, Bliss digs the group out with her bare hands.

Vicky Bliss narrates her own stories. Although she is relatively circumspect when describing her romantic life, it is evident that her statuesque good looks often act as an impediment to her crime fighting. Female suspects and witnesses seem to take an instant dislike to her, and she is constantly harassed by male admirers. Tony Lawrence, a six-foot-five-inch faculty colleague, is a particular pest. Lawrence assists Bliss with some of her detection, but he also offers her repeated, unwanted proposals of marriage. Bliss is willing to have Lawrence serve as her consort, but she is not willing to join him in wedlock. Marriage for a woman, Vicky Bliss believes, is to agree to become "a twenty-five-hour-a-day maid."

Barbara Gross Mertz was born in Canton, Illinois. She received a Ph.D. in 1972 from the University of Chicago Oriental Institute. She has published professional works in cultural anthropology and archeology under her own name, and under the pseudonyms Barbara Michaels and Elizabeth Peters she

has written numerous romances and mysteries. *The Seventh Sinner* (551) and *The Murders of Richard III* (567), two non-Vicky
Bliss novels issued under the alias Elizabeth Peters, appear
in the second section of this bibliography. The sleuth in both
of these novels is Jacqueline Kirby, a middle-aged college librarian. A Barbara Michaels mystery, *Someone in the House*
(627), also appears in the bibliography's second section.

Vicky Bliss Bibliography

303. *Borrower of the Night*. New York: Dodd, Mead and Co.,
      1973; London: Cassell and Collier Macmillan, 1974.

304. *Street of the Five Moons*. New York: Dodd, Mead and
      Co., 1978.

THEODORA ("THEA") WADE CRAWFORD (1973)

Creator: Mann, Jessica

    Theodora ("Thea") Wade Crawford is a professor of archeo-
logy and head of her department at the "University of Buriton,"
a British institution in Cornwall. In early middle age, Crawford is very attractive. She has long black hair, a slim figure, and "Wedgwood blue eyes of startling size." Crawford is
also a thoroughly modern academic woman. She is married to
Sylvester Crawford, a globe-trotting television commentator,
but neither she nor her husband subscribe to the idea of lim-
iting their sexual relationships to each other. While Sylvester has his "diversions" in far-off locales, the professor
attempts to juggle teaching, research, and sleuthing with
extra-marital liaisons of her own. Considering her crowded
schedule, it is little wonder that Crawford is "an intellectual prig" who reads very little outside of her academic
specialities. But at Buriton, where personality and appearance seem to count for more than deep intellectual commitment,
Crawford does not find her narrow literary tastes a handicap.
With her "low and incisive" voice, she both commands the respect of her students and attracts the attentions of her male
colleagues.
    Thea Crawford is a sleuth by happenstance. Events occur
which force her to investigate crimes. Her primary motivations in these instances are to resolve the mysteries in
question in order to rid her environment of distracting (and/
or dangerous) influences. When engaged in sleuthing, Crawford

employs the sharp observational powers which she has developed
in her archeological studies. She also has the physical stamina necessary to conduct exhausting fieldwork. And she remains objective at all times. Not the warmest person among the
professorial series-character detectives surveyed in this bibliography, Crawford admits to an inability to experience em-
pathy with other people. Even in the midst of great human
tragedy, she can stand outside a situation and apply cool,
dispassionate logic.

Both of Thea Crawford's published cases are set at the
University of Buriton. In *The Only Security* (305) she is
plunged into detection when a male member of her department
displays the curious habit of entombing contemporary corpses
in ancient burial sites. And in *Captive Audience* (306) she
finds herself in the midst of a deadly campus political battle
brought on during demonstrations by radical students. *Captive
Audience* is narrated, in part, by Sylvester, who is recuper-
ating at Buriton from a broken leg incurred in the Far East.
Sylvester provides some of the detection in this book. Another noteworthy character in *Captive Audience* is Lewis Rochester, the principal of Buriton. An ambitious man, Rochester
hopes to use the unrest at his school as a vehicle for attain-
ing a bigger and better administrative post in the British
academic world.

Jessica Mann was born in London. She holds a B.A. and
M.A. in archeology from Newnham College, Cambridge, and an
LL.B. from the University of Leicester. Married to a professor of archeology, she lives in Truro, Cornwall. A master
of the surprise ending, Mann is one of Great Britain's most-
respected mystery writers. *The Sticking Place* (564), a non-
Thea Crawford novel by Mann, appears in the second section of
this bibliography.

Theodora Crawford Bibliography

305. *The Only Security*. London: Macmillan, 1973. Published
       in the United States as *Troublecross*. New York: David
       McKay, 1973.

*306. *Captive Audience*. London: Macmillan, 1973; New York:
       David McKay, 1975.

IRA COBB (1974)

Creator: Winsor, Roy (1912-)

One of the world's leading interpreters of the works of

Jonathan Swift, Ira Cobb was once a tenured professor of English at Brown University. He resigned his post, however, after brutally beating an instructor at the Rhode Island School of Design. The instructor had stolen the affections of Cobb's young wife, Pam. Tall, gaunt, and a pipe-smoker, Cobb is now in his late forties, a year-round resident of Nantucket Island, and something of a recluse. He lives alone in an old, grey-shingled house which looks out over the sea. He supports himself by giving occasional lectures, by writing short, cynical novels, and by publishing detective fiction under the pseudonym A.S. Howland. For diversion he reads, drinks (but not to excess), and serves as Nantucket's amateur sleuth-in-residence.

Cobb has a close working relationship with Tony Romano, Nantucket's chief of police. Romano devours all of Cobb's mystery stories and calls upon the professor for help when he has thorny detection problems of his own. Some of Cobb's assistance is rendered in the form of armchair deduction, but he does not rely entirely upon evidence generated by the police. He collects some of his own evidence, and he is not beyond voluntarily placing himself in physical danger in order to trap a criminal. One factor in Cobb's willingness to leave his snug if rustic home in pursuit of wrongdoers is his desire to escape Mrs. Pellagrin, his daily housekeeper. This lady, a Christian fundamentalist, worries constantly about the professor's soul, and she makes repeated (but unsuccessful) attempts to have him accompany her to prayer meetings.

The Cobb novels are narrated by Steve Barnes, one of the professor's former students. During the course of the Cobb series, Barnes rises from graduate student to associate professor of English at Columbia University. In *The Corpse That Walked* (307), Barnes happens to be visiting his former mentor on Nantucket when Cobb resolves the matter of a summer visitor, killed in an automobile accident, who apparently drags his own corpse hundreds of yards from the scene of his death. In *Three Motives for Murder* (308) Cobb travels to the suburbs of New York City to offer assistance when the brother of Barnes' fiancée is murdered. The scene in *Always Lock Your Bedroom Door* (309) is, once again, Nantucket. Barnes is paying Cobb another visit when the professor finds the killer of Addie Hill, a wealthy old lady whose many relatives all stand to reap large financial profits from her death. Barnes emerges from the Cobb stories as an intelligent, well-mannered young man with a promising academic career ahead of him. Nonetheless, Cobb is often patronizing toward his Watson and generally treats him as though he were still one of his undergraduates at Brown.

Roy Windsor was born in Chicago and received an A.B. (mag-

na cum laude) from Harvard in 1936. Most of his career has
been spent as a writer and producer of radio and television
dramas. *The Corpse That Walked* won an Edgar from the Mystery
Writers of America in 1974 as the best original paperback
mystery published that year. Most reviewers of the Cobb novels have seen the professor as a throwback to the amateur
sleuths of the "Golden Age" of mystery fiction. Some have
seen the Cobb-Barnes relationship as echoing that between Nero
Wolf and Archie Goodwin.

Ira Cobb Bibliography

307. *The Corpse That Walked*. Greenwich, Connecticut: Fawcett/
     Gold Medal, 1974.

308. *Three Motives for Murder*. Greenwich, Connecticut: Faw-
     cett/Gold Medal, 1976.

309. *Always Lock Your Bedroom Door*. Greenwich, Connecticut:
     Fawcett/Gold Medal, 1976.

LOREN MENSING (1975)

Creator: Nevins, Francis M(ichael), Jr. (1943-)

Loren Mensing is a professor of law at "City University,"
an urban institution in the American Midwest. Independently
wealthy, thanks to money left him by his late father (a prominent attorney), Mensing has the personal financial security
which allows him to be active in various liberal political
causes. Early in his career he practiced law with his father's
firm, but he found it distasteful to represent the interests
of the firm's affluent clients. He then became a clerk to
Judge Ben Richmond. He and the judge became good friends,
and it was Richmond who steered him into academe. Mensing is
now in his late-thirties, vigorous, and a bachelor. He has
many female companions, but in *Corrupt and Ensnare* (311) he
seems about to forge a lasting relationship with Val Tremaine,
a beautiful female private detective. Mensing is also an active writer. Already the co-author of a best-selling textbook, he is currently researching an exhaustive history of
the legal philosophy of the Third Reich. Perhaps because his
life is so full, he has none of the eccentricities which
characterize most professorial series-character sleuths.

Loren Mensing once served as deputy legal advisor to the local police commissioner. His official duty was to "root out" illegal practices in the city's criminal justice system, but during the course of his service he also became involved in criminal investigations. Although the professor no longer holds his official post, he is still consulted by the authorities when they face difficult cases. In his role as a sleuth, Mensing makes good use of his legal knowledge, and he is proficient at logical deduction (some of which he does while sitting alone in the university law library). But his detection strategy includes extensive fieldwork as well, and many of his activities are reminiscent of those of the great fictional private eyes of the 1930s and 1940s. Searching out witnesses and suspects, Mensing frequently encounters nubile young ladies who find him devastatingly attractive, and he has a tendency to walk into situations which present him with serious personal danger.

Both of the novels in which Loren Mensing appears have on-campus scenes, but neither is a college mystery. In *Publish and Perish* (310), the professor deals with the murder of a novelist. He is drawn into this case because an old girl friend is serving as secretary to the victim's wife. In *Corrupt and Ensnare*, he undertakes the task of preserving Judge Ben Richmond's good name after Richmond dies of cancer, and after a shoe box containing $50,000 in small bills is found in the judge's home. This caper eventually involves Mensing with the CIA, with a multinational oil company, and with international terrorists.

Francis Michael Nevins, Jr., was born in Bayonne, New Jersey. He received an A.B. from St. Peter's College in 1964 and a J.D. from New York University in 1967. He joined the faculty of the St. Louis University School of Law in 1971. Nevins is well-known to mystery buffs for his book reviews and for the many articles about the history of the genre which he has published in such magazines as *The Armchair Detective*. *Publish and Perish* was his first novel, but prior to the book's publication Nevins employed Loren Mensing as the protagonist of several short stories.

Loren Mensing Bibliography

310. *Publish and Perish*. New York: G.P. Putnam's Sons, 1975; London: Robert Hale, 1977.

311. *Corrupt and Ensnare*. New York: G.P. Putnam's Sons, 1978; London: Robert Hale, 1979.

HANNAH LAND (1976)

Creator: MacKay, Amanda [Smith, Amanda Joan MacKay]

Five-feet-eleven-inches tall, Hannah Land is a "lanky"
assistant professor of political science at Duke University
in Durham, North Carolina. Now in her mid-thirties, Land
spent ten years as a typical suburban housewife before she
tired both of domesticity and of her husband, Michael. After
her divorce, she enrolled at Columbia University for doctoral
studies, and her post at Duke is her initial post-Ph.D.
appointment. A scholar of great potential, Land has already
published her first book, *Power in Community Organizations:
Or How Much Good Do the Do-Gooders Do?"* Unlike most academic
monographs, this one is enjoying healthy sales. Attractive
with long, dark-red hair, Land has a sizeable circle of friends
in the Duke community. Her closest feminine companion is Rachel Halifax, a sharp-tongued, black woman who teaches in
Duke's psychology department. Land's most devoted male friend
is Ralph Rutledge, a thirty-seven-year-old, bachelor political
scientist. Rutledge entertains ideas of asking Land to marry
him, but Land makes it clear whenever marriage enters their
conversations that she is not yet ready to tie herself to
another husband.

Hannah Land is reluctant to engage in sleuthing, but she
finds herself at the center of murderous events on and near
the Duke campus. Bright, inquisitive, and sometimes riddled
with guilt about staying uninvolved when she feels she might
be of assistance to the police, Land inevitably shucks off her
hesitancy and plunges into detection. A collector of clues--
often through chance observations and/or through casual conversations with the principals in her cases--she "puts two and
two together and comes up with five and one-half." Land
works closely with Detective Lieutenant Robert E. ("Bobby
Gene") Jenkins of the Durham Police Department Investigation
Squad. An easy-going man, Lieutenant Jenkins has a secret
crush on Hannah. He worries about her welfare, and in *Death
on the Eno* (313), he provides her with a small short-wave radio transmitter with which she can summon him in case of imminent personal danger.

Death Is Academic (312), Land's first published adventure,
is (as its title implies) a thoroughly academic mystery. The
victim in the story is Dr. Bradley Brown, a long-time member of
the Duke political science department. Dr. Brown falls dead
at a departmental retirement dinner after eating a fruit cocktail topped with squirrel poison. Virtually all of the sur-

viving members of the political science staff and their spouses (as well as the department's secretaries) are suspects, and Land resolves the matter only after discovering more than she cares to know about the private lives of some of her colleagues. *Death on the Eno* is set in large part in the countryside around Durham, and a central character is Maynard Turnbull, a widower professor of political science at Duke. In this novel, Land probes the suspicious death of Turnbull's brother, Luther, who expires after a canoeing mishap. Ralph Rutledge, Land's would-be husband, has plenty of cause to fret during *Death on the Eno*. Land's sleuthing puts her in serious danger, and Professor Turnbull, gracious to a fault despite his bereavement, shows signs of developing his own romantic interests in Duke's resident professorial detective.

Amanda MacKay did her undergraduate work at Radcliffe/Harvard and received an M.A. in political science from Columbia University. She is the wife of James Barber, a noted professor of political science at Duke University.

Hannah Land Bibliography

*312. *Death Is Academic*. New York: David McKay, 1976; London: Robert Hale, 1980.

313. *Death on the Eno*. Boston: Little, Brown, 1981.

ROBERT ("MONGO") FREDERICKSON (1977)

Creator: Chesbro, George C(lark) (1940-)

Robert "Mongo" Frederickson is a professor of criminology at a university in New York City. He also works as a for-hire private investigator. Among the professorial series-character sleuths surveyed in this bibliography, Frederickson has three distinctions. First, he is the best armed. Because he holds a blackbelt in Karate, his hands are lethal weapons. He packs a Baretta pistol in a shoulder holster. And, for good measure, he carries razors embedded in the soles of his shoes. Second, Frederickson is the only academic detective to have a personal interview with the late Shah of Iran. This encounter comes in *City of Whispering Stone* (315), when he travels to Teheran in an escapade which involves him in Iran's pre-revolutionary ferment. And, finally, there is the matter of his size. Mongo Frederickson is the only professorial series-character detective who happens to be a dwarf.

Born in Nebraska, Frederickson began his working life as a dwarf-acrobat ("Mongo the Magnificent") in a circus. But after tiring of being a professional freak, he underwent psychoanalysis, gave up show business, studied for a Ph.D. and entered the world of academe. An extremely popular teacher, he now entertains his classes with tales of his circus days and with stories about his on-going sleuthing exploits. Every seat in his classrooms is filled. Thanks to his sometimes-cynical good humor—he has a large fund of self-deprecating wisecracks about himself—Frederickson gets along well with his colleagues and with his department chairperson, Walter Manning. The officious chancellor of the university is concerned, however, that Frederickson's extra-curricular detective work is taking too much time from his "contracted teaching duties." Frederickson does not yet have tenure, and he fears that he may not be offered a new contract at the university when his current one expires.

Despite his diminutive physique, Frederickson conducts his detective business in vintage private-eye style. He maintains a small, dingy office in downtown Manhattan—"dirty windows, a desk, a chair, and an answering service"—but he spends little time there. Instead, he travels far and wide, searching out people who possess the information which allows him to bring his cases to successful conclusions. In *Shadow of a Broken Man* (314) he journeys to Duke University's Institute of Parapsychology in an attempt to trace the whereabouts of a supposedly dead architect. Frederickson's trip to Iran in *City of Whispering Stone* comes in connection with a job involving a missing circus strongman. And in *An Affair of Sorcerers* (316) he takes his tiny body from one end of New York City to the other in order to clear up a matter which concerns murder and witchcraft. He frequently receives assistance from his brother Garth, a normal-sized New York City police detective. Frederickson narrates his own stories. Although he provides readers with great detail about most aspects of his capers, he is less forthcoming regarding his sex life. Frederickson is a bachelor, but it is clear that he does not want for feminine companionship. At one point in *City of Whispering Stone* a bosomy young lady offers to take him to her bed. Frederickson refuses, because he is in the midst of an urgent investigation, but he notes that women frequently issue such invitations in order to see "if I [am] dwarf all over."

George Clark Chesbro was born in Washington, D.C. and received a B.S. from Syracuse University in 1962. He combines mystery writing with work as a special education teacher in Rockland County, New York.

Robert ("Mongo") Frederickson Bibliography

314. *Shadow of A Broken Man*. New York: Simon and Schuster,
      1977; London: Severn House, 1981.

315. *City of Whispering Stone*. New York: Simon and Schuster,
      1978; London: Severn House, 1981.

316. An Affair of Sorcerers. New York: Simon and Schuster,
      1979; London: Severn House, 1980.

RAYMOND ("RAY") GUINNESS (1978)

Creator: Guild, Nicholas (1944-)

     Born some thirty-odd years ago in Newark, Ohio, Raymond
Guinness attended Ohio State University as an undergraduate
and then did graduate work at the University of London. He
ran out of money in London, however, and in order to finish
his studies he hired on as a paid assassin for Great Britain's
M-16. He married while in M-16 service and had a daughter,
but his wife Kathleen left him (and took the girl with her)
when she found out the sinister nature of his duties. Eventually, Guiness resigned from M-16 and took an assistant professorship in English at "Belmont State College" in California.
During his six "grinding years" at Belmont he graded innumerable sophomore themes and tried to lead a normal academic
existence with Louise, his second wife. His old enemies
caught up with him; Louise was murdered; and Guinness rejoined
the world of international intrigue, this time in the service
of the CIA. Guinness is now one of the CIA's best agents,
but occasionally he thinks about returning to the cloistered
world of academe. If he ever tries to secure a new academic
post, his application will certainly raise eyebrows within
those faculty recruitment committees which have the opportunity to review his fascinating résumé.
     As a CIA agent, Guinness can engage in deductive reasoning
when necessary, but his real forte is erasing the people who
stand in the way of the successful completion of his missions.
Adept at various killing techniques, Guinness can be cold, even
brutal at times. Yet, perhaps because of his six years as a
college faculty member, his character includes some elements
of softness. In lonely motel rooms while on assignment, he
reads poetry. And he must constantly watch his weight because
he has a craving for junk foods. Raymond Guinness is the only
professorial series-character in this bibliography who sub-

sists largely on Big Macs, Baskin-Robbins' ice cream sundaes, and cinnamon doughnuts bought in packages of a dozen from grocery stores.

The Summer Soldier (317), Guinness' first published escapade, centers on the murder of Louise, upon Guinness' efforts to avenge her death, and upon his re-entrance into the business of covert intelligence. *The Summer Soldier* offers several views of Guinness at Belmont State College. *The Old Acquaintance* (318) takes the former assistant professor to South Carolina, when he deals with the attempted sabotage of an atomic energy facility. During this novel Guinness makes several appearances on the campus of Clemson University and, for a brief time, he is reunited with his first wife Kathleen and his daughter "Rocky." *The Favor* (319) is set largely in Amsterdam, where Guinness works to rescue the daughter of an East German spy, a man who once saved his life. In both *Old Acquaintance* and *The Favor*, Guinness must do battle with an archfiend, "The Flycatcher," a cunning and unscrupulous international terrorist.

Nicholas Guild was born in San Mateo, California. He received an A.B. from Occidental College in 1966 and a Ph.D. from the University of California at Berkeley in 1972. He was an assistant professor of English at Clemson University from 1973 until 1975, and he has been a member of the department of English at Ohio State University since leaving Clemson. A non-Raymond Guinness novel by Guild, *The Lost and Found Man* (574), appears in the second section of this bibliography. *The Lost and Found Man*, Guild's first full-length work of fiction, has as its protagonist a one-time commando, now turned academic, named William Lukas. Although Lukas and Raymond Guinness have slightly different personal histories, the two characters are in most respects very, very similar.

Raymond Guinness Bibliography

317. *The Summer Soldier*. New York: Seaview Books, 1978; London: Magnum Books, 1979.

318. *Old Acquaintance*. New York: Seaview Books, 1978.

319. *The Favor*. New York: St. Martin's Press, 1981.

PETER SHANDY (1978)

Creator: MacLeod, Charlotte (1922-)

     Peter Shandy is a zany, tenured professor of agrology at
"Balaclava Agricultural College," an institution which is located somewhere in rural Massachusetts. In his mid-fifties,
Shandy is a moderately wealthy man thanks to royalties he receives from seed companies for his great scientific creation,
a giant rutabaga known as "The Balaclava Buster." In *Rest You
Merry* (320) Shandy is a bachelor, living alone in a house by
the Balaclava campus. However, during the course of this
story he meets Helen Marsh, a librarian; and by the beginning
of *The Luck Runs Out* (321), Helen has become his bride.
     Short, overweight, and bespectacled, Shandy does not cut
an imposing physical figure. Nor does he have exceptionally
gracious manners. In fact, Shandy tends to tell people exactly
what he is thinking (however unflattering to his listeners
these thoughts may be), and he is also aggressively iconoclas-
tic in his behavior. In *Rest You Merry*, for instance, he decides that the annual display of Christmas illuminations in his
neighborhood is offensive. Seeking to underline his displeasure, he covers his small brick home with plastic Santa Clau-
ses and flashing lights, blares "All I Want for Christmas Is
My Two Front Teeth" from a loudspeaker, sets his electrical
system at "on," and leaves town for a cruise aboard a tramp
steamer. And in all three of his published adventures Shandy
takes special delight in tweaking Thorkjeld Svenson, Balaclava
Agricultural College's officious president. One of Shandy's
favorite cocktail party stories is about the time President
Svenson slipped and fell into a pile of cow manure while es-
corting the United States Secretary of Agriculture on a tour
of the school's experimental farm.
     Although Professor Shandy possesses some reasonably well-
developed powers of deduction, his sleuthing is best characterized as frenetic, and it takes place in conjunction with
perilous personal situations into which he falls as a result
of his idiosyncratic lifestyle. His detective work in *Rest
You Merry* comes about when he returns from his sea voyage to
find his home dark and silent and a neighbor-woman, who apparently broke in to disconnect his Christmas gadgets, murdered
in his living room. *The Luck Runs Out* has Shandy attempting to
stop what he sees as the unfortunate wedding of one of his
faculty colleagues. In the wake of his intervention his own
wife is kidnapped, a dinner guest at the Shandy domicile is
killed, and Belinda, Balaclava Agricultural College's nine-

hundred-pound, pregnant prize sow, turns up missing. Most of
Wrack and Rune (322) takes place in the hamlet of Lumpkin Cor-
ners, a town near the Balaclava campus. In this escapade Shandy learns about the deadly qualities of quicklime. And he
learns, too, that it is unwise for a 102-year-old man (in this
case, President Svenson's Uncle Sven) to consort with older
women.

Charlotte MacLeod was born in Bath, New Brunswick, Canada.
Trained as an artist, she joined the Boston advertising firm
of N.H. Miller and Co. in 1952. By the time *Rest You Merry*
appeared she was a vice-president of the agency. MacLeod's
Peter Shandy books have generally been praised by critics as
witty, clever satires which, nonetheless, offer their readers
puzzle-solving challenges. In addition to her Peter Shandy
series, MacLeod has published other detective fiction and
several mainstream novels for adults, books for children,
and many articles for popular American magazines. Some of
her work has been issued under the pseudonym Mathilda Hughes.

Peter Shandy Bibliography

320. *Rest You Merry*. Garden City, New York: Doubleday and
      Co., 1978; London: William Collins, 1979.

321. *The Luck Runs Out*. Garden City, New York: Doubleday
      and Co., 1979; London: William Collins, 1981.

322. *Wrack and Rune*. Garden City, New York: Doubleday and
      Co., 1982.

NEIL KELLY (1982)

Creator: S.F.X. Dean (pseud.)

Neil Kelly is a middle-aged professor of English literature at "Old Hampton College," a high-quality liberal arts
institution in the central Massachusetts town of "Oldhampton." Quiet, introverted, and unfailingly polite, Kelly
is well-known in his discipline for his work on seventeenth-
century British poets. A dedicated teacher, Kelly painstakingly prepares his lectures and grades student papers
with scrupulous care. Although he shuns administrative duties,
he is constantly being visited or called by classmates (Kelly
is an Old Hampton graduate with a Harvard Ph.D.) who erron-

eously think that he wields power within the Old Hampton establishment. These former friends and acquaintances want Kelly
to use his influence to have their less-than-academically
qualified offspring admitted as Old Hampton freshmen.

Kelly is a widower. Georgia, his wife of twenty-one years,
died of cancer. Kelly now lives alone (with occasional stu-
ent lodgers) in the rambling old house hear the Old Hampton
campus where he and Georgia raised two daughters. Both of his
girls are now grown, and both are married to academics and
live in California. In addition to research and teaching,
Kelly dispels his loneliness by following the fortunes of the
Boston Red Sox, and he sometimes meditates at length on the
team's problems. Various hostesses in the Oldhampton community see Kelly as a prospective husband for their widowed or
divorced friends, and they invite him to frequent cocktail
and dinner parties. But the professor is only bored by these
intrusive attempts at matchmaking. In *By Frequent Anguish*
(323) Kelly finds his own new life's companion, Pril Lacey,
a bright and sprightly co-ed. Pril is the daughter of Barbara Lacey, an old girlfriend from his younger days. Kelly
and Pril plan to marry, but the young lady is mysteriously
shot dead in the underground stacks of the college library.
Certainly the most tragic figure among the professorial series-character sleuths surveyed in this bibliography, Professor Kelly seems destined to spend the rest of his days
without a mate, mourning the two great loves of his life.

Neil Kelly serves as a sleuth only with extreme reluctance,
and only when his services are expressly requested. In his
first exploit, *By Frequent Anguish,* he is emotionally devas-
tated by Pril's murder, entering the search for her killer
only when Barbara Lacey and her millionaire-industrialist
husband Morgan become disenchanted with the fumbling efforts
of the Oldhampton police. Barbara and Morgan beg Kelly to
employ his highly developed research skills in the case, and
though he is at first too distraught to do so, the professor
eventually enters the investigation in an unofficial but effective capacity. Morgan Lacey is subsequently killed by a bomb
concealed in a gift-package in *Such Pretty Toys* (324), and
Barbara Lacey is permanently blinded by the same explosion.
Kelly becomes involved in this unhappy affair when the CIA,
with whom Barbara Lacey had clandestine dealings, convinces
him that he is the only person who has the contacts within
the Lacey extended family necessary to identify the sender
of the lethal present. Neither a superbrain nor an egotist,
Kelly detects principally by interviewing suspects, witnesses,
and knowledgeable parties, and by doggedly following leads to
their logical conclusions. Perhaps his greatest asset as a

sleuth is his ability to employ his anger in controlled ways. In both of his exploits he is strongly motivated by personal considerations to resolve the crimes in question, and though he hesitates before launching his investigations, once he begins his inquiries he is determined to see them through despite the many obstacles which line his path.

Such Pretty Toys contains a few Old Hampton scenes, but most of the action takes place in Arizona, where the Laceys made their home. *By Frequent Anguish*, on the other hand, is on-campus college mystery fiction at its best, and Professor Kelly's detection leads him to see many of Old Hampton's administrators, faculty members, and students in new and revealing lights. The title of the book is taken from a poem by E.E. Cummings. The tale incorporates clever detection, a host of well-drawn academic characters, and a May-October love affair (between Pril and Kelly) which is so sensitively portrayed that the novel is raised to a literary level seldom reached by detective stories.

S.F.X. Dean is the yet-to-be-revealed pseudonym of a professor at a high-quality, liberal arts college in a small New England town.

Neil Kelly Bibliography

*323. *By Frequent Anguish*. New York: Walker and Co., 1982.

324. *Such Pretty Toys*. New York: Walker and Co., 1982.

II.
Free-Standing
College Mystery Novels

325. Lathrop, George Parsons (1851-1898). *In the Distance.*
Boston: James R. Osgood, 1882.

In the Distance is set, in large part, at "Marle
College" in New Hampshire. Robert Burden, a theology
student, vies with Richard Whitcot, a civil engineer,
for the affections of Edith Archdale, the daughter of
a Marle professor. When Whitcot is found dead in the
nearby woods, his skull shattered by a heavy stick,
Burden is arrested and tried for murder. At the last
moment, however, Burden is exonerated when Idy Hiss,
a local waitress (and Burden's long-lost sister), reveals
the identity of the actual killer. There is no real
detection in the book, although Sheriff Brown--whose
uniform includes a "broken silk hat bound with a faded
blue ribbon"--does track Burden down in the foothills
of Mount Monadnoc. Indeed, Sheriff Brown is mistakenly
convinced that Burden is the murderer, and while the
trial is proceeding he discusses with his cronies the
proper length and weight of rope for the hanging. The
only professor to appear in the plot is Edith's father,
the wise Dr. Archdale, whose sympathies in the Burden-
Whitcot battle for his daughter definitely lie with
Burden. Some of the story takes place in Savage's Hotel,
provided over by "Mother" Savage, a frumpy woman who
smokes a pipe and reads novels. Mother Savage's three
sons--Absalom, Epenetus B., and Serious--play significant roles. Serious, who routinely drums on his teeth
when talking, is the hotel manager. And it is Epenetus
B. (along with his pet hound, Epenetus B. Dog) who finds
Whitcot's body.

George Parsons Lathrop was born in Honolulu, Hawaii.
Educated in New York City and in Dresden, Germany, he
was assistant editor of the *Atlantic Monthly* from 1875
until 1877, editor of the *Boston Courier* from 1877 until
1879, and secretary of the American Copyright League from
1883 until 1895. A prolific writer, Lathrop was the
author of several historical works and literary studies
in addition to many melodramatic novels.

326. Allen, (Charles) Grant (Blairfindie) (1848–1899). *For Maimie's Sake: A Tale of Love and Dynamite*. London: Chatto and Windus, 1886; New York: D. Appleton and Co., 1886.

Maimie Llewellyn is a flirtatious young British girl with a habit of cuddling and kissing all of the men of her acquaintance. One of her more ardent admirers is Adrian Pym, a tutor at Oriel College, Oxford. Since Adrian walks with "a regular Oxford lounging manner," and since he costumes himself with a straw hat adorned with college ribbons, it is little wonder that Maimie hopes to marry him. But Adrian is already secretly married to Bessie, an Oxford barmaid with whom he had a child-producing dalliance during his student days. Hearing of Adrian's existing attachments, Maimie weds Sydney Chevenix, a dynamite manufacturer. Angered by this distressing event, Adrian gives vent to his displeasure by overloading his wife's already alcohol-damaged liver with fatal quantities of French brandy. Then, after castigating Adrian for not adopting the murder-by-liquor technique years before, Maimie stages an accident in which she shoots husband Sydney with an experimental dynamite-firing pistol which is kept lying around the house. To reveal more would be to give away too much of the book's plot, but it can be noted that the moral of this early-day crime story seems to be that bad people, even evil academics, may sometimes live happily ever after.

Charles Grant Blairfindie Allen was born in Kingston, Ontario, Canada. He received a bachelor's degree from Oxford. Allen married during his undergraduate years, and because his wife quickly became an invalid, he was constantly in need of funds. After leaving Oxford he wrote scientific and philosophical books, but these yielded little revenue and, in hopes of larger royalties, he turned to popular novels and mystery stories. Although his fiction did, indeed, provide him with a substantial income, his works—many of which ran counter to Victorian codes of literary decency—often were denounced by critics. After characterizing *For Maimie's Sake* as "flashy and coarse," the reviewer for *Literary World* (April 17, 1886) added: "We wish [Allen] no better fortune than that his wife and children may never chance to see a copy [of the book]."

327. Savidge, Eugene Coleman (1863–1924). *Wallingford: A Story of An American Life*. Philadelphia: J.B. Lippincot, 1887.

This miasmic melodrama follows the young adult careers of two men from the Pennsylvania town of Wallingford, a a suburb of Philadelphia. The first of the protagonists, Windom Travers, finds his calling in architecture. The other, Burt Sheldon, studies to become a physician, and it is Burt's adventures which propel the book into this bibliography. As a penurious medical student at Bellevue Medical College in New York City, Burt works at several jobs in order to finance his education. But shortly after his graduation he is arrested for the murder of a young lady named Fanny, and the last portion of the story deals in detail with his trial. Various of Burt's associates from Bellevue Medical College testify and/ or work behind the scenes to influence the outcome of the proceedings. Kindly Dr. Foster, a Bellevue professor who is Burt's surrogate father, does his best to have Burt released, as does William Bellows, a Bellevue classmate whose real talents seem to lie less in medicine than in white collar crime. And then there is Mr. Piggins, who owns an "eating house," near the Bellevue campus. Mr. Piggins, whose "features [seem] to have been formed by the accretion of meteorites," knows all about the habits of the students who dine at his establishment. There is no classical detection in the story; the facts about the murder come out during the course of Burt's trial. Ruby Fuller, a young lady from Wallingford (and a religious evangelist), contributes the crucial evidence which allows Burt to receive the justice to which he is due.

Eugene Coleman Savidge was a Maryland-born physician who lived and worked in New York City. He was the author of several turn-of-the-century melodramas.

328. Hawthorne, Julian (1846–1934). *The Professor's Sister*. Chicago, New York, and San Francisco: Bedford, Clarke and Co., 1888. Published in Great Britain as *The Spectre of the Camera; Or, The Professor's Sister*. London: Chatto and Windus, 1888.

Set in Germany, this romantic, melodramatic tale has as its protagonists three virile American lads taking post-graduate courses at a university in Dresden. The university has on its staff a distinguished young philosopher, named Conrad Hertrugge, who dabbles in sci-

entific experimentation. Professor Hertrugge has a
beautiful sister, Hildegarde, who marries one of the
Americans. Hildegarde meets a mysterious death, but
through a wonder serum of his own invention, Professor
Hertrugge is able to preserve his sister's body from
decay. At a climactic point in the plot Hildegarde awakes
and assists in the capture of her killer. Though the
three Americans spend little time in the classroom during
the course of this epic, the extracurricular life of American students at nineteenth-century German universities
is explored in considerable detail.

Julian Hawthorne was the son of famed American author
Nathaniel Hawthorne. On the advice of his father, who
discouraged him from trying to follow in his own literary footsteps, Julian studied engineering at Harvard and
at the University of Dresden. But after a brief episode
as a hydrographic engineer for the New York City Department of Docks, Julian disregarded his father's advice
and turned his hand to writing. During the late-nine-
teenth and early-twentieth centuries he produced nearly
one hundred novels and books of short stories. Some of
Julian Hawthorne's works were undiluted detective mysteries. In particular, he pioneered the American police
procedural with a series of books about Inspector Byrnes,
the chief detective of the New York City police force.
Julian Hawthorne's literary career was aborted in 1913
when he was sentenced to a year in a Federal penitentiary
in connection with a stock swindle. After his release
he became a book review editor for the *Pasadena [Cali-
fornia] Star* and took pleasure in the success of his
daughter, Hildegarde, as she became a well-known author
of children's books.

329.   Darnell, Henry Faulkner (1831-1917). *The Craze of
       Christian Englehart.* New York: D. Appleton and Co.,
       1890.

       This wordy novel has as its protagonist one Hugo Wil-
derhalt, a distinguished professor of science at an unidentified university in New York City. Hugo receives
a late evening visit from Christian Englehart, a total
stranger, who tells him of bizarre visions he has experienced. Then Christian disappears into the post-
midnight darkness, leaving behind a packet of papers
which Hugo is to open, if not given contrary instruc-
tions, in three months. As the three-month interval is

ending, Hugo reads that Christian has been killed in a
California mine disaster. Upset by this dismal news,
Hugo travels to Christian's native Denmark where he seeks
out the Englehart family. Christian's aging mother,
Theodora blames Hugo for her son's death, and when Hugo
studies the papers which Christian left behind, he is
inclined to agree with her accusation. There is no
detection in the story. Nor are there any on-campus
scenes. But there is considerable mystery, and toward
the end of the book readers are treated to a detailed
portrait of Hugo as a penitent scholar. Moreover,
present-day New Yorkers can learn that the perils associated walking after dark in their city are not of recent origin. When Christian visits Hugo, he carries
with him a pistol. Afraid at first that his uninvited
guest has come to murder him, Hugo soon finds that Christian merely has armed himself against the street bandits
who make nocturnal strolling a life-threatening event
in late-nineteenth-century Manhattan.

Henry Faulkner Darnell was born in Great Britain.
Most of his life was spent as an Episcopal clergyman in
Avon, New York. A prolific author, Darnell wrote melo-
dramas, histories, works of theology, and poetry.

330. Anonymous [Gull, Cyril Arthur Edward Ranger (1876-1912)].
The Hypocrite. London: Greening and Co., 1898.

The protagonist of this early-day academic morality
tale is Yardly Gobin, a student at Exeter College, Oxford. A rake and a rounder, Yardly takes unfair romantic advantage of Maude, an Oxford shopgirl, and he also
runs up massive bills with local tradesmen. Yardly's
father disowns him, and the lad goes to London where,
sometimes in the company of another hedonistic Oxonian
Mordant Sturtevant, he attempts to execute a number of
shady schemes intended to finance a lavish lifestyle.
One of Yardly's projects is to sell lurid but false
articles to publications specializing in scandal (he
gets his start with a piece on "The Gambling Evil at
the Universities"), and another is to blackmail a young
aristocrat for whom he procures a prostitute. Yardly's
activities make him many enemies, and as the story progresses his fortunes wane. He must constantly move to
new and ever more squalid quarters in order to avoid both
the police and the angry private persons to whom he has
done harm. At one of his last abodes, Yardly meets the
Reverend Peter Belper, yet another Oxford man, who has
committed some great misdeed which he is unwilling to
specify. Belper, now a hulking, disheveled drunk, describes himself only as a "moral object lesson." There

is no detection in the story, and the mystery is what
will happen to Yardly as he sinks deeper and deeper into his life of sin. Yardly's fate will not be revealed
in this bibliography. But it can be told that Mordant
Sturtevant, who has the presence of mind (and the money)
to flee London for a cruise on the Mediterranean when
his involvement with Yardly places him in jeopardy, eventually becomes a wealthy attorney and a judge.

For reasons lost to literary history, *The Hypocrite* was
published anonymously. Cyril Arthur Edward Ranger Gull,
the book's author, was an Oxford graduate who, like Yardly Gobin, began his working life as a journalist. In
1900 Gull became a full-time creative writer, and in
the twenty-three years before his death he produced more
than twenty-five novel-length works of fiction. In addition to popular, melodramatic tales for adults, his output included adventure books for juvenile readers.

331.   Conrad, Joseph [Korzeniowski, Joseph Conrad Theodore
       (1857-1924)]. *Under Western Eyes*. London: Methuen
       and Co.; New York: Harper and Brothers, 1911.

Under Western Eyes tells the bitter story of Kirylo
Sidorovitch Razumov, a student of philosophy at St.
Petersburg University in Imperial Russia. One of Razumov's student colleagues, a revolutionary named Victor
Victorovitch Haldin, assassinates an evil government
minister. Haldin then confesses his crime to Razumov,
who in turn goes to the police with his information.
The police keep Razumov's help a secret; Haldin's anti-
government friends are led to believe that Razumov is a
fellow revolutionary; and Razumov is both riddled with
guilt and afraid that his duplicity will become known.
Much of the story takes place in Geneva, where Razumov
meets and falls in love with Haldin's sister Nathalia.
Although several monographs about mystery fiction cite
Under Western Eyes as an exemplar of the art, and even
though the story offers considerable suspense, the book
is perhaps better seen as a searching study of moral
corruption and its attendant degradations. The early
chapters provide many glimpses of fear-laden student
life under the Czars.

Few users of this bibliography need an introduction to
Joseph Conrad. Born in Poland, the son of a revolutionary, Conrad spent most of his adult life in Great Britain, where he became one of the giants of modern English literature. *Under Western Eyes* was his eleventh
novel. The book is often cited by literary scholars as

a prototypical exploration into human guilt and self-doubt. Conrad was inspired to write the novel after the assassination in 1904 of V.K. Plehve, the Russian minister of the Interior.

332. Hastings, W(ells) S(outhworth) (1879-1923) and Brian Hooker (1880-1946). *The Professor's Mystery*. Indianapolis: Bobbs-Merrill, 1911.

Mr. Crosby, a young professor at a university in the New York area, meets Miss "Lady" Tabor on a train. Crosby and the beautiful Miss Tabor are only slight acquaintances. But after the professor comforts her when the train has a slight accident, Lady graciously invites the traveling scholar to stay overnight at her ancestral mansion. Awakened by noises in the small hours of the morning, Crosby finds that he is locked in his room. Then Lady suddenly appears and tells him that for his own good he should leave the house without delay. Crosby does as he is told, but he stays in the nearby town of Stamford making inquiries. His sleuthing convinces him that Lady is in great danger, and he returns to the Tabor abode to root out the evil lurking there. An involved melodrama, *The Professor's Mystery* eventually brings Crosby into contact with spiritualists, with counterfeiters, with Lady's sinister father and brother, and with her mentally warped mother. It also has a happy ending as Professor Crosby and Lady Tabor announce their engagement. Unresolved at the story's conclusion, however, is the question of whether or not Crosby, who now has access to the sizeable Tabor fortune, will remain a humble tiller of the academic soil. Presumably, he would like to try his hand at other pursuits. Early in his narrative, during his chance meeting with Lady on the train, he laments to his wife-to-be that he tired of "telling things I care about to a lot of kids that aren't old enough to care about anything."

Wells Southworth Hastings was born in New Haven, Connecticut. A writer of many popular turn-of-the-century novels, he seems to have left few biographic traces. Brian Hooker, Hastings' collaborator on *The Professor's Mystery*, was also born in New Haven. He received a B.A. from Yale University in 1902 and an M.A. from Yale in 1904. After his student days, Hooker taught at Yale until 1909, when he gave up the academic life for full-time creative writing. Before his death in 1946, he wrote mainstream novels, plays, and librettos for operas. *The Professor's Mystery* was his only venture into mystery fiction.

333. Belloc, (Joseph) Hilaire (1870-1953). *The Green Over-
     coat*. Bristol, Great Britain: J.W. Arrowsmith, 1912;
     New York: McBride, Nast and Co., 1912.

     Professor Higginson, a psychologist at "Guelph Univer-
     sity" in the British town of "Ormeston," attends a bor-
     ing party one evening. He finds it raining when he
     attempts to make an early departure and, in desperation,
     he "borrows" a green overcoat which he finds in the
     cloakroom. On his walk home, Higginson is kidnapped by
     two Cambridge students named Jimmy and Melba. These two
     lads mistake him for the coat's real owner, Mr. Blessing-
     ton, a wealthy businessman. Jimmy and Melba are owed
     large gambling debts by Mr. Blessington's son, and it
     is their intent to force the father to pay these debts.
     After being held for some days by his adversaries—and
     unable, all the while, to convince them of his real
     identity—Professor Higginson escapes and returns to his
     lodgings, only to find that his landlady has alerted the
     police to his mysterious disappearance. At this point,
     not wishing to reveal his theft of the overcoat, the
     professor makes up a grandiose story about having gone
     into a trance and having heard, during his blackout,
     "heavenly voices." Higginson's tale is picked up by the
     press, and he suddenly becomes a prominent authority on
     ghosts. But his new fame does not bring him happiness.
     As the novel continues, Higginson must concoct new false-
     hoods to cover old ones. His old adversary, Jimmy, re-
     appears; Mr. Blessington enters the story; and the pro-
     fessor nearly lands in prison. Written more as farce
     than as a serious mystery, *The Green Overcoat* poses few
     riddles and incorporates little suspense. But it offers
     an abundance of satire directed at psychology, at aca-
     deme, and at bumbling professors. Higginson, who looks
     out on the world with a "sin-laden" gaze after purloin-
     ing Mr. Blessington's coat, is depicted in embarassing
     situation after embarassing situation. He survives his
     troubles, but trapped by his edifice of lies, he must
     spend the rest of his life reviewing "the wildest books
     about spooks" and lecturing until "thin as a rail (often
     for nothing) about the same subject."
         Educated at Balliol College, Oxford, Joseph Hilaire
     Belloc was one of Great Britain's most versatile men of
     letters during the early part of this century. *The
     Green Overcoat* was the first of five light-hearted mys-
     tery novels which he wrote during his career. In addi-
     tion to mysteries, Belloc wrote children's stories,
     political tracts, historical studies, travel books, and

literary parodies. From 1906 until 1910 he served as a
liberal member of Parliament. Belloc was a close friend
of that eminent British artist, journalist, and mystery
writer, G.K. Chesterton, and *The Green Overcoat* is graced
by several Chesterton illustrations.

334. Onions, (George) Oliver (1873-1961). *In Accordance with
     the Evidence*. London: Martin Secker, 1912; Boston:
     John W. Luce, 1913.

   This grim, early-day psychological mystery takes its
readers deep inside the mind of James Herbert Jeffries,
an evening student at a shabby business college in London's Holburn district. Jeffries falls in love with Evie
Soames, a classmate, but Evie becomes engaged to Archie
Merridew, still another member of the college's student
body. Jeffries narrates the tale, telling his readers about his grinding poverty, about his anguish over
Evie's betrothal, and about his growing determination to
extinguish Mr. Merridew's life. There is no detection
in the book; the galvanizing issue is whether or not
Jeffries will carry out his elaborate plans for Merridew's murder. The business college is described in relentless detail, and readers are offered intensive views
of the school's classrooms, its courses, and the ambitions, fears, and problems of its students.
   George Oliver Onions was born in Bradford, Yorkshire,
Great Britain. He studied for three years at the Royal
College of Art before launching what was to become a
successful career as a writer of mainstream novels, mysteries, and ghost stories. *In Accordance with the Evidence* is often considered a minor classic of early-twentieth century "realistic" mystery fiction. It was reprinted in 1976 as part of Garland Publishing's "Fifty
Classics of Crime Fiction" series, edited by Jacques
Barzun and Wendell Hertig Taylor.

335. Webster, Henry Kitchell (1875-1932). *The Butterfly*.
     New York: D. Appleton and Co., 1914.

   The protagonist of this frothy mystery-romance is Brinsley Butler, a young professor of drama at an unidentified state university in the American Midwest. Brinsley
falls in love with Elaine Arthur, a celebrated dancer-
actress who brings her new show to the university town
for three pre-Chicago tryout performances. A murder
takes place in the hotel in which Elaine is staying. The

victim is an elderly woman, and State's Attorney James
Dorgan, the official detective of the case, soon learns
that Elaine and the woman were acquainted. Dorgan suspects Elaine but, of course, Brinsley doesn't agree.
Thanks in no small part to some energetic amateur sleuthing by the professor, the issue is eventually resolved in
Elaine's favor. Most of the action in the story takes
place off campus, but there is one noteworthy scene in
the home of the university's president, a former professor
of astronomy named VanDyck. The president, whose beard is
so full that all that is visible of his face are his
"cold blue eyes," wants to fire Brinsley for consorting
with a lady of the stage. Brinsley and Elaine visit Van-
Dyck in order to dissuade him from this dastardly plan,
and Elaine charms the old presidential curmudgeon into
a state of fawning adoration. Brinsley's job is saved
by Elaine's seductive behavior, but by the end of the
book it appears as though the professor may be leaving
the university after all. He and Elaine are about to
be married. Furthermore, Brinsley's new play, the plot
which he has lifted from *The Fairie Queen*, is being set
to music as a new vehicle for Elaine's many talents, and
the professor hopes to leave academe forever and make his
future living as a playwright.

Henry Kitchell Webster was born in Evanston, Illinois.
He received a bachelor's degree from Hamilton College
in 1897. After one year as an instructor of rhetoric
at Union College, he turned to creative writing. During
the early years of this century, Webster was one of America's most popular and best-remunerated fiction writers.
A novelist, a mystery writer, and a frequent contributor
of stories to popular magazines, he is reputed to have
dictated his prose to a stenographer at the rate of
20,000 words per week. *The Butterfly* was the third of
eleven full-length mysteries which Webster published
during his lifetime.

336. Wells, Carolyn (1869-1942). *The Mystery Girl*. Phila-
     delphia and London: J.B. Lippincott, 1922.

John Waring, the bachelor president-elect of the "University of Corinth" in New England, dies in his locked
study after his jugular vein is pierced by a stilleto-
like instrument. The death-dealing weapon cannot be
found (and no one can determine how the killer left the
scene without unlatching the door or windows), but suspects are not in short supply. Emily Bates, a widow who
was scheduled to become Waring's bride, stands to inherit

oodles of money from her betrothed's estate. Gordon
Lockwood, Waring's private secretary, was known to have
been in the president-elect's residence during the night
of his employer's demise. And then there is Anita Austen, a beautiful young lady from New York City, who was
once seen kissing Waring's photograph. Anita, "the mystery girl" referred to in the title, claims to have come
to Corinth to paint pictures of the school's environs in
winter, but none of the other characters in the novel
believes that story for a minute. The local police are
thoroughly baffled, and Maurice Trask, a headstrong lawyer who wants to clear Anita of suspicion so that he
might marry her, hires Fleming Stone to bring matters to
a speedy and satisfactory conclusion. Stone is a scholarly Carolyn Wells series-character private detective.
Accompanied by Terrence "Fibsy" McGuire, his ever-present factotum, Stone arrives at the university on page
272. By the time the book ends, a mere seventy-seven
pages later, the whole matter has, indeed, been resolved.
The crucial clue in the case is literary in nature, but
the emphasis of *The Mystery Girl* is on the social rather
than the academic life at Corinth.

Carolyn Wells was one of the pioneers of American mystery fiction. Born in Rahway, New Jersey, she lived
most of her life in New York City. Wells wrote more than
eighty mystery novels during her career. Sixty-one of
her mysteries featured Fleming Stone as sleuth. *The
Mystery Girl* was Stone's twelfth published exploit.

337. Martin, Wyndham (1875-). *The Bathurst Complex*. London:
      Herbert Jenkins, 1924. Published in the United States
      as *The Murder in Beacon Street*. New York: Robert M.
      McBride, 1930.

The sleuth in this often-labored exploration into the
peccadilloes of Boston high society is John Southard, a
Harvard professor of modern literature. John is thirty-
three-years-old, a bachelor, and an avocational writer of
detective sagas. He enters the story when he assists
Rhona King, a young instructor of English at Radcliffe,
after she becomes a suspect in a murder committed in the
Beacon Street mansion of millionaire Curtis Bathurst.
John's detection is not made easier when the victim's
body disappears and when the principal police detective
on the case is fired from the force after a drunken
sail on the Charles River. Nor does the attitude of
Curtis Bathurst help John resolve matters. Bathurst
refuses to admit that anyone was killed in his home,

and in retaliation against what he sees as unwanted prying on John's part, he takes the ultimate punitive step
of trying to have the professor expelled from the Boston
University Club. John prevails, however, and as he un-
ravels the several related mysteries in the book, he even
wins Bathurst's friendship. Moreover, John receives a
monetary bonus for his efforts. Rhona, to whom he has
become engaged, inherits uncounted millions from her late
father, the Dartmouth-educated "cranberry King" of Cape
Cod. Upon learning of her riches, Rhona immediately resigns her teaching post. John plans to follow suit after
his marriage and to spend the rest of his days as a gentleman detective.

Wyndham Martin was born in London. His early ambition
was to be a mining engineer, and to this end he attended
the Bruselies School of Mines and the London College of
Assaying. He found his career not in mining, however,
but in writing, and during the early years of this century he produced a veritable torrent of plays, melodramatic thrillers, mainstream novels, short stories for
popular magazines, screenplays, and mysteries. Martin
spent much of his adult life in the United States and
was a resident of Santa Monica, California.

338.   Knox, Richard Arbuthnott (1888–1957). *The Viaduct Mur-
        der*. London: Methuen and Co., 1925; New York: Simon
        and Schuster, 1926.

Four British golfers find the body of a man near a
railroad viaduct which is adjacent to their golf club.
The four men form themselves into an ad hoc team of detectives in order to establish both the identity of the
deceased and the cause of his death. One of the quartet
is William Carmichael, a retired don. Carmichael acts as
the theorist for the would-be sleuths. An archeologist
by profession, Carmichael is inclined to incorporate as
many false clues as real ones in his ratiocinative musings. Nonetheless, by the end of the book the mystery
has been resolved, and Carmichael is once again enjoying
a quiet retirement.

Ronald Arbuthnott Knox, the fourth son of the Anglican
Bishop of Manchester, was educated at Eton and at Balliol
College, Oxford. After serving for five years as the
Anglican chaplain of Trinity College, Oxford, Knox con-
verted to Roman Catholicism, and in 1925 he became the
Catholic chaplain of Oxford University. A prolific wri-
ter, Knox is best remembered for his sometimes whimsical
and often satirical essays on religious and moral matters.

He was also a serious student of mystery and published many commentaries on the genre. Knox wrote six mystery novels of his own. Five of the stories feature Miles Bredon, an investigator for an insurance company, as sleuth. *The Viaduct Murder,* Knox's first mystery novel, is his only non-Bredon tale. Now considered a classic work of detective fiction, the book incorporates many overt (and covert) references to pre-1925 fictional detectives and their exploits. Some historians of mystery fiction have seen Carmichael and his three associates as embodying satirical commentaries which Knox wished to make about "great" amateur detectives in literature.

339. Cole, G(eorge) D(ouglas) H(oward) (1889-1959) and Margaret (Isabel)(Postgate) Cole (1893-1980). *The Murder at Chrome House.* London: William Collins Sons, 1927; New York: Macmillan, 1927.

The protagonist of this stylish novel is James Flint, a thirty-two-year old lecturer in economics at a college in London. James is vaulted from his untroubled academic life into an unaccustomed role as a sleuth in a murder case when he finds, in a book he has borrowed from the Westminister Library, a photograph of one man shooting another. James shows the strange photo to Sydney Underwood, a solicitor and a fellow member of the St. Martin's Club. Underwood immediately recognizes the victim in the picture as Henry Wye, the former owner of Chrome House in Berkshire, who was murdered a few months earlier. Furthermore, he identifies the assailant in the scene as Oliver de Bellew, one of Underwood's clients, who was tried but found not guilty of the crime. At Underwood's urging, James sets out to get to the bottom of the grisly matter, and his investigations take to various locales in London and to Chrome House itself. As the complex case develops, James discovers that detection is more interesting than offering tutorials, and real-life professors will appreciate the inventive excuses which James generates to shirk his teaching duties. They will appreciate, too, the graceful, clue-fitting writing (laced with some subtle satire) through which readers are led along with James to the story's conclusion.

George Douglas Howard Cole was educated at St. Paul's School and at Balliol College, Oxford. A fixture on the British intellectual scene until his death in 1959, George Cole was a socialist economist, a fellow of the Fabian Society (from 1947-1951), and a prolific writer of professional books, political tracts, and (with his wife,

Margaret) mystery novels. Margaret Isabel Postgate Cole
received her education at Roedean School and Girton College, Cambridge. The sister of mystery writer Raymond
Postgate, Mrs. Cole combined writing with political acti-
vism as a long-time Socialist member of the London County
Council. Critics generally applauded the Coles' mysteries as intelligent, well-crafted, and entertaining,
though most historians of the genre now see the Coles'
output as uneven in its quality. In addition to *The Murder at Chrome House*, three other mysteries by the Coles
appear in this bibliography. These works are *Off With
Her Head!* (385), *A Knife in the Dark* (394), and *Toper's
End* (397).

340. Gordon, Neil [Macdonell, Archibald Gordon (1895-1941)].
     The Professor's Poison. London: Longmans, Green and
     Co., 1927; New York: Harcourt, Brace and Co., 1928.

     James Arnold, a scholarly British professor of chem-
istry, has the misfortune of creating by accident a
colorless and odorless poison gas. James, who lives
near the Chelsea Embankment in London, suddenly becomes
the focus of international espionage. Various governments want his discovery. However, James is a pacifist
and knows that these governments will employ his gas
as a terrible tool of war. So the professor refuses to
disclose the ingredients of his compound (even to the
British War Office), and instead he begins work on the
antidote to the horrible weapon which he has inadvertently brought into being. When spies steal the formula
for his gas, James turns into a sleuth. Although Inspector Fleming of Scotland Yard becomes involved in the
case, it is James--with the help of Reverend Robert Wil-
iamson, a man of the cloth from London's East End--who
eventually makes the world safe (at least temporarily)
from destruction. Despite the deaths of a London policeman and three delegates to a disarmament conference
during the course of the book, the story is written not
as a serious thriller, but as a satirical fable. For
example, one of the murdered conference delegates is
from Cuba, and when his body is returned to his native
land, his funeral is "attended by all who could obtain
leave of absence from the cigar factories." And James
Arnold, whose precise academic affiliation is never revealed, is the sort of often-befuddled professor who
wanders the streets in his slippers and who casually asks
London bobbies if they have the latest learned articles
in chemistry journals.

Archibald Gordon Macdonell was born in Aberdeen, Scotland. After service as an artillery officer in World War I, he was during the 1920s a member of the Geneva headquarters staff of the League of Nations. A mainstream novelist, a writer of travel books and biographies, and the author of a dozen mysteries, Macdonell infused many of his works with satire. During the early days of World War II, Macdonell became a commentator on the BBC's overseas radio service. This career was cut short when he was killed in an air raid on January 17, 1941.

341. MacIsaac, Frederick John (1886-1940). *The Vanishing Professor*. New York: Henry Waterson, 1927; London: Methuen and Co., 1939.

"Omega College," a high-status institution in the eastern United States, has a well-earned reputation "for securing more brilliant professors for less money than any college in the country." Frank Leonard, for example, is a twenty-eight-year-old Harvard Ph.D. in physics who is already a full professor but who earns only $2400 per year. After President Jeffries refuses his request for a $500 raise, Frank angrily resigns his post and goes off to New York City to seek his fortune. But Frank is not your everyday fiscally aggrieved professor. He has invented a "black box" which, when activated, sends out light rays which make its holder invisible. With his box under his arm, Frank undertakes a series of daring money snatches from New York banks. All goes well for a while, but then John Craven, one of Frank's former students, steals the box and undertakes a one-man crime wave of his own. At this juncture, Frank's Harvard background begins to tell. He repents for his sins and, along with Foster Gaines (a private detective working for various New York banks), undertakes a search for the evil Mr. Craven. As part of his amateur detection, Frank constructs a second black box, and the climax of the story occurs when Frank and John Craven, both invisible, engage in mortal physical combat. Although *The Vanishing Professor* strays perilously close to science-fiction fantasy, it is included in this bibliography because it contains some orthodox detection. Moreover, several of the book's characters display decidedly real-world attitudes toward academe. Frank Leonard chaffs at Omega College because his salary is less than that of local day laborers. And Tom Ransome, a director of many of the banks from which Frank and John Craven steal mon-

ey, does not want his "delectable" daughter (a Vassar
graduate) to accept Frank's proposal of marriage. Mr.
Ransome is oblivious, of course, to Frank's career in
crime. He knows only that "a carpenter makes more than
a college professor" and that "[professors] lack guts;
that's why they hide in colleges and earn a miserable
salary instead of going out and bucking real life."

Frederick John MacIsaac was born in Cambridge, Massachusetts. He was a playwright and mainstream novelist
as well as a writer of mysteries. *The Vanishing Professor* was the second of fourteen mystery novels which
MacIsaac published during his lifetime.

342.   Huntington, John [Phillips, Gerald Williams (1884-)].
        The Seven Black Chessmen. London: Gerald Rowe, 1928;
        New York: Henry Holt, 1928.

        Professor William Cheney, now retired but once a che-
        mist of great international reputation, lives quietly
        with his wife and nubile young daughter at Cheney Park,
        an estate in the English Midlands. One day the pro-
        fessor is found dead in his automobile, the apparent vic-
        tim of a heart attack. Though the local police are in-
        clined to dismiss Cheney's death as due to natural cau-
        ses, two inquisitive holidaymakers believe that the pro-
        fessor was murdered. One of the vacationmakers, a man
        named Kent, narrates the story. The other, Mr. Horton
        Forbes, does most of the sleuthing. The solution to the
        mystery lies in a cryptic coded message (apparently a
        chess problem) which Cheney was carrying in his coat poc-
        ket, and thanks to the Kent-Forbes duo the professor's
        killer meets a singularly gory end. Although the book
        incorporates many interesting characterizations of local
        villagers, Professor Cheney is the only academic in the
        plot. Cheney dies in the first chapter; hence his actual
        participation in the goings on is limited. But Cheney
        Park, the professor's exquisite seventeenth-century home-
        stead, is described in detail in later portions of the
        book. And beauteous Mary Cheney, whose favorite past-
        time is feeding the pigeons on Cheney Park's spacious
        lawn, proves to be a girl whose coolness under stress
        would have made her father proud.

*343.   Broome, Adam [James, Godfrey Warden (1888-)]. *The Ox-
         ford Murders*. London: Geoffrey Bles, 1929.

        "St. Anthony's College," Oxford, is thrown into some-
        thing of an uproar when Anthanasius Septimus Konti ar-

rives to begin his undergraduate studies. A black prince from West Africa, "Septic" (as he quickly comes to be known) brings with him a large ceremonial drum, a great quantity of expensive wearing apparel, and two wives. Since women are not allowed to reside in St. Anthony's, the wives are dispatched with great fanfare to a hotel. For a time, Septic is the major topic of discussion in the Oxford community, but the attention of the locals soon turns to other matters--the murders of three dons and an unsuccessful attempt on the life of another. In each killing the victim is knocked unconscious and a hole is drilled through his skull into his brain. Various representatives from the British police establishment become involved in the case. However, the crucial sleuthing is provided by Reggie Crofts, who is depicted first as a St. Anthony's student and then as a junior colonial administrator in West Africa, and by Barbara Playfair, Reggie's ladylove and the niece of an Oxford faculty member. Few regular consumers of mysteries will be surprised at the identity of Oxford's assassin-by-drill. But since the killer sucked out the brains of his victims in order to improve his own intellect, most professorial readers will want to stop and ponder the threatening implications of the crimes.

The Oxford Murders was the second of twelve mystery novels which Godfrey Warden James published during his career. All of his mysteries were issued under the Adam Broome pseudonym. A later James mystery novel is entitled *The Cambridge Murders* (London: Geoffrey Bles, 1936). *The Cambridge Murders* was not available for annotation.

344.   Cohen, Octavius Roy (1891-1959). *The May Day Mystery.* New York: D. Appleton and Co., 1929.

The murder of Pat Thayer, a senior at coeducational "Maryland College," brings fat, cheroot-smoking Jim Hanvey onto the campus for some slow-paced sleuthing. Hanvey is in the employ of the "Banker's Protective Association," and he happens to be in the vicinity doing detective work on a bank heist. The late Mr. Thayer, who was stabbed in his room in the Psi Tau Theta House, was a card cheat, a bootlegger, and a notorious love-'em-and-leave-'em womanizer, and his death proves to be connected with the bank robbery which is the reason for Hanvey's presence in the Marland area. As the title indicates, Pat Thayer was killed on May Day. Marland

College is a picturesque institution in the American
South. Along with Jim Hanvey's sometimes infuriatingly
sluggish detection, the book offers many, many passages
about the beauty of the Maryland environment in the spring.

Octavius Roy Cohen was born in Charleston, South Carolina and graduated from Clemson College in 1911. Admitted to the South Carolina bar in 1913, he abandoned
the practice of law two years later to write fiction.
Known primarily for his Negro dialect stories and for his
detective novels, Cohen also wrote stage dramas. *The
May Day Mystery* was the second of four Cohen mysteries
to feature Jim Hanvey.

345.   Davidson, T.L. [Thompson, David Landsborough (1901-1964)].
       The Murder in the Laboratory. London: Methuen and Co.,
       1929; New York: E.P. Dutton, 1929.

Set at an unidentified British university, this competently crafted story begins with the death of Walter
Sheppary, a research fellow in toxicology. Walter expires in his laboratory after consuming cyanide. His
body is found by Dr. Martin Blythe, one of the university's most distinquished junior scientists, and by
George Wroxham, a medical student. Dr. Blythe quickly
calls the police, and Detective Inspector Mellison of
Scotland Yard is soon on the scene. Dr. Blythe, George
Wroxham, and Mellison then engage in sleuthing. They
first determine that Walter was murdered; then, and after
establishing this dismal fact, they set out to rid the
university of his killer. One of the trio's prime suspects is sinister Professor Franklin, the head of the
toxicology department. A laconic man, with an inexpli-
cable aversion to smoking his pipe in public, Franklin
is indeed a suspicious character. It is not until the
three detectives probe the details of Walter Sheppary's
private life, however, that the case can be closed. In
contrast to some university-laboratory mysteries, this
occasionally satirical novel does not dwell on the chemical properties of exotic poisons. The stress, instead,
is on alibis, motives, and deep, dark family secrets.

David Landsborough Thompson was born in Aberdeen, Scotland and educated at Grenoble and Cambridge Universities. A long-time professor of biochemistry at McGill
University in Montreal, he wrote several well-regarded
scientific textbooks. *The Murder in the Laboratory*
was his only mystery novel.

346. Fairlie, Gerald (1899-). *The Exquisite Lady.* London:
      Hodder and Stoughton, 1929. Published in the United
      States as *Yellow Munro.* Boston: Little, Brown
      and Co., 1929.

      Down in Hampshire, in the quaint British village of
      Bitterme, there lives a brilliant professor named Alex-
      ander Weighton. The professor is inventing an advanced
      form of X-ray, and each night brilliant flashes of light
      and sharp, explosive sounds emanate from the windows of
      his home. Because Yellow Munro, a terrifying, red-head-
      ed criminal of international infamy, wants the invention,
      he has Weighton murdered. The scientific secrets which
      Yellow is after elude him, however, thanks to the efforts
      of Ian Murray, a young British World War I veteran. Ian
      enters the affair after various characters in the story
      mistake him for his cousin, John Murray, one of Yellow
      Munro's paid hoodlums. During the course of his hostil-
      ities with Yellow, Ian several times comes close to los-
      ing his own life, but he is more than compensated for his
      pains by winning the heart of Loyalty Elliot, a super-
      beauty with her own aptitude for survival. There are no
      campus scenes in the story and, indeed, Professor Weigh-
      ton's academic affiliation is never made explicit.
      Nonetheless, modern-day professorial readers may enjoy
      this 1920s thriller if only because Chink, a brutish
      Chinese torture expert in Yellow Munro's employ, may
      remind them of some administrators they have known.
      Gerald Fairlie was born in London and educated at the
      Royal Military College at Sandhurst. He served in the
      Scots Guards from 1917 until 1924 and then became a full-
      time writer. During the course of his career Fairlie
      wrote mysteries, mainstream novels, biographies, plays,
      and scripts for both British and American motion pic-
      tures. He is best known to mystery buffs as the author
      of the later "Bulldog Drummond" novels. Fairlie con-
      tinued that highly successful series after the death of
      H.C. McNeile, Drummond's creator, in 1937.

347. Lilly, Jean. *False Face.* New York: E.P. Dutton, 1929.

      Natica Crane is in love with Granville Perkins, but
      Granville is infatuated with Poppy Brown. Poppy hopes
      to marry K.C. Gildersleeve, but K.C. years for Natica.
      All of the participants in this unhappy, lovelorn circle
      are students at an American institution of emotional
      suffering known as "Jefferson University." Two of the

group are the children of faculty members and one--K.C.
Gildersleeve--is the son of Jefferson's president. The
only non-academic offspring, Granville Perkins, compensates for his inferior lineage by being the son of a millionaire, and it is Granville who becomes the victim in
the story. He is shot dead in his car late one night
outside of his fraternity house. Natica is the prime
suspect because she is the last person known to have
seen young Mr. Perkins alive. Natica's plight naturally
discomforts her father, William Rutherford Crane, Jefferson's stellar Shakespearean scholar, and he undertakes
some sleuthing in order to save his daughter from arrest.
Also functioning as detectives in the saga are Chief Simmons and Inspector Mannie of the local police, and Bruce
Perkins, who is Granville's older brother and an attorney. Meantime, the other faculty father in the affair,
Harrison Brown, stays at home cramming calories into his
corpulent body and preparing lectures on Teutonic literature, even though his own daughter could well have ended Granville's life. And as for President Gildersleeve,
he tries to put the best face on things by claiming that
no one connected with his university could possibly be
a murderer. Brimming over with clues, the book is short
on action but long on talk, since the major characters
spend most of their time interrogating each other. Modern-day academics may not find *False Face* to be the
most exciting mystery in this bibliography, but they
will appreciate the now-extinct lifestyles of the Jefferson faculty. The Cranes employ a live-in black maid
named Melissa, and the Browns' needs are attended to by
Keno, a Japanese houseboy.

The identity of Jean Lilly is not revealed by any ex-
tant bibliographic sourcebook. *False Face* was the second of four mysteries which she published. Attorney
Bruce Perkins, who debuts in *False Face*, sleuths again
in Lilly's third and fourth novels.

*348. Orr, Clifford (1899-1951). *The Dartmouth Murders*. New
       York: Farrar and Rinehart, 1929; London: Hamish Hamil-
       ton, 1931.

       Three Dartmouth students are killed. Two die as the
       result of steel needles which are mysteriously fired in-
       to their skulls. The third is shot accidently-on-pur-
       pose as a posse of Dartmouth vigilantes searches for the
       killer of the first two victims. Fortunately for what
       remains of the Dartmouth student body, Joseph Harris

happens to be in Hanover. The father of the undergrad-
uate-narrator of the story, a Big Green alumnus, and a
lawyer who writes mystery novels as a hobby, Harris is
asked by Dartmouth's president to become the school's
temporary detective-in-residence. With the help of his
son--whose own sleuthing actually breaks the case--Har-
ris resolves matters by the end of the book, but not before some members of the Dartmouth community become tired
of his officious behavior. Included in the story's large
roster of characters is a rustic-but-sagacious local
sheriff, a host of undergraduates (many of them exceedingly wealthy), and Professor "Bossy" Bostwick, an
ingratiating professor of English who makes his bachelor
digs the command post for the investigation. Although
some of the idiomatic language in the novel is now badly
dated, modern-day readers will not complain about a lack
of real and false clues. Nor will devotees of action-
mysteries be disappointed in the chases through the picturesque New England countryside which borders the beautiful Dartmouth campus.

Clifford Orr was born in Portland, Maine, and graduated from Dartmouth. Most of his career was spent as an
editor for *The New Yorker*. A sometimes song lyricist,
as well as a sometimes mystery writer, Orr wrote the
words to the 1929 hit "I May Be Wrong, But I Think
You're Beautiful." *The Dartmouth Murders* was adapted
for a 1935 motion picture. The Chesterfield Productions
film was directed by Charles LaMont and starred Robert
Warwick as Joseph Harris. Although Orr made his home
in New York City, he returned to the Dartmouth environs
in June of 1951, after learning he had a terminal illness. He died, four months later, in a Hanover, New
Hampshire, nursing home.

349. Van Dine, S.S. [Wright, Willard Huntington (1888-1939)].
     The Bishop Murder Case. New York: Charles Scribner's
     Sons, 1929; London: Cassell and Co., 1929.

Professor Bertrand Dillard, one of the world's greatest mathmatical physicists, lives in semi-retirement in
a large house on West 75th Street in New York City.
Sharing his abode are Belle Dillard, his attractive young
niece, and Sigurd Arnesson, his adopted son. Arnesson,
nearing forty, is an associate professor of mathematics
at Columbia. The story begins with the murder (by bow
and arrow) of Joseph Robin, a young playboy and one of
Belle's acquaintances. Called in on the case is the
effete Philo Vance, an illustrious S.S. Van Dine series-

character detective who was once one of Professsor Dillard's students. Vance unmasks the killer. As the clues
pile up, readers learn a great deal about the dark se-
crets which underlie the seemingly placid professorial
lives of Dillard and Arnesson. It will not give too
much of the plot away, perhaps, to note that two years
after the culprit in the case is brought to justice, one
of the two professors wins a Nobel prize.

Willard Huntington Wright was born in Charlottesville,
Virginia. He did his undergraduate work at St. Vincent
and Pomona Colleges in California and took graduate work
in English at Harvard. He also studied art in Munich and
Paris. From 1907 until 1923 he held a variety of editing positions with American newspapers and magazines.
He also attempted, without great success, to become a
best-selling novelist. Wright did not begin his mystery-
writing career until he suffered a mental breakdown in
1923. During his two-year convalescence he read over
two thousand detective novels and determined to try his
own hand at the craft. Wright's extremely popular Philo
Vance series, aimed primarily at educated readers,
earned him the immense royalties which had eluded him
during his earlier, abortive career as a writer of mainstream fiction.

350. Bristow, Gwen (1903-1980) and Manning, Bruce. *The Invi-
      sible Host*. New York: The Mystery League, 1930. Also
      published as *The Ninth Guest*. New York: Popular Li-
      brary, 1975.

Eight New Orleans socialites are invited to a mysterious surprise party in the penthouse of a high-rise office building. Each member of the party has a grudge
against one or more of the other guests. When dinner is
over, a radio suddenly comes on, and the unseen host for
the evening announces over the airwaves that the penthouse is sealed shut, and that during the next few hours
most or all of the assembled partygoers will die. Two
of the diners are Dr. Murray Chambers Reid, the president
of a local university, and Henry Abbott, a former professor whom Reid fired for his left wing politics. As
the soiree proceeds, most of the eight guests perish,
and the survivors take turns accusing each other of staging the macabre affair. Of course, the fundamental plot
of this story was used again, with perhaps more chilling
effects, in Agatha Christie's *Ten Little Niggers* (London:
William Collins Sons, 1939. Published in the United
States as *And Then There Were None*. New York: Dodd,
Mead and Co., 1940). But *The Invisible Host* has the

distinction of offering long, lingering looks at two
academics under severe stress. Faculty readers will especially enjoy the portrait of Dr. Reid, a man whose
"reputation in the local academic circles where he was
reverenced was due to the fact that he never gave the
impression that was being told something for first time."
Gwen Bristow was born in Marion, South Carolina. She
received an A.B. from Judson College in 1924, and during
the 1924-1925 academic year she attended the Columbia
University School of Journalism. She was a reporter for
the *New Orleans Times-Picayune* from 1925 until 1934.
The Invisible Host, written in collaboration with her
husband, Bruce Manning, was her first novel. The book
was adapted for the stage by Pulitzer Prize winning
dramatist Owen Davis, and the play, titled *The Ninth
Guest*, opened on Broadway to mixed reviews on August 25,
1930. Davis's play was subsequently transformed into a
motion picture. The film, also titled *The Ninth Guest*,
was released in 1934 by Columbia Pictures. Spurred
by the success of their first effort, Bristow and Manning collaborated shortly thereafter on a second mystery
novel, *The Guttenberg Murders* (351), which also appears
in this bibliography. In later years Bristow and Manning migrated from New Orleans to Hollywood, where Manning became a successful film writer and Bristow turned
her hand to historical novels.

351.   Bristow, Gwen (1903-1980) and Bruce Manning. *The Guten-
       berg Murders*. New York: The Mystery League, 1931.

Set in New Orleans, this competently written mystery
begins with the theft of nine pages of a Gutenberg Bible
from the "Sheldon Memorial Library." The sleuth in the
book is Wade, a reporter for the "New Orleans Creole."
Wade is "so extremely ugly that there [is] a queer fascination in looking at him." Wade's physical repulsive-
ness is offset in the plot, however, by the many handsome, wealthy people who, in one way or another, become
the subjects of his inquiries. Among the New Orleans
socialites whom Wade interrogates are Professor Alfredo
Miguel Gonzales y Castillo and his dazzlingly beautiful
wife, Winifred. Before Wade's denouement, Winifred is
murdered (as is Quentin Ulman, Winifred's paramour), and
Alfredo emerges as the most likely suspect. Alfredo, a
professor at a major university in the New Orleans area,
is an expert in rare books. "Tall and sunburnt," he
can be "both gracious and cruel ... but never otherwise
than elegant." Alfredo is shown only once on the university campus, but as head trustee of the Sheldon Mem-

orial Library, he plays a major part in the story.
An earlier mystery by Bristow and Manning, *The Invisible Host* (350), also appears in this bibliography.

352. Fitzsimmons, Cortland (1893-1949). *70,000 Witnesses*.
New York: Robert M. McBride, 1931.

"State College" is an American football powerhouse,
and Walter Demuth is its star halfback. When State College plays its big home game of the season against "University," 70,000 spectators pack the stadium in hopes of
watching Walter lead his team to victory. Walter performs in his usual stellar fashion until, later in the
contest, he falls dead while scoring a touchdown. Was
Walter's sudden collapse the result of a heart attack,
or was it murder? An autopsy is inconclusive, and Jack
Kethridge, the local police detective on the case, has
the State College team re-enact the sequence of plays
which led up to Walter's fatal run. At the end of the
mock scrimmage, Rudolpho Cannero, Walter Demuth's stand-
in, falls dead as he strides into the end zone. *70,000
Witnesses* is a how-did-he-do-it as well as a whodunit,
and not until the very end of the story does Detective
Kethridge discover the method by which Walter Demuth
and Rudolpho Cannero were killed. Meanwhile, he interrogates a bevy of suspects. The possible murderers include Ranny Buchan (Walter Demuth's roommate), Dorothy
Demuth (Walter's sister), the whole of the State College
football squad, and even referee Harry Collins (who, as
a Harvard graduate, is naturally a suspicious character).
Bootlegging, gambling, jealousies over girlfriends, and
legacies (Walter and his sister Dorothy are the heirs to
a vast fortune) enter into Kethridge's calculations. The
guilty party is eventually captured. But without Walter
Demuth in the closing quarter of its game with University, State College loses by a score of twenty-seven to
thirteen.

Cortland Fitzsimmons was the creator of Percy Peacock
(221-222), a professorial series-character detective.
70,000 Witnesses, the third of seventeen mystery novels
Fitzsimmons wrote during his lifetime, appeared eleven
years before the first of his two Percy Peacock sagas.
70,000 Witnesses was adapted for a 1932 Paramount Pictures film. The motion picture, in which the names of
the central characters were altered significantly from
those in the novel, starred Phillips Hulmes, Dorothy Jordan, Charles Ruggles, Johnny Mack Brown, and "Big Boy"
Williams.

353. Strange, John Stephen [Tillett, Dorothy Stockbridge

> Doubleday, Doran and Co., 1931. Published in Great
> Britain as *The Murder Game*. London: William Collins
> Sons, 1931.
>
> The "Yorke University" versus "Winslow" game is always
> one of America's outstanding football spectacles. This
> particular year there is an extra-added attraction.
> Coach Diederich of Yorke is shot and killed just as the
> first half is ending. Jim Gaynor, a sports reporter for
> *The New York Sphere*, asks his friend Van Dusen Ormsberry
> to investigate. Ormsberry, a John Stephen Strange ser-
> ies-character detective, finds that Coach Diederich had
> many enemies and that most of them were in the grand-
> stands, within easy shooting distance, when the fatal
> bullet was fired. By the conclusion of this book, the
> murderer has been brought to justice, and, one assumes,
> the Yorke University athletic department has recruited
> a new football coach so that the games may go on.
>   Dorothy Stockbridge Tillett was the author of more
> than twenty mystery novels published between 1928 and
> 1961. All of her works were issued under the John Ste-
> phen Strange pseudonym. *Murder on the Ten-Yard Line*
> was the last of three Van Dusen Ormsberry sagas. Tillett
> is best remembered by mystery buffs for her eight novels
> which featured Pulitzer Prize winning photographer Barney
> Gantt as sleuth.

354. Wees, Frances Shelly (1902-). *The Maestro Murders*. New
York: The Mystery League, 1931. Published in Great
Britain as *Detectives, Ltd*. London: Eyre and Spottis-
wood, 1933.

> Theresa ("Tuck") Torrie and Bunny Temple, two recent
> college graduates with liberal arts degrees, run a
> stenography service in a major American city. Since the
> two young women specialize in translating and transcri-
> bing French and German documents, it is only natural
> (one must suppose) that many of their regular clients
> are professors. Old Professor Seeley, from the local
> university, is one of their patrons, but he ceases to
> bring the young ladies his business after he is shot
> dead in his house. Then the Torrie-Temple office is
> burglarized, and it is clear that someone is looking for
> the last piece of work which the professor asked the
> girls to type. Along with Michael Forrester, a congen-
> ial young attorney, Tuck and Bunny launch a rather fren-
> zied investigation, soon linking the professor's death
> to a ring of international jewel thieves headed by a

man known as "The Maestro." As matters turn out, Professor Seeley's role in the story is relatively insig-
nificant. However, even as Seeley is written out of the
plot, another academic figure enters. This individual,
named Adrian, is a psychologist. Dr. Adrian does research
at the university (which has just awarded him an honorary
degree), and he acts as a consultant to the local police.
An affable man, with a passion for Chinese rugs and Li-
moges table settings, Dr. Adrian is a crucial figure
as the case comes to its tumultuous conclusion.

Frances Shelly Wees was born in Gresham, Oregon. She
received a teacher's certificate from the Saskatoon
(Canada) Normal School in 1923. She was director of
the Canadian Chautauquas when *The Maestro Murders*, her
first novel, was published. In later years Wees was an
account executive for a Toronto public relations firm,
a director of the United Nations Relief and Rehabilita-
tion Agency in Ottawa, and a public relations consultant for the Toronto Art Gallery. Her publishing credits
include many books for children, as well as ten mystery
novels. Wees' second mystery novel, *The Mystery of the
Creeping Man* (335), also appears in this bibliography.
The Mystery of the Creeping Man is set on and near a
university campus, and it features Michael Forrester and
his new bride Tuck as sleuths.

355.   Wees, Frances Shelly (1902-). *The Mystery of the Creep-
       ing Man*. Philadelphia: Macrae-Smith, 1931; London:
       Eyre and Spottiswood, 1934.

       Professor Edgar Murchison disappears. The head of the
       physiology department at an unidentified American uni-
       versity, Murchison drops from sight on the last day of
       the spring semester. Ordinarily, the disappearance of a
       prominent professor in a mystery novel brings out armies
       of professional and amateur sleuths, but in this instance
       no one seems overly concerned. A man of unusual habits,
       Murchison has been known to disappear before. And,
       what's more, the anti-vivisectionists in the local commu-
       nity are glad to see him go, because it is well known
       that he has been conducting painful research on animals.
       Murchison lived in a university-owned house, and some
       weeks after he vanishes the school rents the home to
       Michael Forrester and his wife Tuck. Michael is the
       very same attorney-sleuth who performed so admirably in
       Frances Wees' *The Maestro Murders* (354), and Tuck was the
       co-owner of a stenography service in the earlier novel.

The Forresters become interested in Murchison's whereabouts because they experience a series of break-ins,
and because they suspect that the uninvited intruder may
be their home's previous occupant. The Forresters' detection eventually leads them to a nearby cave, in which
they come dangerously close to dying as unwilling guinea
pigs in a physiological experiment. Real-life academic
scientists often complain about the inadequacy of their
laboratory facilities. After reading about the Forresters' subterranean adventures, they are likely to be
thankful that their own laboratories are, at least,
above ground.

*356. Ford, Leslie [Brown, Zenith Jones (1898-)]. *By the
       Watchman's Clock*. New York: Farrar and Rinehart, 1932.

"Landover College," a private, all-male institution in
Maryland, forms the backdrop for this sometimes wordy,
but sometimes fast-paced mystery-of-manners. The victim
in the story is Daniel Sutton, a wealthy businessman
who resides near the college and who, through his dona-
tions, is the school's chief benefactor. Daniel bullies
unmercifully all of those around him. Hence, when he is
shot dead in his study one night, there is a long list
of people who had ample motive for the crime. The story
is narrated by Martha Niles, the wife of Ben Niles, a
Landover professor of anthropology. Ben is a suspect
in the case, because the truculent Mr. Sutton had threatened to withdraw his support for the anthropology department, but the finger of suspicion also points toward
several of Sutton's houseguests, his two adult offspring,
and several members of Landover's impoverished black
community. Martha does some of the sleuthing, but the
detection is shared by a number of other characters as
well, including courtly Dr. Knox, Landover's president.
Academic readers may feel ambivalent about the novel's
conclusion. Daniel Sutton's killer seems to escape justice, but under the terms of Daniel's will Landover College receives 250,000 acres of oil-rich land in New Mexico.
     Zenith Jones Brown was born in Smith River, California.
She attended the University of Washington. In 1921 she
married Ford K. Brown, who later was to become a professor at St. John's College, Annapolis, Maryland. During the 1920s the Browns spent time in Oxford, where
Ford Brown was conducting research, and Mrs. Brown began
her writing career with a series of mysteries (under the

pseudonym David Frome) with British settings. By the
early 1930s, Mrs. Brown began to write mysteries set in
and around her Annapolis home, and thereafter some of
her works were laid in Great Britain and some in the
United States. She employed the pseudonym Leslie Ford
on her American mysteries. *By the Watchman's Clock* was
her second Leslie Ford novel. One of Mrs. Brown's David
Frome mysteries, *Mr. Pinkerton Finds a Body* (366), is
also included in this bibliography.

357. King, C(harles) Daly (1895-1963). *Obelists at Sea*. Lon-
      don: John Heritage, 1932: New York: Alfred A Knopf,
      1933.

The oceanliner *S.S. Meganaut* is sailing from New York
to Southhampton when Victor Smith is shot dead in the
ship's crowded ballroom. Smith was one of America's
richest industrialists and, apparently, one of its most
hated men as well. The leading suspect is a Mr. de Bras-
to, a New York lawyer who is found to be carrying a
discharged revolver, but anyone of hundreds of people
could have committed the foul deed. Four psychologists
on their way to a convention in London are on board the
Meganaut, and they volunteer to identify Smith's killer.
There is a slight problem, however. Each of the psychologists has his own pet professional orientation, and
each of the four savants pinpoints a different person
as the murderer. As matters turn out, each of the psychologists is incorrect. The four psychologists are Dr.
Frank Hayvier (an advocate of conditioning theory), Dr.
Malcolm Plecks (a psychoanalyst), Dr. Love Rees Pons
(who has recently created a theory dealing with dominant
personalities), and Professor Knott Coe Mittle (a cau-
tious man whose professional tastes tend toward "middle
ground" approaches). The first three manqué-detectives
seem to be private psychological practitioners. Professor Mittle, however, is a tried and true academic,
though his university affiliation is never made explicit.
Written both as farce and as serious mystery (in terms
of its unrelenting emphasis on ratiocination), the
story is preceded by a full roster of its many, many
important characters, and it is followed by a paginated
list of the crucial clues in the plot.
Charles Daly King was born in New York City and received a B.A. from Yale. After serving as an artillery
lieutenant in World War I, he entered the cotton and
wool business. Late in the 1920s King returned to

school for an M.A. (from Columbia) and a Ph.D. (from
Yale) in psychology. Thereafter he operated a private
psychology practice, published several well-received professional books on psychological matters and wrote six
mystery novels. *Obelists at Sea* was his first venture
into the mystery field. Connoisseurs of the genre generally give King's mysteries high marks for their original
plotting and structure. The five mystery novels which
followed *Obelists at Sea* all feature Michael Lord, a young
New York City police investigator, as sleuth. Dr. Love
Rees Pons, one of the four bumbling psychologists in
Obelists at Sea, serves as Lord's Watson throughout the
series. And what is an obelist? In a special note at
the beginning of *Obelists at Sea*, King defines the term
as "one who harbours suspicions."

358. Propper, Milton (Morris) (1906-1962). *The Student Fra-
ternity Murder*. Indianapolis: Bobbs-Merrill, 1932.
Published in Great Britain as *Murder of an Initiate*.
London: Faber and Faber, 1933.

Stuart Jordon, a student at the "University of Philadelphia," is murdered by poison while being initiated
into a fraternity. Tommy Rankin, a Philadelphia police
detective and an experienced Milton Propper series-character sleuth, handles the investigation. Rankin finds
that the late Mr. Jordan had mortal enemies off as well
on the Philadelphia campus, and in order to apprehend
the killer he must probe deeply into Stuart's unusual
life history. *The Student Fraternity Murder* is noteworthy as an early-day American police procedural. It
also offers considerable insight into fraternity life
in the 1930s. And, as an extra added attraction, it
provides a how-to-do-it course for young ladies who
might want to pass as men and live undetected in all-
male dormitories.

Although Milton Morris Propper is not included in any
of the standard biographical compendia of American literary figures, he was the subject of an extended essay
by Francis M. Nevins, Jr. in the July 1977 issue of
The Armchair Detective (Vol. 10, No. 3). According to
Nevins, Propper was born in Philadelphia in 1906 and
received an LL.B. from the University of Pennsylvania
Law School in 1929. An aspiring writer, Propper did not
apply for admission to the Pennsylvania bar. Instead,
he wrote mystery novels and short stories and, early in

his career, experienced significant critical and financial success. By the mid-1930s, however, Propper's literary popularity faded, and he took a position with the
Social Security Administration, serving first in Philadelphia and then in Atlanta. During the 1950s Propper
suffered from bouts of depression and was placed under
psychiatric care. In 1962 he committed suicide.

*359. Whitechurch, Victor Lorenzo (1868-1933). *Murder at the
College*. London: William Collins Sons, 1932. Pub-
lished in the United States as *Murder at Exbridge*.
New York: Dodd, Mead and Co., 1932.

"St. Oswald's College," of "Exbridge University" in
Great Britain has a reputation for the scholarly attain-
ments of its fellows. The college's image takes a bit
of a beating, however, when a visitor is stabbed to
death in the rooms of one of its more illustrious dons.
Detective-Sergeant Ambrose handles the investigation. An
intelligent, pipe-smoking man of about thirty, Ambrose
refuses to be awed by a long list of accomplished but
eccentric academic suspects. One of those upon whom
Ambrose focuses his attentions is Mr. Hewitt, a man so
dedicated to the intellectual life that he seldom leaves
his quarters. Another is Dr. Blake, a professor of theology who fancies himself a master of disguise. Though
Ambrose discovers the killer's identity, the culprit escapes capture. Instead of the usual detective-explains-
to-all denouement, the last chapter of this book consists
of a long, revelatory letter from the murderer. Written
from hiding to a former colleague at the college, the
letter explains the killer's motives and methods for
the crime.
      Victor Lorenzo Whitechurch was born in Norham, Great
Britain. An Anglican clergyman, he served in a number
of Midlands parishes before becoming, in retirement,
honorary canon of Christ Church, Oxford. Whitechurch's
extensive literary ouevre includes romantic novels,
books on theology, and eight works of mystery fiction.
Written while he was convalescing after a long illness,
Murder at the College was Whitechurch's last book.

*360. Masterman, J(ohn) C(ecil) (1891-1977). *An Oxford Tragedy*.
London: Victor Gollancz, 1933.

The dons of "St. Thomas's College," Oxford, gather in
the common room after an especially amusing dinner with

Ernst Brendel, a visiting lawyer-criminologist from Vienna. One by one, the dons drift away until only Brendel and Francis Winn, vice-president of St. Thomas's, are left chatting over cigars. Then Dean Maurice Hargreaves bursts in, almost beside himself with agitation. "My God!" he exclaims. "Come up quickly. Someone's shot Shirley--in my room." Hargreaves' announcement thus plunges St. Thomas's into what eventually becomes a murder-suicide, and it thrusts Brendel and Winn (who narrates the tale) into one of the most carefully written and purely academic mysteries to appear in this bibliography. Shirley, as Winn informs us, was an unpopular fellow in classics who had a sizeable list of enemies. Eight dons emerge as suspects, as do Callendar (the St. Thomas's butler) and several of the college's undergraduates. In the end, it is Brendel who deduces the truth about the matter, but the killer avoids arrest by consuming a fatal dose of prussic acid. Jacques Barzun and Walter Hertig Taylor in *A Catalogue of Crime* (see footnote 7, introduction) call *An Oxford Tragedy* "a masterpiece," and it would be difficult to quarrel with this evaluation. The book is rich with Oxford atmosphere, and it incorporates enough real and false clues to satisfy even the most demanding readers. Moreover, the actions and reactions of its participants are entirely in keeping with real-life academic behavior. As the novel concludes, the surviving St. Thomas's dons seem to have quickly forgotten the deaths of their two colleagues. They are, instead, bickering over the redecorations of the college rooms left vacant by the unfortunate affair.

John Cecil Masterman was born in Kingston Hill, Surrey He received a B.A. in 1913 and an M.A. in 1914 from Worcester College, Oxford. A lecturer and tutor at Christ Church, Oxford, from 1913 until 1947, Masterman then became provost of Worcester College and vice-chancellor of the University. A second Masterman novel, *The Case of the Four Friends* (464), also appears in this bibliography. Published in 1957, *The Case of the Four Friends* describes Ernst Brendel's return to St. Thomas's College after an absence of twenty years. In addition to *An Oxford Tragedy* and *The Case of the Four Friends*, Brendel can be found as the central character in two extended short stories contained in J.C. Masterman's *Bits and Pieces* (London: Hodder and Stoughton, 1961).

*361. Morrah, Dermot (Michael)(MacGregor) (1896-1874). *The Mummy Case*. London: Faber and Faber, 1933. Published in the United States as *The Mummy Case Mystery*. New York: Harper and Row, 1933.

After a fire destroys most of the bursary at "Beaufort College," Oxford, the charred remains of a body are found in the rooms of Professor Peter Benchley. Is the body that of Benchley or is it that of a mummy which the professor was seen examining in his bedroom only hours before the conflagration? In a burst of pure academic democracy, the fellows of Beaufort vote to declare that the body is Benchley's, but Denys Sargent and Humphrey Carver, two of the college's junior members, decide to conduct further inquiries. Their exploits, and their many discoveries in the course of their investigation, provide the ingredients for as witty a story as can be found in all of college mystery fiction. A bitter feud among world-famous Egyptologists, a faked drowning, an (off-stage) sword duel between professors, the loss of a favorite Meershaum pipe, and a scenic, fact-finding trip to the Isle of Wight are only a few of the many elements which are worked into the plot of this highly civilized, sometimes-satirical, and always entertaining story.

Dermot Michael MacGregor Morrah received an N.A. (first class honors) from New College, Oxford, in 1921. From 1921 until 1928 he was a fellow of All Souls College, Oxford. In 1928 he began a long career as a leader-writer and editor for various London newspapers. Morrah's oeuvre includes historical works and many studies of the British royal family. Something of a joiner, at different points in his life Morrah was a fellow of the Society of Antiquaries, chairman of the Press Freedom Committee of the Commonwealth Press Union, director of the British Wine Society, and a councillor of honor of the Monarchist League. *The Mummy Case* was his only mystery novel. The book was reprinted by Garland Publishing in 1976 as part of Garland's "fifty classics of crime fiction" series.

362. Patrick, Q. [Webb, Richard Wilson (1901-)]. *Murder at Cambridge*. New York: Farrar and Rinehart, 1933. Published in Great Britain as *Murder at the Varsity*. London: Longmans, Green and Co., 1933.

The protagonist of this lively, atmospheric mystery is Hilary Fenton, an American graduate studying English at "All Saints College," Cambridge. Hilary has a B.A. from

Harvard, a father who is a Justice of the United States
Supreme Court, and an effervescent personality. Even
the murder by shooting of Julius Baumann, a South African fellow student, and the stabbing of Hankins, an All
Saints College gyp, cannot depress him for long. Nor
is Hilary subdued by his failure to impress Dorothy Du-
puis, a Newnham College undergraduate whose wondrous phy-
siognomy has earned her the nickname "The Profile." The
murders are investigated by Inspector Horrocks of the
Cambridge Police, but Hilary manages to lend an enthusiastic hand. Who is the killer loose in All Saints? It
is not Stuart Somerville, the loud-mouthed aristocratic
oarsman whom Hilary first suspects. But it is someone
who is present in All Saints on a daily basis. And what
is a gyp? A gyp is a Cambridge male servant (at Oxford
he is called a scout). The term is defined, along with
a host of other Cambridge colloquialisms, in a four-page
glossary following the text of the story.

Richard Wilson Webb was born in Great Britain but spent
most of his adult life in the United States. He employed
the Q. Patrick pseudonym on mystery novels which he wrote
by himself and on novels which he wrote with various
collaborators. Webb's most lengthy collaboration was
with Hugh Callingham Wheeler. Another Q. Patrick academic mystery, *Death and the Maiden* (389), appears in
this bibliography. *Death and the Maiden* is a work by
Webb and Wheeler.

*363.   Sproul, Kathleen. *Death and the Professors*. New York:
        E.P. Dutton, 1933. Published in Great Britain as
        Death Among the Professors. London: Eyre and Spottis-
        woode, 1934.

There's trouble in the physics department at "Dunster
College," an exclusive institution for men in New England. Old Professor Clarence Shearer and upstart Professor Peter Storm don't get along. Part of the problem
is that Storm is having an affair with Shearer's young
wife. Storm collapses and dies after a dinner party at
which Shearer is also a guest, and then the next evening
Shearer is found dead in his home with his throat cut
from ear to ear. Richard Van Ryn Wilson, a Kathleen
Sproul series-character sleuth, happens to be spending
the semester at Dunster giving lectures in criminal psychology, and he leaps into action. A wealthy New York
City consulting detective when he is out of his academic
guise, Wilson is assisted by Manners, his butler, and
by his long-time friend Dr. Eric Dieterlee, a New York

physician. Dr. Dieterlee, by yet another happy coincidence, is paying Wilson a visit. The sleuths' attentions first center on Professor Shearer's widow, Lillian, but since the author sees fit to parade before her readers virtually the entire Dunster faculty and student body, and several townspeople as well, new suspects emerge right up until the end of the 252-page story. Among the possible killers are Timothy Bates (a mathematics professor with a terrible temper), Leavitt Walz (a brilliant student who was expelled from the college for having an affair with Ruth Storm, Peter's teenage sister), Alicia McSorley (an attractive laboratory assistant in the physics building), and Gracien Lowell (a dotty old lady who wanders the campus at night getting mysterious scratches on her face). Even prim and proper Dr. Parmer, Dunster's president, is thought capable of the crime, and he certainly had a motive since the deaths of Storm and Shearer restore peace to the physics department. Richard Wilson finally sorts through all of the suspicious characters, of course, and along with identifying the guilty party, he finds that Storm's demise was brought about by a highly ingenious method which is not employed by any other villain in college mystery fiction. The book is ideal reading for those who like a plethora of clues and characters. And nostalgia buffs will enjoy the scene in which one of Leavitt Walz' former fraternity associates tells sleuth Wilson how the brothers angrily stripped Walz of his membership pin when they found that he had had sexual relations without the benefit of marriage.

The identity of Kathleen Sproul remains in the realm of research opportunities for the biographically curious. *Death and the Professors* was the second of five mystery novels which she published between 1932 and 1946, and it was the second of four Richard Van Ryn Wilson adventures.

364. Berkeley, Anthony [Cox, Anthony Berkeley (1893-1970)].
Panic Party. London: Hodder and Stoughton, 1934.
Published in the United States as *Mr. Pidgeon's Island*.
New York: Doubleday, Doran and Co., 1934.

Guy Pidgeon, a fifty-year-old reader in Greek at "St. Mary's College," Oxford, inherits millions and sudddenly becomes one of the of the richest men in England. Weary of teaching "idle youths," he buys a yacht and an uninhabited island in the mid-Atlantic. Then, in a burst of professorial perversity, he invites a dozen non-academic acquaintances for an extended cruise, strands them on his

island, and startles his marooned party by announcing
that one of its members is guilty of a pre-cruise murder.
Hardly the perfect host, Pidgeon's intent is to observe
his guests' frenzied machinations as they attempt to detect the killer in their midst. Unhappily for Pidgeon,
he soon meets his demise in a suspicious fall over a
cliff and thus misses all the fun. One of Pidgeon's
guests is Roger Sherington, an Anthony Berkeley Cox series character detective and a former student of the Oxford don. By the end of the long (320-page) novel,
Sherington has unravelled the complex mystery and has
shepherded the surviving merrymakers back to Great Britain. Although the story takes place far from Oxford's
spires, Cox's treatment of the prankish if ill-fated Guy
Pidgeon is a noteworthy portrait of an academic.

Anthony Berkeley Cox was one of the leading figures of
the inter-war "Golden Age" of detective fiction. A one-
time cartoonist for *Punch*, Cox began writing mysteries
in the early 1920s and stopped, for some as yet unexplained reasons, in 1939. He employed the pseudonyms
A.B. Cox, Anthony Berkeley, and Frances Iles. His Cox
and Berkeley stories tend to be richly satirical puzzlers.
His works as Francis Iles are more somber. The most famous Iles mystery, *Malice Aforethought* (London: Victor
Gollancz, 1931; New York: Harper and Brothers, 1931), is
now rated as a classic of the genre. Before launching
his mystery-writing career, Cox published comedy novels
with indifferent commercial success. One of his early,
non-mystery efforts was *The Professor on Paws* (London:
William Collins and Sons, 1926; New York: Dial Press,
1927), the story of a cat which receives the transplan-
ted brain of a brilliant and arrogant professor.

*365. Boyd, Marion [Havinghurst, Marion Margaret Boyd (?-1974)].
       Murder in the Stacks. Boston: Lothrup, Lee, and Shep-
       ard Co., 1934.

"Kingsley University," in the American Midwest, is an
untroubled institution to which evil is almost a complete
stranger. When Donald Crawford, the school's reclusive
assistant librarian, is found dead of a fractured skull
in the library stacks, everyone assumes that his demise
was the result of an unfortunate fall. Everyone, that
is, except Tom Allen, a young member of the English department. Tom brings his dark suspicions to the attention of President Mittoff, who authorizes him to do some
unofficial sleuthing. Although Tom bungles the job rather

badly at times, he is able to show by the book's conclusion that Crawford was murdered. And, from the dozen or
so faculty and librarian suspects who come to his attention, he is able to pick out Crawford's killer. As his
reward, Tom wins the heart of Carla Robinson, a pretty
instructor of French who occupies an office on the library's second floor. Furthermore, President Mittcoff,
apparently unconstrained by any rules about following
departmental recommendations for salary increases, gives
Tom an on-the-spot raise for restoring Kingsley University to its former state of languid academic bliss.

   Marion Margaret Havinghurt received an A.B. from Smith
College in 1916 and an M.A. from Yale in 1926. Married
to a professor of English at Miami University of Ohio,
she held teaching positions in the Miami English department at various times throughout her adult life. A well-
respected poet and mainstream novelist, she began and
ended her mystery writing career with *Murder in the
Stacks*. The reason her foray into the detective-story
field was so brief may be suggested by a notation on the
book's dustjacket. The blurb tells us that Marion Boyd
started the story in a library, "but the surroundings
became so fearsome to her that she finished the book
elsewhere.... It is a good writer who can scare herself
with her own thoughts."

366. Frome, David [Brown, Zenith Jones (1880-)]. *Mr. Pinker-
      ton Finds a Body*. New York: Farrar and Rinehart, 1934.
      Published in Great Britain as *The Body in the Turl*.
      London: Longmans and Co., 1935.

      Sir William Brame, a millionaire clothing manufacturer,
      is shot dead one evening in Trul Street, just outside the
      gates of "St. Jude's College," Oxford. The case is in-
      vestigated by blustery Inspector J. Humphrey Bull of
      Scotland Yard and by his unofficial assistant, Evan Pin-
      kerton, a timid little man with an extraordinary talent
      for sleuthing. Before these two David Frome series-char-
      acter detectives crack the case, two more murders occur.
      The additional victims are Ronald Brame, Sir William's
      St. Jude's-student son, and Beulah, Ronald's secret wife.
      Before marrying Ronald, Beulah was the commoner grand-
      daughter of Higson, an aged college servant. Whimsical
      in tone, *Mr. Pinkerton Finds a Body* is exceedingly rich
      with Oxford atmosphere. Careful descriptions are pro-
      vided both of the university and the commercial portions
      of the city. The most likely suspects are old Higson
      (who, at one point, makes a false confession), an Oxford

senior tutor named Kewly-Smith, and Ronald's sister Natalie. As it happens, however, the murderer turns out to be a mostly unlikely individual, and the motive for the crimes, while non-academic in nature, is very, very British.

Mr. Pinkerton Finds a Body was the tenth of sixteen mystery novels which Zenith Jones Brown published under the pseudonym David Frome. Another mystery by Zenith Jones Brown, *By the Watchman's Clock* (356), appears earlier in this bibliography. *By the Watchman's Clock* was issued under the pseudonym Leslie Ford.

367. Keene, Faraday [Jarrett, Cora Hardy (1877-)]. *Pattern in Red and Black*. Boston: Houghton Mifflin, 1934; London: Arthur Barker, 1934 (as by Cora Jarrett).

Handsome Creek is the name of an old Southern mansion, now restored to its ante-bellum opulence. The edifice is inhabited by Shadwell Dunn, a self-made millionaire, and by the members of Shadwell's large extended family. Rumor has it that the mansion is cursed. Nevertheless, from time to time guests come for lengthy visits. Matthew Voorhees, one of Shadwell's old schoolmates,is one such visitor, and the curse seems to be working when Matthew is stabbed to death in the library. When the local sheriff proves unable to discover Matthew's killer, the Dunns retain Mr. Hoopes, a private detective from Washington, D.C. Hoopes also fails to break the case, and the task then falls on Leonidas Ames, a retired professor of ornithology who is another houseguest at Handsome Creek. Professor Ames, who believes that a detective should look for simple explanations before constructing elaborate hypotheses, brings the affair to a successful conclusion. Professorial readers will be impressed by Ames' amateur sleuthing. They will be even more impressed, however, by his fiscal resources. Apparently a man of considerable means, Professor Ames seems to fit effortlessly into the ultra-affluent Dunn milieu, and he travels with Robinson, his personal valet.

Cora Hardy Jarret was born in Norfolk, Virginia. She received a B.A. from Bryn Mawr in 1899 and then did graduate work at the Sorbonne, the College de France, and Oxford. After a brief career as a teacher of English. in private secondary schools in the South, Jarrett married, left the teaching profession, and became a successful creative writer. A mainstream novelist and short story writer, as well as an author of mysteries, Jarrett

employed the pseudonym Faraday Keene for some of her
detective fiction. *Pattern in Red and Black* was issued
in America under the Keene alias but published in Great
Britain under Cora Jarrett's real name. The book is interesting for its clever implementation of clues, for
its ingenious plotting, and for its application of the
British country-house theme to an American setting. Although it is not widely mentioned in histories of mystery fiction, some connoisseurs consider it a minor classic of the genre.

368. Stout, Rex (1886-1975). *Fer-de-Lance*. New York: Far-
      rar and Rinehart, 1934; London: Cassell and Co., 1935.

      Peter Oliver Barstow, the president of "Holland Univ-
ersity," dies of an apparent heart attack while playing
golf. Because Peter's wife, Ellen, is not satisfied
that her husband's death was natural, she places a newspaper advertisement requesting information about Dr. Barstow's killer. Urbane private detective Nero Wolfe and
his energetic assistant, Archie Goodwin, investigate and
bring the guilty party to justice. *Fer-de-Lance* provides
its readers with some details about Dr. Barstow's personal history, but, in part because Nero Wolfe never
leaves his brownstone home, it generally ignores life
on the campus of Holland U. Nonetheless, at one point
in the narrative Wolfe offers his opinion of academic
criminology. When reminded that Holland's Professor
Gottlieb has written a famous text titled *Modern Crime
Detection*, Wolfe responds disparagingly that it is "a
book that an intelligent criminal should send as a gift
to every detective he knows."
      Rex Stout was born in Noblesville, Indiana. He did
not attend college. Only modestly successful at writing
mainstream novels during his early career, he turned to
detective fiction in his middle-age. *Fer-de-Lance*
published when Stout was forty-eight-years-old, was his
first Nero Wolfe-Archie Goodwin adventure. Before his
death in 1975 Stout published seventy-one more Wolfe-
Goodwin novels and novellas. The series brought him
wealth, fame, and critical approbation. Scholars of detective fiction consider Wolfe and Goodwin two of the
greatest series-character creations in the genre.

369. Dane, Joel Y. [Delaney, Joseph Francis (1905-)]. *Murder
      Cum Laude*. New York: Harrison Smith and Robert Haas,
      1935. Published in Great Britain as *Murder in College*.
      London: George Bell and Sons, 1935.

This novel is set at "Cardaff University," an institution located in the New York City suburbs. When a male undergraduate is shot dead on the campus, the case is assigned to Police Sergeant Cass Hartly. A World War I veteran, Hartly is a tough cop with little sympathy for collegiate fripperies. As he begins his investigation, another male student is murdered. The second victim is stabbed, and his body is discovered among the cadavers being readied for dissection in the university's medical school. After some dogged detection Hartly roots out the murderer, but not before he learns more than he cares to know about student pranks, left-wing political protest, and secret societies. Faculty members and administrators are limited to token performances. However, one administrator is at least accorded a good description. Dr. Averill P. Coife, Cardaff's pompous dean, is portrayed as resembling "a Shakespearian actor of the old school who [has] gone badly to seed."

Joseph Francis Delaney published four detective novels in the 1930s. All of them featured Sergeant Cass Hartly as sleuth, and all were issued under the Joel Y. Dane pseudonym. *Murder Cum Laude* was the first work in the Cass Hartly series.

370. Eberhard, Frederick G(eorge) (1889-). *The Microbe Murders*. The Macauley Co., 1935.

The body of Professor Larkin, an Egyptologist at an American university, is found disembowled and mummified in the Larkin home. Fortunately, ex-Inspector O'Hare of Scotland Yard happens to be in the United States, and the baffled local police call upon him for assistance. The title of the book gives away the method of the murderer, but not until the end of the novel is the motive revealed and the culprit unmasked. The suspects include "Smooth" Larkin, the professor's confidence-man brother, and a host of the professor's male and female scientific colleagues. Reviewing the book in the *New York Times* (March 31, 1935), Isaac Anderson noted that *The Microbe Murders* "is a wild tale, and the telling of it is marred by some exceedingly bad writing."

Frederick George Eberhard was born in South Whitley, Indiana. After an undergraduate education at the University of Chicago, he received an M.D. from Northwestern in 1912. *The Microbe Murders* was the last of five mystery novels published by Eberhard during his literary career.

371. Fairway, Sidney [Daukes, Sidney Herbert (1879-)]. *The Long Tunnel*. London: Stanley Paul, 1935; Garden City, New York: Doubleday, Doran and Co., 1936.

Seton Holbrook, a research scientist at "St. Botolph's Medical College" in London, dies after ingesting poison. Richard Carford, a young, bachelor professor of bacteriology at the college, is arrested as Holbrook's murderer. Carford stands trial and is acquitted, but his colleagues at St. Botolph's still believe him guilty of the crime. Ostracized by his former friends, Carford sets out to find Holbrook's real killer and, in the process, to clear his own name. He eventually succeeds in accomplishing both tasks. The motive for the crime, as Carford discovers, was rooted in the race for a cure for cancer, and the book is replete with detail about medical research in Britain in the 1930s. The book also includes a heavy dose of romance since the busy Carford takes time from his sleuthing to court Ruth Jessel, the daughter of a country parson. Academic readers will find the unflattering portraits of Carford's fellow St. Botolph's faculty members of more than passing interest. And they will appreciate, too, the book's ending. After the guilty party commits suicide, and after Carford's workmates are finally convinced of his innocence, our professorial protagonist relocates with his wife Ruth to the idyllic Isle of Jersey where he operates a marine biology research station.

Sidney Herbert Daukes was a prominent London medical practitioner who wrote fiction as an avocation. He published nine mystery novels during his lifetime. Most of his stories centered on the medical profession.

*372. Sayers, Dorothy L(eigh) (1893-1957). *Gaudy Night*. London: Victor Gollancz, 1935; New York: Harcourt, Brace and Co., 1936.

Dorothy Leigh Sayers was born in Oxford. The only child of the headmaster of Christchurch Cathedral Choir School, she was one of the first women to obtain an Oxford degree (first honors in medieval literature from Somerville College in 1915). Sayers taught modern languages at a girls' high school in Yorkshire from 1915 to 1917, was a reader for Blackwell Publishers in Oxford for one year during World War I, and then spent ten years as an advertising copywriter in London. In 1926 she married journalist Oswald Atherton Fleming, and in 1931 she retired from the advertising business to pursue her own writing on a full-time basis. A poet, playwright, editor, screen and radio writer, translator of Dante, expert on medieval culture, historian of mystery fiction, and a feminist long before feminism was a popular or even acceptable orientation, Dorothy Sayers is best remembered by modern-day mystery buffs for her series of elegant detective novels and short stories featuring ` suave and urbane Lord Peter Whimsey. *Gaudy Night* is the twelfth novel in the Whimsey canon. Unlike most of the other books in the series, however, *Gaudy Night* pays far less attention to Whimsey's exploits than it does to the adventures of Harriet Vane, Lord Peter's mystery-writing lady friend (and future wife). And, unlike any of the other books in the Whimsey series, *Gaudy Night* takes place in an academic setting.

Harriet Vane has recently been acquitted of a murder. Her nerves jangled from the experience, she is therefore responsive to an invitation to attend a presumably pleasant reunion at "Shrewsbury College," her Oxford alma matter. During her stay in Oxford, Harriet receives several threatening notes. When she returns to London, she is contacted by the administration of Shrewsbury and asked to come back to Oxford in order to investigate various other ominous happenings which have been taking place at the college. Putting her mystery-writer's skills at sleuthing to work, Harriet succeeds in developing a long list of Shrewsbury faculty and staff who could be disrupting the college's scholarly tranquility. She succeeds, too, in finding herself in physical danger. Lord Peter, who has been observing Harriet's labors from afar, finally enters the case. In as long and as intricate a denouement as can be found in any college mystery, he identifies the perpetrator of Shrewsbury's reign of evil deeds. Some critics have found the murderless *Gaudy Night* too long (483 pages in the original Gollancz edition), too wordy, and/or too prone to digress from detection in order to concentrate upon Harriet's blossoming romance with Whimsey. Nonetheless, the book is filled with engaging academic characters, and it is overflowing with between-the-wars Oxford atmosphere.

373. Simmons, Addison (1902-). *Death on the Campus*. New York: Thomas Y. Crowell, 1935.

Death on the Campus is 293 pages long, considerably longer than the usual academic mystery. And no wonder!

Twenty people meet violent deaths; five sleuths work
more or less independently of each other; and there are
ten major suspects in the case. The tale is set at an
unidentified American university. The first victim is
Philip Yerkes, a professor of English, who is shot
dead in his office. An amateur detective, Yerkes was investigating the apparent suicide of a faculty colleague.
Professor Ben Ingram, yet another member of the school's
English department, discovers Yerkes' body. He then
calls President Meade, and even before they telephone
the police, Ingram and Meade begin to interrogate individuals who were near Yerkes' office at the time of his
death. Only after Ingram and Meade fail to identify
the killer do they ask for official assistance, and in
response to their belated call District Attorney Kent
Bloomingdale and Captain Packer of the local homicide
squad arrive on the scene. At this point the carnage
begins in earnest. Most of the likely suspects in the
affair are killed by unknown assailants and another,
Professor John Hardwick Bailey, tries unsuccessfully to
commit suicide. As the story develops, it becomes evident that an underworld "mob" is at the bottom of all
the evil. Professorial readers will revel in the scene
toward the end of the book in which the aging Thaddeus
Davis, still another professor of English, opens fire
with his hair-triggered submachine gun on a gaggle of
gangsters. Because the book incorporates so many plotting elements, and because it includes such a massive
list of characters, it cannot be summarized adequately.
Indeed, the author takes fifteen pages of text to provide the denouement. It can be noted with reasonable
dispatch, however, that by the finale of this saga the
university's English department has many, many faculty
vacancies.

*374.   Innes, Michael [Stewart, John Innes Mackintosh (1906-)].
        Death at the President's Lodging. London: Victor Gol-
        lancz, 1936. Published in the United States as *Seven
        Suspects*. New York: Dodd, Mead and Co., 1936.

        John Innes Mackintosh Stewart was born in Edinburgh,
Scotland, and received a B.A. (honors) from Oriel College,
Oxford, in 1928. He was a lecturer in English at the
University of Adelaide, Australia, from 1935 until 1945,
a lecturer at Queen's University, Belfast, from 1946 to
1948, and a fellow of Christ Church, Oxford, from 1949
until his retirement in 1973. Under his own name Ste-

wart has published more than fifteen mainstream novels, and he has written and/or edited many full-length studies of such literary giants as Shakespeare, Kipling, and Thomas Hardy. Under the pseudonym Michael Innes, Stewart has published over forty mystery novels. Most of his mysteries feature John Appleby in the role of sleuth. Appleby is an erudite, Oxford-educated, New Scotland Yard inspector. Although Innes' mysteries adhere to no particular structural formula, many have Oxbridge settings and/or involve Oxbridge dons in important roles. Crammed with literary allusions, witty donnish dialogue, and incorporating very, very cunning puzzle development, the droll Innes tales of murder and detection in academe are generally acknowledged to set the standards against which the academic mysteries by other authors are measured.

Death at the President's Lodging was Stewart's first foray into the mystery field, and most aficionadoes of the genre now consider it a classic piece of detective fiction. The setting is "St. Anthony's College," Oxbridge, and the crime in the case is the late-night murder of Josiah Umpleby, St. Anthony's president. Umpleby is found shot dead in his locked college rooms. John Appleby arrives from London to investigate, and he discovers that several of St. Anthony's dons had sufficient motive and opportunity for ending President Umpleby's life. The clues in the affair have to do with the physical locations of the suspects' own rooms in the college, the dons' access to keys to various college doors, and the professional jealousies which pervade St. Anthony's faculty milieu.

One of the crucial characters in *Death at the President's Lodging* is Giles Gott, a young literary scholar and junior proctor at St. Anthony's. Gott, who writes his own academic mystery novels (and whom many critics have seen as John Stewart's fictional version of himself) renders valuable assistance to Inspector Appleby. Gott appears again as a Michael Innes character in *Hamlet, Revenge!* (378). In addition to *Hamlet, Revenge!*, six other Innes mysteries appear in this bibliography. They are *The Weight of the Evidence* (405), *Operation Pax* (432), *Old Hall, New Hall* (454), *Appleby Plays Chicken* (462), *The Long Farewell* (470), and *A Family Affair* (528). John Appleby appears in all of the Innes' novels included in the bibliography except *Old Hall, New Hall*.

*375. Post, Mortimer [Blair, Walter (1900-)]. *Candidate for
        Murder*. Garden City, New York: Doubleday, Doran and
        Co., 1936.

        "Chatham University," somewhere in the United States,
        is thrown into disarray by four murders. The first vic-
        tim is Carl Schact, a young, anti-Nazi chemist from Ger-
        many. Carl dies after eating nicotine-laden peppermint
        candies. The second victim is Geoffrey Nye, the chair-
        man of the political science department. Nye is stabbed
        with an icepick in a dark corner of the Chatham Faculty
        Club. Next to go is Babette Whipple, Nye's young and
        attractive niece. Babette, too, is the recipient of ice-
        pick hospitality at the faculty watering hole. And,
        finally, Henry Winston joins the ranks of the deceased.
        Henry is a foundation executive and the executor of Geo-
        ffrey Nye's estate. He is killed when he opens the door
        of his hotel room, trips off a booby-trapped shotgun,
        and literally loses his head in the excitement. The
        local police enter the affair, but the real sleuthing in
        the story is by four professors who band together to
        pool their amateur talents. Lowell Gaylord, the sixty-
        year-old, portly chairman of Chatham's English depart-
        ment, is the leader of the group. His assistants are
        Angus McDermott (a professor emeritus of medicine), Lens
        Penga (chairman of the biology department), and Arthur
        Churchill (a professor of law). Likely suspects include
        Karl Stein (a visiting Nazi academic from Germany), Avery
        Cox (a physician), Lynn Hazlitt (a chemist), and John
        Cannon (the desk clerk at the faculty club). Using
        logic, processes of elimination, and some personally
        perilous entrapment schemes, the four professorial de-
        tectives eventually get their man. Written with some
        light touches, despite an unremitting buildup of real
        and false clues, the book offers several unusual acad-
        emic situations. At one point in the story Professor
        Gaylord becomes so engrossed in the murder that he los-
        es his customarily cheerful and pacifying disposition.
        As a result, the department over which he presides ex-
        plodes with long-simmering jealousies and animosities.
        Toward the end of the book, the four professorial gum-
        shoes dress in costumes and attempt to snare their
        quarry at a gala masked ball at the Faculty Club. And
        both the police and the professor-detectives spend a
        great deal of time interrogating the late Professor Nye's
        retinue of servants. The resident of a large, imposing
        house near the Chatham campus, Nye employed a maid, a

housekeeper, a chauffeur, and a gardener.

Walter Blair was born in Spokane, Washington. He received his undergraduate education at Yale and then obtained an M.A. and a Ph.D. from the University of Chicago. From 1929 until his retirement in 1968, he was a member of Chicago's English department, and from 1951 until 1960 he served as department chairman. A critic, a biographer, and an authority on humor and folklore, Blair has published extensively, but *Candidate for Murder*, which he issued under the pseudonym Mortimer Post, is his only mystery novel.

376. Steel, Kurt [Kagey, Rudolph Hornaday (1904-1946)]. *Murder Goes to College*. Indianapolis: Bobbs-Merrill, 1936.

The institution of higher learning referred to in the title of this character-crammed novel is "Chelsea College," a high-prestige, private school in New York City. The murder is the shooting of Thomas Kelly, a Chelsea professor of mathmatics. Tom was using his skills in addition and subtraction to moonlight as a financial consultant to Strike Fusil, a notorious Harlem racketeer. Strike is a suspect in the case, but so, too, are at least a dozen other principals in the story. Among the academic suspects are Chancellor Walter MacShean, Dean Everitt James, Paul Broderick (a black-bearded professor of English who writes mysteries of his own as a sideline) and Howard Sayfort (a professor of psychology). The sleuthing is done by Henry Hyer, a Kurt Steel series-character private detective. Hyer is appropriately tough-talking and cynical, and he finds that Chelsea's genteel veneer covers not only Kelly's involvement with the underworld, but embezzlement and widespread faculty wife-swapping as well. Real-life college teachers will savor the portrait of Dean James. A small, "ferret-eyed" man, James is systematically looting Chelsea's treasury, and when caught in the act by Hyer (who calls him "weasel face"), he collapses in tears and begs for mercy. And serious students of college mystery fiction will be interested in the depiction of Decker, Chelsea's black elevator operator. Whereas college porters are the sources of crucial information in many British mystery tales, Decker serves in this capacity in *Murder Goes to College*. The faculty and staff of Chelsea are housed in a high-rise building, and Decker monitors all of the conversations between his passengers.

Rudolph Hornaday Kagey was born in Tuscola, Illinois, and was educated at the University of Illinois and Columbia University. From 1928 until his death in 1946, he

was a member of the philosophy department at Washington
Square College of New York University. At the time of
his death he was acting director of the evening division
of NYU. Kagey wrote ten mystery novels during his lifetime, nine of which starred private eye Hank Hyer in the
role of sleuth. *Murder Goes to College* was the third
book in the Hank Hyer series. All of Kagey's mysteries
were published under the pseudonym Kurt Steel.

*377.   Boucher, Anthony [White, William Anthony Parker (1911-
        1968)]. *The Case of the Seven of Calvary*. New York:
        Simon and Schuster, 1937; London: Hamish Hamilton,
        1937.

The sleuth in this riddle-filled story is John Ashwin,
a professor of Sanskrit at the University of California
at Berkeley. Assisted by Martin Lamb, a research fellow in German, Ashwin gets to the bottom of two related
murders. The first is the apparently motiveless stabbing of the "unofficial" ambassador from the Swiss Republic. The second is the poisoning of a young instructor of history named Paul Lennox. An amateur actor,
Paul brings a new sense of realtiy to the Berkeley stage
by actually expiring while acting out a death scene in
a university production of *Don Juan Returns*. Professor
Ashwin and Martin Lamb are both avid readers of mystery
fiction, and the book incorporates many references to
classic works of the genre. Due, no doubt, to their
familiarity with the tactics of other fictional sleuths,
Ashwin and Lamb are ever alert for red herrings. Furthermore, they are sufficiently sophisticated to realize that two murders need not be the work of one murderer. Most of the suspects in the case are residents
of Berkeley's International House, where Martin Lamb
is one of the few American lodgers. Professor Ashwin,
who never ventures out of his study during the course
of the story, utters one line which can serve as useful advice for all sleuths in genteel, academic detective stories. At the end of the book Ashwin gathers
the principal surviving characters and announces which
of them murdered the Swiss diplomat. Immediately thereafter he offers the killer a glass of scotch. "A mere
accusation of murder," says Ashwin, "should never stand
in the way of hospitality."
    William Anthony Parker White was born in Oakland, Cal-
ifornia. He received a B.A. from the University of
Southern California in 1932 and an M.A. from the University of California at Berkeley in 1939. *The Seven of*

Calvary was the first of four mystery novels which White published during his lifetime. His third novel, *The Case of the Baker Street Irregulars* (New York: Simon and Schuster, 1943), includes in its cast of characters one Drew Furness, a professor of English at the University of California at Los Angeles. Since Professor Furness is only a catalytic character in the story, the book is not accorded a separate entry in this bibliography. White employed the pseudonym Anthony Boucher throughout his career. And it is under this alias that he is remembered (and often revered) for the penetrating reviews of mystery fiction which he offered to readers of *The New York Times* from 1951 until his death in 1968.

378. Innes, Michael [Stewart, John Innes Mackintosh (1906-)].
      Hamlet, Revenge! London: Victor Gollancz, 1937; New
      York: Dodd, Mead and Co., 1937.

This extremely literate and unusually intricate mystery takes place at "Scamnum," an architectural folly in the English Midlands serving as the home of Crispin family. The Crispins are both rich and eccentric, and they decide to stage an amateur production of Hamlet as the centerpiece for a glittering houseparty. Giles Gott, a fellow in Elizabethan bibliography at "St. Anthony's College," Oxbridge, arrives to organize the show. In addition to producing amateur Shakespearean theatricals for wealthy patrons, Gott also writes detective novels He is doubly in his element, therefore, when Lord Auldearn, the Lord High Chancellor of England, is shot dead on stage while playing Polonius. As the investigation of Lord Auldearn's death gets underway, Gott is reunited with Inspector Appleby of New Scotland Yard, with whom he collaborated once before, in *Death at the President's Lodging* (374). Appleby does the heavy detection; Giles Gott advises and theorizes; and what appears at first glance to be a simple case of high-society mayhem turns into a case of espionage. American academic readers will be pleased to find that the story includes one of their own, a Dr. Bunny from "Oswego, U.S.A." Dr. Bunny, a phoneticist, is one of the Crispins' houseguests. Though he is not Lord Auldearn's murderer, he is nonetheless what in some circles would be called a party-pooper. As part of his study of various accents, Dr. Bunny scurries among those assembled at Scamnum asking each person to say "Bunchy cushiony bush" into his portable dictaphone.
      Hamlet, Revenge! was the second of more than forty mystery novels which have been produced by John Innes Mackintosh Stewart under the pseudonym Michael Innes. The book met with signal critical acclaim. Moreover,

it served as inspiration to Robert Bruce Montgomery, the
creator of professorial series-character sleuth Gervase
Fen (223-233). Montgomery's professorial detective was
named after Gervase Crispin, one of Innes' *Hamlet, Revenge!* characters, and Montgomery's own pseudonym, Edward Crispin, in the name of yet another fictional participant in the *Hamlet, Revenge!* proceedings. All told,
eight Michael Innes mystery novels appear in this bibliography. In addition to *Death at the President's Lodging* and *Hamlet, Revenge!*, these novels are *The Weight
of the Evidence* (405), *Operation Pax* (432), *Old Hall,
New Hall* (454), *Appleby Plays Chicken* (462), *The Long
Farewell* (470), and *A Family Affair* (528).

379. MacDuff, David (1905-). *Murder Strikes Three*. New York:
      Modern Age Books, 1937.

It is commencement day at an unidentified liberal arts
college in the eastern United States. Professor Russell
Stearne Finley, a distinguished archeologist, is scheduled to read the names of the graduates as they step
forward to receive their diplomas. But Professor Finley
does not appear. He is found shot dead in his office
at the Swann Museum. And, what's more, Finley's prize
mummy, "Benny," is missing from the museum's exhibits.
That same afternoon George Goeckler of the Latin department is stabbed dead in an automobile. And a few days
later Professor Otto Goeckler (an archeologist, and no
relation to George) turns up drowned in a nearby river,
his face apparently eaten away by extremely hungry fish.
The sleuthing in the story is done by Reuben Mallock,
the chief of detectives of Buckhill County, and by Geoffrey Fowler, a young instructor at the college. Fowler
is an early suspect in the case, but Anne Faulconer,
Professor Finley's attractive secretary, and Andrew Finley, the professor's hunchbacked, dwarfish son, emerge
as more-likely culprits as the mystery deepens. *Murder
Strikes Three* offers relatively little of the civilized
dialogue usually associated with college mysteries, but
it contains many interesting on-campus scenes. Professorial readers will appreciate the vignette, early in
the book, in which Geoffrey Fowler and several of his
junior faculty cronies fortify themselves with gin ric-
keys before heading reluctantly for what they expect
will be a long and tedious graduation ceremony.

Murder Strikes Three was David MacDuff's one and only
mystery novel. The tale was issued as part of an early-
day experiment, by Modern Age Books, in the publication

and mass marketing of paperback novels. Presumably worried that the book's sales would be hurt if prospective
readers thought the saga to be a conventional, slow-moving college mystery yarn, Modern Age took pains to pro-
mote the story as a hard-hitting detective epic. The
blurb on the cover of the book reads in part: "Tough
fast, terse, this story of a campus murder has no academic flavor to it."

380. Miller, John [Samachson, Joseph (1906-)]. *Murder of a
     Professor*. New York: G.P. Putnam's Sons, 1937; Lon-
     don: Robert Hale, 1937.

The professorial victim referred to in the title of
this novel is Ellsworth Owen, a member of the chemistry
department of a large, unidentified American university.
After years of suffering from slowly spreading cancer,
Professor Owen apparently takes his own life with an
overdose of painkiller. Sergeant Fogerty of the Homicide Squad is not content to rule out foul play, however,
and Fogerty's investigation not only establishes that the
professor was murdered, but it also leades to the identification of his killer. The story is told from the
perspective of Philip Waring, one of Professor Owen's
junior colleagues. Along with several other university
chemists, Philip becomes a suspect in the case, and he
must engage in some sleuthing of his own in order to
avoid arrest. Although *Murder of a Professor* is not one
of the more inspired examples of mystery fiction in this
bibliography, it does keep its readers guessing until
the end. Moreover, for those who are interested in
chemical analysis, the book offers some fine examples
of in-the-laboratory detective work.
    Joseph Samachson was born in Trenton, New Jersey. He
received a B.S. from Rutgers in 1926 and a Ph.D. from
Yale in 1930. Samachson's primary career was as a chemist. After holding a variety of posts with commercial
firms and hospitals, he became an associate clinical
professor of biochemistry at the Stritch College of
Medicine in Chicago in 1968. As a writer, Samachson collaborated with his wife, Dorothy, on several books about
music and the theatre. Under the pseudonym William
Morrison, he also published many science-fiction stories. *Murder of a Professor* was Samachson's only mystery
novel.

381.   Owens, Hans C. *Ways of Death*. New York: Green Circle
       Books, 1937.

       It is "Tap Day" at an American university which very
       much resembles Yale. Bob Somers, a junior, confidently
       expects to be offered membership in one of the insti-
       tution's most prestigious secret societies, and his fa-
       ther, Judge Albert Somers, has traveled up from New York
       City to witness the great event. Bob gets his cherished
       invitation, but, even as the selection ceremonies are
       taking place outside in the quadrangle, Judge Somers is
       shot dead in Bob's dormitory room. The local police
       quickly identify Johnny Redfield, a campus security
       guard, as the judge's probable killer. When Redfield
       is murdered, however, the police admit their bewilder-
       ment, and President Davenport asks Percival Trout, dean
       of the university's school of psychology, to pick up the
       threads of the case. Trout, a major in army intelli-
       gence during World War I, possesses an M.D., a Ph.D.,
       and an LL.D. He also possesses an imperious manner and
       is given to such endearing outbursts as, "Shut up ... If
       you had my brains, even you might amount to something."
       Playing no favorites, the deanly detective treats every-
       one (including President Davenport) as a suspect before
       announcing the name of the guilty party. Neither the
       murderer nor his motive turn out to have university con-
       nections, but, in addition to the depiction of Dean
       Trout, the book contains some arresting academic por-
       traits. Of special interest to modern-day president
       watchers will be the characterization of courtly Presi-
       dent Davenport. A gentleman of the old school, Daven-
       port buys all of his black derby hats from a shop on
       Ludgate Hill, London, and for male guests in his home
       he keeps on hand a supply of the finest Havana cigars.

382.   Sloane, William Milligan (1906-1974). *To Walk the Night*.
       New York: Farrar and Rinehart, 1937; London: Arthur
       Barker, 1938.

       Jerry Lister and Bark Jones, two recent college grad-
       uates, revisit their alma mater to attend a football
       game. Their school is a high-status university within
       a half-day's drive of New York City. After the game
       Jerry and Bark decide to walk to the university obser-
       vatory to visit old Professor Le Normand, for whom Jerry
       once worked as a research assistant. As expected, Le
       Normand is in his study, but he is dead of burns which
       cover his body. The two young men then call the univer-

sity's president, a man named Murray, who comes to the
scene and notes with proper presidential wisdom that
although Le Normand is burned, the rest of the room is
untouched by fire.   After telephoning the police Jerry,
Bark, and President Murray visit Selena Le Normand, the
professor's very young and startingly gorgeous wife.
Struck not only by Selena's beauty, but also by her
calmness when told of her husband's demise, Jerry Lister
proposes to her a few weeks later, and the pair is soon
married.   It would not be fair to go into any more detail about the plot of this novel except, perhaps, to
note that Jerry does not survive until the end of the
tale, and that as the book moves to its conclusion Selena displays an unusual skill in starting fires without
matches.   Because *To Walk the Night* incorporates elements of the supernatural, it is now sometimes considered a pioneering work of science fiction.   It was
reviewed as a mystery when it appeared, however, and it
earned lavish praise as an inventively plotted exemplar
of the genre.

William Milligan Sloane was a prominent publishing
executive.   From 1946 until 1955 he headed his own firm,
William Sloane Associates.   In 1955 he became director
of the Rutgers University Press; in 1969 and 1970 he
was president of the Association of American University
Presses.

383.   Storme, Peter [Stern, Philip Van Doren (1900-)].   *The
       Thing in the Brook*.   New York: Simon and Schuster,
       1937; London: Robert Hale, 1937.

James Whitby is a struggling young assistant professor
of biology at "State College," an institution located
in a distant suburb of New York City.   James desperately
wants to finish his book on myxomcetes, but instead he
finds himself dealing with a different kind of slime--
that produced by murder.   It all begins when James discovers the body of Howard Stanton, an unpopular local
farmer, hanging from a tree.   When Captain Macready of
the State Police is unable to identify Stanton's killer,
James invites his friend, Henry Hale, to come out from
Manhattan to resolve the case.   Although Henry is a
"cotton converter" by profession, he has learned all
there is to know about detection by reading mystery novels.   Captain Macready takes a dim view of Henry's
interference, but with James' help the amateur sleuth
eventually sees that justice is done.   Before the story

ends, however, the town drunk and a Spanish-American War
veteran become additional murder victims, and James, so
engrossed in the goings on that he feels compelled to
narrate the story, falls far behind with his professional
writing.

Philip Van Doren Stern was born in Wyalusing, Pennsylvania, and received a Litt. B. from Rutgers University
in 1924. After a brief career in the advertising business,
he turned to publishing, becoming in 1945 vice-president
in charge of editorial work for Pocket Books. Stern's
extensive literary output includes mainstream fiction,
travel books, biographies, and historical studies of the
Civil War. Although *The Thing in the Brook* was widely
praised at its appearance as a pleasant, inventive
detective-puzzler, it was Stern's only mystery novel.

384.   Tilton, Alice. [Taylor, Phoebe Atwood (1909-1976)].
       Beginning with a Bash. London: William Collins Sons,
       1937; New York: W.W. Norton, 1972.

Bonds worth $40,000 are stolen from the treasury of
"The Anthropological Society," and Harvard Professor
John North, the president of the organization, accuses
Martin Jones of the crime. Martin is a young Yale graduate and a junior member of the Society's staff. When
North is bludgeoned to death deep in the musty stacks
of a Boston secondhand bookstore, Martin becomes the
primary suspect in the case. But Leonidas Xenophon
("Bill") Witherall believes Martin to be innocent, and he
sets out to find North's real killer. Witherall, an
Alice Tilton series-character sleuth, was once a teacher
of English in a private secondary school, and Martin
was one of his pupils. Now retired, but with his pen-
sion erased by the Depression, Witherall is the janitor
in the bookstore where the murder occurred. He begins
his detection by investigating the customers who were in
the shop at the time of North's murder. He soon turns
his attentions toward North's personal life, however,
uncovering a curious relationship between the professor
and Dr. Maria Langford, an aggressively homely female
anthropologist, who is well-known for her research among
tribesmen in the Pacific. There are no campus scenes in
the novel--though there is some action in and around Harvard Square--but skullduggery within the discipline of
anthropology is central to the plot.

Phoebe Atwood Taylor was born in Boston. She received
a B.A. from Barnard College in 1930. She began her writing career with a series of humor-filled mysteries featuring Asey Mayo, a dour Yankee sleuth from Wellfleet,
Cape Cod. *Beginning with a Bash* first appeared in *Mystery League Magazine* in 1933. It was then published in

book form in Great Britain in 1937, but it did not appear between hard covers in the United States until
1972. It was the initial story in what was to become
a series of eight light-hearted tales starring Leonidas
Xenophon Witherall. A man who bears an uncanny resemblance to William Shakespeare, Witherall rises during
the series from "janiting" to owning "Meredith's Academy," a private school for boys. Although she employed
her own name on her Asey Mayo novels, Taylor used the
pseudonym Alice Tilton on all of her Leonidas Witherall
books. As published in *Mystery League Magazine*, however,
Beginning with a Bash is by Phoebe Atwood Taylor.

*385. Cole, G(eorge) D(ouglas) H(oward) (1889-1959) and Mar-
      garet (Isabel) (Postgate) Cole (1893-1980). *Off with
      Her Head!* London: William Collins Sons, 1938; New
      York: Macmillan, 1939.

The severed head of a woman is delivered in a biscuit
tin to the room of an Oxford undergraduate. When it
rested atop its body, the head was the property of a
shady lady-of-the-town whose charms had been shared with
many members of the Oxford academic community. Called
in to assist the local police with their inquiries is
Tom Fairford, a young, bachelor Scotland Yard inspector.
Fairford has no shortage of suspects. Some are undergraduates. Some are unsavory London types who have taken up temporary residence in Oxford. And one is Dr.
John Holland, an accomplished surgeon and a temporary
member of the Oxford faculty. Fairford solves the case
with the assistance of Ann Maitland, the niece of Dr.
George Milligan, the master of "St. Simon's College."
Fairford and Ann also fall in love, much to the master's
distress. Dr. Milligan, a paragon of stuffiness whose
idea of an opening conversational gambit is to offer an
opinion on the arts of primitive Africa, does not relish
the thought of a policeman in the family. Written with
a light touch and replete with satirical references to
Oxford personages and folkways, the book is a classic
British academic mystery.
  George Douglas Howard Cole and his wife, Margaret,
were leading socialist intellectuals in Great Britain
whose joint avocation was mystery writing. Three other
Cole collaborative mystery novels appear in this bibliography. These works are *The Murder at Chrome House*
(339), *A Knife in the Dark* (394), and *Toper's End* (397).

386. Crofts, Freeman Wills (1879-1957). *Antidote to Venom*.
     London: Hodder and Stoughton, 1938; New York: Dodd,
     Mead and Co., 1939.

Although he is seventy-four years old, Professor Burnaby is still an active member of the University of Birmingham (Great Britain) faculty. In fact, Professor
Burnaby has just been granted a research leave so that
he might accelerate in his study of cobra venom. But
the professor dies, apparently from the bite of a snake
mysteriously slithering loose in his home. Was it an
accident or murder? George Surridge knows. George is
the director of the Birmingham Zoo, and it is through
his office that Burnaby obtained the snakes for his research. George is also bankrupt, the keeper of a mistress, and the husband of a shrewish wife, Clarissa.
And Professor Burnaby was a wealthy man whose will left
a considerable sum of money to one of George's unscrupulous friends. There are no campus scenes in the book.
Nevertheless, the novel may intrigue professorial scholars of detective fiction, not only because it includes
a brief but trenchant portrait of a dedicated academic,
but because it represents Freeman Wills Crofts' attempt
to combine the direct and inverted mystery. The first
portion of the story deals with George Surridge's growing motivation for murder. The second part follows Inspector Joseph French, a Freeman Wills Crofts' series-
character detective, as he moves with sure-handed sleuthing competence toward uncovering the facts surrounding
Professor's Burnaby's death.

Freeman Wills Crofts was born in Dublin. Most of his
early adult years were spent as a civil engineer for
various railway companies in what is now Northern Ireland. He began writing detective stories during a long
illness in 1919, and by 1929 he had given up engineering
for a second career as a mystery writer. One of the
major contributors to the "Golden Age" of detective fiction, Crofts was best known for his careful attention to
detail. *Antidote to Venom* includes copious marginalia
about snakes and zoo management, and in an author's note
Crofts thanks E.G. Boulenger, director of the aquarium
and curator of reptiles at the London Zoo, for technical
advice.

387. Evermay, March [Eiker, Mathilde (1893-)]. *They Talked
      of Poison*. New York: Macmillan, 1938; London: Jar-
      rolds, 1939.

Harry Curry is a professor of sociology at "Penfield
University," a high-status institution in the eastern
United States. He and his wife invite the Reverend Per-
ley to a pleasant dinner, but the local parson expires
after enjoying the Currys' hospitality. Then the family
fox terrier dies, and the diagnosis in both cases is

strychnine. Enter Inspector Glover of the Penfield
police! He solves the case, with Harry's help, and life
at the Currys' returns to normal. Harry's niece, Elinor,
a student at Penfield, is also involved in the sleuthing
The mystery in the story is non-academic in nature, but
professorial readers may find the portrait of the Curry
family of great interest. Harry is nearing retirement
and his wife, a mystery-novel fan, urges him to write
an academic detective story in order to make money for
their old age. Meantime, Harry lovingly executes his
teaching duties, even holding evening seminars in his
home. Mrs. Curry, whose appreciation of Harry's pedagogic efforts seems to be minimal, routinely interrupts
the sessions with coffee and cookies at 10 p.m. to indicate that it is time for the students to return to
their dormitories.

Mathilde Eiker was born in Washington, D.C. and received a B.A. in 1914 from George Washington University.
She was well-known in the 1920s and 1930s for her romantic mainstream novels. Eiker also published two mysteries, both of them under the pseudonym March Evermay.
Both mysteries incorporate Professor Harry Curry and his
family as characters. The second of these works, *This
Death was Murder* (391), appears later in this bibliography.

388. Alington, Adrian Richard (1895-1958). *The Amazing Test
Match Crime*. London: Chatto and Windus, 1939.

Written as farce, *The Amazing Test Match Crime* has as
its principal villain a man known only as "The Professor." A renegade academic from continental Europe, The
Professor has quit his research post at a university because he realizes that "however long he lives, he can
never know more than he does now." Hoping to occupy his
restive mind, he has put together a three-man gang of
criminals--known as "The Bad Men"--and the trio hires
itself out for political assassinations, murders-on-de-
mand, and particularly lucrative bank robberies and
jewel heists. As *The Amazing Test Match Crime* opens,
The Bad Men have been retained by unidentified "International Interests" for no less than a task than the
overthrow of the British Empire. Pondering the difficulty of the group's assignment, The Professor decides
that it is the game of cricket which holds the Empire
together, and during most of the book he and his merry
men work to disrupt the test match between England and
"The Commonwealth of Imperia." The professor's two
compatriots-in-criminal-zaniness are Carlo, a tough-
talking American, and Ralph, a British public-school

dropout. There is some frenzied detection in the tale, by a Scotland Yard Inspector to whom everyone refers as "Steady as a Rock." But The Professor, who directs the drugging of Britain's best batsmen, who engineers the kidnapping of Great Britain's captain, and who orders his henchmen to machine-gun the Oval Cricket Grounds from an airship, is clearly the star of the story.

   Adrian Richard Alington was born in Oxford and educated at Oxford University. Best-known to the British reading public as the author of many popular, mainstream novels, Alington published two comic mysteries during his lifetime. *The Amazing Test Match Crime* was the second of these comic epics. *The Vanishing Celebrities* (London: Chatto and Windus, 1938), Alington's first farcical mystery, did not include The Professor as a character, but it did introduce readers to Steady as a Rock.

389.   Patrick, Q. [Webb, Richard Wilson (1901-) and Hugh Cal-
         lingham Wheeler (1913-)]. *Death and the Maiden*. New
         York: Simon and Schuster, 1939; London: Cassell and
         Co., 1939.

   This intricate, clue-crammed story is set at "Wentworth College," an institution in the New York City area. When Grace Hough, a Wentworth coed, is found dead after a "severe blow" to the back of her head, Lieutenant Timothy Trant of the New York Homicide Squad is put in charge of the case. Grace was blackmailing her professor of French, but as Trant learns after considerable sleuthing, the professor was not the only person on the Wentworth campus who wanted to extinguish her life. The story is narrated by Lee Lovering, Grace's roommate. Everyone's friend, Lee deliberately deceives Lieutenant Trant on a number of occasions in order to protect persons who, in her view, are not possibly capable of murder. But Trant is a Princeton graduate as well as an experienced Q. Patrick series-character detective. Knowing that evil may lurk where it is least suspected, he eventually sees through Lee's deceptions. College mystery buffs will have to be alert when reading this novel; the book probably contains more red herrings than other work in this bibliography.

   An earlier Q. Patrick academic mystery, *Murder at Cambridge* (362), also appears in this bibliography. *Murder at Cambridge*, published in 1933, was written by Richard Wilson Webb. *Death and the Maiden* was the result of a subsequent collaboration between Webb and Hugh Callingham Wheeler. Born in Northwood, a London suburb, Whee-

ler took an honors degree in English at the University
of London in 1932. After a chance meeting, Webb invited
Wheeler to write with him under the Q. Patrick alias
and, in 1933, Wheeler emigrated to Philadephia, where
Webb was employed with a pharmaceutical firm. The Webb-
Wheeler collaboration endured for nearly two decades, until Webb's health forced him into retirement. Wheeler
then utilized a new pseudonym, Patrick Quentin, on some
of his works. *The Crippled Muse* (434), a mystery novel
published in 1951 under Wheeler's own name, appears
later in this bibliography.

390.   Clark, Wesley Clarke (1907-). *Murder Goes to Bank Night*.
       Boston: Hale, Cushman, and Flint, 1940.

It is "bank night" at a motion picture theatre in "Go-
shen," a summer resort in the mountains of central Pennsylvania. The winner of the $300 lottery is Jane Wether-
ell, a young heiress who hardly needs the money. And,
in fact, Jane doesn't keep the prize very long because
just as she receives the award, the lights of the theatre go out, she is stabbed to death, and the cash disappears. In the audience is Chattin "Chat" Whyte, an
associate professor of political science at the University of Pennsylvania. Chat, who was once a crime reporter for *The Pittsburg Press*, and who also was one of
Jane's teachers at Penn, insists on helping the local
police with their investigations. Chat's detecting
slows his progress on the article he is writing for
Public Opinion Quarterly. However, because he quickly
becomes a prime suspect in the case, he is more than
willing to assign second priority to his professorial
activities. There are no on-campus scenes in the novel.
Nonetheless, professorial readers may find the book worthy of their attentions. Chat Whyte, who at one point
advocates ending proletarian political revolutions by
offering free showings of "dirty movies" to the lower
classes, displays many of the sharp ratiocinative powers
usually associated with professorial sleuths. Moreover,
Sarah Whyte, who actually beats her husband in a race
to identify Jane Wetherell's killer, is one of the more
astute faculty wives in detective fiction.
     Wesley Clarke Clark was born in Cleveland, Ohio. He
received an A.B. from Marietta College in 1930 and a
Ph.D. from the University of Pennsylvania in 1942. A
long-time professor of journalism at Syracuse University, Clark was dean of the Syracuse School of Journalism during the later stages of his career. *Murder Goes
to Bank Night* was his only mystery novel.

391. Evermay, March [Eiker, Mathilde (1893-)]. *This Death
      Was Murder*. New York: Macmillan, 1940; London: Jar-
      rolds, 1940.

      Teresa Haskill, a young heiress, has reason to believe
      that Erich Humphrey, her penniless stepfather, killed
      her wealthy mother. Teresa lives in the town of Pen-
      field, the site of "Penfield University," an elite Amer-
      ican institution. Fearing that Teresa may need protec-
      tion, Inspector Glover of the local police sends the
      distraught girl to stay with Professor Harry Curry and
      his wife. Harry is a professor of sociology who really
      cares about young people, and Mrs. Curry is a charming,
      if overbearing woman who serves the best roast lamb and
      lemon chiffon pie in town. Mrs. Curry is also a detec-
      tive-story buff, and it is largely through her insights
      that Glover is able to resolve Teresa's problems. The
      crime components of this novel are non-academic, and
      there are no campus scenes. However, the portrait of
      the Currys is a noteworthy characterization of a faculty
      family.
          This Death Was Murder was Mathilde Eiker's second and last
      mystery novel. Her first mystery, *They Talked of Poison*
      (387), also includes Professor and Mrs. Curry in signi-
      ficant roles, and it, too, is included in this biblio-
      graphy.

392. Fearnley, John Blakeway. *Murder by Degrees*. London:
      Robert Hale, 1940.

      "Branstead University" is a British institution in which
      the hazing of new students is a major part of the curri-
      culum. One of the victims doesn't appreciate having his
      bed torn apart and his rice pudding doused with mustard.
      He retaliates by sending his tormentors threatening let-
      ters signed with the pseudonym A.B. Clinton Ellison.
      The lads of Branstead try in vain to discover the iden-
      tity of the elusive Mr. Ellison, but since none of them
      suffers more than petty theft after receiving the mis-
      sives, they eventually dismiss the whole business as an
      inventive collegiate joke. However, after Ellison's pen
      pals graduate from Branstead--halfway through the book--
      the mood of the narrative changes. Ellison begins to
      kill his antagonists one by one, and this time in self-de-
      fense, the survivors of his murderous activities renew
      their efforts to find out who he is. Readers are offered
      anonymous glimpses of Ellison at several junctures in
      the story, and the suspense is heightened by graphic
      accounts of his chronic headaches and his paranoid musings.

393. Mersereau, John (1898-). *Murder Loves Company*. Phila-
     delphia: J.B. Lippincott, 1940.

     James Yates Biddle is a professor of horticulture at
     the University of California at Berkeley. In addition
     to his teaching duties, he oversees an experimental for-
     est near the campus. When two men are found dead of
     cyanide poisoning in his "garden," Professor Biddle
     turns sleuth. He is assisted by Kay Ritchie, a sprightly
     female reporter for a San Francisco newspaper, and im-
     peded by Police Inspector Angus Drift, a dour minion of
     the law who holds professor-detectives in low regard. A
     vigorous man in his mid-thirties, Biddle steals time
     from his many responsibilities to romance Kay. Some of
     his courting is done to the melodious strains of "Davy
     Doolittle's Dizzy Drudges," the house band at the "Ral-
     eigh Rainbow Room" in Oakland. Captivated by Biddle's
     intellect and charm, Kay is willing to overlook most of
     his many eccentricities. The good professor drives a
     sports car which he has christened Xantrippe. He awakes
     each morning to his "happy chimes" alarm clock. And he
     refuses to read any books containing split infinitives.
         John Mersereau was born in northern Michigan but moved
     with his family to California when he was eight years
     old. He attended the University of California at Ber-
     keley. At the time *Murder Loves Company* was published,
     Mersereau was a Hollywood screenwriter. Although his
     characterization of James Yates Biddle included many of
     the qualities which contribute to a successful profes-
     sorial series-character detective, Mersereau began and
     ended Professor Biddle's literary life with this single
     adventure.

394. Cole, G(eorge) D(ouglas) H(oward) (1889-1959) and Mar-
     garet (Isabel)(Postgate) Cole (1893-1980). *A Knife
     in the Dark*. London: William Collins Sons, 1941;
     New York: Macmillan, 1942.

     A Knife in the Dark is set at "Stamford University,"
     an institution two-hours train ride to the north of Lon-
     don. In a foreword to the book the Coles call Stamford
     a "dream university," but the place takes on night-
     marish qualities when Kitty is stabbed through the
     heart with a Maori dagger. Kitty, so it seems, was
     something of a one-woman hospitality squad, and various
     of her academic and non-academic lovers come under sus-
     picion for her murder. A number of individuals share
     the detection in this story. Colonel Gries, Superinten-

dent Codd, and Inspectors Johnson and Jackson, all of
the Stamford police force, have a hand in the investi-
ations. The case is finally resolved, however, by Mrs.
Elizabeth Warrender, a distant relative of the Lakes and
an infrequently employed G.D.H. and Margaret Cole series-
character sleuth. The time is 1940. Refugees from continental Europe have relocated in the town of Stamford,
and though the story incorporates many references to
university matters, it also deals in detail with the
fears of wartime Britishers that Nazi spies have entered
their midst.

Leaders in the socialist movement in Great Britain
for nearly forty years, George and Margaret Cole also
collaborated to produce many literate, well-constructed
mysteries. *The Murder at Chrome House* (339), *Off With
Her Head!* (385), and *Toper's End* (397) are other mystery novels by the Coles which appear in this bibliography.

395. MacInnes, Helen (1907-). *Above Suspicion*. Boston: Little, Brown and Co., 1941; London: George G. Harrap,
1941.

It is June of 1939, and Richard and Frances Myles are
enjoying the soft summer days of Oxford. Richard, a junior fellow at one of the university's colleges, has just
published a book on English lyric poetry. But Frances,
whose appreciation for the mellow Oxford atmosphere seems
inexhaustible, fears that ominous world events are about
to bring their idyllic academic existence to an end.
And, in fact, when Peter Gait comes to call, Richard
and Frances are soon propelled out of Oxford and into
the thick of pre-World War II espionage. An old friend,
Peter is now doing secret work for the British government.
He recruits the Myles to travel to the Continent in order
to assist in the smuggling of anti-Nazis out of Germany
into France. Before their odyssey is over, Richard and
Frances find themselves well inside The Third Reich,
where they experience nearly fatal personal perils and
gain even a greater appreciation for the relative calm
and serenity of British university life. In terms of
its plot structure, *Above Suspicion* is a conventional chase-
and-be-chased professorial spy melodrama. In contrast to
the usual stories of this type, however, the author of *Above
Suspicion* spends an unusual amount of prose explaining the
protagonists' transformations from gentle Oxonians into
heroic, if reluctant cloak-and-dagger operatives.

Helen MacInnes was born in Glasgow, Scotland. She received an M.A. from Glasgow University in 1928 and a diploma in librarianship from University College, London, in 1931. The wife of Gilbert Highet, the noted Columbia University classicist, essayist, and literary critic, MacInnes came to the United States in 1931 and became a naturalized American citizen in 1951. *Above Suspicion* was her first novel. The book met with almost universal critical praise, launching MacInnes on a distinguished writing career which was to bring her into the front ranks of "thriller" writers. *Above Suspicion* was adapted for film; the Metro-Goldwyn-Mayer motion picture, released in 1943, starred Fred MacMurray and Joan Crawford.

396. McCloy, Helen (1904-). *The Man in the Moonlight*. New York: William Morrow, 1941; London: Hamish Hamilton, 1941.

"Yorkville University" in New York City is in a state of turmoil. Professional jealousies and domestic difficulties are tearing apart its faculty. Nazi spies are skulking between its buildings. Evil capitalists are trying to usurp for themselves the profits from scientific breakthroughs made in the school's laboratories. And the institution's finances are in such poor condition that faculty salaries have just been reduced. No wonder that Yorkville's president (whose paycheck, presumably, has not been cut) is off on an extended lecture tour of South America. During (but not because of) the president's absence, corpses of murdered faculty members and their spouses begin to turn up on and near the campus. Dr. Basil Willing, a prominent New York psychiatrist who happens to be a Yorkville graduate as well as a Helen McCloy series-character detective, is asked to help investigate the killings. Though he cannot hope to deal with all of his alma mater's problems, Dr. Willing does at least end the spate of murders. Overstuffed with academic and international intrigues. *The Man in the Moonlight* features a large and generally unpleasant cast of academic characters.

Helen McCloy was born in New York City. After attending the Sorbonne in 1923-1924, she served as a correspondent for various American and British newspapers in Paris and London. She began to publish detective fiction in 1938. McCloy's Dr. Basil Willing series is generally held in high esteem by mystery buffs. *The Man in the Moonlight* was the second of eleven Basil Willing novels.

397. Cole, G(eorge) D(ouglas) H(oward) (1889-1959) and Mar-
      garet (Isabel) (Postgate) Cole (1893-1980). *Toper's
      End*. London: William Collins Sons, 1942; New York:
      Macmillan, 1942.

      Dr. Percy Sambourne is a cantankerous, former profes-
      sor of chemistry who has left the British academic
      world after "a row" at his university. A wealthy man,
      he now conducts research at his Berkshire home, "Excal-
      ibur House." The time is early in World War II, and
      Sambourne is hosting a gaggle of demanding refugee pro-
      fessors who have fled continental Europe in advance of
      Adolph Hitler. Also residing in the Sambourne manse
      are Mr. and Mrs. Mudge, a pair of insolent servants, and
      a collection of the professor's offensive relatives.
      Completing the cast of disagreeable characters at Excal-
      ibur are assorted tradesmen and local villagers who
      visit the house from time to time. As might be expected,
      the Sambourne residence becomes a theatre of bickering.
      The arguments escalate until one guest is dead of cyan-
      ide poisoning and Dr. Sambourne himself nearly expires
      after morphine is slipped into his beer. The local
      police are baffled by the professor's repugnant collec-
      tion of associates, and the case is finally cracked by
      Superintendent Henry Wilson of Scotland Yard, G.D.H. and
      Margaret Cole's celebrated series-character detective.
      Wilson has a host of academic suspects from continental
      Europe to interrogate, and in the course of his inves-
      tigation he probes deeply into several professorial
      minds. The pre-murder portion of the book is written
      largely as farce. After Superintendent Wilson comes on
      the scene, however, the stress is on serious detection.
         Three other mystery novels by George and Margaret Cole
      are included in this bibliography. These novels are
      The Murder at Chrome House (339), *Off with Her Head*!
      (385), and *A Knife in the Dark* (394). Superintendent
      Henry Wilson, who plays the role of sleuth in *Topper's
      End*, is a diligent, workaholic police official who
      stars in many other of the Coles' books. Though he
      does not appear as a character in either *The Murder at
      Chrome House* or *A Knife in the Dark*, he puts in a cameo
      appearance in *Off with Her Head*! Wilson's most notable
      intrusion onto academic turf occurs in a story-length
      piece entitled "The Oxford Mystery." In this test of
      his detection abilities, Wilson copes with the murder
      of Maurice Austin, one of the most popular students at
      "St. Philip's College," Oxford. "The Oxford Mystery"
      can be found in a collection of stories titled *Super-
      intendent Wilson's Holiday* (London: William Collins Sons,
      1928; New York: Payson and Clarke, 1929).

398. Holman, (Clarence) Hugh (1914-1981). *Death Like Thunder*. New York: Phoenix Press, 1942.

Mike Leiter, a radio scriptwriter from New York City,
accepts a position at "Abecton College" in rural South
Carolina. Mike's job is to organize a "department of
radio." He makes little progress, however, because
shortly after his arrival in the steamy heart of Dixie,
he finds himself in jail after being falsely arrested
for the murder of an Abecton history professor. Only
Norman Travis, a local boy who has recently established
a law practice in Abecton after ten years with a prestigious New York law firm, stands between Yankee Mike
and the full force of Southern justice. With the help
of Juanita Dickens, his sharp-tongued, attractive secretary, and Ruth Dessauseux, Mike's impulsive girlfriend,
Norman is able to identify the professor's actual killer.
The unmasking of the murderer comes during Mike's trial,
but much of the action preceding the courtroom scenes is
set on the Abecton campus, and most of the suspects in
the case are Abecton faculty members and administrators.
Dr. Arnold Jarvis Taine (an instructor of history), Dr.
Isaac Hews (an aged psychologist), Dean William Andrew
Thomas, and President Yates Thorndyke Bell are all crucial figures in the story. Real-life academics may enjoy the vignette in which the stuffy Dean Thomas breaks
down and cries on the witness stand, and flesh and blood
presidents will appreciate Yates Thorndyke Bell's description of his presidential duties. When asked to summarize his role at Abecton, Bell says that he is a "combination of circus barker, press agent, and professional
beggar." The book incorporates an abundance of clues,
several sub-plots, and a few explanations (offered by
Norman Travis) of the prejudices which small-town South-
erners harbor against carpetbaggers from the North.
    Clarence Hugh Holman was born in Cross Anchor, South
Carolina. He received a B.A. from Presbyterian College
in Clinton, South Carolina, in 1938 and a Ph.D. from
the University of North Carolina in 1949. At the time
Death Like Thunder was published, Holman was serving as
"director of radio" and instructor of English at Presbyterian College. In 1946 Holman moved to the University
of North Carolina as a graduate student and instructor
in French. He eventually became Keene Professor of English at North Carolina, provost of the university, and
chairman of the board of governors of the University of
North Carolina Press. *Death Like Thunder* was the first
of five mystery novels which Holman published during his
lifetime. One of his subsequent mysteries, *Up This Crooked
Way* (414), appears later in the bibliography.

*399.   Johnson, W. Bolingbroke [Bishop, Morris Gilbert (1893–
        1973)]. *The Widening Stain*. New York: Alfred A.
        Knopf, 1942; London: John Lane, 1943.

The Wildmerding Library, on the campus of a high-status but unidentified university in the eastern United
States, is known far and wide for its great collections
of rare manuscripts. But when Mademoiselle Coindreau,
an assistant professor of French, is found dead of a
broken neck after a suspicious fall from one of the
building's galleries, the Wildmerding begins to acquire
a new, less-edifying reputation. Gilda Gorham, the
library's chief cataloger, looks into Mademoiselle Coindreau's demise. However, just as Gilda pinpoints old
Professor Hyett of the classics department as the most-
likely murderer, Hyett becomes the second library visitor to expire on the premises. More sleuthing is required, and Gilda, with help from Lieutenant Kennedy of
the local police, is equal to the task. Laced with li-
mericks and peppered with false as well as real clues,
The Widening Stain is one of the brightest and wittiest
of all American academic mysteries. Many, many professors appear in the story, and each of the pedants has
his or her unique set of eccentricities. The surprising
motive for the killings, which is revealed in the last
chapter, may give modern-day academic feminists additional ammunition for their arguments.
  Morris Bishop was born in Willard, New York. He received an A.B. and a Ph.D. from Cornell. A long-time
professor of romance languages at Cornell, Bishop wrote
in a wide variety of fields. His oeuvre includes textbooks,
biographies, poetry, and a history of Cornell. *The Widening Stain* was his only mystery novel.

400.   Lewis, Lange [Brandt, Jane Lewis (1915–)]. *Murder Among
        Friends*. Indianapolis: Bobbs-Merrill, 1942; London:
        Bodley Head, 1950.

Kate Farr takes a job as secretary to Ulysses Calder,
the wise and humane dean of a university medical school
somewhere in America. Kate's predecessor, Garnet Dillon,
was a beautiful young woman who was efficient as a ty-
pist but, as Dean Calder puts it, "not necessarily
good" when it came to sexual conduct. Garnet has mysteriously disappeared. But Kate, taking an introductory
tour of the medical school's facilities, finds Garnet's
dead body laid out in the embalming room. Detective
Richard Tuck of the local police enters the case at
this point. An autopsy shows that Garnet was both poi-

soned and pregnant, and Tuck's sights fall upon various
male medical students, all of whom were known to have
been smitten by Miss Dillon's charms. Kate, meantime,
falls in love with Johnny Greenwood, one of the stu-
dent-suspects, and she also provides sleuth Tuck with
some amateur assistance. The ending of the story is
unusual, and readers may find it difficult to disting-
uish between the good guys and the bad ones.

Jane Lewis Brandt was born in Oakland, California,
and received an A.B. from the University of Southern
California in 1939. *Murder Among Friends* was her first
detective novel. Two other mysteries by Jane Lewis
Brandt, *Juliet Dies Twice* (406) and *The Passionate Victims* (437), appear in this bibliography. Both of these
works, like *Murder Among Friends*, were published under
the pseudonym Lange Lewis. And both employ Richard Tuck
in sleuthing roles.

401. Millar, Margaret (Ellis) (Sturm) (1915-). *The Weak-
      Eyed Bat*. Garden City, New York: Doubleday, Doran
      and Co., 1942.

Henry Frost, a divorced professor of Greek, has two
daughters, both of whom spend the summers on Lake Rosseau in Canada. Susan, Henry's oldest offspring, is
single, in her early twenties, and an apparent paragon
of virtue. Joan, the professor's younger daughter, is
eighteen, blonde, and a singularly nasty, man-crazy
hellion. Joan is thoroughly disliked by all of the
residents in the small lakeside vacation colony in
which the Frost cottage is located; even her father
detests her. Joan is killed by an unknown assailant
(her skull is bashed in and her body is dumped in the
lake), and everyone except Dr. Paul Prye, a Margaret
Millar series-character sleuth, secretly rejoices at
her death. Dr. Prye, a Detroit psychiatrist who is on
holiday at Lake Rosseau, suspects Tom Little, a married
man with whom Joan had been having an affair. When
Little is murdered, however, Dr. Prye must begin his
detection afresh, and his attentions turn quickly to
Professor Frost and Susan. There are no campus scenes
in the sometimes-whimsical story, but the book offers
many intensive views of a trouble-plagued faculty family.

Margaret Millar was born in Kitchener, Ontario, Canada, and attended the University of Toronto. A highly
respected writer of both mainstream and mystery novels,
She is married to Kenneth Millar whose own novels, *The*

Dark Tunnel (410) and *The Chill* (490), appear later in
this bibliography. Written very early in her long and
illustrious career, *The Weak-Eyed Bat* was Margaret Millar's second full-length work of detective fiction and
the second of three Dr. Paul Frye tales.

402. Mitchell, Gladys (1901-). *Laurels Are Poison*. London:
      Michael Joseph, 1942.

Miss Murchan, the warden of Athelstan Hall at "Cataret
Training College," disappears during a school dance.
Miss du Magne, the principal of the institution, sends
for Mrs. Beatrice Bradley, Gladys Mitchell's famed series character detective. Installed as Athelstan's temporary warden, Mrs. Bradley gets to the bottom of the
affair. The story, written with Gladys Mitchell's usual
blend of neo-fantasy, semi-satire, and genteel dialogue,
includes a murder (of Athelstan Hall's cook), many college "rags," and a discussion of the "fetishism" involved
in the preparation of vegetables. The staff, faculty,
and students of Cataret College (all of them female)
display various sportive eccentricities. As for Mrs.
Bradley (who is required to teach in the story as well
as act as sleuth), real-life academics will marvel at
the ease with which she delivers off-the-cuff lectures
on a dizzying array of arcane topics.
    Gladys Mitchell was born in Cowley, Oxford, Great Bri-
tain. She was a student at Goldsmith College from 1919
until 1921 and received a diploma in history from the
University of London in 1926. Miss Mitchell taught
English, history, and games at several British girls'
schools until her retirement in 1961. Her first Beatrice
Bradley mystery novel, *Speedy Death*, was published by
Victor Gollancz in 1929. *Laurels Are Poison* was the
fifteenth book in the Bradley series. A later Beatrice
Bradley exploit, *Spotted Hemlock* (472), also appears in
this bibliography. Permanently middle-aged, though her
sleuthing career spans nearly half a century, Mrs.
Bradley is the protagonist of more than fifty Mitchell
novels. Many of the characters who are introduced in
Laurels Are Poison appear in subsequent Bradley adventures.
Laura Menzies, a Cataret student, eventually becomes Mrs.
Bradley's secretary. And Kitty Trevelyan, another of Mrs.
Bradley's charges at Athelstan Hall, becomes "Kitty Vinni-
combe," an internationally known hair-stylist in *Pageant
of Murder* (London: Michael Joseph, 1965).

403. Wallis, J(ames) H(arold) (1885-1958). *Once off Guard*.
      New York: E.P. Dutton, 1942; London: Jarrolds Publish-
      ing Ltd., 1943. Also published as *The Woman in the*
      Window. Cleveland: World Publishing Co., 1944.

Richard Wanley is fifty-four-years-old and still an
assistant professor of English at "Gotham College" in
New York. One summer evening, while looking at the
painting of a beautiful woman displayed in the window
of a Manhattan sales gallery, he is approached by Alice
Rete, a seductive lady of doubtful virtue whose face
resembles that in the portrait. Yielding to the siren
call of lustful temptation, Wanley accompanies Alice to
her apartment. Another of Alice's male friends bursts in
upon the scene and attacks Wanley, and in self-defense the
professor stabs his assistant to death with a pair of
scissors. The dead man proves to be Claude Mazzard, an
internationally famous Wall Street financier. Wanley
drives Mazzard's corpse to deepest New Jersey, dumps it
in a field, and returns to New York in hopes of resuming
his normal, bland routine. All of these events occur
in the first third of the novel. From that point the
primary question is whether or not Wanley will be able
to harness his own conscience. The phrase "I killed a
man" runs constantly through his head, and he finds himself perpetually on the brink of admitting his crime to
his friends. The details of Wanley's guilt-ridden machinations cannot be revealed in this bibliography without destroying the story for prospective readers. However, it can be noted that the author employs a number
of clever plotting devices, both to heighten the tension
and to introduce irony into the narrative. Academic
readers of junior rank will be especially interested in
the episode in which Wanley receives a surprise promotion to full professor. In order to minimize his chances of capture, Wanley has not told Alice Rete his real
name. Gotham College, however, publicizes his sudden
full professorship by arranging for articles containing
his picture and his complete biography to appear in all
of New York City's daily newspapers.
    James Harold Wallis was born in Dubuque, Iowa. He
received a B.A. from Yale in 1906. After a career in
the newspaper business--as a reporter and editor for the
Dubuque Times Journal and, later, as owner and publisher
of the *Dubuque Daily News*--he moved to Scarsdale, New
York, in the late 1920s to pursue a second career as a
creative writer. Though Wallis wrote poetry, mainstream
novels, and political commentaries, he achieved his grea-

test commercial success with mysteries. *Once off Guard* was the ninth of ten mysteries he published before his death in 1958. The book was adapted for a major motion picture in 1944 titled "The Woman in the Window." The film was directed by Fritz Lang and starred Joan Bennett, Dan Duryea, Raymond Massey, and Edward G. Robinson.

*404.   Campbell, Mary Elizabeth (1903-). *Scandal Has Two Faces*. Garden City, New York: Doubleday, Doran and Co., 1943.

It is June of 1939 and at a large state university in Ohio the English department is about to give final examinations. Trouble arises, however, when the questions to one of the tests turns up in a fraternity house. Then the widely disliked director of the freshman English program, a man who is also the university's dean of liberal arts, is found murdered in his office. Matthew Craig, the local prosecuting attorney, takes personal charge of the murder case. In the process of discovering the identity of the dean's killer, he also plugs the leaks in the English department's security system. A great many faculty members, most of them teachers of freshman English, pass across the pages of this story and more than one of them proves to have a suspicion-provoking secret life. Moreover, several of the faculty spouses in the plot are something other than happy, loving helpmates. *Scandal Has Two Faces* is on-campus detective fiction in undiluted form. Readers who enjoy excavating for dirt beneath the clean surface veneers of academe will find that this book more than meets their requirements.

Mary Elizabeth Campbell was born in Cambridge, Ohio. She received an A.B. and A.M. from Radcliffe and a Ph.D. from Yale. At the time *Scandal Has Two Faces* was published, Campbell was a member of the English department at Indiana University. *Scandal Has Two Faces* was the second of two mystery novels which she published during her literary lifetime.

*405.   Innes, Michael [Stewart, John Innes Mackintosh (1906-)]. *The Weight of the Evidence*. New York: Dodd, Mead and Co., 1943; London: Victor Gollancz, 1944.

Detective Inspector John Appleby, who made his debut as a Michael Innes series-character sleuth in *Death at the President's Lodging* (374), ventures onto academic turf once again in *The Weight of the Evidence*. This time, however, the scene is not Oxbridge. Instead, it

is "Nesfield University," a seedy provincial institution
somewhere in the North of England, where the members of
the faculty mask their professorial shortcomings with
pretense and pomposity. The crime which brings Appleby
to Nesfield is the murder of Professor Pluckrose, a bio-
chemist, who is crushed by a meteorite. The object does
not fall from the sky. Rather, it is pushed onto him
from atop a university building while he sits taking the
sun in a deck chair. The major suspects in the bizarre
affair are all Nesfield teachers and administrators, and
while few of these worthies have convincing alibis to
offer, most are quite willing to provide Appleby with
preposterous, self-serving explanations for Pluckrose's
death. *The Weight of the Evidence* is one of the more
ingeniously constructed mysteries in academic detective
fiction. It also includes great swaths of sharp satire
as well as innumerable references to obscure and not-so-
obscure literary figures, to pioneers of modern science,
and to heroes of ancient myths.

Eight John Mackintosh Stewart mystery novels (all as
by Michael Innes) appear in the bibliography. In addition to *Death at the President's Lodging* and *The Weight
of the Evidence*, these novels are *Hamlet, Revenge!* (378),
Operation Pax (432), *Old Hall, New Hall* (454), *Appleby
Plays Chicken* (462), *The Long Farewell* (470), and *A Family Affair* (528).

406.   Lewis, Lange [Brandt, Jane Lewis (1915-)]. *Juliet Dies
Twice*. Indianapolis: Bobbs-Merrill, 1943; London:
Bodley Head, 1948.

Everyone stays awake in Professor Edwin Brewer's psychology class at "Southwest University" in Los Angeles.
They keep alert because the professor likes to have his
students learn by doing. When he teaches about homicidal behavior, for example, he pours ketchup over one
student, hides his "murder victim," and then instructs
other members of the class to go through the classroom
building in search of the bogus corpse. On the occasion
chronicled in *Juliet Dies Twice*, the student-searchers
find a real corpse, that of Ann Laird, a young lady who
was about to star in Southwest's production of *Romeo and
Juliet*. Ann is discovered, with her head bashed in, lying on the floor of the prop room used by the drama department. One prime suspect, of course, is Professor
Brewer, but several other faculty members, as well as a
host of students and townspeople, could have put an end
to poor Ann's acting career. The only non-suspects in

the story are Lieutenant Richard Tuck of the Los Angeles
Homicide Squad, who does the sleuthing in the case, and
Dr. Trinklehaus, Southwest's president. The tall, lean
Tuck is not the culprit because he is a Lange Lewis series-character detective. And Dr. Trinklehaus, who wanders the campus muttering "This is a terrible thing,"
is clearly too incompetent to have committed what seems,
on initial appearances, to be a murder without clues.

Two other Jane Lewis Brandt novels are included in
this bibliography. They are *Murder Among Friends* (400)
and *The Passionate Victim* (437).

407. Magoon, Carey [Carey, Elizabeth, and Marion Austin Waite
      Magoon (1885-)]. *I Smell the Devil*. New York: Farrar
      and Rinehart, 1943; London: Cassell and Co., 1949.

      Miss Christopherson, the custodian of the rare books
      room at "Cowabet College" in Michigan, is a "tiresome"
      protector of her literary treasures, but no one has an
      apparent reason for murdering her. Yet murdered she is,
      stabbed in the back in her office. Since there are no
      immediate suspects in the case, all of the regular users
      of the rare books room are interrogated by State Police
      Sergeant Robert Morningstar. These individuals include
      Adelaide Stone and Henrietta Fellows, two spinster tea-
      chers of English at "Kenneth State Teachers College,"
      who are spending a year doing graduate work at Cowabet.
      The story is narrated by Adelaide, who writes with con-
      siderable self-depreciating humor, especially about her
      weight (187 pounds), and whose amateur sleuthing even-
      tually brings Miss Christopherson's killer to his just
      reward. Much of the plot revolves around the value of
      a rare collection of Cyprian's sermons which Adelaide
      is using in her dissertation research. Though she cer-
      tainly is no fool, Adelaide mixes serious detection with
      frequent flights of mental fancy. The title of the nov-
      el refers to her conviction, based on laborious readings
      of medieval texts, that she can detect evil by its le-
      gendary odor ("a combination of fresh-blood, moldy lea-
      ther, and a dead rat in a trap for a week").

*408. Stein, Aaron Marc (1906-). *The Case of the Absent-Mind-
      ed Professor*. New York: Doubleday, Doran and Co.,
      1943.

      The absent-minded professor in the title of this clas-
      sic academic mystery is Alpheus Chambers, a world-famous
      anthropologist at a small college in the American Midwest.

Chambers finds the corpse of a small-time hoodlum in the manuscript room of the college library. Since he claims not to remember his actions before his discovery, everyone in the school's indigenous community is prepared to believe that he is the gangster's murderer. Only Tim Mulligan and Elsie Mae Hunt, a pair of Aaron Marc Stein series-character sleuths, doubt that Chambers committed the crime. Tim and Elsie Mae are itinerant archeologists who happen to be on campus cataloging the "Horton Collection" of rare gold pieces. Quickly familiarizing themselves with the institution's internal politics, they identify the guilty party and, while doing so, blow open a host of smoldering college scandals. The large roster of suspects includes faculty members, students, and the college's belligerent football coach. Readers who enjoy president watching will be particularly interested in the portrait of President Webster and his vacuous, "birdlike" wife, Sarah. When informed of the murder, Dr. Webster utters those time-honored administrative words, "This is profoundly disturbing." When Tim Mulligan suggests to Sarah Webster that the school's football players are dull-normal louts, she counters by proclaiming, "All our football men are fine, clean-living youths."

Aaron Marc Stein was born in New York City. He received an A.B. from Princeton in 1927. *The Case of the Absent-Minded Professor* was the fourth book in the sixteen-work Tim Mulligan-Elsie Mae Hunt series. Stein's immense output of mystery fiction also includes the Inspector Schmidt series (published under the pseudonym George Bagby) and the Jeremiah Gibson collection (published under the pseudonym Hampton Stone). Before launching his mystery-writing career, Stein produced a mainstream novel which might be of interest to academic readers. *Spirals* (New York: Corici, Friede Publishers, 1930) is a stream-of-consciousness narrative detailing the four undergraduate years of Tony Todd, a Princeton undergraduate.

409. La Roche, K. Alison. *Dear Dead Professor*. New York: Phoenix Press, 1944.

This book is set at "Roseview College," an exclusive women's college in the eastern United States, and the eponymous "dear dead professor" is Walter Morton, chairman of the Roseview chemistry department. Walter is stabbed dead in his laboratory. One of the more dedicated faculty philanderers in academic mystery fiction,

Walter had two student girl friends (one of them pregnant) and a female laboratory assistant with whom he
shared more than an interest in the poison gas research
he was conducting for the United States Government. All
three of Walter's extramarital lady friends are suspects
in the case, although one of them (non-pregnant student
Gloria Knight) quickly exits from the story when she becomes the second corpse on the Roseview scene. And then
there is Althea, Walter's long-suffering wife. A woman of
action, Althea has compensated for Walter's wanderings by
taking up with Albert Townes, a Roseview professor of
astronomy. The task of sifting through the list of Walter's
many possible killers falls to Rufus Albert Jones, the
Gary Cooperish local police chief, and to Barbara Crew, a
perky Roseview student enlisted as Rufus' temporary, on-
campus stenographer. Rufus and Barbara find the double-
murderer, though not before Barbara almost becomes yet
another fatality. Furthermore, in what appears to be an
inevitable consequence of any male-female interaction at
the Roseview campus, Rufus and Barbara fall in love. At
the end of the story they are preparing to elope to Florida.
Competently written and laden with both clues and clichés,
Dear Dead Professor offers the clear message that women's
colleges are pervaded with sexual frustrations. Neither
handsome nor nice, Walter Morton is uncharitably described
by Barbara Crew as "a latin type with oily black hair and
lips too red for a man." And yet, in the Roseview hothouse
atmosphere, he is able to pick and choose among the nubile
young ladies populating the school.

The identity of K. Alison La Roche continues to elude
literary biographers. It is evident, however, that he
or she had more than a passing familiarity with the extracurricular customs at institutions such as Roseview
College. In any event, *Dear Dead Professor* was La
Roche's only mystery novel.

410. Millar, Kenneth (1915-). *The Dark Tunnel*. New York:
      Dodd, Mead and Co., 1944. Also published as *I Die
      Slowly*. New York: Lion Books, 1945.

Set during World War II, at "Midwestern University,"
this lively novel includes murder, espionage, detection,
and suspense. The protagonist-narrator is Robert Branch,
a professor of English. Alarmed over security leaks at
Midwestern, Robert conducts an unofficial investigation.
In the process, he encounters Nazi agents, alluring ladies with mysterious pasts, the body of a murdered professor of German, and a psychotic homosexual. An un-

convincing disclaimer at the end of the book announces that although Midwestern University "bears a certain physical resemblance to University of Michigan," the institution is in fact "a figment of the author's imagination."

Kenneth Millar was born in Los Gatos, California. Raised in Canada, he attended the University of Western Ontario as an undergraduate and then received a Ph.D. in English literature from the University of Michigan. *The Dark Tunnel* was Millar's first novel. He is known to mystery readers primarily for his Lew Archer Series, published under the pseudonym Ross MacDonald. One of Millar's Lew Archer novels, *The Chill* (490) is included in this bibliography. *The Dark Tunnel* was originally published under Millar's real name, but in reprint editions it appears under the Ross MacDonald pseudonym.

411. Lewis C(live) S(talples) (1898-1963). *That Hideous Strength: A Modern Fairy-tale for Grown-Ups.* London: John Lane, 1945; New York: Macmillan, 1946.

That Hideous Strength is the third volume of a complex and allegorical C.S. Lewis trilogy which explores (among other matters) the interplay between good and evil. The first two novels in the series are *Out of the Silent Planet* (London: Bodley Head, 1938; New York: Macmillan, 1943) and *Perelandra* (London: John Lane, 1943; New York: Macmillan, 1944). Both of these books are primarily science fiction in form. The principal setting of *Out of the Silent Planet* is Mars, and most of *Perelandra* takes place on Venus. *That Hideous Strength*, on the other hand, is set in Great Britain during the immediate post-World War II period. Although it incorporates elements of science fiction (especially in the closing chapters), it is unlike its two predecessors in the sense that it has the basic structure and much of the "realism" of a conventional adventure thriller.

The protagonist of *That Hideous Strength* is Mark Studdock, a young, up-and-coming fellow in sociology at "Bracton College" of "Edgestow University." Mark accepts part-time employment with the National Institute for Co-ordinated Experiments (N.I.C.E.), an organization which is in the process of purchasing some of Bracton College's property for the purpose of building a massive research facility. Following several puzzling misadventures at N.I.C.E., and after meeting the bizarre staff of the enterprise, Mark discovers that N.I.C.E. has as its nefarious goal nothing less than

the full re-ordering of human life and culture. Meantime, Mark's wife Jane becomes affiliated with a rival
group headquartered in a manor house in the village of
St. Anne. The St. Anne organization, Lewis' collective
metaphor for good, wages various modes of combat against
N.I.C.E. It is led by a Mr. Fisher-King, who in the
first two novels of the series bore the name Ransom.
Before undertaking his crusade against evil, Ransom was
a professor of philosophy at Cambridge. In addition to
Mark Studdock and Ransom, a sizeable number of other
academics appear in *That Hideous Strength*. Some of
them are faculty members at Bracton College, and some,
like Mark, hold appointments at N.I.C.E. One of the
non-academic staffers at N.I.C.E. is Fairy Hardcastle,
the sadistic, lesbian chief of the institute's secret
police. Fairy may or may not have been C.S. Lewis' projection of the female of the future, but she is given
one cutting piece of dialogue which clearly summarizes
Lewis' views of sociology. Shortly after assuming his
post at N.I.C.E., the still naive Mark asks Fairy how
he, as a sociologist, will fit into the institute's
operations. Chomping on her ever-present cheroot, Fairy
tells Mark that he probably will be helping her devise
new punishments for criminals. "There's no distinctiion
in the long run between police work and sociology," she
says. "You and I've got to work hand in hand."

    Clive Staples Lewis was born in Belfast, Ireland in
1898, served as a lieutenant in the Somerset Light In-
fantry in World War I, and took three firsts (in classical moderations, ancient history and philosophy, and
English language and literature) at Oxford University
in the early 1920s. In 1925 he was elected to a fellowship in English language and literature at Magdalen College, Oxford; he continued in that position until 1954.
He was a prolific writer, his oeuvre including fifty-
eight books and his output spanning a vast range of genres. Lewis was an atheist until the late 1920s, when he
became an ardent, fundamentalist Christian. Most of his
books contain Christian themes and messages. The precise
themes and messages embedded in *That Hideous Strength*
remain a matter of continuing debate by students of modern English literature.

412. Wallis, Ruth (Otis) Satwell (1895-1978). *Blood from a
      Stone*. New York: Dodd, Mead and Co., 1945; London:
      Hammond, Hammond and Co., 1955.

      Set deep in the Pyrenees Mountains, just north of the

Spanish border, *Blood from a Stone* has as its protagonist a beautiful, red-headed American girl, Susan Kent. Susan, a student at a progressive and expensive college for women in the eastern United States, is getting credit for one of her undergraduate years by participating in amateur archeological digging in French caves. Detection is not part of her official study plan, but she becomes a sleuth nonetheless when she uncovers various non-ancient skeletons during the course of her underground explorations. "Archeological dig" mysteries are generally excluded from this bibliography, but *Blood from a Stone* is not the usual anthropologist-on-location story. Although Susan spends considerable time brushing centuries of dust and dirt from objects of antiquity, the plot of the story hinges on modern-day, pre-World War II espionage. Susan survives the many perils which she encounters during her adventure, but the college in which she is enrolled never has the chance to grade her outstanding performance. Not content with mere digging and detection, Susan falls in love with Marc de l'Arize, a wealthy local lad who serves on occasion as a French secret service agent. At the end of the book, Susan and Marc are preparing to marry and to live, pending the soon-to-come German invasion of France, in the sumptuous, hilltop Chateau de l'Arize.

Ruth Sawtell Wallis was born in Springfield, Massachusetts. She received an A.B. from Radcliffe in 1919, an M.A. from Radcliffe in 1923, and a Ph.D. from Columbia in 1929. During her writing career Wallis held a variety of posts in academe and in government before becoming a professor of sociology and anthropology at Annhurst College in Putnam, Connecticut. Wallis wrote many anthropological monographs, most of which were well received in professional circles. *Blood from a Stone* was the second of five mystery novels which she published during her lifetime. One of Wallis' later mysteries, *Cold Bed in the Clay* (422) is also in this bibliography.

*413. Eustis, Helen (1916-). *The Horizontal Man*. New York: Harper and Brothers, 1946; London: Hamish Hamilton, 1947.

Serious students of mystery fiction universally rate *The Horizontal Man* at or near the top of their lists of best academic murder novels. Set at "Hollymount College," an exclusive women's college in New England, the brooding, psychological story centers on the murder of Kevin Boyle, a twenty-nine-year-old bachelor member of

the Hollymount English department. His skull crushed by
a blunt instrument, Boyle is discovered dead in his
apartment at 7 P.M. one evening, and by the next morning
several Hollymount students, faculty members, and administrators find that their lives will never be the same.
Particularly aggrieved by Boyle's murder are Leonard
Marks and George Hungerford, two of the deceased's faculty colleagues. Leonard, another young member of the
English department, feels guilt because he and Boyle
carried on a continuing rivalry. And Hungerford, a
burnt-out hulk of a man, experiences emotional torment
because he feels as though he has lost a son. Some
of the detection in the story is by the timid and self-
tortured Leonard, and some is by Jack Donnelly, a local
newspaper reporter. Jack is assisted in his investigations by Kate Innes, the editor of the student paper on
campus, and the generally light-hearted banter between
Jack and Kate acts to offset the serious and weighty
dialogue offered by most of the book's other characters.
Mention should be made, too, of President Baimbridge,
a man who wishes the whole affair had never occurred.
In the interests of his school, Baimbridge makes some
inquiries of his own. All of the sleuthing proves to
be unnecessary, however. At the climax of the tale,
in as effective a scene as one is likely to encounter
in a college mystery, the villain gives himself away.

   Helen Eustis was born in Cincinnati. She received
a B.A. from Smith College in 1938. *The Horizontal Man*
won the Mystery Writers of America Edgar for the best
first mystery novel of 1946. Eustis' only other full-
length mystery, *The Fool Killer* (New York: Doubleday,
and Co., 1954; London: Secker and Warburg, 1955), does
not deal with academe and was given only fair notices
by reviewers.

*414.   Holman, (Clarence) Hugh (1914-1981). *Up This Crooked
        Way*. New York: M.S. Mills, 1946; London: William
        Foulsham, 1951.

        Up This Crooked Way is set at "Abecton College" in
        South Carolina. It begins with the shooting of Walter
        Perkins, the unpleasant, miserly owner of a lodging
        house occupied by unmarried members of the college's
        faculty and staff. The most likely suspect-tenant is
        Philip Kent, an associate professor of English. Phil-
        ip has already been acquitted of another murder, and
        most members of the Abecton community are ready to be-
        lieve that he is a pathological killer. But Sheriff

"Mac" Macready is not willing to leap to conclusions based on Philip's lurid past. Macready finds that Perkins's wife, Olga, had reason to kill her husband. And he learns, too, that Steel Carlise (an Abecton physicist), Jackie Dean (a nubile young college librarian), and Robert Herbert (an instructor of history), all had motives for exterminating their landlord. Crisply written and crammed with real and false clues, *Up This Crooked Way* incorporates some sly humor. For example, Sheriff Macready is an elected official who feels it necessary to pretend he is illiterate in order to get votes from the non-college portions of his constituency. But Macready is, in fact, a closet Chaucer buff. When he attends one of Philip Kent's classes, as part of his detection activities, he cannot prevent himself from rising and offering a long, off-the-cuff quotation from *The Canterbury Tales*.

Death Like Thunder (398), an earlier mystery by Clarence Hugh Holman, also appears in this bibliography. Like *Up This Crooked Way, Death Like Thunder* is set at Abecton College. However, none of the principal characters in either story appears in both books. Sheriff Macready is a Holman series-character sleuth, but he is absent from the scene in *Death Like Thunder*. And Yates Thorndyke Bell, the forthright president of Abecton College in *Death Like Thunder*, has been replaced by Dr. Bruce F. Walsh by the time the events in *Up This Crooked Way* take place. Dr. Walsh is a more usual presidential character-type. A man who revels in the status of his office, Dr. Walsh takes particular delight "in the thick nap of the carpet of his long, austere office."

*415. Kyd, Thomas [Harbage, Alfred Bennett (1901-)]. *Blood Is a Beggar*. Philadelphia, J.B. Lippincott, 1946; London: Hammond, Hammond and Co., 1949.

Professor Oscar Biddler, the chairman of the English department at a large university in the eastern United States, is showing a film to his drama class, and Anne Ridgeway, his young, attractive secretary, is operating the projection equipment. Biddler is shot dead as the film unreels, and when the lights are turned on, Anne is hunched over the professor's corpse, Although Anne is not holding the fateful pistol (it has been thrown into a far corner), the thirty students in the classroom are convinced that she committed the dirty deed. But Sam Phelan, the local police detective assigned to

the case, is not so certain. Captivated by Anne's good
looks, Sam insists upon developing a long list of other
suspects, most of whom are members of the university's
faculty. Sam's eye falls in particular upon Professor
"Clockworks" Partridge, the English department's director of graduate studies, with whom Biddler once had a
bitter quarrel over the worthiness of a Ph.D. dissertation. And he looks hard, too, at Professor Twines, an
extremely popular teacher of English whom Biddler was
trying to get fired on the grounds of grade inflation.
A thoroughly academic mystery, *Blood Is a Beggar* introduces its readers to a host of university characters
and situations, and it incorporates considerable not-so-
veiled satire directed both at academe and at college
mystery novels. Moreover, some clever literary irony
is built into the book's structure. Casual consumers
of mystery fiction may have little difficulty guessing
Professor Biddler's killer. But serious students of the
genre, who have been conditioned to discount the obvious
in detective yarns, may have to work their ways through
to the book's denouement in order to discover the identity of the guilty party.

Alfred Bennett Harbage was born in Philadelphia. He
received an A.B. from the University of Pennsylvania in
1924 and a Ph.D. from the same institution in 1929.
After teaching at the University of Pennsylvania and at
Columbia University, Harbage became a professor of
English and comparative literature at Harvard in 1952.
In 1960 he was named Cabot Professor of English Literature at Harvard. A Shakespearean scholar of international renown, Harbage published four mystery novels
during his lifetime. *Blood Is a Beggar* was his first
venture into the mystery field. Harbage's second and
third mysteries both star Sam Phelan in their sleuthing
roles, but neither is concerned with academic matters.
Harbage's final mystery, *Cover His Face* (427), does not
include Sam Phelan as a character. The protagonist of
Cover His Face is Gilbert E. Wheldon, an instructor of
English who journeys to Great Britain in search of long-
lost literary treasures. The book is described later
in this bibliography.

416. Tey, Josephine [Mackintosh, Elizabeth (1896-1952)]. *Miss
      Pym Disposes*. London: Peter Davies, 1946. New York:
      Macmillan, 1948.

      Lucy Pym is a middle-aged spinster of independent
      means. The author of a best-selling critique of modern

psychology, she is invited to give a lecture at "Leys Physical Training College," a genteel institution for females. The lecture is a great success. Moreover, Miss Pym finds herself embroiled, quite by happenstance, in an interlocking series of disturbing events. These including a case of cheating on a final examination and the death of a student after a suspicious fall in the school's gymnasium. Though Miss Pym is reluctant to get involved, her curiosity gets the better of her, and by the end of the story she has tied together and resolved both mysteries. A very quiet book, with considerably more feminine chit-chat than gore or detection, *Miss Pym Disposes* probably will have little appeal for modern-day devotees of action-filled mysteries. On the other hand, those who detest contemporary academe's institutional food will appreciate the descriptions of the almond-fingers and eclairs which are standard Leys College fare at tea time.

Elizabeth Mackintosh was born in Inverness, Scotland. She attended the Anstey Physical Training College in Birmingham and for a time held various positions as a physical training instructor. In 1924 she retired to her parents' home in a small village near Loch Ness to nurse her ailing mother. Upon her mother's death, she remained in the family homestead to keep house for her father. Mackintosh wrote novels, plays, and detective mysteries. The pseudonym Josephine Tey, which she employed on most of her detective works, was the name of her great-great grandmother. She also used the pseudonym Gordon Daviot. The Daviot alias appeared on the title page of Macintosh's first mystery novel, *The Man in the Queue* (London: Methuen and Co., 1929; New York: E.P. Dutton, 1929), but thereafter it was reserved for her mainstream novels and dramas.

*417. Thomas, Carolyn [Duncan, Actea Caroline (1913-)]. *Prominent Among the Mourners*. Philadelphia: J.B. Lippincott, 1946; London: Cherry Tree Books, 1949.

John Herron, the president of "Larkin College," is stabbed dead during a faculty reception in his home. An anomaly among fictional academic presidents, Herron was a kindly man without dedicated enemies, and thus the only immediate suspects are a few neurotic professors who had trivial grievances against him. The sleuthing in the case is provided by Sheriff Townsend, a perceptive local policeman, and by Susan Eyerly, Larkin's newly hired director of publicity. Sheriff Townsend

and his attractive assistant eventually bring Herron's murderer to justice, but not until two more killings occur. Larkin College is a venerable coeducational institution in the American Midwest, and the roots of
the riddle lie in the school's past. President Herron
was writing a history of Larkin, and the moral of the
story seems to be that college presidents should concentrate on their school's present-day problems and
allow long-forgotten scandals to remain dormant. In
addition to Herron and Susan Eyerly, the book contains
a great many other academic characters, some of whom
are drawn with venom-laden ink. Social scientists may
want to take special note of the portrait of Scott Gerald Ball, a boorish young sociologist. Scott Gerald
Ball insists on being addressed by his full name and,
though he is not quite capable of physical murder, verbally assassinates anyone who doubts his interpretations
of "the significance of rural-urban curve variations."

418. Connington, J.J. [Stewart, Alfred Walter (1880-1947)].
      Common Sense Is All You Need. London: Hodder and
      Stoughton, 1947.

      Set in the British village of Ambledown, this novel
centers on the mysterious death by hanging of George
Pickford, a local librarian. The detective is Sir Clinton Driffield, the local chief constable and a well-
known J.J. Connington series-character. One of Driffield's assets is his willingness to seek expert advice
when investigating crimes; on this occasion he calls
upon Professor Howard Dundas, a chemist at nearby "Tren-
don University." A methodical man, who carries a magni-
fying glass and a tape measure as part of his standard
equipment, Dundas examines the death scene and provides
Sir Clinton with important information. The professor
also discourses at one point on the difficulties he
experiences with his self-identity. He dislikes being
called "Professor" because people confuse him "with a
conjurer or a chiropodist." If called "Doctor," he is
forever having to explain that he is not "a medic."
And if he describes himself as a chemist, people "seem
to think I wear a white apron and serve behind the
counter in a druggist's shop."
      Educated at the Universities of Glasgow and Marburg
and at University College, London, Alfred Stewart was
one of Europe's leading professors of chemistry during
the early part of this century. Holding chairs at
Queens University, Belfast, and the University of Glas-

gow, Stewart produced a series of chemistry textbooks which became the classic works of their era. He was also one of the first prominent academics to write detective fiction. His first detective story was *Death at Swaying Court* (London, Ernest Benn, 1926; Boston: Little, Brown, 1926). In 1927 he introduced Sir Clinton Driffield as the sleuth in *Murder in the Maze* (London, Ernest Benn, 1927; Boston: Little, Brown, 1927), and Sir Clinton appeared in sixteen more works before Stewart's death in 1947. *Common Sense Is All You Need* was Stewart's last book.

419. Freeman, Kathleen (1897-1959). *Gown and Shroud*. London: Macdonald and Co., 1947.

Augustus Spencer, a professor of archeology at a new (but unidentified) British university, has an affair with Miss March, his resident housekeeper. When Augustus decides to end the liaison, in order to marry his cousin, Miss March is no longer content to clean his abode and cook his meals. She threatens to provoke a campus scandal and, shortly thereafter, she is found dead in her quarters, her skull smashed by a series of blows delivered from behind. Augustus seems to be the prime suspect in the case, but as the story unfolds into a series of subplots, other murders are committed and other potential villains are introduced. Police Inspector Poole successfully sorts through all of the complications to produce a seventeen-page denouement. In addition to Augustus' tangled home life, Poole must cope with the disputed ownership of archeological treasures brought back from the Island of Xanthos, undergraduate rivalries over a university scholarship, and the problem of whether of not Sir Thomas Hyde, the wealthy squire of Viccam Court, will continue to provide the university with sizeable financial contributions.

Kathleen Freeman was born in Birmingham, Great Britain, and educated at the University of Cardiff. A long-time lecturer in Greek at University College, Cardiff, she was a prolific writer of mystery fiction. Most of her detective works were issued under the pseudonym Mary Fitt. *Gown and Shroud* was the only novel-length mystery which she published under her real name.

420. Gray, Jonathan [Taylor, Jack]. *Untimely Slain*. London:
      Hutchinson and Co., 1947.

      Set in the days just before World War II, this novel
      begins as a conventional British academic mystery and
      turns into a spy thriller. Humphrey Wayne, a tutor in
      medieval history at "St. Michael's College," Oxford, is
      found murdered in the college library. It turns out
      that Humphrey, a one-time British undercover operative,
      was killed by Nazi agents because he was in possession
      of crucial information about Germany's ambitions toward
      Poland. Sir Harker Mulready, the head of British Intel-
      ligence, recruits Geoffrey Tarleton, a junior research
      fellow in history at St. Michael's, to travel to Poland
      in order to foil the German plans. Since Sir Harker's
      last words to Geoffrey are "God rest the souls of the
      gallant men who have gone before," Britain's newest
      espionage agent knows that the road ahead will be
      fraught with peril. And, indeed, during the second part
      of the book, Geoffrey surmounts a vast array of obsta-
      cles before completing his mission. Though the latter
      portion of the story digresses into almost pure derring-
      do, the initial chapters contain especially well-drawn
      portraits of St. Michael's characters, heavy doses of
      academic atmosphere,and interesting on-campus detection.
      The identity of Jack Taylor has escaped the editors of
      the standard biographic sourcebooks. However, Jacques
      Barzun and Wendell Taylor, in *A Catalogue of Crime* (see
      footnote 7, Introduction) report that Jack Taylor was
      an economist at the University of Rochester (New York)
      who possessed an M.A. from Oxford. *Untimely Slain* was
      Taylor's only venture into the field of mystery fiction.

421. Mitchell, Ronald Elwy (1905-). *Design for November*.
      New York: Harper and Brothers, 1947.

      Design for November is set at "Creston University,"
      an institution in the American Midwest. The first half
      of the story is a conventional mainstream novel of aca-
      demic manners. Sam Forrester, a graduate assistant in
      the art department, struggles against poverty and hopes
      desperately for appointment to a vacant instructorship.
      But a European emigré, one Dr. Konopka, arrives at Cre-
      ston and is given the post instead. At this point Sam's
      wife, Catherine, takes charge of the Forrester family
      affairs. After she secretly murders Dr. Konopka by
      adding poison to his liquor, Sam, who does not know
      of his spouse's evil deed, happily accepts an offer to

assume Konopka's duties and salary. Detection does not figure prominently in the plot of this broken-backed story. However, there is considerable second-half suspense built around the question of whether of not Catherine can surmount her conscience and get away with her crime.

Ronald Elwy Mitchell was born in London. He received his undergraduate training at Kings College, University of London, and did graduate work at Yale. At the time *Design for November* was published, Mitchell was a professor of speech and theatre at the University of Wisconsin.

422. Wallis, Ruth (Otis) Sawtell (1895-1978). *Cold Bed in the Clay*. New York: Dodd, Mead and Co., 1947.

Cold Bed in the Clay is set at a state university in the American Midwest. Don Adriance, an instructor of freshman English, who has just arrived at the school, is found dead in a roadside ditch. Adriance is the apparent victim of a hit-and-run accident. But Eric Lund, an ex-FBI agent and a Ruth Sawtell Wallis series-character sleuth, happens to be at the university as a guest lecturer in criminology. Lund suspects that Adriance's death may have been murder, and his eye falls first on Audrey, Don's wife, a young lady with a shocking secret in her past. By the end of the tale, however, Lund's attentions have turned to several other faculty wives and their husbands. Written in a rich, sometimes-obscure style more often encountered in avant-garde mainstream novels than in detective stories, *Cold Bed in the Clay* takes its readers deep inside a troubled faculty milieu. Furthermore, through Cadwallader, an inquisitive dog-about-campus, it opens to public view the contents of the garbage cans into which faculty families toss the unwanted flotsam from their lives.

Cold Bed in the Clay was the second of three novels by Ruth Sawtell Wallis which featured Eric Lund as their detective-protagonist. *Blood from a Stone* (412), a non-Eric Lund story by Ruth Sawtell Wallis, appears earlier in this bibliography.

423. Lockridge, Frances Louise (1896-1963) and Richard Lockridge (1898-). *Murder Is Served*. Philadelphia: J.B. Lippincott, 1948; London: Hutchinson and Co., 1950.

It is final examination time at "Dyckman University" in New York City, and John Leonard, an associate pro-

fessor of psychology, is grading the blue books turned
in by the students in his experimental psychology course.
The exam of Peggy Mott, an aspiring Broadway actress, is
entitled "Hatred" and contains so much bitter prose that
John is convinced that Peggy is about to commit a murder. Looking for guidance, John telephones Jerry North,
his publisher. Jerry, one-half of Frances and Richard
Lockridge's celebrated amateur detective team of Mr.
and Mrs. North, is at first inclined to dismiss John's
call as the ranting of an eccentric intellectual. But
when John Mott, Peggy's husband, is stabbed dead in a
restaurant by an unknown assailant, Jerry and his amazingly intuitive wife, Pam, drop all of their other
responsibilities to engage in sleuthing. Assisted by
Lieutenant Bill Wiegand and Sergeant Aloyius Mullins of
the New York Police, the Norths find the villain. For
his part, poor Professor Leonard is quickly tabbed by
the Norths as a likely suspect; then he barely survives
an attack by the book's mysterious, knife-wielding
assassin. Much of the story takes place in central Manhattan. However, the novel's first chapter, in which
John Leonard is depicted ruminating in his classroom
about the frustrations of college teaching, contains
some of the most insightful academic introspection in
mystery fiction.

Frances Louise Lockridge was born in Kansas City,
Missouri. She attended the University of Kansas. Richard Lockridge was born in St. Joseph, Missouri, and
attended Kansas City Junior College and the University
of Missouri. At the time the Lockridges were married,
in 1922, Richard was a reporter for the *Kansas City
Star*. The couple moved to New York City shortly after
their wedding and Richard joined the staff of the *New
York Sun*. The Lockridges published their first mystery
novel in 1940--a Mr. and Mrs. North adventure--and until Frances' death in 1963 they collaborated on nearly
sixty more full-length detective stories. In addition
to the Norths, the Lockridges created a number of other
series-character sleuths. These include New York City
Police Captain Bill Wiegand, New York Homicide Detective
Nathan Shapiro, New York City Assistant District Attorney Bernie Simmons, and New York State Police Captain
Merton Heimrich. Many of the Lockridges' novels feature
more than one of their series-characters. Richard Lockridge has continued to write mysteries after Frances'
death. Most of his solo efforts have employed Merton
Heimrich in starring roles. Dyckman University and/or
members of its faculty figure prominently in six Lock-

ridge novels. After *Murder Is Served*, Frances and Richard returned to Dyckman in *Accent on Murder* (471), *Murder Is Suggested* (476), and *The Drill Is Death* (482).
Richard then utilized Dyckman in two post-Frances stories, *Murder Can't Wait* (492) and *Twice Retired* (535).

424.   Muir, Dexter [Gribble, Leonard Reginald (1908-)]. *The
Pilgrims Meet Murder*. London: Herbert Jenkins, 1948.

Stephen Pilgrim is an affluent young professor of
criminology at the "University of Westminster" in his
native Great Britain. With his American-born-and-bred
wife, Lola, he travels to his Dorset holiday home
(appropriately named Mayflower Cottage) in search of rest
and relaxation. He no sooner arrives than he is visited
by his old friend, Chief Inspector Max Hunter of Scotland Yard. Hunter, in Dorset investigating two local
murders, asks Professor Pilgrim for assistance. Before
the novel concludes--with the twin mysteries solved--
Lola is kidnapped, Pilgrim is trapped in an ancient
quarry running under his property, and several smugglers do battle among themselves. A man who tries
assiduously to keep emotion out of his sleuthing, Professor Pilgrim nonetheless becomes exceedingly angry
when Lola falls into evil hands. He displays pique,
too, when Mrs. Rimmer, his housekeeper and an anti-
smoking zealot, hides his ashtrays, thus making it difficult for him to smoke his pipe while engaged in heavy
ratiocination. There is one classroom scene (in the
book's first chapter), but the lion's share of the story
takes place amidst the coves, caves, and villages along
Britain's southwest coast.
    Leonard Reginald Gribble was born in London. The au-
thor of more than two hundred books (most of them mystery novels), Gribble has employed the pseudonyms Sterry
Browning, Landon Grant, Leo Grex and Louis Grey as well
as Dexter Muir. Gribble is best known to mystery fans
for his more than twenty Superintendent Anthony Slade
novels. The Slade stories appear under his real name.

425.   Bronson, F(rancis) W(oolsey) (1901-1966). *The Bulldog
Has the Key*. New York: Farrar and Straus, 1949.

The sleuth in this uniquely premised novel is Ed Brake-
ly, a United States Government intelligence agent and a
member of the Yale class of 1922. It is June of 1947,
and Ed is sent to New Haven, under the guise of attending his twenty-fifth reunion, to investigate an inter-

national jewel smuggling operation. One government
agent already has been killed on the case, and Ed
Brakeley almost meets his own death several times before
the novel reaches its conclusion. On his way to the
resolution of the affair, Ed comes into contact with
several Yale professors and administrators, with a
beautiful and mysterious blonde, and with a host of his
convivial classmates. And he revisits many of his old
haunts, including the Taft Hotel, Woolsey Hall, and Yale
baseball field. Moreover, in one arresting scene, Ed is
forced to kill an antagonist in a Yale dormitory room.
Although the motives behind the mayhem in *The Bulldog
Has the Key* are not academic in nature, Yale is an
integral part of the story. The book will have special
appeal for Yalies, but it can be read with enjoyment by
anyone who appreciates solid, on-campus mysteries.

Francis Woolsey Bronson was born in Minneapolis and,
like Ed Brakeley, was a member of the Yale class of 1922.
Known to generations of Yale men as "Bus," Bronson was
from 1937 until shortly before his death the editor of
the *Yale Alumni Magazine*. *The Bulldog Has the Key* was
the last of three mystery novels which Bronson published
during his lifetime.

426. Hodgkin, M(arion) R(ous) (1917-). *Student Body*. New
      York: Charles Scribner's Sons, 1949; London: Victor
      Gollancz, 1950.

"Carodac College" is a coeducational American institution in which the students pay considerably less attention to their studies than to their social lives.
In fact, the most hated man on campus is the night watchman, known to everyone but his immediate family as "The
Goon," who sneaks around the school's cloisters surprising unsuspecting couples with a flashlight. Carodac's
relentless pursuit of academic mediocrity is temporarily
forgotten, however, when three of its undergraduates
meet mysterious deaths. One of the victims, a girl
named Candy, was the roomate of Nora Pickham, a senior
who majors in English literature between coed gossip
sessions. As Nora turns amateur detective, her suspects include fellow students, The Goon, administrators,
faculty wives, and even bombastic old Professor Beacon.
The latter, at one point, incriminates himself by warn-
ing Nora in a typical-for-the-book faculty monologue:
"Young woman ... does it occur to you that a murder has
been done, that the murderer is still at large, that it
might very well be myself, and that you have by sheer

ignorance, stumbled upon a situation in which I, for one, have little interest, but which is of quite stupendous importance to others?" Slow-paced, and not among the most suspense-filled mysteries in this bibliography, the book is nonetheless noteworthy for views it presents of Carodac's intellectually empty environment.

Born in New York City, Marion Rous Hodgkin received a B.A. from Swarthmore College in 1939. *Student Body* was the first of two novels which she wrote during a brief excursion into the field of mystery fiction.

427. Kyd, Thomas [(Harbage, Alfred Bennett (1901-1976)].
      Cover His Face. Philadelphia: J.B. Lippincott, 1949.

A lowly instructor of English at the "University of Allegheny" in the eastern United States, Gilbert E. Wheldon yearns for an assistant professorship at a more prestigious institution. He wants, too, to improve upon his $2500 per year salary so that he might marry Ethel Macomber, his fiancée. Hoping to make a literary name for himself through one bold piece of research, Gilbert flies to Great Britain in search of a cache of "unpublished" writings by Samuel Johnson. This treasure trove, so Gilbert believes, rests somewhere on a farm, owned by his British relatives, near the thatched village of "Fenny Dasset." But when Gilbert arrives at his destination, he becomes embroiled in a family feud, in a murder, and in a series of situations which almost put an end to his own life. Written with polished satirical humor, *Cover His Face* pokes fun at literary research and, through Gilbert Wheldon, tweaks overzealous literary scholars as well. For example, when Wheldon is asked about his experiences as a marine in the South Pacific during World War II, he replies in all seriousness: "The library facilities were terrible!" Wheldon does not find the lode of Samuel Johnson writings on the family farm. But at the end of the story, even though he is battered and bruised from his perilous exploits, he is still running down obscure clues about the whereabouts of the papers.

Alfred Bennett Harbage was an internationally famous Shakespearean scholar and professor of English at Harvard. An earlier mystery by Harbage, *Blood Is a Beggar* (415), also appears in this bibliography.

428.   Mais, S(tuart) P(etre) B(rodie) (1885-1975). *Who Dies?*
       London: Hutchinson and Co., 1949.

       Why did C.E. Venables, a lecturer in chemistry at Ex-
       eter College, Oxford, suffocate while returning to his
       lodgings one bitter cold evening? Did he fall accidently
       into a snowbank, as the authorities assume, or was he
       murdered? Who is Philip Winslow, the protagonist of
       this story? As the book opens Philip seems to be a
       colorless teacher at an Oxford public school, but as
       the plot unfolds it becomes evident that he is far more
       knowledgeable than most school teachers about the inner
       workings of the British secret service. And what is the
       meaning of the encoded message (P M C D L R 72 B_7
       109 Y_{13} 21 F_8 37 N_4) that Winslow finds concealed
       in a coat hanging in Vincent's Club, a watering spot for
       Blues in Oxford's Oriel Lane. The answers to these and
       many other riddles are provided by the end of the book,
       but not before readers are taken through a dark and
       well-constructed literary maze complete with enigmatic
       characters, ill-fated love affairs, and scenes in var-
       ious Oxford pubs, in Blackwells, and in the Bodleian
       Library. Set during the days of extreme austerity in
       Britain just after World War II, *Who Dies?* is less a
       conventional detective novel than an espionage thriller.
       Nevertheless, it contains more than enough riddles and
       Oxford atmosphere to satisfy the most discerning con-
       noisseurs of orthodox academic mysteries.
         Stuart Petre Brodie Mais was born in Matlock, Great
       Britain. He received a B.A. (with honors) and an M.A.
       from Oxford. He began his working life as a school-
       master but soon turned to newspaper work, radio com-
       mentary for the BBC, and creative writing. Mais' enor-
       mous oeuvre includes studies in English literature,
       mainstream novels, and travel books. *Who Dies?* was the
       tenth of eleven mystery novels which Mais wrote during
       his lifetime.

429.   Hubbard, Margaret Ann [Priley, Margaret (1909-)]. *Mur-*
          der Takes the Veil. Milwaukee: Bruce Publishing,
          1950.

       "The College of St. Aurelian" is a Catholic institution
       for young women, located deep in the bayous of Louisiana.
       Mother Theodore, the superior of the college, hires three
       men as new lay instructors. One of the new recruits has
       committed an off-campus murder, and he sets out to elim-
       inate the only person who can implicate him, a St. Aure-

lian student named Trillium Pierce. Trillium suffers
far more than her fair share of terror-filled moments
during the story. Meantime, once they become aware of
what is happening, Mother Theodore and the other nuns
on the St. Aurelian staff attempt to discover which of
their new recruits is making poor Trillium's life so
miserable. With the help of a wise local sheriff, the
troublemaker is identified and hauled off to pay for
his misdeeds. Casual readers of mysteries may have
difficulty identifying the culprit before the end of
the story. On the other hand, dedicated devotees of
college detective novels will have no such problems.
For these fortunate individuals, the author provides a
bold-faced onomastic clue on page four.

Margaret Priley was born in Souris, North Dakota.
She received a B.S. in 1932 from the University of Minnesota and then began a successful career as a writer
of adventure books for juveniles. *Murder Takes the
Veil* was the first of four mystery novels which she
wrote for adult consumption.

430.   Carr, John Dickson (1905-1977). *The Devil in Velvet.*
       London: Hamish Hamilton, 1951; New York: Harper and
       Brothers, 1951.

Nicholas Fenton, a professor of history at "Paracelus
College," Cambridge, searches obsessively for the details about a murder committed in London in 1675. Unable to find any but sketchy records of the case, he ex-
changes his soul with the Devil for a trip back to Restoration England. After arriving in the seventeenth
century, Professor Fenton engages in sword fights, finds
romance, and even manages to change the course of world
events. And, through some unusual sleuthing, he emerges as history's earliest successful professorial detective. Written with verve, invention, and close attention to historical detail, the book is the only work
surveyed in this bibliography to conclude with five
pages of "Notes for the Curious" about Restoration London's characters and customs. Moreover, it is the only
work listed in the bibliography in which the Devil has
a speaking part.

One of the giants of the "Golden Age" of detective
fiction, John Dickson Carr was born in Uniontown, Pennsylvania, and attended Haverford College. He lived much
of his adult life in Great Britain where, in addition to
producing a stream of popular, puzzle-filled mystery
novels, he also wrote radio scripts for the BBC. An-

other of Carr's mysteries, *The Dark Man's Knock* (466),
appears in this bibliography. *The Dead Man's Knock*
features Dr. Gideon Fell, the best-known of Carr's many
character sleuths, as its protagonist.

431. Hare, Cyril [Clark, Alfred Alexander Gordon (1900-1958)].
      An English Murder. London: Faber and Faber, 1951;
      Boston: Little, Brown, 1951.

      It is Christmas eve at stately "Warbeck Hall," and
      the members of the Warbeck family, plus some invited
      guests, are assembling to celebrate the holiday season.
      One of the merrymakers is Wencelaus Bottwink, a pro-
      fessor of modern history at the University of Prague,
      who is staying at the Hall to examine some George III-
      period letters in Lord Warbeck's possession. The Christ-
      mas festivities cease, however, when Robert Warbeck,
      heir to the family fortune, dies after drinking cham-
      pagne laced with cyanide. Then it begins to snow and
      the party is stranded. After two more highly suspic-
      ious deaths take place, Professor Bottwink turns
      sleuth. Along with Bottwink and Robert Warbeck, the
      players in this country-house mystery include Britain's
      Chancellor of the Exchequer, the wife of an up-and-com-
      ing British bureaucrat, and Warbeck Hall's butler, whose
      daughter has borne Robert Warbeck's illegitimate son.
      In the end, the alien professor solves the case by util-
      izing his vast academic knowledge of English history and
      culture.
           Alfred Alexander Gordon Clark received a first in his-
      tory at New College, Oxford, and then became an attorney.
      He wrote nine detective novels during his lifetime, and
      drew many of his plots from real-life cases-at-law in
      which he was involved. Clark's pseudonym, Cyril Hare,
      was taken from Hare Court, Temple, in which he was em-
      ployed during the early part of his legal career. At
      the time *An English Murder* was published, Clark was a
      county-court judge in Surrey.

432. Innes, Michael [Steward, John Innes Mackintosh (1906-)].
      Operation Pax. London: Victor Gollancz, 1951. Pub-
      lished in the United States as *The Paper Thunderbolt*.
      New York: Dodd, Mead and Co., 1951.

      A group of scientists, some of whom hold posts at Ox-
      ford, plots to develop a secret weapon which will bring
      it power over the world. This sinister band is foiled,
      however, by Inspector John Appleby of New Scotland Yard,

Michael Innes' tireless series-character sleuth, and by Jane Appleby, John's twenty-one-year-old sister who is an Oxford undergraduate. A dizzying tale, which intermixes pulsating chase sequences, dark satire, and serious detection, *Operation Pax* defies easy description. The book's final scenes, which take place in the book-storage vault underneath the Bodleian Library, are among the more gripping pieces of writing in academic mystery fiction. And, told in Innes' unique, urbane style, the story offers some irreverent glimpses of Oxonians committing devilish deeds.

Seven other Michael Innes mysteries appear in this bibliography. These books are *Death at the President's Lodging* (374), *Hamlet, Revenge!* (378), *The Weight of the Evidence* (405), *Old Hall, New Hall* (454), *Appleby Plays Chicken* (462), *The Long Farewell* (470), and *A Family Affair* (528).

433. Van Arsdale, Wirt [Davis, Martha Wirt (1905-1952)]. *The Professor Knits a Shroud*. Garden City, New York: Doubleday and Co., 1951.

Henry Von Fliegel, a best-selling novelist, is shot dead while a guest at the upstate New York farm owned by Niles Carter, his publisher. By a happy coincidence, another guest at the Carter farm is Pedro Jose Maria Guadaloupe O'Reilly Apodaca, a professor of archeology at a New York City university. Professor Apodaca, whose idea of relaxation is to sip whiskey and knit socks, takes on the sleuthing chores in the story. With his knitting needles clicking furiously, he identifies Von Fliegel's murderer. Apodaca, known as "Uncle Pete" to his friends, is a short, stubby man in his fifties. Of Spanish-Irish descent, he has "electric blue" eyes, skin "as pink and white as a cherub," and a keen capacity for logical deduction. *The Professor Knits a Shroud* may well have been intended as the first exploit in a Professor Apodaca series, but the knitting pedant's detection career was never carried forward beyond this novel. While some professorial readers may find themselves mourning Professor Apodaca's literary demise after only one adventure, others are likely to be even more depressed over the fact that Marita Brenner, Henry Von Fliegel's luscious "secretary," also faded from the fiction scene after *The Professor Knits a Shroud*. Still another guest at Niles Carter's rustic retreat, Marita has "smooth golden hair," an "exquisite" figure, and an exceptional ability to enliven otherwise long, dull nights in the country.

Martha Wirt Davis was born in Denver, Colorado, and attended the University of Denver. She also studied at the Art Students League in New York City. The wife of author Clyde Brion Davis, she lived much of her adult life in Salisbury, Connecticut. *The Professor Knits a Shroud* was her only mystery novel.

434. Wheeler, Hugh Callingham (1913-). *The Crippled Muse.* London: Rupert Hart-Davis, 1951; New York: Rinehart and Co., 1952.

The central character in this scenic professor-on-sabbatical story is Horace Beddoes, a middle-aged professor of English literature at "Wentworth College" in Ohio. In hopes of writing a biography of Mecape Sloane, once America's foremost poet, Horace travels to Capri, where Miss Sloane is reported to be spending her last years in seclusion. After arriving on Capri, Horace finds that another would-be Sloane biographer is already on the scene. When his rival dies after being stabbed and then pushed over a cliff, Horace becomes the prime suspect in the case. Then, to make matters worse, Horace meets but cannot capture Girlie Winters, a suntanned beauty who has two muscular beachboys as paramours. There is little detection in the novel although Horace, who tends to drown his sorrows in alcohol, makes some besotted attempts at clearing his name. As for Merape Sloane, all things are not as they initially seem to be, and the climax of the novel revolves less around Horace's problems with the law than around the question of why Miss Sloane has not published any new works for over thirty years.

Writing under the pseudonym Q. Patrick, Hugh Callingham Wheeler collaborated with Richard Wilson Webb on many mystery novels and short stories published in the 1930s and 1940s. One of these collaborations, *Death and the Maiden* (389), appears in this bibliography. *Death and the Maiden* also is set at a "Wentworth College." But whereas the Wentworth College in *The Crippled Muse* is in Ohio, the Wentworth College in *Death and the Maiden* is located in the New York City metropolitan area.

435. Wylie, Philip (Gordon) (1902-1971). *Experiment in Crime.* New York: Avon Publications, 1951.

Experiment in Crime chronicles the exploits of Luther Martin Burke, a professor of "socio-psychology" at the

University of Miami, as he tumbles in a whimsical whirl
from his academic pedestal into a short-lived but enervating adventure with gun molls, gangsters, and FBI
agents. It all begins when Burke, who routinely lectures to his classes that criminals are "intellectually
defective," is challenged by his students to go off campus and actually meet some underworld characters.
Though he does not expect his opinions of criminals to
change, Burke decides to spend an evening at the Club
Egret, a well-known illegal-gambling spot in Miami
Beach. The place is raided; Burke finds himself an unwilling participant in the perilous dealings of an international smuggling ring; and he almost loses his life
when a mobster threatens to push him out of an airplane
high over the Caribbean. There is no detection in the
novel, and because the author's emphasis is on entertaining his readers with clever, light-hearted prose,
the book is also devoid of tension. While no one should
read the book expecting thrills, chills, or riddles,
many real-life academics may find the ending to their
liking. Since Burke has received considerable newspaper
publicity for his escapade, and because he is now a famous name among socio-psychologists, President Tolver of
the university makes him department head at double his
previous salary.

Philip Gordon Wylie was born in Beverly, Massachusetts.
He attended Princeton from 1920 until 1923. One of America's most prolific writers, Wylie wrote mainstream novels, books of history, social commentaries, and radio
and television scripts as well as mysteries. His best-
selling analysis of America's pre-World War II social
ills, *Generation of Vipers* (New York: Farrar and Rinehart, 1942), introduced the term "momism" into the English language. In addition to its Avon paperback edition, *Experiment in Crime* appeared as one of three novellas bound together in hardback in Philip Wylie's
Three to be Read (New York: Rinehart and Co., 1951).
Another mystery by Wylie, *The Smuggled Atom Bomb* (436),
also appears in this bibliography.

436. Wylie, Philip (Gordon) (1902-1971). *The Smuggled Atom
      Bomb*. New York: Avon Publications, 1951.

Allan Diffenduffer Bogan is a twenty-four-year-old
student in physics at the University of Miami. Rooming
in a private home owned by the Yates family, he has
eyes for Eleanor, the Yates' oldest daughter. There is

another lodger in the house, one Harry Ellings, a fifty-year-old bachelor automobile mechanic. Young Mr. Bogan works off some of his rent by helping Mrs. Yates with housekeeping. While cleaning Hary Ellings' room, he comes across a mysterious box which contains an odd metal object. Bogan identifies the object as part of an atomic bomb. He notifies the FBI, but Special Agent Slater Higgins is inclined to dismiss his story as a youthful hallucination. When Bogan is savagely beaten, however, and when Harry Ellings commits suicide, Agent Higgins' interest is finally aroused. As the plot moves forward, Bogan and Eleanor Yates supplement Higgins' official detection with some energetic amateur sleuthing. At the conclusion of the yarn, the grateful President of the United States gives Bogan a full government scholarship so that he may pursue his Ph.D. without further need to wield a mop and broom.

The Smuggled Atom Bomb is a light novella, designed more to entertain readers than to pose to them any serious challenges in vicarious deduction. In addition to the self-contained Avon paperback edition of the work, the tale was published in hardback form as one of three stories in Philip Wylie's *Three to be Read* (New York: Rinehart and Co., 1951). *Experiment in Crime* (435), another one of the pieces in *Three to be Read*, and another mystery with an academic character as its protagonist, also was published separately. It is accorded its own entry in this bibliography.

437. Lewis, Lange [Brandt, Jane Lewis (1915-)]. *The Passionate Victims*. Indianapolis: Bobbs-Merrill, 1952; London: Bodley Head, 1953.

The year is 1945 and Brigit Estees, the only woman member of the Los Angeles homicide squad, is investigating the murder of a high-school girl. As Brigit searches for clues, she is ambushed by an unknown gunman. Badly wounded, she lies in a hospital, hoping that other members of the Los Angeles police force will be able to pick up the threads of the case. But as Brigit rests and recuperates, who should turn up in Los Angeles but Mordecai Fentwell, her long-lost great uncle. Mordecai is a world-famous British professor of philosophy, a former student of Sigmund Freud, and a man whose own ideas have influenced Einstein, Churchill, and Robert Hutchins. Mordecai is also a proficient amateur detective, and since he will be in Los Angeles for several weeks to deliver a series of lectures at the University of Southern California, he insists on helping Brigit find her assailant. Buoyed by Mordecai's presence, Brigit rises from her bed, and the curious pair of crime-fighters goes forth to resolve all and sundry matters. Joining in the action is Richard Tuck, another Los Angeles homicide detective, who just happens to be one of Mordecai Fentwell's greatest admirers. Although Tuck's role in the story is limited he does provide readers with insight into Uncle Mordecai's philosophies by quoting, on occasion, from the professor's monographs. Indeed, Tuck seems to have memorized large sections of *The Void After Freud*, that classic treatise on human will which vaulted Fentwell into the front rank of Anglo-American intellectuals.

Murder Among Friends (400), and *Juliet Dies Twice* (406), two other mysteries by Lange Lewis, are included in this bibliography. Neither Brigit Estees nor Mordecai Fentwell appear in either of these works. But Richard Tuck, a hard-working series-character, does the heavy sleuthing in both stories.

438. Muir, Thomas. *Death Under Virgo*. London: Hutchinson and Co., 1952.

Professor Cleghorn, an anthropologist at an unspecified Scotish university, takes his family for what he hopes will be a quiet holiday on the Island of Camorach. A beautiful and rustic "Highland paradise," Camorach lies "just north of Skye." The Cleghorns are not long at their vacation retreat, however, before teenaged daughter Valerie finds the corpse of a young girl in a derelict tugboat anchored at a pier. The police are called, but before they can arrive from the mainland, the girl's body disappears. Then, a few days later, the cadaver washes up on a Camorach beach, but now the features of the deceased young woman have been eaten away by acid. Professor Cleghorn, a droll, chubby man in his early sixties, it tempted to play detective. But Roger Crammond, a Thomas Muir series-character detective, happens to turn up, and Cleghorn contents himself with serving as Crammond's assistant. When Crammond, a pipe-smoking marine biologist, lands on Camorach to conduct research for the British Seaweed Development Council, he discovers that smuggling and family feuds among the island's inhabitants are at the root of the local nastiness. Professor Cleghorn, who has never before been so close either to a murder or to a marine-biologist detective, gains a fund of anecdotes to tell to his classes.

Death Under Virgo was the third of four Thomas Muir
mystery novels to star marine biologist Roger Crammond
in the role of sleuth. Muir's identity constitutes a
mystery of its own, but between 1948 and 1957 he published nine full-length mysteries, each of which had
the word "death" at the beginning of its title.

*439. Vulliamy, C(olwyn) E(dward) (1886-1971). *Don Among the
       Dead Men*. London: Michael Joseph, 1952.

Kerris Bowles-Ottery, a professor of chemistry at the
"University of Ockham" in Great Britain, discovers a
traceless compound which, when mixed with food or drink,
produces in its recipients heightened feelings of well-
being and amusement. Those who ingest the concoction
laugh, sing, dance, and otherwise display the symptoms
of advanced euphoria. They also fall dead in a matter
of hours but, as Bowles-Ottery rationalizes, they expire
happily. With this lethal but humane compound at his
disposal, Bowles-Ottery sets out to rid the university
of his enemies. The first to go merrily to his maker
is Professor Gasson-Brown, the institution's faculty
bully and a man who "thunderously occupied the chair
of Greek Literature." Then a host of other vicitms
follow. Since the author intersperses his narrative
with excerpts from Bowles-Ottery's diary, readers have
no doubts about the professor's guilt. The question,
instead, is whether or not he will get away with his
crimes. Written as satire, the book includes little
serious detection but offers some of the wittiest prose
in academic mystery fiction. Set in 1928, the book also
provides many sardonic insights into the behavioral and
intellectual foibles of genteel academic folk in Great
Britain in between the wars.
    One of Great Britain's more diverse early-twentieth-
century writers, Colwyn Edward Vulliamy did not attend
a university. After receiving a private education at
home, he studied art and then anthropology before embarking on a long and illustrious literary career. Best
remembered for his biographies of such historic personages as Voltaire, Boswell, and William Penn, Vulliamy
turned in his later years to social satires and to mysteries. *Don Among the Dead Men*, which combines both of
his late-in-life interests, was the fifth of ten mystery
novels which he published before his death in 1971, and
it was the first to bear his real name. His first four
mysteries were issued under the pseudonym Anthony Rolls.
Like *Don Among the Dead Men*, most of Vulliamy's other
mystery novels tell of individuals who incorrectly sup-
pose that they have developed the perfect method for

murder. Widely respected among Great Britain's literati, Vulliamy was a Fellow of the Royal Society of Literature. A later Vulliamy mystery, *Tea at the Abbey* (484), also is included in this bibliography.

440. Wallace, Francis (1894-1977). *Front Man*. Rinehart and Co., 1952.

When head football coach Pop Tierney dies of a heart attack, Chancellor Paxton of "State University" hires Johnny Stone as Pop's replacement. Stone, a former star halfback at State, wants to continue Pop's winning tradition, but powerful gambling interests have other plans for the team. As the Saturday afternoons pass during Stone's first season at the Midwestern American football factory, a number of wealthy alumni prove that they put their own interests ahead of State's gridiron fortunes, a truly dedicated booster named Benny Bomas is murdered, and Stone himself is kidnapped. Most of the investigatory work in the story is handled by Stone, who feels that his responsibilities as coach extend to off-the-field concerns. But when Stone is held against his will in a shack far out in the countryside, the detective chores fall to Ruth Dee, the athletic department's attractive secretary. Ruth, who is described early in the book as an "excellent specimen of female on the hoof," is a resourceful woman. However, neither she nor Stone can compete with Nip, the football team's canine mascot, for real sleuthing skill. It is Nip who captures the principal villain of the piece, even as State is in the process of defeating its archrival, "Prairie," by a score of 24 to 23. As for Chancellor Paxton, he becomes a born-again athletic purist. Realizing toward the end of the book that he has allowed intercollegiate football to become his institution's main reason for being, Dr. Paxton quotes from the Bible and asks God to forgive him for his administrative sins.

A graduate of Notre Dame University, Francis Wallace spent most of his working life as a New York City sportswriter. From 1937 until 1948, he wrote "Pigskin Review" for the *Saturday Evening Post*, and he continued this column for *Colliers* from 1949 until 1956. Wallace also wrote many fiction and non-fiction books about sports. One of his novels, a prizefighting story titled *Kid Galahad* (Boston: Little, Brown and Co., 1936), was adapted for a 1937 motion picture of the same title. The film starred Wayne Morris, Edward G.

Robinson and Bette Davis. *Kid Galahad* was remade as a
1962 musical starring Elvis Presley. *Front Man* was the
second of two mysteries which Wallace wrote during his
career.

*441. Waugh, Hillary (Baldwin) (1920-). *Last Seen Wearing*.
       Garden City, New York: Doubleday and Co., 1952;
       London: Victor Gollancz, 1953.

A classic police procedural, *Last Seen Wearing* begins
with the mysterious disappearance from "Parker College"
of Marilyn Lowell Mitchell, an eighteen-year-old freshman. Parker College, a fashionable institution for females, is located in the town of "Bristol," Massachusetts, and the case is handled by Chief Ford and Sergeant Cameron of the local police. Through diligent
sleuthing, the two Hillary Waugh series-character cops
find Miss Mitchell's body in a nearby river, determine
that she was murdered, and then apprehend her killer.
Among the possible culprits in the case are male students at nearby "Carlton College," a campus security
guard, and several members of the Parker College faculty.
Though Ford and Cameron are clearly adept at policework, academic readers may find one slight flaw in their
reasoning processes. Early in their investigation they
discover that Miss Mitchell was two months pregnant and
decide that her death was most probably the work of the
man who impregnated her. Going through the roster of
males on the Parker campus, they come to the school's
president, an individual named Howland. After reviewing
Dr. Howland's long list of degrees (from Yale, Harvard,
and Columbia) and after noting that he is, after all,
a college president, the two detectives immediately dismiss him from their list of suspects.
     Hillary Baldwin Waugh was born in New Haven, Connec-
ticut, and received a B.A. from Yale in 1942. After
service as a naval aviation officer in World War II,
he began what proved to become a highly successful
career as a mystery writer. *Last Seen Wearing* was his
fourth mystery novel. Some of Waugh's books have been
published under the pseudonyms H. Baldwin Taylor and
Harry Walker.

442. Levin, Ira. (1929-). *A Kiss Before Dying*. New York:
      Simon and Schuster, 1953; London: Michael Joseph, 1954.

Two sisters, the daughters of a millionaire copper
magnate, are murdered. At the time of their deaths the

girls are students at two different but nearby institutions of higher learning in Wisconsin. Then the third,
surviving sister--a Columbia University graduate living
in New York City--finds herself in jeopardy. The villain in all three instances is a mentally unbalanced
young man who romances the heiresses in hopes of gain-
ing access to the family fortune. Written as a psychological thriller, the book has little classical detection, but it incorporates many sudden, spine-chilling
discoveries by its characters. Much of the plot tran-
spires at "Stoddard University," the school attended by
the first victim. Stoddard is graced by one of the more
zealous administrators in academic fiction. Almost before the first sister's body is cold, Dean Welch has the
presence of mind to suggest that her family might like
to make a sizeable cash contribution to the university
in her memory.

Ira Levin was born in New York City and graduated
from New York University in 1950. *A Kiss Before Dying*
was his first novel. In 1956 the book was adapted for
a United Artists motion picture starring Jeffrey Hunter,
Joanne Woodward, and Robert Wagner. Levin followed *A
Kiss Before Dying* with such horror-mystery blockbusters
as *Rosemary's Baby* (New York: Random House, 1967; London:
Michael Joseph, 1967) and *The Stepford Wives* (New York:
Random House, 1972; London: Michael Joseph, 1972).

*443. Mainwaring, Marion. *Murder at Midyears*. New York:
Macmillan, 1953; London: Victor Gollancz, 1954.

A quintessential academic mystery, *Murder at Midyears*
is set at "Collins College," a New England institution
for high-status young women. The book begins with a
short history of Collins, and then moves quickly to a
meeting of the school's department of English literature. Presiding over the gathering is Gabriel Mersey,
the dictatorial and corrupt head of the department.
Indeed, Gabriel is so loathsome that neither his colleagues nor the book's readers are especially surprised
when, three chapters later, someone slips the evil old
autocrat a lethal dose of cyanide. The sleuth in the
story is Toby Sampson, a local assistant district attorney. Helped by Henry Dane and Jill Carey, two junior
members of the English literature staff, Toby explores
the late Dr. Mersey's full closet of skeletons before
announcing the identity of the murderer. Professorial
readers will appreciate the setting for Toby's denouement speech. It is delivered at yet another department

meeting. The story abounds with real and false clues,
and the murderer, as Toby reveals, had a thoroughly academic motive.
     Marion Mainwaring was born in Boston. She received
a B.S. from Simmons College in 1943 and a Ph.D. from
Radcliffe in 1949. She then taught English at Mt. Holyoke College from 1949 until 1952. Following her short
academic career, Mainwaring served as an editor for
Houghton Mifflin, as a newspaper correspondent in
Europe, as survey director for the Massachusetts Council
on the Arts and Humanities, and as a translator and
writer for UNESCO. *Murder at Midyears* was the first of
two mystery novels which she produced during the mid-
1950s.

444. Postgate, Raymond William (1896-1971). *The Ledger Is*
      Kept. Michael Joseph, 1953.

     The sudden death of Henry Proctor, presumably from a
virulent case of leukemia, prompts the suspicious Desmond Maverick to investigate. Proctor was a high-level
British civil servant with access to atomic weapons
secrets, and Maverick, an assistant secretary to the
Ministry of Supply, was at Oxford with the deceased
during their days as undergraduates. Most of the story
takes place in and around a hush-hush scientific research station near the rural town of "Chellerton."
But the middle section of the story contains a long and
vivid flashback in which Maverick offers his recollec-
tions of Proctor at Oxford. A scholarship student and
possessed of decidedly leftist political leanings, Proctor was something of an outcast among his peers. Also
at Oxford during Proctor's stay was one John Blunt, himself a left-wing pariah at the university, and Blunt reappears at the end of the mystery to play a significant
role in its denouement. It may be a total literary
coincidence, but eighteen years after the publication
of this urbane, "insiderish" espionage yarn, the British
Government admitted that Anthony Blunt, later a noted
art historian, had been a real-life Soviet spy recruiter
while an undergraduate at Cambridge in the 1930s.
     Raymond Postgate was born in Cambridge. He attended
St. John's College, Oxford. A fellow of Trinity College,
Cambridge, Postgate was a noted social historian, a
dedicated socialist, and the author and/or editor of
more than forty books. Most of Postgate's works were
non-fiction, but *The Ledger Is Kept* was the last of
three mysteries which he produced during his lifetime.

Postgate may be best remembered today for *The Plain Man's Guide to Wine* (London: Michael Joseph, 1951), a book which has been reprinted in many, many editions.

445. Wakefield, R.I. [White, Gertrude Mason (1915-)]. *You Will Die Today*. New York: Dodd, Mead and Co., 1953.

This novel of academic nastiness and murder takes place at "Greene University," an expanding school in the American city of "Lockport." Jim Hatch, an expert in Celtic literature, is found strangled in his office. The humanities department's resident busybody, Hatch gained his primary pleasure in life from spying on his fellow faculty members and then gossiping about their darkest secrets. Since Hatch did not lack for enemies, there are suspects aplenty in the case, and Lieutenant Marshall, of the Lockport police, has no shortage of possible professorial killers to interrogate. Lieutenant Marshall is aided in his work by Judy Meadows, the newest member of the humanities department. Judy is of great help to Marshall, but her attentions to her unofficial duties are sometimes diverted by Bill Griffith, a male colleague with romance on his mind. Neither Judy nor Bill Griffith is Jim Hatch's killer. That individual, as readers will discover, had an unusual (and non-academic) reason for putting an end to Hatch's vicious tattletales.

Gertrude Mason White was born in Pawtucket, Rhode Island. She received an A.B. from Mount Holyoke College in 1936, an M.A. from Columbia in 1937, and a Ph.D. from the University of Chicago in 1950. *You Will Die Today* was her first novel. Prior to the book's publication, White had taught English at the University of Chicago, McGill University, and Wayne State. At the time the book appeared, White was employed by the University of Maryland's Overseas Division as an instructor of English at Ruislip Air Force Base in Middlesex, Great Britain. In later years, White became a professor of English at Oakland University in Rochester, Michigan.

446. Armstrong, Charlotte (1905-1969). *The Better to Eat You*. New York: Coward-McCann, 1954; London: Peter Davies, 1954. Also published as *Murder's Nest*. New York: Pocket Books, 1955.

Sarah Shepard, an attractive coed at "Lowell College" in California, thinks of herself as cursed. A boyfriend once died in an automobile accident, and a husband suffered a fatal collapse as he and Sarah walked from their wedding chapel. Professor David Wakeley, a thirty-four-year-old bachelor professor of history, does not believe in curses. He looks for other explanations for Sarah's troubles and finds them at "Colony Cove," the exclusive residential community where Sarah resides with her wealthy, ex-vaudevillian uncle Bertrand Fox. There are several scenes on the Lowell campus, but most of the important events in the story take place at the Fox abode. A romantic suspense story, *The Better to Eat You* has what is presumably a happy ending. Sarah is free at last from the non-academic evils which have controlled her life. But now she is preparing to spend the rest of her days with Professor Wakeley and to enter, as his bride, the perilous faculty milieu at a small liberal arts college.

Known as "The Mistress of the Macabre," Charlotte Armstrong was one of America's most highly acclaimed writers of mystery fiction. She was the creator of Mac-Dougall Duff (218-220), an ex-professor of history who starred as a series-character sleuth in her first three novels. *The Better to Eat You* was Armstrong's tenth mystery novel, and her seventh post-Duff venture. Two later non-Duff Armstrong novels, *A Dram of Poison* (453) and *The Witch's House* (486), also appear in this bibliography.

447. Cassill, R(onald) V(erlin) (1919-). *Dormitory Women*. New York: Lion Books, 1954.

Millie Doran, a coed at "Blackhawk University," en-counters misfortune wherever she turns. Dolphin Myers, her big-man-on-campus boyfriend, is killed in an auto-mobile accident after making an unsuccessful attempt on her virtue. Professor Penard of the English department begins to receive threatening telephone calls after appointing Millie his research assistant. And Millie's roommate mourns the mysterious disappearance of her pet baby chicken during a panty raid on the girls' residence hall. Beset by all of these depressing events, poor Millie is suffering a breakdown. *Dormitory Women* is not a conventional mystery. Nor, despite its sugges-tive title, is it an exposé of the sexual habits of fe-male undergraduates. Rather, it is a skillfully written psychological suspense story detailing one girl's mental dissolution on a midwestern American campus.

Ronald Verlin Cassill was born in Cedar Falls, Iowa. He received a B.A. from the State University of Iowa in

1939 and an M.A. from the same institution in 1947.
Cassill taught at the Iowa Writers' Workshop from 1948
until 1952 and from 1960 until 1966. In 1966 he joined
the faculty of Brown University. *Dormitory Women* was
Cassill's second novel. Perhaps because it was published in paperback or because of its unfortunate title,
the book received only a few, brief reviews. Many of
Cassill's later works, however, have met with extensive
critical acclaim. Known primarily as the author of mainstream fiction, Cassill's list of publications includes
two non-mystery novels set in academe. These are *Night
School* (New York: New American Library, 1961) and *The
President* (New York: Simon and Schuster, 1965).

448. Bawden, Nina [Kark, Nina Mary Mabey (1925-)]. *Change
      Here for Babylon*. London: William Collins Sons, 1955.

A slow-moving but well-crafted exercise in ambiguities,
Change Here for Babylon is narrated by Tom Harrington,
a lecturer at an unidentified provincial university in
Great Britain. Tom has a fight with David Parry, his
wife's obnoxious, alcoholic brother. Shortly thereafter David dies of a cerebral hemorrhage; thus Tom may
have been instrumental in producing his brother-in-law's
death. Then Emily Hunter, Tom's mistress, apparently
commits suicide by swallowing an excessive quantity of
sleeping tablets. But Geoffrey Hunter, Emily's suave
and sophisticated husband, may have engineered his
wife's demise by lacing some chocolate with extra portions of the fatal compound. Inspector Walker of the
local police investigates the matters surrounding both
unpleasantries, and his sleuthing leads to an arrest, a
murder conviction, and an execution. However, since one
of the book's central characters withholds crucial evidence at a critical moment in the proceedings, neither
Inspector Walker nor the book's readers can be entirely
certain that an innocent person has not gone to the
gallows. There are a few on-campus scenes in the tale,
but most of the important events take place away from
the university.
Nina Mary Mabey Kark was born in London. She received
a B.A. and an M.A. from Oxford. She is a writer of
children's books as well as adult mainstream novels and
mysteries. *Change Her for Babylon* was her sixth work
of adult fiction.

449. Brown, Frederic (1906-1972). *The Wench Is Dead*. New
      York: E.P. Dutton, 1955.

      The protagonist of this story is Howard Perry, a gra-
      duate student in sociology at the University of Chicago.
      Because Howard is writing a thesis about life on skid
      row, he travels to Los Angeles, adopts the guise of a
      down-and-out alcoholic, and pretends to be just one of
      the winos. Unfortunately, Howard finds that he is a
      real alcoholic, and as his study proceeds he begins to
      lose his self-identity through periodic binges which
      blur his perception. When a B-girl, Mame, is murdered,
      Howard becomes a prime suspect. The plot centers on
      his efforts to extricate himself from the mixture of
      messes into which he has fallen. Textbooks in sociology
      often describe the virtues and shortcomings of "partici-
      pant-observation" as a research device. *The Wench Is
      Dead* is better than any textbook in detailing the meth-
      od's pitfalls.
          Born in Cincinnati, Frederic Brown attented the Uni-
      versity of Cincinnati and Hanover College but did not
      graduate from either school. During the early years of
      his working life, he was a proofreader and writer for
      the *Milwaukee Journal*. In 1947 Brown's first mystery-
      novel, *The Fabulous Clipjoint* (New York: E.P. Dutton,
      1947), won him the Mystery Writers of America Edgar for
      the best first novel of that year. With that achieve-
      ment Brown became a full-time writer of both mysteries
      and science-fiction stories. His two best-remembered
      mysteries, *The Screaming Mimi* (New York: E.P. Dutton,
      1949; London: T.V. Boardman, 1950) and *Madball* (New
      York: Dell Publishing, 1953; London: Frederick Muller,
      1962), were transformed into successful motion pictures.
      The latter, retitled "Crack-Up," was released by RKO in
      1964 and starred Pat O'Brien, Claire Trevor, and Herbert
      Marshall.

450. Christie, Agatha (1890-1976). *Hickory Dickory Dock*.
      London: William Collins Sons, 1955. Published in
      the United States as *Hickory Dickory Death*. New
      York: Dodd, Mead and Co., 1955.

      Strange doings at 26 Hickory Road, London! Small,
      apparently inconsequential articles begin disappearing
      from the rooms of several University of London students
      who lodge at that address. Then Celia Austin, one of
      the residents of the coed rooming house, is poisoned to
      death. Mrs. Hubbard, the manager of the ill-fated

residence, is the sister of Miss Lemon, secretary to
Agatha Christie's famed series sleuth, Hercule Poirot.
At Miss Lemon's urging, Poirot involves himself in the
investigation. He must sift through a host of student
and non-student suspects while practicing his usual
cerebral detection. Of course, any Agatha Christie
novel is worth reading, but for regular consumers of
college mysteries, *Hickory Dickory Dock* has a special
virtue. Whereas many academic detective stories lay out,
in full detail, the evil acts of faculty members, *Hickory Dickory Dock* provides literary insight into the
depths of depravity of which students are capable.

Few users of this bibliography will require a biographic identification of Agatha Christie. The queen
of Anglo-American mystery writers, Mrs. Christie created
such classic series-character detectives as Superintendent Battle, Tuppy and Tommy Beresford, and Miss Jane
Marple in addition to Hercule Poirot. A former Belgian
police officer, Poirot emigrated to Great Britain during
World War I, became a London private detective, and subsequently starred in thirty-seven Christie novels and
collections of short stories. Perhaps because Agatha
Christie never attended college, few of her many works
deal even indirectly with academe. She did, however,
compose a quintessential "archeological dig" mystery,
Murder in Mesopotamia (London: William Collins Sons,
1936; New York: Dodd, Mead and Co., 1936). Since archeological dig mysteries *per se* fall outside of the scope
of this bibliography, this book is not accorded a separate history. However, it should be noted that the
book features in its cast of characters one Eric Leid-
ner, a sinister American professor from the "University
of Pittstown," who heads a team of international exca-
vators which is working in Iraq. And users of the bibliography might be interested, too, in *Verdict*, an Agatha
Christie drama for the stage which had a brief London
run in 1958. More a series of character studies than
a conventional mystery play, *Verdict* is built around the
involvement of a university professor named Karl Hendryk
with an aggressive female student. The drama focuses
first on the killing of Hendryk's invalid wife Anna, and
then it moves on to the murder trial which follows Anna's
death.

451.   Hardwick, Elizabeth (1916-). *The Simple Truth*. New
York: Harcourt, Brace and Co., 1955; London: Weidenfeld and Nicholson, 1955.

The Simple Truth is a multi-level courtroom drama. It
not only describes the usual examinations and cross-exam-

inations of witnesses; it also explores the relationship
which develops between two people who meet for the first
time in the spectator's gallery. The defendant is Rudy
Peck, a University of Iowa undergraduate. Rudy is accused of strangling Betty Jane Henderson, an Iowa coed,
in his room in an off-campus boardinghouse. The focal
members of the audience are Joseph Parks, a twenty-
eight-year-old Iowa graduate student, and Anita Mitchell,
the young wife of a university professor of chemistry.
Fascinated by the moral and legal aspects of the case,
Joseph and Anita attend almost every session of the
lengthy trial and meet each afternoon after court
adjourns for extended discussions of the day's proceedings.   A serious, sometimes poignant novel, *The
Simple Truth* is neither a conventional mystery nor an orthodox crime novel. But as it progresses it nevertheless offers its readers two riddles. Will Rudy Peck be
found guilty or not guilty? And will Joseph and Anita
be content to confine their relationship to conversations about Iowa's criminal justice system?

Elizabeth Hardwick was born in Lexington, Kentucky.
She received an A.B. from the University of Kansas in
1938 and an M.A. from Columbia University in 1939.   She
married poet Robert Lowell in 1949; they were divorced
in 1972. *The Simple Truth* was Elizabeth Hardwick's
second novel.

452.   Keyes, Frances Parkinson (1885-1970). *Station Wagon in
Spain*. New York: Farrar, Straus and Cudahy, 1955.
Published in Great Britain as *The Letter from Spain*.
London: Eyre and Spottiswood, 1959.

This slow-móving, romantic mystery tells the story of
Allan Lambert, a fiftyish bachelor professor of Spanish
at a "small select college" in New England, after he inherits a large fortune from his uncle. Bored by his
academic duties and frightened by the marital overtures
of Charlotte Wendell, the daughter of a local automobile
dealer, Allan sails for Spain (taking his newly pur-
chased station wagon along) in response to a "Spanish
prisoner" letter which he has received in the mail.
Although Allan correctly suspects that the letter is a
fraud, he does not anticipate the five deaths which will
take place as a result of his Spanish sojurn.   Nor, during the course of his travels, is he able to avoid several wolf-in-sheep's-clothing characters who seek to
separate him from his money.   Professorial readers may
find it difficult to comprehend Allan's behavior at the

end of the tale. After surviving his various predica-
ments, Allan marries Milagrita, a beautiful young new-
stand clerk at a Spanish hotel. He then has the opportunity to spend the rest of his fiscally secure life in
Spain doing research and lolling in the sun, although
not necessarily in that order. Yet he elects to return
to his teaching post because now, after his Spanish experience, he can give his students "something he [has]
never been able to give them before." Professorial
readers will not find the behavior of the college dean
hard to understand, however. This worthy welcomes
Allan's return because he knows rich professors seldom
demand salary increases.

Frances Parkinson Keyes was born in Charlottesville,
Virginia. She was the wife of Henry Wilder Keyes, the
governor of New Hampshire from 1917 until 1919 and the
United States Senator from that state from 1919 until
1931. After the death of her husband in 1938, she con-
centrated on creative writing and became one of America's
most popular novelists. Most of her novels focused upon
upperclass life in America and Europe. *Station Wagon
in Spain* was the third of three mysteries which Mrs.
Keyes wrote during her lifetime. Although Mrs. Keyes
did not attend college, she was awarded honorary degrees
by George Washington University, Bates College, and the
University of New Hampshire.

453. Armstrong, Charlotte (1905-1969). *A Dram of Poison.*
New York: Coward-McCann, 1956; London: Peter Davies,
1956.

The world suddenly looks bright and inviting to Kenneth Gibson, a fifty-five-year-old teacher of English at
a small California liberal arts college, after he marries Rosemary James. Rosemary, in her early thirties,
is the daughter of a recently deceased faculty colleague.
But clouds make their appearance in Kenneth's sky when
he and Rosemary are injured in an automobile accident
and when Ethel, Kenneth's domineering old-maid sister,
arrives to care for the newly married couple during
their convalescence. It would not be fair to prospective
readers to provide the melancholic details of Kenneth's
subsequent relationships with Ethel, with Rosemary, and
with Paul Townsend, the genial chemical engineer who
owns the cottage in which the Gibsons make their home.
It can be stated, however, that although the plot of
this very dark story is not grounded in academic issues,
the author offers one of the more penetrating portraits
of an introspective college teacher in mystery fiction.

Existential in tone, yet not without its action sequences,
A Dram of Poison won the 1957 Edgar Allen Poe Award of
the Mystery Fiction Writers of America.
Charlotte Armstrong began her illustrious mystery-
writing career with three novels featuring professorial
series-character sleuth MacDougal Duff (218-220). *A
Dram of Poison* was her twelfth full-length work of mystery fiction. Two other non-Duff mysteries by Armstrong,
The Better to Eat You (446) and *The Witch's House* (486)
also appear in the second section of this bibliography.

454. Innes, Michael [Stewart, John Innes Mackintosh (1906-)].
      Old Hall, New Hall. London: Victor Gollancz, 1956.
      Published in the United States as *A Question of Queens.*
      New York: Dodd, Mead and Co., 1956.

      More a satirical exploration into academic non-manners
      than a conventional mystery story, *Old Hall, New Hall* is
      set at a provincial university somewhere in Great Bri-
      tain. The central character is Colin Clout, a young
      graduate of the university, who has just returned with a
      B. Litt. from Oxford to join the English faculty as an
      "Alderman Shuffleman Fellow." Colin has two lady
      friends. One is Sadie Sackett, a university librarian.
      The other is Olivia Jory, a ravishingly beautiful and
      wealthy girl-about-town. All three of the participants
      in this romantic triangle, in addition to many other
      members of the local community, search for a mysterious
      treasure trove supposedly hidden somewhere on or near
      the university campus. There are no murders in the
      story, although there is an abundance of verbal assass-
      ination. And since all of the major characters are ei-
      ther addled or at least mildly larcenous, there are no
      easily identifiable heroes in the plot. Colin, whose
      constant bumbling cannot help but remind readers of James
      Dixon in Kingsley Amis' *Lucky Jim* (London: Victor Gol-
      lancz, 1953; Garden City, New York: Doubleday and Co.,
      1953), is best characterized as ingenuous. Professor
      Gingrast, Colin's immediate supervisor in the English
      department, develops a sudden interest in archeology
      halfway through the novel and begins to dig up large
      sections of the university's lawn. Milton Milder, a
      Yankee professor "from either Yale or Princeton," offers
      research appointments in America in exchange for infor-
      mation about the treasure. And George Lamb, another
      junior faculty member (who jousts with Colin for the
      affections of both Sadie and Olivia), stutters so badly
      that his listeners often lack the patience to allow him

to finish his sentences.

Old Hall, New Hall is an atypical Michael Innes academic mystery, not only in the sense that it lacks a murder, but because John Appleby, Innes' learned, New Scotland Yard series-character detective, does not put in an appearance. Seven other Innes academic mysteries, all of which include murders, and all of which feature John Appleby as sleuth, appear in this bibliography. These novels are *Death at the President's Lodging* (374), *Hamlet, Revenge!* (378), *The Weight of the Evidence* (405), *Operation Pax* (432), *Appleby Plays Chicken* (462), *The Long Farewell* (470), and *A Family Affair* (528).

455. Kelly, Mary (1927-). *A Cold Coming*. London: Secker and Warburg, 1956; New York: Walker and Co., 1968.

Two undergraduates at the University of Edinburgh are mysteriously drugged, and then just-as-mysteriously released (separately) in remote, rural areas of Scotland. The students, Alec Starmer and Roy Plunkett, have no idea of what they have done to deserve such treatment, nor at first does Inspector Brett Nightengale of Scotland Yard. But as Nightengale investigates the affair, he learns that Alec and Roy are unwitting pawns in a large-scale and murderous conspiracy involving new bacteriological serums which can be used for good or for evil. He finds, too, that some of the sinister business can best be investigated by attending an opera being staged at London's Covent Garden. Not the most academically oriented of the mysteries included in this bibliography—very little of the action takes place on university grounds—the well-written story nonetheless keeps its surviving participants (and its readers) on their sleuthing toes until its conclusion.

Mary Kelly was born in London and received an M.A. from the university of Edinburgh in 1951. She is a well-respected writer of lucid yet intricate mysteries. *A Cold Coming* was her first novel. A later Kelly novel, *Dead Man's Riddle* (463), also appears in this bibliography.

456. Levin, Meyer (1905-1981). *Compulsion*. New York: Simon and Schuster, 1956; London: Frederick Muller, 1957.

Compulsion is a fictionalized but slavishly accurate recapitulation of the infamous Leopold-Loeb murder case. In the actual 1923-1924 series of events, Nathan Leopold and Richard Loeb, two brilliant, teen-aged University of Chicago students, kidnapped and murdered a fourteen-year-old-boy named Bobby Franks. In *Compulsion*, the victim is named Paulie Kessler and the two killers are Judd Steiner and Artie Strauss. The novel covers the detection in the case--Leopold dropped his eyeglasses during the kidnapping, and the glàsses provided the Chicago police with their most important clue--and also describes the highly publicized trial which followed the boys' arrests. At the actual trial, Clarence Darrow acted as defense attorney and saved the killers from the death penalty. In the novel, the chief defense counsel is Jonathan Wilk, and he, too, saves his clients from capital punishment. There are several scenes at the University of Chicago in the early part of the story.

Meyer Levin was born in Chicago. A well-respected novelist, dramatist, and editor, Levin received a Ph.B. from the University of Chicago in 1924. While still a student at Chicago, he served as a reporter for the *Chicago Daily News*. The narrator of *Compulsion* is Sid Silver, a University of Chicago student who covers the Steiner-Strauss case for a Chicago newspaper.

*457.   Robinson, Robert (Henry) (1927-). *Landscape with Dead Dons*. London: Victor Gollancz, 1956; New York: Rinehart and Co., 1956.

The theft of pages from the Bodleian Library's rarest edition of *Paradise Lost* brings Inspector Autumn of Scotland Yard to Oxford. Autumn, a man of stolid working-class experiences, initially finds the elite Oxford scene both distasteful and frustrating. When old Professor Manchip (the cantankerous master of "Warlock College") is murdered, however, Autumn begins to warm to his sleuthing tasks. And when the Reverend Bow-Parley (the chaplain of Warlock College) is killed shortly thereafter, Inspector Autumn finds that the mysteries of Oxford are not so impenetrable as he had supposed. More than vaguely Inneseque, with its emphasis on droll professorial dialogue, and with many sketches of eccentric Oxford dons, this novel represents witty academic mystery fiction in its most advanced state. Though the book includes some set pieces, as well as some semi-stock characterizations, it also incorporates considerable inventiveness. When Professor Manchip is killed, for example, the culprit drags the master's body onto the college roof for public display. And toward the end of the story, a horde of naked male Oxonians, inter-

rupted while swimming *au naturel* in a secluded bywater
of the River Cherwell, chases a possible suspect through
the Oxford streets past all of the city's major land-
marks.

Robert Robinson was born in Liverpool and received an
M.A. from Exeter College, Oxford. He has been a newspaper columnist, a film critic, and a BBC television
personality. *Landscape with Dead Dons* was his first
novel.

458.   Turngren, Annette (1902-1980). *Mystery Walks the Campus*.
       New York: Funk and Wagnalls, 1956.

The mystery in the title of this innocuous story is
the whereabouts of a young woman who sends her baggage
off to "Endicott College" but fails to appear for
freshman registration. In today's world, where the
number of freshman enrollees is an exceedingly vital
academic statistic, the disappearance of a prospective
first-year student probably would send a college president out on a personal search. At Endicott in the
1950s, however, President Fillmore continues to tend his
chrysanthemums as if nothing significant has occurred,
and it is up to a small band of inquisitive undergraduates to determine the fate of the missing girl. Endicott is a coed college in the midwestern town of "Grove-
land." Near the campus is the ominous old Thurson mansion, presided over by the reclusive widow of a former
college benefactor. Before the book's conclusion the
student-sleuths learn some long-hidden secrets about
the Thurson family's real involvement in Endicott's history.

Annette Turngren was born in Montrose, Minnesota, and
received a B.S. from the University of Minnesota. After
a brief career as a schoolteacher, she entered the publishing business, holding editorial positions with a
number of magazines, book publishers, and newspapers.
A prolific author, she was best known for her mysteries
and self-help books for young people. Since *Mystery
Walks the Campus* is one of only a very few college mysteries to lack a murder, it probably was intended for
a juvenile audience. Nonetheless, because the story
includes (perhaps unintentionally) some rich satirical
passages about Endicott faculty members and administrators, it is suitable for adult readers who are properly
cynical about academe.

459. Du Maurier, Daphne (1907-). *The Scapegoat*. London:
      Victor Gollancz, 1957; Garden City, New York: Double-
      day and Co., 1957.

      John, a bachelor British academic, meets his double
      in a French railway cafe. John's look-a-like, Jean
      Compte de Gue, is fleeing his unhappy family, his tire-
      some mistress, and his tangled business affairs. John,
      who has just completed a research project in France, is
      anxious to return to his university. But after four
      drinks with Jean, he passes out. When he awakes, he
      finds himself in Jean's clothing and in the company of
      Jean's chauffeur, who insists upon addressing him as
      Monsieur le Compte. John's experiences as Jean last for
      a week, until the missing Frenchman suddenly reappears.
      During this time John, who speaks French like a native
      finds both danger and romance in his unwanted role.
      There are no campus scenes in the story, but John em-
      ploys his academic expertise in French culture to sur-
      vive his adventure.
          Daphne du Maurier was born in London. She is univer-
      sally acknowledged as the queen of quiet but tension-
      filled novels of suspense. Another of DuMaurier's no-
      vels, *The Flight of the Falcon* (496), is also included
      in this bibliography.

460. Hardy, William (Marion) (1922-). *Lady Killer*. New
      York: Dodd, Mead and Co., 1957.

      Earl Borstleman, a fortyish professor of mathematics
      at an American state university, wants to kill his
      dumpy wife. An extremely systematic man, Earl calcu-
      lates the advantages and disadvantages of various death-
      dealing methods before settling on strangulation. Then
      he decides that the probabilities of escaping suspicion
      will be better if he strangles two other dowdy, middle-
      aged women first, thereby creating the illusion that a
      mad killer is on the loose. The first of Earl's vic-
      tims is the mathematics department's secretary. The
      second is a local landlady. And then wife Sarah goes
      to her reward. Although campus security officers, the
      local police, and state troopers all involve themselves
      in the affair, the most inspired detection in the novel
      comes from Bob Adams and Anne Miner, two of Earl's stu-
      dents. Bob, a suspect in the case, becomes an amateur
      sleuth largely out of a sense of self-preservation.
      Anne, a lovely young lady whose charms have not escaped
      Earl's methodical observations, discovers firsthand

that the notion of a madman loose on the university campus is, in fact, no illusion.

William Marion Hardy was born in Norfolk, Virginia. He received a B.S. from Duke University in 1943 and an M.A. from the University of North Carolina in 1954. He was an assistant professor of communications at Purdue University when *Lady Killer*, his first novel, was published. A later Hardy mystery, *A Little Sin* (469), also appears in this bibliography.

461. Hocking, Anne [Messer, Mona Naomi Anne (189?-)]. *The Simple Way of Poison*. London: W.H. Allen, 1957; New York: Ives Washburn, 1957.

Jocelyn Waring, a professsor of drama at Oxford, is a philanderer, a liar and cheat, and something of a prankster. One night he invites all of his many enemies to meet and mingle at a party. During the course of the bizarre evening, one of his guests slips him a lethal dose of poison and, unloved by all, Jocelyn departs this world. Scotland Yard Superintendent William Austen, a Mona Messer series-character detective, is called in by the local police. The prime candidate for the gallows is Juliet Waring, Jocelyn's non-grieving widow, but Superintendent Austen knows better than to center his investigations on the most likely suspect. Some of the other individuals whom Austen interrogates before identifying the actual killer are Oxford students and faculty members, but his attentions fall on a number of non-academics as well. Members of the Oxford-area homosexual community occupy a prominent place in the story. And Juliet Waring, a writer of mystery fiction who is ever alert for new ideas, presumably trades a nefarious husband for the plot of her next detective epic.

Mona Naomi Anne Messer published over forty mystery novels between 1933 and 1960. All but one of these novels were issued under the pseudonym Anne Hocking.

462. Innes, Michael [Stewart, John Innes Mackintosh (1906-)]. *Appleby Plays Chicken*. London: Victor Gollancz, 1957. Published in the United States as *Death on a Quiet Day*. New York: Dodd, Mead and Co., 1957.

A "reading party" from Oxford journeys to the village of "Nymph Monachorum" on Dartmoor in search of the quiet it needs to prepare for examinations. David Henchman, the most studious member of the group, takes a

stroll on the moor and finds a corpse. David also finds
that he is not alone at the death scene. An old man
"smelling of tweed and tobacco" arrives shortly after
David flèes across the moor, and the elderly gentleman
pursues him. Fortunately for David, Sir John Appleby,
Michael Innes' redoubtable series-character sleuth from
New Scotland Yard, happens to be in the area. Sir John
puts an end to the chase, investigates matters, and resolves the several mysteries which have lèft poor David
breathless and in no condition to study his medieval history. *Appleby Plays Chicken* is written with Michael Innes' customary wit and skill. In addition to David
Henchman, several other Oxford undergraduates appear in
the story, and an aging tutor, Pettifor (the head of the
reading party), plays a significant role. The word "chicken" in the British title of the work refers to a quaint
American game which the members of the reading party play
early in their stay at Nymph Monachorum. With stiff Oxford upper lips, they get into an automobile, drive it
at breakneck speed without anyone giving the car direction, and wait to see who will be the "chicken" who
first grabs for the steering wheel.

Eight Michael Innes mysteries appear in this biblio-
graphy. In addition to *Appleby Plays Chicken*, these
mysteries are *Death at the President's Lodging* (374),
Hamlet, Revenge! (378), *The Weight of the Evidence* (405),
Operation Pax (432), *Old Hall, New Hall* (454), *The Long
Farewell* (470), and *A Family Affair* (528).

463. Kelly, Mary (1927-). *Dead Man's Riddle*. London: Secker
and Warburg, 1957; New York: Walker and Co., 1967.

A pleasant, inoffensive German philologist is beaten
to death in the library of the University of Edinburgh.
The victim, a man named Seifert, seems to have had no
enemies, and the local police are baffled. Persuaded
to enter the case is Scotland Yard Inspector Brett
Nightengale, in Edinburgh to attend a concert by his
wife Clarissa, a mezzo-soprano. Nightengale has very
few early clues from which to work. Seifert had pro-
pounded a controversial interpretation of the Runic in-
scriptions on a Celtic cross in the nearby town of Ruth-
well. And he had recently written a will. Starting from
this meager basis, Nightengale builds his evidence, and
eventually the identity of Seifert's killer is established. Along the way readers are exposed to the rudi-
ments of the Runic alphabet and treated to a vivid ac-

count of a student riot as the undergraduates of "Old College" campaign for their candidates for the office of rector. Moreover, readers learn, too, that quiet German philologists may have lurid pasts. *Dead Man's Riddle* is the second of two Mary Kelly novels included in this bibliography. The first, *A Cold Coming* (455), also takes Inspector Nightengale, a series-character sleuth, to the University of Edinburgh.

464. Masterman, J(ohn) C(ecil) (1891-1977). *The Case of the Four Friends*. London: Hodder and Stoughton, 1957.

One of the most unusually structured novels in this bibliography. *The Case of the Four Friends* recounts a tale of murderous intrigue told during the small hours of the morning in the senior common room of "St. Thomas's College," Oxford. The teller of the story is Ernst Brendel, a Viennese lawyer and expert criminologist, whose sleuthing led to the resolution of a murder-suicide at St. Thomas's in *An Oxford Tragedy* (360). Twenty years after his work in *An Oxford Tragedy*, Brendel is again a guest at St. Thomas's; this time he spins what he calls a story in "pre-detection" for the eager dons. Brendel's yarn is itself non-academic. It involves corruption, rivalry, and retribution within a London law firm. Nor does anyone die violently in the story, because events transpire to prevent any of the four "friends" in the narrative from committing murder. But as Brendel goes through his recitation, his St. Thomas's listeners try to guess who would have murdered whom had the opportunities presented themselves. Some of those who form Brendel's audience were witnesses to his sleuthing in *An Oxford Tragedy*. Readers with a fondness for wrestling with difficult criminological puzzles will find that *The Case of the Four Friends* offers a real challenge. And those who frequent Oxford senior common rooms late at night, after the servants have retired, will learn that at St. Thomas's an extra bottle of whiskey is kept hidden behind the "aesthetically distressing" bust of the Founder.

*465. Asimov, Isaac (1920-). *The Death Dealers*. New York: Avon Books, 1958. Also published as *A Whiff of Death*. New York: Walker and Co., 1968; London: Victor Gollancz, 1968.

Louis Brade is a member of the chemistry department department of a large, North American university. A

man of strong convictions, he refuses to publish until
he has something truly significant to communicate to his
professional peers. As a consequence of the nearly
blank publications page of his résumé, Brade has been
an assistant professor, without tenure, for eleven years.
When one of his graduate students dies in what appears
to be a laboratory accident, Brade's department chairman, Professor Littleby, suggests that the loss of promising Ph.D. candidates through careless laboratory
safety practices is not a way to speed up promotion.
Adding to our troubled assistant professor's woes is
Jack Doheny, a local police detective, who is not convinced that the student's death was accidental and who,
moreover, harbors suspicions that Brade is a murderer.
In the end it is Brade who discovers the truth of the
matter. Before its denouement the book touches upon
faculty rivalries, the "fudging" of research data, and
the poisonous properties of a host of chemicals.

Isaac Asimov was born in the Soviet Union and was
brought to the United States at the age of three. He
received B.A., M.A., and Ph.D. degrees from Columbia
University. A veritable Renaissance man of letters,
he has written scientific texts, novels, science fiction stories, mysteries, and a variety of other works.
The Death Dealers was his first mystery. At the time
the book was published Asimov was an associate professor
of biochemistry at the Boston University Medical School.

*466.   Carr, John Dickson (1905-1977). *The Dead Man's Knock*.
        New York: Harper and Brothers, 1958; London: Hamish
        Hamilton, 1958.

Mark Ruthven, a professor of English at "Queens College" in "Queenshaven," Virginia, has made an important
literary discovery. An expert in the life and times of
detective-story pioneer Wilkie Collins, Ruthven has
found three letters from Collins to Charles Dickens.
The letters, written in 1869, outline the plot of a
sealed-room mystery which Collins planned to write but
never actually set down on paper. Ruthven would like
to give his new treasures painstaking scrutiny, but
events intervene. First, his wife leaves him after a
family tiff. Then Rose Lestrange, a beautiful bachelorette friend of many of Queens' male faculty members, is
stabbed to death behind the locked doors of her bedroom.
Happily for all concerned, with the exceptions of Rose
and her murderer, Dr. Gideon Fell happens to be visiting
the Queens campus in order to inspect the Collins letters.

A fat, wheezy British lexicographer, Fell is an internationally celebrated detective and John Dickson Carr's
most famous series-character sleuth. Perhaps because
he has had some prior experience with American higher
education--he once gave a series of lectures at Haver-
ford--Dr. Fell is able to cut through the intricate romantic and political entanglements within the Queens
College community and to bring forth a solution to
the school's own sealed-room killing.

John Dickson Carr modeled Dr. Gideon Fell after G.K.
Chesterton, one of his favorite writers. A man of immense erudition and many eccentric mannerisms, Dr. Fell
specializes in locked-room murders and other crimes that
defy solution. An earlier, non-Gideon Fell mystery by
John Dickson Carr, *The Devil in Velvet* (430), also
appears in this bibliography.

467. Cooper, Briån (1919-). *A Path to the Bridge*. London:
     William Heinemann, 1958. Published in the United
     States as *Giselle*. New York: Vanguard Press, 1958.

Although much of *A Path to the Bridge* is set at "St.
Margaret's College," Cambridge, and even though it presents its readers with several sudden deaths and a series of related puzzles, the book is not an orthodox Oxbridge mystery. It is, instead, a pensive, romantic
tale of lost love before and during World War II. Rod
McKinnon and Mark Endersleigh enter Cambridge in 1936,
and both men are attracted to Giselle Masson, a young
French girl living near the university. Mark emerges
victorious in the combat for Giselle's heart, but Claire
Ainsley, Mark's aunt, discovers that Giselle bears a
striking resemblance to Christine, Mark's mother.
Christine, who died when Mark was three, was known to
have had extra-marital liaisons, and Claire suspects
that Giselle is really Mark's half-sister. Rod undertakes the task of investigating Giselle's ancestry, but
before he can ascertain the truth of the matter, the
war breaks out, and Giselle is trapped in occupied
France. What happens next is best left unrecorded in
this bibliögraphy. However, it can be noted that the
author builds suspense into the plot until the very
end. And it can be mentioned, too, that the many Cambridge scenes in the book reflect both the exhilarations
and the sorrows of undergraduate life.

Brian Cooper was born in Stockport, Cheshire, Great
Britain. He received an M.A. from Jesus College, Cambridge, in 1945. At the time *A Path to the Bridge* was

published, Cooper was a senior history master at a British secondary school in Derbyshire. *A Path to the Bridge* was his second novel.

468.   Daniels, Harold R(obert) (1919-). *The Accused*. New
       York: Dell Publishing, 1958; London: Andre Deutsch,
       1961.

The Accused is a gnarled psychological tale about an instructor of English who is arrested and put on trial for killing his wife. The instructor is Alvin Morlock, a morose, masochistic member of the faculty at "Ludlow College" in Massachusetts. Alvin's wife, Lolly, dies after a mysterious fall from a cliff. Before her demise, Lolly had affairs with various men (including at least one of Alvin's students), greatly overspent the family budget, and generally made her husband's life miserable. Thus, Alvin certainly had enough motive to murder her. But did he actually shove Lolly to her death? And regardless of the truth of the matter, what will the jury decide? Moreover, whatever the verdict, how will Alvin cope with the decision? The story is told though courtroom dialogue mixed with flashback narrative, and readers must persevere to the final page in order to discover Alvin's destiny. The book contains no classical detection, but it does include several scenes at Ludlow College. A dingy, disagreeable institution, Ludlow caters to a surly and dull-normal student clientele. It is singularly fortunate, however, in having George Gorham as its academic dean. Although he can be properly pompous, Gorham has an astonishingly deep concern for the well-being of Ludlow's teaching staff. Indeed, real-life college instructors may think they have wandered into a science-fiction epic when (on page 11) Gorham offers to dip into his savings to help Alvin Morlock pay off the huge debts which Lolly has accumulated.

Harold Robert Daniels was born in Winchendon, Massachusetts. He did not attend college. He began his working career as a laborer and mechanic. After serving in the U.S. Army during World War II (and rising to the rank of major), he became a freelance writer. *The Accused* was his third full-length mystery. In addition to msytery fiction, Daniels has written articles and books on metalworking, and from 1958 until 1972 he served as senior associate editor of *Metalworking Magazine*.

469. Hardy, William (Marion) (1922-). *A Little Sin*. New
      York: Dodd, Mead and Co., 1958; London: Hamish Hamil-
      ton, 1959. Also published as *The Case of the Missing
      Coed*. New York: Dell Publishing Co., 1960.

      Bruce Graham has a spell of ill luck. A forty-two-
year-old professor of mathematics at "Dryden University"
in North Carolina, Bruce is asked by a coed admirer to
meet her (for purposes unspecified) at a deserted hun-
ting lodge near the campus. But when he arrives the
girl is dead of strangulation. Fearing for his reputation, Bruce makes quick tracks for home. This tactic
backfires, however, because he is eventually arrested
for murder, put on trial, and the key element in his
conviction is his rapid exit from the scene of the crime.
As Bruce's execution nears, it appears as though nothing
can save him. His wife is immobilized by grief. The
police are apathetic. And only Karen Gordon, a news-
paperwoman who is the girlfriend of Bruce's defense
attorney, seems capable of action. What happens next
cannot be revealed without giving away too much of the
book's plot. However, it can be noted that Karen's life
is forever changed as a result of her involvement in the
case. And Bruce acquires enough death row stories to
regale his companions at the faculty club for years to
come.
    Lady Killer (460), an earlier mystery novel by William
Marion Hardy, also appears in this bibliography.

470. Innes, Michael [Stewart, John Innes Mackintosh (1906-)].
      The Long Farewell. London: Victor Gollancz, 1958;
      New York: Dodd, Mead and Co., 1958.

      Why should a man such as Lewis Packford shoot him-
self? An independently wealthy literary scholar, Packford seemed just before his death to be vibrant, healthy,
and in full pursuit of the enjoyment of life. Sir John
Appleby, Michael Innes' scholarly series-character detective, journeys to Urchins, Packford's country home.
to look into the matter. There, even as two more
shooting deaths take place, the New Scotland Yard inspector meets three representatives from the academic
world. The first is Ruth Packford, Lewis' widow, a
teacher at an unidentified women's college. The second
is Professor Prodger, an aging bibliophile who seems
to be a semi-permanent houseguest in the Packford home.
And the third is Professor Charles Rushout from the
"University of Nesfield," that daffy, provincial bastion

of higher learning which was the setting for Michael
Innes' *Old Hall, New Hall* (454). Rushout is at Urchins
to examine a rare manuscript which Packford had in his
possession. All three members of this learned trio become suspects in the case, although Appleby quickly dis-
misses Professor Prodger from his list because he "would
scarcely make a convincing villain even in a milieu of
low comedy in the Anglo-Irish theater." There are no
campus scenes in the novel. But there is a barrage of
literary allusions as the academic and non-academic
characters in the story discuss with Inspector Appleby
such questions as whether or not Shakespeare ever visited Italy.

The Long Farewell is the seventh of eight Michael
Innes mysteries to appear in this bibliography. The
six Innes novels which precede it are *Death at the Pres-
ident's Lodging* (374), *Hamlet, Revenge!* (378), *The
Weight of the Evidence* (405), *Operation Pax* (432), *Old
Hall, New Hall* (454), and *Appleby Plays Chicken* (462).
The Innes novel which follows *The Long Farewell* in the
bibliography is *A Family Affair* (528).

471.   Lockridge, Richard (1898-) and Frances Louise Lockridge
       (1886-1963). *Accent on Murder*. Philadelphia: J.B.
       Lippincott, 1958; London: John Lang, 1960.

       It is June, and Walter Brinkley, a retired professor
       of English from "Dyckman University" in New York City,
       decides to hold a party for some nonacademic friends in
       his posh Westchester County home. The party goes well,
       but the next day one of his guests is found shotgunned
       dead on a nearby beach. The victim is Carolyn Wilkens,
       the wife of a naval officer. Carolyn's death is inves-
       tigated by Captain Merton Heimrich of the New York State
       Police. Captain Heimrich seems to be failing at his
       task until Professor Brinkley comes with the vital clue,
       the regional American accent in the murderer's speech.
       Brinkley, you see, is one of the nation's foremost ex-
       perts in regional dialects. Professorial readers will
       find the mystery element in *Accent on Murder* arresting,
       but they are likely to be more interested in Professor
       Brinkley as a character-type. A wealthy man, Brinkley
       employs a black butler named Harrison. He drives an MG,
       works assiduously on late-in-life scholarship, and oc-
       casionally pops in at the Dyckman Faculty Club for lunch
       with about-to-retire former colleagues. Brinkley also
       keeps a pistol in his home, and toward the end of *Accent
       on Murder* he rounds up a gaggle of suspects at the point

of his gun.

Three other Richard and Frances Lockridge mysteries
appear in this bibliography. They are *Murder Is Served*
(423), *Murder Is Suggested* (476), and *The Drill Is Death*
(482). Two Richard Lockridge stories, written after
Frances' death in 1963, also appear. They are *Murder
Can't Wait* (492) and *Twice Retired* (535). Professor
Brinkley reappears in both *Murder Can't Wait* and *Twice
Retired*. In the former he plays only a minor role. In
Twice Retired, however, he is an important character.

472. Mitchell, Gladys (1901-). *Spotted Hemlock*. London:
Michael Joseph, 1958.

"Highpepper Hall" is an agricultural training college
for men in the British county of Berkshire. "Calladale
College," twenty-five miles away, is an agricultural
training school for women. As might be expected, the
romantic traffic between the two institutions is considerable, and one evening the dead body of a female,
presumably a Calladale student, is discovered in an
ancient stagecoach on the Highpepper grounds. Because
her nephew, Carey LeStrange, is serving as a tutor in
piggery at Calladale, series-character Dame Beatrice
LeStrange Bradley arrives on the scene to offer her own,
uniquely energetic brand of detection. With thirty published exploits already behind her, Dame Beatrice is not
fazed when the corpse turns out to have a mysterious
identity. Nor is she put off by the rats and rhubarb
which litter the Calladale grounds as the result of
a prank perpetrated by the Highpepper farmers-in-train-
ing. By the end of this light-hearted and entertaining
story, Dame Beatrice has found the killer, and readers
have learned a good deal about pig farming. In fact,
Spotted Hemlock is the only college mystery to reveal
the dietary regimen for piglets with oedema--sloppy
bran mash mixed with an ounce and a half of Epsom salts.

An earlier Gladys Mitchell mystery, *Laurels Are Poison* (402), also appears in this bibliography. *Laurels
Are Poison* also features Dame Beatrice LeStrange Bradley as sleuth.

*473. Pilgrim, Chad. *The Silent Slain*. New York and London:
Abelard-Schuman, 1958.

"Jonas B. Steele College for Women" in New England is
beset by problems. President Charles Rutledge Westbridge
(whose wife is known on the campus as "The Faded Bat")

is being blackmailed by Isabel Respy, the cruel and
crafty head of the philosophy department. Isabel was
once President Westbridge's secret lover. Isabel now
has a secret husband, R. Pramley Thatcher, a professor
of philosophy, and Thatcher has his own set of worries.
He is trying to live down several instances in which he
was accused of plagiarizing the writings of others. Bachelor Professor Robert Glynn, whose academic field is medieval French literature, has a wandering eye for his
more attractive students. And Regan Bogue, one of Professor Glynn's favorite pupils, seems about to have a
nervous breakdown. The difficulties at Jonas B. Steele
become acute when Regan disappears and is then found
dead of a broken skull in a remote area of the school's
pastoral property. Matt Ruffins, the local police
chief, is called in, but just when he decides that Professor Glynn is the guilty party, the professor is shot
dead in his apartment. At this point, virtually everyone in the Jonas B. Steele community becomes a suspect.
Matt continues his sleuthing, striking up a romantic
relationship with President Westbridge's daughter, Lou-
isa, in the process. He stages his denouement over
sherry in the library of the president's mansion. Laden
with clues, characters, and sub-plots, and graced by
occasional flashes of sardonic humor, *The Silent Slain*
is an exemplar of spiteful college mystery fiction. Isabel Respy is described as "a cat, all but the whiskers."
Professor Thatcher, who suffers from ulcers, is "a
bland person on a bland diet." And President Charles
Rutledge Westbridge, who raises pomposity to a high art,
is "conscious of each syllablè of his impressive name."
     The identity of Chad Pilgrim is not revealed by any
of the usual biographic sourcebooks. *The Silent Strain*
was his or her only mystery novel.

474. Fenwick, Elizabeth [Way, Elizabeth Fenwick (1920-)].
      A Long Way Down. New York: Harper and Brothers, 1959;
      London: Victor Gollancz, 1959.

      "Stanton College," one of the oldest and most dis-
tinguished schools for men in the United States, is
rocked by two mysterious deaths. First, the fiancée of
a young instructor of English expires after tumbling off
the town's highest bridge. Then someone shatters the
skull of old Professor Gibson, the campus eccentric,
all over the floor of the professor's dining room. Ordinarily, one might assume that two such violent occur-
ences would overtax the resources of a campus police

force. But Stanton College is fortunate to have Matthew
Holley as its security chief. Though Matthew is more
accustomed to handing out parking tickets than investigating murders (after all, in his ten years at Stanton
the most serious incident has been a student suicide),
he calls upon his full reservoir of latent sleuthing
talent. And, after a few false starts, he brings Stanton's reign of terror to an end. As Matt conducts his
investigations, readers' attentions are focused upon a
lady landlord, a properly sanctimonious college president, a loud and nasty faculty wife, and an instructor
of romance languages who, during his own undergraduate
days, elected such criminally easy courses as practical
mechanics and coed cooking.

An accomplished and commercially successful mystery
writer, Elizabeth Fenwick Way is best known for grisly
stories set in isolated or tightly bounded communities.
A Long Way Down was her fifth novel.

475. Graaf, Peter [Youd, Samuel (1922-)]. *The Sapphire Conference*. London: Michael Joseph, 1959; New York:
Ives Washburn, 1959.

Joe Dust, a Peter Graaf series-character, is a wisecracking American private eye plying his trade in London. His friend, Detective-Superintendent Hebden, invites Joe to take a holiday with him at "Iron Head College," where the superintendent is to attend a gathering
of noted scientists. Hebden once had ambitions to be
a physicist, and he wants to listen in at Iron Head's
"Sapphire Conference" in order to keep abreast of the
latest developments in nuclear technology. Joe and his
policeman-host no sooner arrive at Iron Head--located in
the town of Minster--than one of the biggest-name participants in the think-sessions disappears. The two
sleuths immediately launch an inquiry which eventually
resolves matters, but not until four murders have been
committed. Hardly one of the most plausible works of
college-mystery fiction, *The Sapphire Conference* nonetheless provides, through Joe Dust's commentaries, some
American views of the British world of higher education.

Samuel Youd was born in Knowsley, Lancashire,
Great Britain. A prolific author, he has written main-
stream novels, children's books, and works on cricket
as well as mystery stories. Peter Graaf is only one of
Youd's many pseudonyms. Among his other aliases are
John Christopher, Hilary Ford, William Godfrey, Peter
Nichols, and Anthony Rye.

476. Lockridge, Frances Louise (1896-1963) and Richard Lockridge (1898-). *Murder Is Suggested*. Philadelphia:
J.B. Lippincott, 1959; London: Hutchinson and Co.,
1961.

The victim in this competently constructed mystery is
Jameson Elwell, a sixty-five-year-old, widowed professor
of psychology at "Dyckman University" in New York City.
Elwell is shot dead one evening in the study of his
home. Because Carl Hunter, the professor's research
assistant, was the last person known to have seen Elwell
alive, he quickly becomes the leading suspect in the
case. Also on the list of possible murderers are Faith
Oldham, a Dyckman coed who was accustomed to visiting Elwell late at night in his home, and Hope Oldham, Faith's
protective mother. The detection is done by Captain
Bill Weigand and Sergeant Aloysius Mullins, of the New
York City police, and by Jerry and Pam North. All four
sleuths are Frances and Richard Lockridge series-characters. Jerry and Pam enter the proceedings because
Elwell's most recent book, *Hypnotism in the Modern
World*, was published by Jerry's firm, North Books, Inc.
And as it happens, hypnotism plays an important role in
the solution of Elwell's killing. Most of the story
takes place off campus, but there is one interesting
scene in Dyckman's opulent Faculty Club. It is there
that Captain Weigand interviews Dr. Eugene Wahmsley,
Dyckman's suave dean of the faculty, and the two men con-
verse in deep, leather armchairs over coffee and brandy
served by a uniformed waiter.
Frances and Richard Lockridge composed three other
mysteries which appear in this bibliography. These novels are *Murder Is Served* (423), *Accent on Murder* (471),
and *The Drill Is Death* (482). *Murder Is Served* is an
earlier Jerry and Pam North adventure set, in part, at
Dyckman University. Two Richard Lockridge stories, written after Frances' death, also appear in the bibliography. They are *Murder Can't Wait* (492) and *Twice
Retired* (535).

477. Butler, Gwendoline (Williams) (1922-). *Death Lives Next
Door*. London: Geoffrey Bles, 1960. Published in
the United States as *Dine and Be Dead*. New York:
Macmillan, 1960.

The central figure in this bizarre psychological story
is Marion Manning, an Oxford University philologist.
Grey-haired, stocky, and in her fifties, Marion shares

her home with a mysterious female named Joyo. Marion
is being hounded by another mysterious person known as
"The Watcher." When this individual claims to be Marion's husband and is then found stabbed dead in her
home, series-character Inspector John Coffin from London launches an investigation. Coffin is given some
assistance in his sleuthing by Ezra Barton, a scholar
who has been existing on grants and bringing forth snip-
pets of new knowledge about *Beowulf* for the past thirteen years, and by Rachael Henson, an anthropology student who is Ezra's girlfriend. Toward the end of the
story Rachael comes down with a near-fatal fever, and
her illness provides Inspector Coffin with the clue
he needs to fathom what is happening. Heavy with miasmic Oxford atmosphere and very effective in generating
suspense, the book is likely to keep most readers guessing (along with Inspector Coffin) until the very end.
    Gwendoline Butler was born in London. She received
an M.A. from Lady Margaret Hall, Oxford, in 1948. The
wife of a professor of medieval history at the University of St. Andrews and a prolific writer of mysteries.
Butler writes under her own name and under the pseudonym Jennie Melville. One of Butler's Jennie Melville
mystery novels, *A New Kind of Killer, An Old Kind of
Death* (537), appears later in this bibliography.

*478. Hull, Helen (1888-1971). *A Tapping on the Wall*. New
       York: Dodd, Mead and Co., 1960; London: William Col-
       lins Sons, 1961.

       Richard Macameny is not the happiest of men. Though
       he takes satisfaction in his work as a professor of Eng-
       lish, his homelife is a shambles. Wife Naomi is both
       a self-styled invalid and a shrew. She even tries to
       pollute his professional world by circulating vicious
       rumors about an attractive female graduate student who
       is his prize pupil. As Naomi's nastiness reaches new
       heights, Richard begins to wish that she were dead. Not
       a whodunit, this novel is instead a willhedoit. Follow-
       ing Richard as he plots to improve his domestic condi-
       tion, the book takes its readers deep into a tortured
       professional mind. And, in the process, it gives vent
       to the malodorous internal politics of the unnamed
       American college at which Richard is employed.
           Helen Hull was born in Albion, Michigan. She attended
       Michigan State and the University of Michigan before re-
       ceiving a Ph.D. from the Univeristy of Chicago in 1912.
       After two years as an instructor of English at Wellesley,

she joined the department of English at Columbia, where
she remained until her death in 1971. *A Tapping on the
Wall* was published after Hull won a $3,000 prize offered
by Dodd, Mead and Company for the best mystery or suspense manuscript submitted by an American or Canadian
college student or faculty member. Though some reviewers found the book cheerless, most praised it for the
skill of its writing, for the surprises contained in the
plot, and for its depiction of the darker side of academe. *A Tapping on the Wall* appeared toward the end of
Hull's distinguished writing career. A prolific writer,
she wrote mainstream novels and textbooks as well as
mysteries. One of her mainstream novels, *The Asking
Price* (New York: Coward-McCann, 1930) tells the story
of yet another henpecked academic husband. Unlike Richard Macameny, however, the protagonist of *The Asking
Price* passively accepts his wife's tongue-lashings because he feels that any domestic scandal will ruin his
chances to become chairman of his department.

479. Leslie, Warren (1927-). *Love or Whatever It Is*. New
      York: McGraw-Hill, 1960.

Hans Grimm, a bachelor professor of music at "Caruth
College," falls in love with Ann Bowen, the daughter of
a faculty colleague. Hans is in his fifties. Ann is
in her mid-twenties. For a time the romance goes
smoothly. But then Ann tells Hans that she has doubts
about their relationship and, in a fit of rage, the
professor stangles Ann to death. Caruth College is located in the picturesque village of "Hester," Massachusetts. The local police suspect Ricki Pulaski, the
town half-wit, of the killing but, of course, Hans
knows better. After Ricki is shot trying to escape capture, the guilt-ridden Hans takes up with "Beavertooth"
Pulaski, Ricki's prostitute sister. What happens next
can only be described as an exercise in human degrada-
tion. There is only a modest amount of sleuthing in
the book, and because readers know that Hans is Ann's
murderer, there is no denouement. Nonetheless, the
story has a surprising (and bitter) ending.

Warren Leslie was born in New York City. He was educated at Phillips Exeter Academy and at Yale. At the time
Love or Whatever It Is was published, Leslie was vice-
president and director of sales promotion for the Nei-
man-Marcus department store in Dallas, Texas.

*480. Dwight, Olivia [Hazzard, Mary]. *Close His Eyes*. New York: Harper and Brothers, 1961.

Andrew McNeill, a visiting poet-novelist at an unnamed university in the American Midwest, dies in a plunge from the library tower. Since McNeill had chronic drunkenness among his many faults, the police dismiss the incident as either an accident or an inebriated suicide. But when John Dryden arrives on the campus to catalogue McNeill's papers, he begins to suspect that McNeill's death may have been murder. John is a Ph.D. candidate in English at Columbia University. Alone on his first academic job, he quickly strikes up a romantic relationship with Gwyneth Jones, a clerk in the office of the institution's president. John pores over McNeill's letters and manuscripts; Gwyneth feeds him information about various faculty members who actively disliked McNeill for his boozing, womanizing, and all-around disagreeable behavior; and together John and Gwyneth identify the poet-novelist's killer. *Close His Eyes* is a college mystery in almost undiluted form. Long on talk and relatively short on action, it is built upon a network of deceptive clues, and the motive for the crime is rooted in faculty politics. Moreover, the book includes among its characters a retinue of professors, administrators, and staff members whom many professorial readers will recognize as possessing traits which belong to real-life people at their own institutions. There is, for example, Horace Wooten, the university's empire-building president, who conveniently forgets about the promises he makes to faculty members. There is Dr. Quinnell, the grand old professor of English, who remains aloof from disputes within his department. And the author renders an especially compelling portrait of Alice Crabbe, the crippled, dwarfish secretary to President Wooten. Alice lionizes her boss and would do anything to protect his reputation.

The identity of Mary Hazzard, who wrote *Close His Eyes* under the pseudonym Olivia Dwight, remains a biographic mystery. It is obvious, however, that she had a first-hand familiarity with the manners and morals of large, midwestern American universities. *Close His Eyes* was Mary Hazzard's first and only mystery novel.

481. Garve, Andrew [Winterton, Paul (1908-)]. *The House of Soldiers*. New York: Harper and Brothers, 1961; London: William Collins Sons, 1962.

The Hill of Tara, outside of Dublin, was the strong-
hold of ancient Irish kings. Sean Connor, an entrepen-
eurial reporter for the *Dublin Record*, offers to stage
a ceremonial pageant there in order to raise the Irish
public's consciousness about the site's historic value.
Sean enlists the expert help of James McGuire, a professor of archeology at Trinity College, Dublin, and
for a time the preparations for the pageant go famously.
But James discovers that Sean's major role in life is
really that of commander of an army of rebellion, and
he discovers, too, that the army plans to use the pageant as a staging area for an armed assault on Dublin.
Only James can stop the impending overthrow of the
Irish government, and he determines to do so, even
though Sean kidnaps his wife and children as hostages
for his silence. *The House of Soldiers* is not, perhaps, the most perspiration-producing suspense story
listed in this bibliography, but at least James McGuire
treats the readers of the saga to a rudimentary lesson
in the structure of the Ogham alphabet. Indeed, it is
James' fluency with this long-unused Irish script which
allows him to preserve the modern Irish Republic which
he knows and loves.

Paul Winterton was born in Leicester, Great Britain,
and received a B.Sc. from the London School of Economics
in 1928. He began his career as a London journalist,
but became a full-time creative writer in 1946. Winterton has more than thirty suspense novels to his credit.
In addition to the Andrew Garve alias, he has used the
pseudonyms Roger Bax and Paul Somers on some of his
works.

482. Lockridge, Frances Louise (1896-1963) and Richard Lock-
        ridge (1898-). *The Drill Is Death*. Philadelphia:
        J.B. Lippincott, 1961; London: John Long, 1963.

It is a foggy November evening and Reginald "Reg"
Grant, a visiting British poet at "Dyckman University"
in New York City, leaves his apartment to deliver a
lecture. In the backseat of the waiting taxi he finds
the corpse of a college-age girl, and he and the cab
driver go by the shortest route to the nearest police
station. Detective Nathan Shapiro, a Frances and Richard Lockridge series-character, commiserates with Reg
on his ill-luck at finding the body and apologetically
sends the poet off in a squad car to his appointment.
Later that evening, however, Reg is picked up by two
bogus policemen and held captive in an uptown tenement.

The dead girl, it turns out, was a Dyckman coed, and
when Shapiro cannot find the visiting Englishman for
further questioning, he puts out an all-points bulletin
for his capture. Meantime, Reg is suddenly released by
his captors, and knowing that he is now wanted by the
police, he launches his own independent investigation
into the whole puzzling business. Before the story
reaches its final pages, Shapiro interrogates a host
of Dyckman faculty members and students, the FBI and
the British Special Branch enter the case, Benjamin
Carter--a long-missing Oxford don--surfaces on the Dyckman campus, and the unfortunate Reg suffers a series of
physical beatings administered by various of the book's
villains. All in all, Reg does not enjoy his stay in
the United States. But at least he finds romance with
Peggy Larkin, the sister of the dead girl, and he presumably takes an American bride back with him to the
relative sanctity of Great Britain.

Murder Is Served (423), *Accent on Murder* (471), and
Murder Is Suggested (476) are earlier Frances and Richard Lockridge works which appear in this bibliography.
Two Richard Lockridge mysteries, *Murder Can't Wait* (492)
and *Twice Retired* (535), also appear in the bibliography.

*483. Robinson, Timothy (1934-). *When Scholars Fall*. London:
New Authors Ltd./Hutchinson and Co., 1961.

When Scholars Fall is both a quintessential Oxford
mystery and a spoof of the classic Oxbridge mysteries of
the 1940s and 1950s. Dr. Ronald George Herriott, a
singularly unpleasant historian, is shot with an eight-
eenth-century dueling pistol in his rooms in "St. Sav-
ior's College," and various of the book's characters
try their hands at sleuthing. Charles Blakelock, Edward Donaldson, Andrew Muir, and John Quince, a quartet
of energetic undergraduates, are four of the would-be
detectives. Another is Dr. Browning, a crashing bore
of a visiting professor from Harvard. And then there
is Inspector Mild of the Oxford police. A graduate of
Balliol, Mild knows that the keys to Oxford murders
are inevitably found in literary quotations. Therefore, in preparation for such cases, Mild spends much
of his free time studying the works of lesser British
writers. Although literary clues prove crucial in solving the mystery of Dr. Herriott's death, the motivation of the killer proves to be rooted in the history
of the university. Another don meets his end before the
book's conclusion, but with the arrest of the evildoer

the university's survivors are free, once again, to engage in the unfettered celebration of their eccentricities. No serious student of the academic mystery can ignore the novel. All of the stock Oxbridgians found in the works of Innes, Masterman, and Crispin parade across its pages in hyperbolized form, and they interact in exaggerated set-piece situations which satirize the plots and styles of the same authors.

Timothy Robinson was born in Croydon, Surrey, and read history at Magadalen College, Oxford. *When Scholars Fall* was his first novel. At the time the book was published Robinson was employed by the Church Commissioners for England in Purley, Surrey.

484. Vulliamy, C(olwyn) E(dward) (1886-1971). *Tea at the Abbey*. London: Michael Joseph, 1961.

They are doing very interesting scientific research at the "University of Mansterbridge" in Great Britain. Working generally in the field of hydrogenetics ("a new science"), they have developed a compound of aminoacids, pyrimidine, desoxyribose, and other substances which can produce marked personality changes in persons who consume it. One of the Mansterbridge hydrogeneticists is Hindley Bascombe, a bachelor senior lecturer. In his thirties, Hindley has become engaged to Violet Oskinlowe, an undergraduate. But Hindley's wealthy aunt, Anna Belinda Mortinghouse, would prefer Diana Starbourne as Hindley's mate. Diana is a socialite, whereas poor Violet is only a scholarship girl. Since Hindley will someday inherit stately Stathering Abbey (Anna's residence), it is important that he marry someone with the proper lineage and graces. Hindley doses Aunt Anna's tea with a liberal quantity of the new Mansterbridge wonderformula. And, lo and behold, Anna suddenly becomes so enthusiastic about his engagement that she invites Violet to a weekend gathering at the Abbey. All does not go entirely according to Hindley's plan, however. Violet is stabbed dead as she strolls alone in the Stathering Abbey gardens. The most likely suspect is Bruce Westerman, Violet's former boyfriend, but any of Anna's weekend guests (or even an interloper) could have committed the bloody deed. Many police officials enter the case, and so, too, does William Arthur Mallingham, the elderly curator of the "small but reputable" University of Mansterbridge Anthropological Museum. A man with an unquenchable passion for minutiae, Mallingham provides the crucial sleuthing through which Violet's

killer is brought to justice. Written with frequent
sardonic jibes at academics and academe, *Tea in the
Abbey* offers several scenes within the "semi-sanct en-
closures" of the University of Mansterbridge. Professorial readers will especially enjoy the episode,
near the middle of the book, in which a clutch of gos-
sipy dons turns the senior common room into a "recep-
tacle" for the "ugly fermentation" of suspicions, sni-
pings, and accusations in connection with Violet's murder.

An earlier mystery by Colwyn Edward Vulliamy, *Don
Among the Dead Men* (439), also appears in this bibliography.

485. Angus, Douglas Ross (1909-). *Death on Jerusalem Road.*
New York: Random House, 1963.

An instructor of psychology at a middling-status university in the eastern United States, Derek Crome is
writing his Ph.D. dissertation on "the atrophy of the
sympathetic imagination in the murder syndrome." In
order to get data for his thesis, he volunteers to assist the local police in cases involving psychopathic
killers. Derek gets all the raw material he needs when
he helps investigate the death of a beautiful high-
school girl found raped and murdered in a deserted mansion. *Death on Jerusalem Road* includes only a few on-
campus scenes because Derek is the only one of the
book's major characters who is connected with the university. Nonetheless, academic readers are likely to
savor the book, if only for its postscript. Derek not
only identifies the girl's murderer, but he completes
and publishes his thesis as well. Then, on the strength
of the excellent reviews which his dissertation receives,
Derek is offered a faculty appointment at Harvard.

Douglas Ross Angus was born in Amherst, Nova Scotia,
Canada. He received a B.A. from Acadia University in
1934, an M.A. from the University of Maine in 1935, and
a Ph.D. from Ohio State University in 1940. He was a
professor of English at St. Larwence University in Canton, New York, when *Death on Jerusalem Road* was published.

486. Armstrong, Charlotte (1905-1969). *The Witch's House.*
New York: Coward-McCann, 1963; London: William Collins
Sons, 1964.

This well-crafted suspense story focuses upon the

efforts of Anabel O'Shea, the wife of a young instructor, to locate her missing husband. Pat O'Shea, the object of Anabel's frantic searching, is a member of the
mathematics department at a university in southern California. Where is Pat? Well, he is being held prisoner by Mrs. Pryde, a senile old woman who thinks that
he is her long-lost son. But Mrs. Pryde is only one of
many villains in the tale. Everitt Adams, one of Pat's
faculty colleagues, is not a nice person, nor are several of Everitt's relatives. And then there is Rex,
Mrs. Pryde's vicious dog. Those professorial readers
who insist upon projecting symbolism upon college mystery novels may find that Rex, whose normal mode of com-
munication is snarling, is a perfect anthropomorphic
representation of a university administrator.

A leading figure in the history of American mystery
fiction, Charlotte Armstrong was the creator of MacDougal Duff, a professorial series-character sleuth (218-
220), who was the protagonist in Armstrong's first three
novels. *The Witch's House* was the nineteenth of twenty-
six mystery novels which Armstrong published during her
lifetime. Two earlier, non-Duff novels by Armstrong,
The Better to Eat You (446) and *A Dram of Poison* (453),
also appear in this bibliography.

487.   Evans, Fallon (1925-). *Pistols and Pedagogues*. New
       York: Sheed and Ward, 1963.

The protagonist of this often-frenzied comic mystery
is Adrian Withers. Short, red-haired, and at the age
of thirty a perpetual graduate student, Adrian is hired
to teach English at "Saint Felicitas College," a Catholic institution in the midwestern American town of
"Stratford." The complicated plot centers on the disappearance of Jim Downey, another member of the school's
English department. Foul play is suspected, and because he quickly becomes the target of the subsequent
police investigation, Adrian turns sleuth in his own
defense. Before the book is over readers are provided
with glimpses of Chicago mobsters, local drug pushers,
and thorougly confused Saint Felicitas' faculty members
and administrators. However, they will look in vain
for anything resembling serious detection.

Born in Denver, Colorado, Fallon Evans received a
B.A. from Notre Dame, an M.A. from the University of
Chicago, and a Ph.D. from Denver University. *Pistols
and Pedagogues* was his first mystery novel. At the
same time the book was published Evans was an associate

professor of English at Immaculate Heart College in Los
Angeles. An earlier, non-mystery novel by Evans also
deals with academe. *The Trouble with Turlow* (Garden
City, New York: Doubleday and Co., 1961) follows the
comedic exploits of Henry Turlow, an associate professor of English, as he attempts to adjust to his
dead-ended professional career at a small Catholic college
for women in the American West.

488. Hopkins, (Hector) Kenneth (1914-). *Campus Corpse*. London: Macdonald and Co., 1963.

The protagonist of *Campus Corpse* is Gerry Lee, a London newspaperman. Gerry travels to the University of
Texas in order to give a series of lectures on the differences between British and American journalism. During his stay in Austin, Gerry is the recipient of some
of Texas' finest hospitality—in the bed of Miss Jose
Sparrow, a dean's secretary—and he turns sleuth when
an assistant professor of English dies in a suspicious
automobile mishap. The plot of the story is very inventive and includes a phony fall-to-the-death from
the Texas Tower, the disappearance from a faculty office
of a complete set of Sir Walter Scott's novels, and the
only tour of the Alamo in college mystery fiction. In
a preface to the narrative, author Kenneth Hopkins notes
that although he "spent some months" at the University
of Texas before writing the book, none of the characters
"is totally based" on anyone he met on the Texas campus.
Hector Kenneth Hopkins is the creator of Professor
Gideon Manciple, a professorial series-character detective (271-273). Gerry Lee, the journalist-sleuth in
Campus Corpse, is another Hopkins' series-character.
Campus Corpse was Hopkins' third Gerry Lee novel.

489. Hubbard, P(hilip) M(aitland) (1910-). *Flush as May*.
London: Michael Joseph, 1963; New York: London House
and Maxwell, 1963.

Margaret Canning, an energetic Oxford undergraduate,
finds the dead body of a man as she hikes near the picturesque village of "Lodstone." When she reports the
news to the Lodstone police constable, he patronizes
her. Then, when the policeman finally agrees to accompany her to the site of the discovery, the body is gone.
Margaret is not so easily discouraged, however. Enlis-
ting the assistance of Jacob Garrod, a young Oxford anthropologist, she snoops around the village until she

convinces herself that she did, indeed, see a corpse.
And, what's more, Margaret suspects that the deceased
was either Sir James Utley, a noted sociologist and BBC
television personality, or his worthless brother John.
So Margaret snoops some more, into the Utleys' odd life
histories and, by the conclusion of the story, knows
considerably more about Sir James than do any of his
most devoted viewers. She also knows that Lodstone,
which has a history even more bizarre than that of the
Utley brothers, is a good place to avoid on future excursions from the university. Although *Flush as May*
includes a great deal of detection, several Oxford characters, and a number of lushly described university
scenes, it is not a conventional academic mystery. The
motive behind the murder in the story is not academic
in nature, and the evil which lurks in Lodstone is, perhaps, even uglier than that which is harbored in most
fictional (or real) institutions of higher learning.

Philip Maitland Hubbard was born in Reading, Berkshire,
Great Britain. He received a B.A. in 1933 and an M.A.
in 1940 from Jesus College, Oxford. A one-time British
civil servant, first in India and then in London, Hubbard became a full-time writer in 1960. *Flush as May*
was his first novel. Although he has published many
suspense novels, mysteries, and children's books since
Flush as May, Hubbard is probably best known to British
readers as a regular contributor of poems and stories
to *Punch*.

490. Macdonald, Ross [Millar, Kenneth (1915-)]. *The Chill*.
     New York: Alfred A. Knopf, 1963; London: William Col-
     lins Sons, 1964.

Dolly Kincaid, a student and part-time librarian at
"Pacific Point College" in California, disappears on
the second day of her honeymoon. Dolly's perplexed husband hires celebrated private detective Lew Archer to
find his missing bride. Because Archer's early sleuthing suggests that the case has its roots at Pacific
Point, much of his time is spent examining Dolly's connections with various members of the school's academic
community. Professorial readers will especially appreciate the information which Archer develops about Dean
Roy Barstow. The only Harvard Ph.D. at the university,
Barstow is desperately anxious for a college presidency.
By probing Barstow's relationship with his mother, Archer provides considerable insight into the deep-seated
psychological factors which prompt such lofty administrative aspirations.

Lee Archer, a cynical private eye with his own code of

ethics, is one of the most popular series-character detectives in contemporary mystery fiction. *The Chill*
was awarded the 1964 Silver Dagger by the Crime Writers'
Association of Great Britain. Kenneth Millar, Archer's
creator, is a past president of the Mystery Writers of
America. An earlier, non-Lew Archer novel by Millar,
The Dark Tunnel (410), also appears in this bibliography.

491. Drummond, June (1923-). *Welcome, Proud Lady.* London:
Victor Gollancz, 1964; New York: Holt, Rinehart and
Winston, 1968.

Out in South Africa, at Cape Town University, James
Porbeagle is perplexed by the sudden downturn in Linda
Walton's academic performance. James is a bachelor,
thirty-two-year-old lecturer in English with a photo-
graphic memory. Linda is an attractive and exceedingly
wealthy second-year student. One of the more dedicated
teachers in college fiction, James begins to explore the
reasons for Linda's ill-prepared recitations and examinations. He finds that the girl is badly shaken by
the mysterious death of her grandmother. From that
point on, James adopts the role of amateur sleuth (sometimes explaining his investigations as "university research"), and he uncovers the key to Linda's troubles
hidden deep within the Walton's large collection of
family secrets. The book includes some descriptions of
the Cape Town University campus, along with some scenes
in James Porbeagle's office, but neither the crime nor
the clues in the story are academic in nature.
June Drummond received an undergraduate degree from
Cape Town University. At the time *Welcome, Proud Lady*
was published, she was a resident of Durham, South Africa. *Welcome, Proud Lady* was her eighth mystery novel.
A later June Drummond mystery novel, *The Gantry Episode*
(515), also appears in the bibliography.

492. Lockridge, Richard (1898-). *Murder Can't Wait.* Philadelphia: J.B. Lippincott, 1964; London: John Long,
1965.

This workmanlike mystery revolves around the murder
of Stuart Fleming, a former football star for "Dyckman University" in New York City. Stuart is killed just
as he is about to volunteer information to the police
about point-shaving by the current Dyckman eleven.
The sleuthing in the book is shared by Detective Nathan
Shapiro, a New York City policeman, and by Captain Mer-

ton Heinrich of the New York State Police. Shapiro and
Heinrich are both series-character detectives. The
pair of investigators uncovers many suspects, but the
one who will be of most interest to academic readers is
Louis Clappinger, a former member of the Dyckman faculty.
Now a rich man, although no one knows the source of his
income, Clappinger has resigned from Dyckman to live
the lush life in suburban Westchester County. Moreover,
Clappinger had a longstanding hatred for the deceased
Mr. Fleming. The handsome all-American halfback, so it
seems, once had an affair with Clappinger's wife. Most
of the story takes place in Westchester County, but
there are numerous references to Dyckman and to its varsity sports program. And Walter Brinkley, the retired
Dyckman professor of English who aided Captain Heinrich
in *Accent on Murder* (471), makes a cameo appearance.

In collaboration with his wife, Frances, Richard Lockridge wrote four mystery novels included in this bibliography. These four novels are *Murder Is Served* (423),
Accent on Murder (471), *Murder Is Suggested* (476), and
The Drill is Death (482). *Murder Can't Wait* was written by Richard Lockridge after Frances' death in 1963.
Another Richard Lockridge solo mystery, *Twice Retired*
(535), also appears in this bibliography.

493. McDonald, Gregory (1937-). *Running Scared*. New York:
     Ivan Obolensky, 1964; London: Victor Gollancz, 1977.

The protagonist of this unique study in human psychology is Tom Betancourt, a wealthy undergraduate at a
world-famous university in the Boston area. Tom's suite-
mate, McKenzie Case, announces his intention to commit
suicide and then withdraws to his bedroom where he
slashes his wrists. Tom (a dedicated student of Scho-
penhauer) sits quietly in the living room, without trying to intervene, while MacKenzie bleeds to death. Only
some hours later does Tom telephone the campus police.
These events occur before the story begins, and the
book itself centers on the efforts of various university
officials, Tom's parents, and several members of the
Case family to fathom Tom's behavior. Meantime, the
remorseless Tom takes his pet cocker spaniel ("Princeton") to New York and then to Cape Cod, where he leaves
further destruction in his wake. No faculty members
appear in the novel, but Manfred Collier, the university's sage dean of students, plays a significant role.
At one point, Dean Collier attempts to attribute Tom's
callousness to his schooling. "Tell me, Betancourt,"

the Dean asks, "are you entirely the product of a private education?" Yes, sir...completely," replies the
lad. Having struck at the core of the matter, Collier
abruptly terminates the conversation with a heartfelt,
"God bless you, Tom."
     Gregory McDonald was born in Shrewsbury, Massachusetts,
and received a B.A. from Harvard in 1958. *Running
Scared* was his first novel. The book was adapted for a
1972 motion picture of the same title. The film, directed by David Hemmings, starred Robert Powell and Gayle
Hunnicutt. McDonald is best known to mystery buffs for
his subsequent series of novels starring that indomin-
able investigative reporter, Irwin Maurice Fletcher
("Fletch"), as sleuth.

494. Roberts, James Hall [Duncan, Robert Lipscomb (1927-)].
      The Q Document. New York: William Morrow, 1964; Lon-
      don, Jonathan Cape, 1967.

     The protagonist of this unusual novel is George Cooper,
a professor of theological history at "Cummerland College" in the eastern United States. After George's
wife and small daughter die in a fire, he takes an emer-
gency leave in order to recover from his grief. He travels to Japan and acquires a temporary job translating
medieval manuscripts for Victor Hawkins, a sinister Englishman who describes himself as a dealer in rare books.
And he meets Willa Cummings, a down-at-the-heels newspaper correspondent, with whom he falls in love. The
primary mystery in the story centers on the authenticity
of a first-century manuscript--"The Q Document"--which
appears to raise serious doubts about the divinity of
Jesus Christ. A dedicated literary sleuth, George
Cooper traces the writing to its surprising source.
Meantime, evil forces (including Victor Hawkins) make
his life difficult. Neither a conventional detective
story nor a conventional thriller, *The Q Document* is instead an exploration into the human condition. Professor Cooper does lonely battle with Japanese bureau-
crats during the course of his adventure; various of
the book's characters (including a Catholic priest)
worry that *The Q Document* might shake the foundations
of Christianity; and through George Cooper's research
readers are offered a look at the Nazi persecution of
Jewish scholars during World War II.
     A well-respected American free-lance writer, Robert
Lipscomb Duncan has ventured into many literary genres
during the course of his career. In addition to mys-

teries, he has published biographies, mainstream novels,
and comedies. He employed the pseudonym James Hall Roberts on several of his early works. Duncan is perhaps
best known to devotees of college and university-orien-
ted fiction for *The General and the Co-Ed* (Garden City
New York: Doubleday and Co., 1963), a light, semi-satirical story about a United States Army general who becomes president of "McDermott College" in California.
The General and the Co-Ed was issued under the name Bob
Duncan.

495. Wilson, Colin (Henry) (1931-). *Necessary Doubt*. London:
      Arthur Barker, 1964; New York: Trident Press, 1964.

Professor Karl Zweig, a refugee from Hitler's Germany,
chances to see Gustav Neumann emerging from a restaurant in the Shepherd's Bush section of London. Gustav
was one of Zweig's students at the University of Heidelberg, and the professor has reason to believe that
his ex-pupil is now a confidence man who attaches himself to wealthy old men and then murders them. In the
company of a good friend, a prominent British police
official named Charles Grey, Zweig tracks Gustav down
and attempts to ascertain whether or not he is a killer.
There are a few flashback scenes from Heidelberg in the
book, but most of the story takes place in London and
in Bury St. Edmunds, where Zweig and Grey finally locate Gustav while a snowstorm rages through the Suffolk
countryside. *Necessary Doubt* is several cerebral not-
ches above most of the works cited in this bibliography.
The character of Karl Zweig is modeled upon Paul Til-
lich, the eminent theologian, and Zweig often interrupts his sleuthing to discourse on moral philosophy.
Moreover, as the plot develops readers are led to consider some of the tacit implications of such matters
as religious conversions, euthanasia, suicide, and modern psychiatry. Gustav Neumann proves that his studies at Heidelberg were not in vain. When confronted
by Professor Zweig, he is able to mount a series of
effective rhetorical arguments to counter those of his
former mentor.
    Colin Wilson was born in Leicester, Great Britain. He
attended school until he was sixteen. A leading exis-
tentialist writer, Wilson's list of publications includes plays, mainstream novels, and works of non-fiction as well as mysteries. *Necessary Doubt* was his
third mystery novel.

496. Du Maurier, Daphne (1907-). *The Flight of the Falcon*.
London: Victor Gollancz, 1965; Garden City, New York:
Doubleday and Co., 1965.

Set in Italy, this unusual mystery has as its protagonist a young, university-educated tour guide, Armino
Fabbio. While conducting a group of English school-
teachers through a cathedral in Rome, Armino finds the
murdered body of a woman who bears a resemblance to his
childhood nurse. In order to satisfy his compulsive
curiosity, Armino returns to his birthplace, the city
of Ruffano, and takes a job as a librarian at the local
university. Armino eventually finds that the killing
in Rome is linked to other, equally lethal events in
Ruffano. During the course of his sleuthing, Armino has
substantial contact with professors, students, and staff
members at the university. Although *Flight of the Falcon* is not a conventional college mystery, it does provide its readers with many lingering looks at life in an
Italian institution of higher learning.

An earlier novel by Daphne du Maurier, *The Scapegoat*
(459), is also included in this bibliography.

497. Fleming, Joan Margaret (1908-). *Nothing Is the Number
When You Die*. London: William Collins Sons, 1965;
New York: Ives Washburn, 1965.

The protagonist of this very different college mystery
is Nuri Bey, an impoverished Turkish philosopher-scholar.
Though he has never before been out of his native land,
Nuri is asked by Torgut Yemish, a wealthy Istanbul businessman, to travel to England in search of Jason Yemish, Torgut's missing son. Jason, when last heard from,
was an Oxford undergraduate. Nuri flies to London and
then takes a train to Oxford where he attempts to ascertain Jason's whereabouts. As the plot develops, Nuri
finds that Torgut Yemish is, in reality, a major figure
in international drug trafficking and that Jason's disappearance is connected with his father's nefarious
dealings. The book contains a number of Oxford views,
as seen through Nuri's eyes, and the amateur Turkish detective even has the opportunity to stay at the Randolph
Hotel and to visit Blackwell's bookshop.

Joan Margaret Fleming was born in Horwich, Lancaster-
shire, Great Britain, and attended the University of Lau-
sanne. A prolific mystery writer, she introduced Nuri
Bey in *When I Grow Rich* (London: William Collins Sons,

1962; New York: Ives Washburn, 1962), a book which won
the 1962 Crime Writers Association critics award. *Nothing Is the Number When You Die* was Nuri Bey's second
literary adventure.

498.   Hart, Janet. *File for Death*. London: T.V. Boardman,
         1965.

Ellie Gerald, an undergraduate at an unnamed American
university, is stabbed dead with a nail file one night
as she walks across the campus. The police assume that
Ellie committed suicide, but Jinsie Cartwright, Ellie's
roommate, thinks otherwise. Sleuthing alongside Richard
Fletcher, her boyfriend, Jinsie proves that Ellie did not
take her own life and, what's more, she unmasks Ellie's
murderer. The latter task puts Jinsie in considerable
personal peril, but she survives her dangerous adventure. In addition to Ellie, Jinsie, and Richard, two
other participants in the story deserve mention. George
Harrington, a professor of English, is noteworthy for
his lectures on the relative merits of murder and suicide. And Big King, one of the "usual pack" of campus
dogs, is the only character in the book to profit from
Ellie's demise. As Ellie lies dying in a pool of blood,
Big King leads his canine compatriots to the murder
scene for a nocturnal banquet.

499.   Household, Geoffrey (1900-). *Olura*. London: Michael
         Joseph, 1965. Boston: Little, Brown and Co., 1965.

It seems like the middle-aged academic's dream come
true. Philip Ardower, a fellow in comparative philosophy at an unidentified Oxford college, is lying in
his Spanish hotel room one night when Olura Manoli, a
beautiful young heiress, quietly slips in through a window and whispers that he should not put on the lights.
But, as a don's luck would have it, Olura only wants
Philip to advise her about the disposition of a corpse
she has just found in the bathroom of her own room.
Summoning all of his British gallantry, Philip not only
advises Olura about her problem; he also stuffs the
dead body into the trunk of a car, drives to a remote
coastal location, and dumps the unwanted cadaver into
the sea. But bodies dumped into the ocean tend to wash
up on shore; soom Lieutenant Pedro Gonzales of the local
police is on the case. He thinks Ardower is a British
secret agent. It is all that Philip and Olura can do,
during the last two-thirds of the story, to disabuse him

of this notion and, in self defense, to get to the bottom
of the mystery. There are no campus scenes in this taut,
well-written novel, but Philip (who, as a fellow, does
not like to be called "Professor") behaves in properly
impulsive professorial ways. And the master of Philip's
college makes a brief appearance when Philip telephones
him for assistance. Reluctant to become involved, the
master says that the college will stand by Philip if he
is engaged in a political scandal, or in a sexual affair,
or if he has committed the murder. "But," the master
warns, "the college cannot be expected to condone scandal,
murder, and fornication simultaneously."

Geoffrey Household was born in Bristol, Great Britain,
and received a B.A. (honors) in English from Magdalene
College, Oxford. He served as a lieutenant colonel in
British Intelligence during World War II. *Olura* was his
tenth mystery novel. Known primarily as a "chase novelist," Household portrays many of his male protagonists
(such as Philip Ardower) in the vein of John Buchan's
Richard Hannay in *The Thirty-Nine Steps* (London: W.
Blackwood and Sons, 1915; New York: George H. Doran,
1915).

500. Kenyon, Michael (1931-). *May You Die in Ireland*. Lon-
      don: William Collins Sons, 1965; New York: William
      Morrow, 1965.

William Foley, an asthmatic and pudgy associate professor of mathematics at a university in the American
Midwest, inherits a castle in Ireland. Naturally, he
calls a travel agent, books a flight to the Emerald
Isle, and flies off to inspect his new property. But
a ring of international spies conceals some microfilmed
allied defense secrets in the packet of papers he receives from the travel agency, and Foley becomes an unwitting courier. When he arrives in Ireland the professor learns to his chagrin that his castle is, in fact,
a rundown manor house, so deteriorated that the cost of
its restoration would far exceed his paltry fiscal resources. Moreover, he finds that international spies
play for keeps, and during his stay in Ireland he is
robbed, beaten, kidnapped, and in various ways preven-
ted from enjoying his first trip to the land of his
ancestors. Smoothly written and incorporating both wit
and humor, *May You Die in Ireland* combines elements of
the conventional mystery with ingredients of modern,
not-to-be-taken-seriously espionage thrillers. Pro-

fessor Foley is portrayed more as a victim of circumstances than as a hero, and some of the scenes--such as
this one, toward the end of the book, where Foley is
pursued by villains to a mock medieval banquet--are
written largely as farce. It will not give too much
of the plot away to report that Foley, though wheezing
and exhausted, survives his harrowing experiences. And
on his return flight to America he is accompanied by
Mary Casey, a comely Irish lass, who is shortly to become his bride.

Michael Kenyon was born in Huddersfield, Yorkshire,
Great Britain. He received a B.A. and an M.A. from Oxford and then did graduate work during the 1954-1955
academic year at Duke University. Before moving to the
Isle of Jersey in 1966, to pursue a full-time career as
a creative writer, Kenyon worked as a reporter and editor for various British newspapers. He was a visiting
lecturer in journalism at the University of Illinois
from 1964 to 1966. *May You Die in Ireland* was Kenyon's
first novel. A later Kenyon mystery, *The Whole Hog*
(510), is also included in this bibliography. *The
Whole Hog* is set at "Illinois State College."

501. Smithies, Richard H(ugo) R(ipman) (1936-). *An Academic
Question*. New York: Horizon Press, 1965. Also published as *Death Gets an A*. New York: Signet Books,
1968.

An Academic Question is a semi-serious takeoff on
drug-related college detective stories. The protagonist of the tale is Campbell Craig, a professor of Latin
literature at New York City's "Kingston University,"
which bears a very strong resemblance to Columbia. One
of Campbell's graduate students, an annoyingly aggressive young lady named Iris Macready, has a $500-per-month
hashish habit. In search of funds, Iris attempts to
blackmail the professor. Campbell, as Iris has discovered, once published under his own name the nearly
completed Ph.D. thesis of a student who died in an automobile accident. When Iris is found dead in Campbell's
office, her throat cut with a bronze letter opener, various amateur and professional sleuths enter the fray in
search of Iris's killer. Professor Campbell is, of
course, involved in the detection, as are Peter Dart
(a customs agent) and Inspectors McAlpin and Golgram
of the New York police. As the story proceeds the author offers his readers a wide assortment of set-piece

situations, literary clues, and academic character-types,
and his players sometimes regale each other with quasi-
witty repartee. And, oh yes, Professor Campbell's wife
is a well-known writer of mystery fiction. She plays
only a minor role in the book, however, because she is
out "in the country," trying to extricate her latest
heroine from the washroom on the Orient Express.
  Richard Smithies was born in Canberra, Australia. He
received a B.A. from Harvard in 1957 and an LL.B. from
Harvard Law School in 1960. *An Academic Question* was
his first novel. Although *An Academic Question* met
with only lukewarm response from reviewers, several of
Smithies' subsequent mysteries--most of them set in suburban Connecticut--have been widely praised.

*502.   Blake, Nicholas [Day-Lewis, Cecil (1904-1972)]. *The Mor-
        ning After Death*. London: William Collins Sons, 1966;
        New York: Harper and Row, 1966.

  Nigel Strangeways, Cecil Day-Lewis' erudite British
series-character detective, comes to America to visit
an old Oxford classmate. His friend, Zeke Edwards, is
now Master of Hawthorne House at "Cabot University" in
New England. Strangeway's sojourn proves to be a bus-
man's holiday, however, when a Cabot professor of classics is found shot dead on the campus. Strangeways
identifies the murderer, but not until he experiences
American chocolate ice cream, a Cabot-Yale football
game, and the sexual delights offered by "Sukie" Tate,
a free-loving graduate student who is writing a dissertation on the works of Emily Dickinson. Despite Strangeways' obvious proficiency as a sleuth, the book contains
little in the way of sophisticated ratiocination. It
is better read, perhaps, as the author's attempt to
thrust his literary knife deep into the corpus of American academic morals and customs.
  Cecil Day-Lewis was born in Ballintubber, Ireland.
The Poet Laureate of Great Britain from 1968 until his
death four years later, he was at various points in his
career a lecturer at Trinity College, Cambridge, and a
professor of poetry at Oxford. Day-Lewis was also a
prolific writer of mysteries, all of which were issued
under the Nicholas Blake pseudonym. *The Morning After
Death*, Day-Lewis' last detective saga, was published
shortly after he returned to Great Britain from Harvard,
where he spent the 1964-1965 academic year as the
Charles Eliot Norton Professor of Poetry. In addition
to *The Morning After Death*, two other Day-Lewis Nigel

Strangeways novels deserve mention in this bibliography.
Though neither of them is sufficiently "academic" to
warrant a separate listing, both incorporate professors
in ancillary roles. *Thou Shell of Death* (London: William Collins Sons, 1936. Published in the United States
as *Shell of Death*. New York: Harper and Brothers,
1936) includes in its cast a dapper British don named
Philip Starling, the world's foremost authority on Ho-
meric civilization and literature. And *The Sad Variety*
(London: William Collins Sons, 1964) describes the kidnapping by Russian agents of Lucy Wragby, whose father
Alfred, is a British professor in possession of valuable
Allied defense secrets.

503. Cadell, (Violet) Elizabeth (1903-). *The Corner Shop*.
      London: Hodder and Stoughton, 1966; New York: William
      Morrow, 1967.

After the death of his mother, Professor Hallam must
catalog the contents of his ancestral home. Hallam is
a fortyish, bachelor professor of medicine at "a famous
[British] university," and his home, "Hill House," is
located near the picturesque Hampshire village of
"Holme." Hallam requires the services of a secretary
for his cataloging task, but the first three women sent
out by a London agency object to the professor's demanding nature, and none of them stays in his employ for
more than a day. Lucille Abbey, the twenty-eight-year-
old, "blonde and beautiful," owner of the agency, travels to Hill House in order to inspect the job first
hand. She stays on, falls in love with Hallam, and
finds that a collection of paintings (which Hallam
naively believes to be worthless) is missing from the
estate. From that point, the plot of the frothy story
incorporates two mysteries: Will Lucille and Hallam
be able to locate the missing paintings? Will Hallam
propose marriage? Much of the action takes place in
Paris, to which Lucille and the professor repair in
search of the purloined art work. There are no murders
in the novel. Nor is there any sophisticated detection.
In fact (as several of the ancillary characters in the
tale observe), the most puzzling aspect of the whole
affair is why the bright, warm-hearted Lucille would
want to wed Professor Hallam. Described by one of Lucille's lady friends as "not animal; he's vegetable and
mineral," Hallam is depicted as nasty, absent-minded,
uninterested in sex, and fully set in his bachelor ways.
Violet Elizabeth Cadell was born in Calcutta, India,

educated in Great Britain, and has spent much of her
adult life in Portugal. Although she has published
several mysteries, she is best known for her nearly fifty
light-hearted, romantic mainstream novels.

504. Davis, Dorothy Salisbury (1916-). *Enemy and Brother*.
New York: Charles Scribner's Sons, 1966; London: Hodder and Stoughton, 1967.

The protagonist-narrator of this involved novel is
John Eakins, a professor of English at an unidentified
American university. Eakins travels to Greece to investigate the murder of Alexander Webb, an American journalist. The murder took place seventeen years earlier,
during the Greek Civil War, and Eakins, then a young
overseas correspondent accompanying Webb at the fighting
front, was falsely arrested for the crime. Mysteriously released shortly thereafter--and sent back to the
U.S.A.--Eakins now wants to learn the real circumstances
behind Webb's death. When Eakins returns to Greece, he
seeks out Paul Stephanov, the man who had accused him of
Webb's murder. Stephanov, now blind, accompanies Eakins
in his search for Webb's killer, and their joint sleuthing leads them to Russian agents, to CIA operatives, and
to a plot to overthrow the Albanian government. As cover for his activities, Eakins pretends to be conducting
research for a biography of Lord Byron. *Enemy and Brother* incorporates many of the plotting devices of an
international espionage thriller, but in contrast to
most such epics, the book is written in quiet, literate
and sensitive prose. While considerable suspense is
built into the narrative, the emphasis is upon the growing relationship between Professor Eakins and Paul Stephanov, two former enemies who are now allied in detection. Much of the tale is told in flashbacks, and the
story is based, in part, upon the real-life 1948 murder
of a C.B.S. correspondent George L. Polk who, at the
time of his death, was covering the Greek Civil War.
Dorothy Salisbury Davis was born in Chicago, Illinois,
and received an A.B. from Barat College in 1938. One of
America's premier mystery writers, Davis served in 1955-
1956 as president of the Mystery Writers of America.
Enemy and Brother was Davis's thirteenth full-length
work of fiction, and it is sometimes considered a mainstream novel rather than a mystery. A more conventional
detective-style mystery by Davis, *Shock Wave* (548),
appears later in this bibliography.

*505. Devine, D(avid) M(cDonald) (1920-). *The Devil at Your Elbow*. London: William Collins Sons, 1966; New York: Walker and Co., 1967.

This suspenseful tale of academic intrigue is set at "Hardgate University," a British institution which is generally conceded, even by its staunchest admirers, to be much inferior to Oxford or Cambridge. Edward Haxton, a non-distinguished economist, is accused of embezzling twenty pounds from the summer school budget. He retaliates by threatening to reveal new facts about an old Hardgate sex scandal. When Haxton is found murdered shortly thereafter, several of Hardgate's dons are suspected of the crime. Inspector Finney of the Hardgate CID leads the investigation, but the author provides a great many real and false clues through which readers can do their own, independent detecting. *The Devil at Your Elbow* is noteworthy for the well-realized academic characters who appear in the story. Edward Haxton, whose chief failing in the minds of some members of the Hardgate community is that he allows the garden around his home to become overrun with weeds, is suitably obnoxious. Peter Bream, a neophyte member of the economics faculty, has all of the charm and good looks which real-life economists often admire in themselves. And Graham Louden, the fortyish, widower dean of the Faculty of Law, is appropriately soberminded as he plays amateur sleuth, finds himself on the list of suspects, and carries on the courtship of a girl who is half his age.

Born in Greenock, Scotland, David McDonald Devine was educated at the University of Glasgow and the University of London. At the time *The Devil at Your Elbow* was published he was deputy secretary of The University of St. Andrews, Scotland. *The Devil at Your Elbow* was his fifth work of mystery fiction. A later Devine mystery, *Death Is My Bridegroom* (522), also appears in this bibliography.

506. Queen, Ellery (pseud). *The Devil's Cook*. New York: Pocket Books, 1966.

Terry Miles, the wife of a professor of economics at an American institution known at "Handclasp University," disappears one evening just before her husband, Jay, returns home for dinner. Terry, a young lady who is "five feet four of scenic stuff and [isn't] particular who explores[s] the scenery," has a habit of wandering

off in search of new sexual experiences. Thus Jay is
not immediately concerned. Two days later, however,
Terry is found strangled to death in a vacant house,
and Jay becomes the number one suspect. Police Captain
Bartholdi is in charge of the case. By probing Terry's
torrid life history, Bartholdi exonerates Jay and roots
out the real killer. Although many of the characters
in the story are Handclasp faculty members and graduate
students, the denouement does not hinge on academic
matters. In fact, the decisive clue is related to the
level of seasoning which Jay likes in his ragout.

The Devil's Cook was written by an anonymous person or
persons under contract to Pocket Books. It was not composed by Frederick Dannay and Manfred Lee, the two originators of the Ellery Queen pseudonym. Another anonymously written Ellery Queen novel, *The Campus Murders*
(530), appears later in this bibliography.

*507. Bernard, Robert [Martin, Robert Bernard (1918-)]. *Death
Takes a Sabbatical*. New York: W.W. Norton, 1967. Pub-
lished in Great Britain as *Death Takes the Last Train*.
London: Constable and Co., 1967.

Forty-four-years-old, a widower, and a professor of
modern history (and sometimes dean) at an unidentified
American university, Richard Halsey takes a sabbatical
leave in Great Britain. Shortly after his arrival, he
finds himself sharing a car on the London underground
with what appears to be a dead body. Richard reports
the incident to the police, travels to his rented cottage in the quaint Oxfordshire village of "Cheswold,"
and prepares to get down to the business of studying
the lives and times of French royal emigrés to England in
the nineteenth century. But the incident in London is
not settled. The police cannot find the corpse which
Halsey claims to have seen. Furthermore, uninvited in-
truders seem to be extremely interested in the contents
of the professor's rented home-away-from-home. As Richard's sabbatical proceeds, the French emigrés remain
largely unresearched, but Richard becomes ever-more-
deeply embroiled in what turns out to be a terror-filled
affair. A classic professor-on-sabbatical mystery, the
book offers several scenes at Oxford, an especially arresting vignette at Blenheim Palace, and a great deal
of atmospheric action in Cheswold and its immediate
vicinity. There are several British police officials
in the story, but Richard does much of his own sleuthing. And he does some romancing, too. Although his
leave turns out to be something less than a success from
the professional standpoint, Richard becomes engaged to
Martha Bryant, a comely Cheswold widow.

Robert Bernard Martin was born in La Harpe, Illinois, and received an A.B. from the University of Iowa in 1943, an A.M. from Harvard in 1947, and a B. Litt. from Oxford in 1950. He was a member of the English department at Princeton University from 1951 until his retirement in 1975. Under his own name, Martin has written and edited many professional works. He employs the pseudonym Robert Bernard on his mysteries. *Death Takes a Sabbatical* was his first mystery novel. His second excursion into mystery fiction, *Deadly Meeting* (533) also is included in this bibliography.

508. Dalmas, Herbert. *The Fowler Formula*. Garden City, New York: Doubleday and Co., 1967, London: Victor Gollancz, 1968.

"Dorset University" is a high-caliber institution snuggled in the recesses of southern New England. John Fowler, a prominent member of the English department, is framed for the murder of a local businessman. Knowing that his arrest is imminent, John leaves his home, goes into hiding, and attempts to discover the identity of the actual killer. Since he chooses to conceal himself for long periods in his campus office, the book provides real-life professors with insight into what happens in faculty office buildings during the wee hours of the morning. Professorial readers also will find instruction in the portrait of Prescott Smith, Dorset's president. Flashing a smile which "he [does] not attempt to make merry," Smith has as his goal the prevention of any damage to the university's good name. Although John Fowler heretofore has been a model academic citizen, President Smith has no difficulty believing him guilty of murder, and he makes every effort to insure John's speedy apprehension and conviction.

509. Keating, H(enry) F(itzwater) (1926-). *Inspector Ghote Caught in the Meshes*. London: William Collins Sons, 1967; New York: E.P. Dutton, 1968.

The Strongbow brothers travel from America for a vacation in India. One of the pair, Hector, is a nuclear engineer. The other, Gregory, is a professor at an unidentified American university and one of the world's leading authorities on hydrodynamics. The brothers separate for a time, and Hector is murdered in what first appears to be a simple highway robbery. Inspector Ganesh Ghote of the Bombay CID is a doubting Thomas, however, who thinks that Hector's death may have been planned. Inspector Ghote is a well-known H.R.F. Keating series-character sleuth. As he inves-

tigates the affair, he must contend with obstructionists
in the Indian police bureaucracy and with Professor
Gregory Strongbow, who insists on conducting unofficial
detective work on his own. Indeed, Gregory's impulsive behavior so impedes Ghote's progress on the case
that the professor emerges as a prime suspect. The
book does not include any campus scenes, but the characterization of Gregory Strongbow will please readers
who appreciate portraits of angry, headstrong American
professors attempting to take the law into their own
hands in foreign locales.

Henry Raymond Fitzwater Keating was born in St. Leo-
nards-on-the-Sea, Sussex. He received a B.A. in 1952
from Trinity College, Dublin. A one-time London journalist and reviewer of crime novels for *The Times,* Keating has won many prizes for his mystery fiction. Inspector Ghote, a fallible but resourceful Indian police
official, has appeared in eighteen of Keating's works.
Inspector Ghote Caught in the Meshes was Inspector
Ghote's ninth published adventure.

510. Kenyon, Michael (1931-). *The Whole Hog.* London: Wil-
liam Collins Sons, 1967. Published in the United
States as *The Trouble with Series Three.* New York:
William Morrow, 1967.

The Whole Hog is the second (and last) story in the
bibliography to deal extensively with academic piggery.
The first, Gladys Mitchell's *Spotted Hemlock* (472), is
set in large part at "Calladale College," an agricultural training school in Great Britain. *The Whole Hog* has
a British protagonist--twenty-nine-year-old Arthur
Appleyard, a visiting swine nutritionist from Leeds
University--but it is set at "Illinois State College"
in the American Midwest. Arthur is at the Illinois
institution under a grant from the United States Air
Force and the National Aeronautics and Space Administration to test various pig feeds. Because pigs have
digestive systems similar to those of human beings,
Arthur's research has important implications for space
travel. International spies, interested in Arthur's
findings, kill his laboratory assistant and kidnap
Humphrey, his prize hog. Captain Petty of the local
police handles some of the detection in the story, but
finding purloined porkers is not really in his line. In
the end, it is up to Arthur and Liz Salucka, Arthur's
American co-worker and girlfriend, to bring the case to
a successful conclusion. And Humphrey, too, has an im-

portant role in the final, climactic scene. Mixing
satire with serious mystery, *The Whole Hog* offers a
wealth of sardonic commentary on space research, on
American police methods, and on life at a large midwestern emporium of higher learning where the experimental animals seem to be at least as intelligent as
the school's human element.

The Whole Hog is the second Michael Kenyon novel to
appear in this bibliography. The first is *May You Die
in Ireland* (500). A one-time editor and reporter for
various British newspapers, Kenyon was a visiting lecturer in journalism at the University of Illinois from
1964 until 1966.

511. Peters, Ellis [Pargeter, Edith Mary (1913-).]. *Black
      Is the Colour of My True Love's Heart.* London: Wil-
      liam Collins Sons, 1967; New York: William Morrow,
      1967.

This combination country-house, gothic, and college
mystery is set at a music school located in a remote
corner of the British Midlands. The institution, known
as "Follymead College," is a branch campus of an unidentified "parent university." Follymead is housed in a
dark, turreted structure which some of the characters
in the book disparagingly refer to as "Nightmare Abbey."
A folk-music festival is being held at Follymead, but
the gaiety is interrupted when Lucien Galt, a world-famous performing artist, mysteriously disappears. Then
Edward Arundale, the dour, humorless warden of Follymead, is found murdered. The police work is handled
by George Felse, a British CID officer who is an Ellis
Peters series-character sleuth. George comes on the
scene because his son Dominic, an Oxford undergraduate,
is a festival participant. Dominic calls his father to
alert him to the problems at Follymead, and he subsequently helps his dad with some of the detection. Although most of the players in this tale are not conventional university students or faculty members, seven-
ty-five-year-old Professor Roderick Penrose from the
parent university is on hand to lend the story some academic status. The master of ceremonies at the folk-
music event, Penrose displays uncharacteristically good
professorial judgement. Toward the end of the book, when
the festival seems to be imploding thanks to ceaseless
talk about the murder, petty jealousies among the assembled guests, and the marathon musical laments of distraught female singers, Professor Penrose packs his bags

and makes a rapid exit from the scene.

Edith Mary Pargeter was born in Horsehay, Shropshire, Great Britain. She served as a petty officer in the Women's Royal Navy Service from 1940 until 1945, and in 1944 she was awarded the British Empire Medal. A woman of diverse literary talents, Pargeter has published mainstream novels (under her real name) as well as mysteries. *Black Is the Colour of My True Love's Heart* was her seventh George Felse mystery. Her first Felse story, *Death and the Joyful Woman* (London: William Collins Sons, 1961; New York: Doubleday and Co., 1962) won the 1961 Mystery Writers of America Edgar for the best mystery novel of that year.

512. Stern, Richard Martin (1915-). *The Kessler Legacy*. New York: Charles Scribner's Sons, 1967; London: Cassell and Co., 1968.

The Kessler Legacy is narrated by Walter Spense, a thirty-year-old bachelor instructor of Germanic literature at Harvard. Walter has just published his first book, a biography of that famous German writer, Heinrich Kessler, who died under mysterious circumstances in Austria in 1938. Walter receives word from one of his book's readers that Kessler may have been murdered. And so, in the interests of scholarly research, he flies off to an Austrian village near Innsbruck to investigate. Walter's exploits in Austria then become the stuff of a colorful mystery-thriller. With the Alps as a backdrop, Walter probes for the real story of Kessler's demise. Five of the people whom Walter meets in his travels die; Walter finds that Kessler left behind a hidden cache of jewels; and Walter finds, too, that Kessler's beautiful daughter, Marta, is as skilled at lovemaking as her father was at writing. There is only one campus scene in the novel (in the first chapter), but throughout the story Walter exhibits all of the stock characteristics of an academic who is discovering for the first time the exhilarations and the perils of international intrigue.

Richard Martin Stern was born in Fresno, California. He attended Harvard. *The Kessler Legacy* was his seventh work of mystery fiction. His first mystery novel, *The Bright Road to Fear* (New York: Ballantine Books, 1958; London: Secker and Warburg, 1959) won a Mystery Writers of America Edgar. In 1971 Stern served as president of the Mystery Writers of America.

513. Wynd, Oswald (Morris) (1913-). *Walk Softly, Men Praying*. London: Cassell and Co., 1967; New York: Harcourt, Brace and World, 1967.

The narrator-protagonist of this unusual novel of international mystery and suspense is Ian Douglas, an itinerant professor of English from Scotland. After a stint at Iowa State, Ian obtains a three-year contract to teach at the Naboshima Higher Technical College in Japan. Upon his arrival in the Land of the Rising Sun, he is recruited by the CIA to report upon anything unusual at his new post. Naboshima, as Ian finds, is the center of a large smuggling operation, and the cargo, destined for Red China, is human. There is some brink-of-peril action in the story, along with romance, sinister Japanese thugs, and international intrigue. Moreover, there are some lessons about the dangers to the Free World of a Sino-Japanese alliance. For most academic readers, however, the major fascination will lie in the descriptions of Naboshima Tech, its native faculty members, and its curriculum. And even though Ian occasionally stumbles in his role as an intelligence agent, British and American academics are likely to find him a highly sympathetic character. After all, it is not every Anglo professor of English who has the courage to lecture modern-day Japanese technology students on the delights of Victorian British poetry.

Born in Tokyo of British missionary parents, Oswald Morris Wynd was educated at the American School in Japan, Atlantic City High School in New Jersey, and Edinburgh University. During World War II he was a British intelligence officer and spent three years as a Japanese prisoner of war. Under his own name, and under the pseudonym Gavin Black, Wynd has written more than twenty adventure stories, romantic novels, and mysteries.

514. Allingham, Margery (1904-1966). *A Cargo of Eagles*. London: Chatto and Windus, 1968; William Morrow, 1968.

Albert Campion, Margery Allingham's illustrious, aristocratic series-character sleuth, receives a request from the British Government to investigate strange doings in "Saltey," an ancient Essex village. Saltey, located at the point where the "River Rattey" runs into the sea, was an infamous "bolt-hole" for criminals fleeing London in the seventeenth century. Now it is a gathering point for motorcycle gangs, smugglers, and worse. Campion brings along Magersfontein Lugg, his

cockney valet, to help him in his detection. And he
enlists, too, the help of Professor Mortimer ("Morty")
Kelly, an archeologist from "Vere University" in "Con-
stance," New Jersey. The youthful Professor Kelly,
still in his twenties, is more interested initially in
studying Saltey's ancient artifacts than he is in
fighting crime. But when an attractive female doctor
in the village begins to receive mailed death threats,
Kelly becomes a dedicated detective's helper. There are
no campus scenes in the novel, but the sometimes-impul-
sive American professor (whose mother was British) plays
a central role in the story.

One of the best-respected British mystery writers of
the 1940s and the 1950s, Margery Allingham was born in
London. *The Cargo of Eagles* was her nineteenth Albert
Campion saga. During the series Allingham made several
changes in Campion's roster of sleuthing assistants. It
is not known whether or not Allingham intended to employ
Professor Kelly in future Campion exploits. She died
when the manuscript for *A Cargo of Eagles* was only partially completed, and the book was finished by Youngman
Carter, her husband.

515. Drummond, June (1923-). *The Gantry Episode*. London:
Victor Gollancz, 1968. Published in the United States
as *Murder on a Bad Trip*. New York: Holt, Rinehart
and Winston, 1968.

Disaster strikes the university town of "Gantry."
Someone pours LSD into the local reservoir. Many of the
town's inhabitants hallucinate; a drug-induced bus accident claims seven lives; and several people are murdered. Units of the army come to restore order, and
David Cope, a government narcotics agent, arrives to
locate the LSD-dropper. Cope's inquiries center on Gantry University's chemistry department, in which LSD has
been manufactured for scientific research. World-re-
nowned scientist Derek Yardley is a suspect, as are
George Grant and Dr. Falck, two other members of the
chemistry staff. The culprit, whom Cope uncovers after
nearly losing his own life, was motivated by an ultra-
serious case of faculty jealousy. Rich with detail
about the composition and the effects of LSD, the book
is less precise about Gantry University's location. A
"senator" who becomes involved in the affair decries
the effects which the incident will have upon the voting
behavior of the members of "both Houses." And, in the
manner of many American institutions of higher learning,

Gantry is supported by private funds. Yet, at the same time, Professor Yardley is described as Gantry's "principal," and several of the characters in the story drive British-made automobiles with British-style license numbers.
An earlier mystery by June Drummond, *Welcome, Proud Lady* (491), also appears in this bibliography.

516. Jay, Simon [Alexander, Colin James (1920-)]. *Sleepers Can Kill*. London: William Collins Sons, 1968; Garden City, New York: Doubleday and Co., 1968.

At the end of World War II, five communist agents were planted in New Zealand. Their mission was to obtain ordinary jobs and wait until called upon. The agents' big moment comes when, fifteen years later, they are ordered to steal the plans of a new laser device being perfected at Ardmore, an engineering college of the University of Auckland. Fortunately for Western civilization, Mike Conner, a former CIA agent now employed by New Zealand Intelligence, is assigned to the case. After much derring-do on and near the Ardmore campus, Mike is able to identify the well-hidden spies and to save the Allied defense establishment from a disaster of serious proportions. Although espionage stories *per se* do not qualify for listing in this bibliography, *Sleepers Can Kill* is included because Ardmore College and several of its faculty members are crucial to the book's plot. And so, too, as readers will discover, are the sinister activities of the college's Chess Club.
A New Zealand physician, Colin James Alexander was a radiologist at Master Miserocordiae Hospital in Auckland when *Sleepers Can Kill* was published. It was his second mystery novel.

517. Lathan, Emma [Latsis, Mary J., and Martha Hennisart]. *Come to Dust*. New York: Simon and Schuster, 1968. Victor Gollancz, 1969.

Not one but three highly publicized scandals hit "Brunswick College," a select, Ivy League school in "Coburg," New Hampshire. A professional fund raiser disappears with a $50,000 negotiable bond intended for the institution's coffers. Someone steals the files of the applicants for next fall's freshman class. And a high-school student visiting the Brunswick campus for an application-interview is stabbed to death in the quaint Coburg Inn. Because much of Brunswick's fund raising is done in conjunction with the Sloan Guaranty Bank in New York, John Putnam Thayer, the bank's urbane senior vice president, becomes involved in the college's affairs. Thayer is an Emma Lathan series-character. He ties together and resolves all three of Brunswick's difficulties, but not before he finds that even Ivy League alumni are not always as wealthy as they seem to be. Thayer does some of his sleuthing on the Brunswick campus and some of it in New York. The New York scenes include rare fictional glimpses of an Ivy League alumni admissions committee as it screens prospective students.

Emma Lathan is a pseudonym employed by Mary Jane Latsis and Martha Hennisart. Both collaborators did graduate work at Harvard. Their John Putnam Thayer novels have received widespread critical acclaim and are among the most commercially successful works in contemporary detective fiction. Under the pseudonym R.B. Dominic, Latsis and Hennisart also have written a series of mystery novels about a congressman named Ben Safford.

518. Malloch, Peter [Duncan, William Murdock (1909-1976)].
    Murder of a Student. John Long, 1968.

Two young women are murdered in an unidentified provincial British university town. The first to die is a librarian; the second is a student at the university. The killings are separated by a few months, but the methods are the same. Both women are bludgeoned dead by blows from a hammer as they walk alone at night. *Murder of a Student* is an inverted mystery; readers know early in the story the identity of the hammer-wielding assassin. He is a demented, third-year history student named Pilgrim, whose self-determined goal in life is to commit "perfect" crimes. Because Pilgrim had no prior contact with either of his victims and because the crimes are apparently motiveless, Inspector Tom Swetman and Inspector Crane of the local police are appropriately baffled. But after some dogged sleuthing, these two upholders of the law manage to end Pilgrim's nefarious nocturnal activities. There are a few university scenes in the novel, but the emphasis is on off-campus policework.

William Murdock Duncan was born in Glasgow, Scotland, and received an M.A. in history from the University of Glasgow in 1934. A full-time and prolific writer of mysteries, Duncan published well over two-hundred tales of murder and detection. In addition to the pseudonym

Peter Malloch, Duncan employed John Cassells, Neill Graham, Martin Locke, and Lovat Marshall as pennames, *Murder of a Student* is starkly written. Duncan tells his
story with considerable skill, but he does not embellish
it with elaborate descriptions of his settings or characters. This bare-bones technique is attributable, one
might suspect, to the fact that *Murder of a Student* was
only one of ten mystery novels which Duncan published
(under his various aliases) in 1968!

519. Woodfin, Henry. *Virginia's Thing*. New York: Harper
      and Row, 1968.

Virginia McReedy, a twenty-year-old-year junior at an
American state university, disappears from campus.
Frank McReedy, the president of The International Dock-
men's Union, hires John Foley, an ex-cop turned private
detective, to find his daughter. As Foley earns his
$200-per-day fee, his sleuthing brings him into life-
threatening contact with an unfriendly black civil
rights leader and into only slightly less-acrimonious
relationships with a succession of university faculty
members. The book includes an especially chilling
portrait of Sybyl Howard, a charmless female sociologist.
An expert in the reactions of people to stressful situations, Dr. Howard verbally abuses her husband, conducts
decidedly unethical research, and takes her left-wing
political involvements very, very seriously.
        Henry Woodfin was born in Buffalo, New York. *Vir-
ginia's Thing* was his first novel.

520. Anthony, David [Smith, William Dale (1929-)]. *The Mid-
      night Lady and the Mourning Man*. Indianapolis: Bobbs-
      Merrill, 1969; London: William Collins Sons, 1970.

Set on and near the lovely, tree-shaded campus of
"Jordan College," in Jordan, Ohio, this complex and
violence-filled story is narrated by Morgan Butler, the
town's lone policeman. Former-marine Morgan has problems. Natalie Clayborne, a beautiful Jordan coed, has
been strangled in her dormitory room, and the county
sheriff, a gruff bully named Jack Casey, insists on
handling the investigation. But Sheriff Casey succeeds
only in arresting a man whom Morgan knows to be innocent. Morgan suspects that Waldo Mason is the guilty
party. Waldo, a professor of history, has a long record of extracurricular contact with his more attractive female students. Meantime, a gang of thuggish

hillbillies tries to beat up Linda Thorpe, a tavern hostess with whom Morgan has fallen in love. And Madge Bell, the seductive wife of a local underworld figure, has a habit of inviting Morgan to her home, stripping off her clothes, and distracting our virile hero from his sleuthing. Before the novel comes to its surprising conclusion, Morgan wrestles with literary clues—a marked copy of *The Brothers Karamazov* is found by Natalie Clayborne's body—and learns that lecherous old professors may not be quite as evil as some people think them to be.

William Dale Smith was born in Holliday's Cove, West Virginia. He received a B.A. from Antioch College in Ohio in 1955. Smith is now a successful writer of both mainstream novels and mysteries. *The Midnight Lady and the Mourning Man* was his first foray into the mystery field.

521. Blackstock, Charity [Torday, Ursala]. *The Melon in the Cornfield*. London: Hodder and Stoughton, 1969. Published in the United States as *The Lemmings*. New York: Coward-McCann, 1969.

The Melon in the Cornfield is set at "Timperley Commercial College" in London. Although the book is cited in several general bibliographies of mystery fiction, it is not a mystery in the usual sense. *The Melon in the Cornfield* is, instead, the disquieting story of an idealistic young instructor of English named Todd Murray who befriends a Nigerian girl who is a student in his classes. Because blacks are not popular at Timperly, Todd Murray (and the girl) suffer various indignities at the hands of racists both in and out of the college community. Meantime, Todd's wife, Tracy, is dying of an incurable illness. There is some violence in the novel, but there is no serious detection. However, readers who are willing to forego the pleasures of classical criminological puzzles will find that the tale offers a gritty depiction of faculty life at a seedy institution on the fringes of the British world of higher education.

A native of Great Britain, Ursala Torday received a B.A. from Oxford University in 1935. A one-time social worker, Torday has written many mainstream novels as well as more than a dozen mysteries. In addition to the pseudonym Charity Blackstock, Torday also has used aliases Paula Allardyce and Lee Blackstock on some of her publications.

522. Devine, D(avid) M(cDonald) (1920-). *Death Is My Bride-*
      groom. William Collins Sons, 1969. New York: Walker
      and Co., 1969.

      Who kidnapped and murdered Barbara Letchworth, a stu-
      dent at "Branchfield University" in Great Britain? Was
      it one or more of the radical students currently demon-
      strating on the Branchfield campus? Barbara, after all,
      was the daughter of Lord Letchworth, a staggeringly rich
      capitalistic chain-store owner? Or was it Michael Den-
      ton, an assistant lecturer in Greek, with whom Barbara
      had been carrying on a tempestuous affair. It certain-
      ly was not Vincent Sempill, the Yale Ph.D. who is Branch-
      field's vice-chancellor. Sempill is sincerely dis-
      traught over Barbara's death; not only because one of
      his undergraduates has been killed, but because he fears
      that Lord Letchworth will withdraw his generous fin-
      ancial contributions to the new and considerably less-
      than-distinguished school. A veritable army of sleuths
      tries to track down Barbara's murderer. Brian Armour,
      a young lecturer in classics, is one of the detectives.
      Hew Rhys-Jones, the do-gooder, ecologist head of the
      faculty union is another. Sheila Rhys-Jones, Hew's
      wife and the secretary to Vice-chancellor Sempill, also
      looks into the matter. Lorna Denton, Michael's older
      sister, arrives from out-of-town to help her brother
      prove his innocence. And Chief-Inspector Christie and
      Inspector Eggo of the local police enter the story in
      their official capacities. Written in the slightly sar-
      donic, clue-dropping tradition of classic academic mys-
      teries, *Death Is My Bridegroom* suffers, perhaps, from
      an overabundance of characters. Nevertheless, it pro-
      vides considerable detail about life and death at a
      recently established British university.
          The Devil at Your Elbow (505), an earlier mystery by
      David McDonald Devine, also appears in this bibliography.

523. Gores, Joseph (1931-). *A Time of Predators*. New York:
      Random House, 1969; London: W.H. Allen, 1970.

      After being gang-raped by four young thugs, Paula Hal-
      stead commits suicide. Paula's husband, Curt, a pro-
      fessor or philosophy at "Los Feliz University" in nor-
      thern California, is a former British commando. The local
      police show little interest in pursuing Paula's attackers,
      and thus Curt--after shaving off a few excess pounds
      by exercising in a gymnasium--sets out to locate and to
      bring to justice those individuals who caused his wife's

anguished demise. The first problem is to establish the
identity of the rapists; Curt manages this through the
good offices of Debbie Marsden, one of his students.
The girlfriend of one of the quartet of nasties, Debbie
provides Curt with crucial information and is herself
gang-raped in retaliation. The climax of the story comes
when Curt, without a gun, stalks his armed quarry to
their cabin on a deserted stretch of California shore-
line. What happens then produces some of the most ana-
tomically detailed scenes of professorial revenge in
fiction. *A Time of Predators* is a far cry from the
quiet, genteel academic mysteries which predominate in
this bibliography. Taken on its own terms, however, it
is a masterfully written tale of retribution. In addition to its considerable violence, the book explores in
detail Curt Halstead's rationalizations as he trans-
forms himself from a mild-mannered professor into a
cold, calculating avenger.

Joe Gores was born in Rochester, Minnesota, and received a B.A. from Notre Dame in 1953 and an M.A. from
Stanford in 1961. A one-time private detective in the
San Francisco area, Gores is now one of America's most-
respected mystery writers. *A Time of Predators* received the 1969 Mystery Writers of America Edgar for
that year's best first novel.

524.   Graham, John Alexander (1941-). *Arthur*. New York:
       Harper and Row, 1969.

The title character of this light but intriguing novel is Arthur Silverman, a chronic graduate student in
mathematics at Harvard. Relaxing from his infrequent
studies, Arthur lounges on the beach north of Glouches-
ter, and there he meets a mysterious "Mr. Hoad." When
Mr. Hoad's lovely female swimming companion is found
murdered, Arthur turns detective. At the age of twenty-
seven, Arthur is making virtually no progress on his
Ph.D. dissertation, and his mother worries that he will
never finish. He does little in this story to ease his
mother's fears. However, he displays some enthusiastic
and inventive sleuthing and indicates, by his deeds,
that detective work, rather than mathematics, might be
the career for which he is best suited.

Born in New York City, John Alexander Graham received
a B.A. from Columbia in 1962 and an M.A. from Brandeis
in 1964. He was an instructor in mathematics at Wellesley College when *Arthur*, his first novel, was published.
A later mystery novel by Graham, *The Involvement of Arnold Wechsler* (541) also appears in this bibliography.

*525. Greenbaum, Leonard (1930-). *Out of Shape*. New York: Harper and Row, 1969; London: Victor Gollancz, 1970.

Rudolph Reichet, an immigrant professor of medieval literature, is found dead in his office, his face blown away by a shotgun blast. The setting is "Milton State University" in Michigan. Lieutenant Paul Gold of the local police, along with Tommy Larkin, the professor's graduate-student research assistant, investigate the killing. Larkin is especially interested in the matter since he received a telephone call, presumably from Reichet, an hour after the professor was murdered. The complex case prompts Gold and Larkin to focus on a growing Neo-Nazi movement on the Milton campus, and it also leads them to probe Professor Reichet's youthful days in pre-World War II Germany. Written with a fine ear for the melodies and rhythms of academe, *Out of Shape* carries its readers through a highly sophisticated series of puzzles before reaching its conclusion. The many Milton faculty members who appear in the story are especially well drawn, and the plot is devoid of the set pieces found in more orthodox college mysteries. Furthermore, the book is certainly one of very few detective stories, of any description, to include two full-page photographs of Adolph Hitler.

Leonard Greenbaum was born in Boston. He received a B.A., an M.A. and a Ph.D. from the University of Michigan. *Out of Shape* was his first novel. At the time the book was published, Greenbaum was an assistant professor of English at the University of Michigan and assistant director and editor of the Michigan Memorial Phoenix Project.

526. Hamilton, Alex (John) (1939-). *The Dead Needle*. London: Hutchinson Publishing Group, 1969.

As this ambiguous, apparently allegorical novel opens, a London park-keeper finds the body of a young man in a chair still standing from the previous evening's band concert. By the time the police arrive, however, the body is gone. In fact, the young man in question, one Nicholas Sturm, was only playing dead, and while the London police attempt to unravel the case of the disappearing corpse, Nicholas returns to his lodging house. Nicholas lives, as it happens, in the home of a Mrs. Granville, who rents most of her rooms to university undergraduates. And, oh yes, Nicholas has been away for a year (and thought dead), so that his landlady and his fellow roomers are startled to see him reappear. At this point Mrs. Granville, her two daughters, and her student-tenants try to determine the cause of Nicholas' lengthy absence. Nicholas, who possibly may have been a student before his disappearance, but who does not now seem to have any academic affiliations, may be a spy or he may simply be insane. Meantime, the student-lodgers take their university examinations, though they find it difficult to concentrate. Nicholas is eventually bitten by a snake, and at the end of the opus he is back in the park, dying from the snakebite, but in possession of a serum which he might decide to take and which might or might not save his life. Though a few policemen appear in the book, there is no significant detection. Readers are required to exercise their own sleuthing talents to decipher the meanings and non-meanings embedded in the plot.

Alex Hamilton was born in Bristol, Great Britain, and received his undergraduate degree at Oxford. *The Dead Needle* was his fourth full-length work of mystery fiction. A full-time writer and editor, Hamilton has written travel books, children's stories, and radio plays for the BBC in addition to mystery novels.

527. Harrison, William (1933-). *In a Wild Sanctuary*. New York: William Morrow, 1969; Victor Gollancz, 1970.

The central characters in this dark, existential novel are four male graduate students at a university in Chicago. All four suffer from severe cases of social maladjustment, and they join together in a suicide pact. After the first two students die, one of their fathers (an Air Force colonel) takes it upon himself to investigate his son's death. What he finds cannot be revealed in this bibliography without destroying the story's suspense for prospective readers. However, it can be noted that many reviewers saw within the work updated overtones of the real-life Leopold-Loeb case of 1923-1924. Highly praised, *In a Wild Sanctuary* was also thought by many critics to be a terrifying statement about the pressures and perils of student life in the late 1960s.

William Harrison was born in Dallas, Texas. He received a B.A. from Texas Christian University in 1955 and an M.A. from Vanderbilt in 1959. *In a Wild Sanctuary* was his second novel. At the time the book was published, Harrison was a member of the English department of the University of Arkansas.

528.   Innes, Michael [Stewart, John Innes Mackintosh (1906-)].
        A Family Affair. London: Victor Gollancz, 1969. Pub-
        lished in the United States as *Picture of Guilt*. New
        York: Dodd, Mead and Co., 1969.

The detective-protagonist in *A Family Affair* is John
Appleby, Michael Innes' estimable series-character
sleuth. Now retired from active duty with New Scotland
Yard, Appleby nonetheless takes it upon himself to end
a series of diabolically clever swindles which are pla-
guing the British art establishment. John Appleby's
assistants in the case are his wife, Judith, and his
youngest son, Bobby, an undergraduate at Oxford. Much
of the story takes place in and around Oxford University. The plot includes an elaborate student prank
which John Appleby stages to trap the villains of the
piece, and the grisly climax takes place on the River
Isis, at a point near the Folly Bridge, while the Oxford
and Cambridge crews are holding a race. A sizeable number of Oxonians appear in the novel, and John Appleby,
himself an Oxford graduate, spends some time reminiscing
about his undergraduate experiences. As for Cambridge,
that venerable institution is represented not only by
its crew, but by Professor John Sansbury as well. Professor Sansbury, a world-famous art historian, proves to
know far more about the provenance of paintings and sta-
tuary than he does about boatsmanship.

A Family Affair is the eighth (and last) Michael Innes
mystery to appear in this bibliography. The others are
Death at the President's Lodging (374), *Hamlet, Revenge!*
(378), *The Weight of the Evidence* (405), *Operation Pax*
(432), *Old Hall, New Hall* (454), *Appleby Plays Chicken*
(462), and *The Long Farewell* (470).

529.   Lafore, Laurence Davis (1917-). *Nine Seven Juliet*. Gar-
        den City, New York: Doubleday and Co., 1969.

Walter Payne, now eighty years old, is a retired professor of English. He lives on a farm in Iowa with his
grandnephew Ritchie, whose leg has been shattered in an
auto accident. One night a small plane lands nearby,
and someone buries the bejeweled body of a woman in a
wooded area which borders Walter's wheatfield. Walter
and Ritchie investigate. Walter's sleuthing takes him
to Paris at one point in the story, and Ritchie, suffering from a serious case of melancholia when the book
begins, finds that amateur detection can restore zest
to one's life. The title of the novel is taken from

the identification number (N9397J) of the body-bearing airplane.

Laurence Davis Lafore was born in Narbeth, Pennsylvania, a suburb of Philadelphia. He received a B.A. from Swarthmore in 1938 and a Ph.D. from the Fletcher School of Law and Diplomacy in 1950. At the time *Nine Seven Juliet* was published, Lafore was a professor of history at the University of Iowa. Lafore is the author of one of the classic comedy novels about academic life. *Learner's Permit* (Garden City, New York: Doubleday and Co., 1962. Published in Great Britain as *The Pride of Parthenon*. London: Victor Gollancz, 1963) describes the life and times of an imposter-instructor of English at a small college in upstate New York.

530. Queen, Ellery. *The Campus Murders*. New York: Lancer Books, 1969.

"Tisquanto State College" is located in that remote area of America known as "upstate." The school was once small and idyllic, but now, at the height of the Vietnam War, it has grown into a vast, sprawling institution complete with hordes of student radicals and an incompetent administration. Tisquanto's troubles finally come to the attention of Governor Sam Holland when Laura Thornton, a sophomore and the daughter of Holland's rival for re-election, mysteriously disappears from the campus. The governor sends Mike McCall, his virile special assistant to investigate. Mike finds Laura, and helps put an end to the student uprisings, but not before he is kidnapped by a gang of mask-wearing male and female students, stripped to the buff, and has his genitals burned with the lighted end of a marijuana cigarette. Although this story will never be rated among the most cerebral of college mysteries, some readers may find that it has one saving grace. At the conclusion of the book, Governor Holland makes a personal visit to Tisquanto. Appalled by the goings-on, he confronts President Wolfe Wade—a man characterized by "jellyfish dampness" —and sends him off to an early retirement.

The Campus Murders marked the debut of Mike McCall, a "two-fisted troubleshooter" who eventually became a series character. The McCall stories were not written by Frederick Dannay and Manfred Lee, the originators of the Ellery Queen pseudonym. Rather, they were composed by mercifully anonymous specialists in mass-market, paperback, action sagas. *The Devil's Cook* (506), a pre-

Mike McCall novel, and yet another bogus Ellery Queen
mystery, also appears in this bibliography.

531. Thomas, Alan Ernest Wentworth (1896-). *The Professor*.
London: Victor Gollancz, 1969.

More a novel of domestic tragedy than a conventional
mystery, this sensitive story nonetheless includes
three sudden deaths and a case of blackmail. The protagonist is John Felbridge, a fiftyish professor of ancient history at an Oxbridge college known as "St. Theo-
bald's." John is a model academic, happiest when alone
with his books, but his cloistered world begins to dis-
solve when his brother, Sir Henry Felbridge, M.P., collapses and dies while giving a speech in London. Sir
Henry, it seems, had a secret sex life, and over the next
few months, as Henry's past comes to light, John finds
that his own life will never be the same. Although some
of this story takes place in London, most of it is set
in the professor's home. There is no detection in the
book, but there is one long and very tension-filled courtroom scene. It would be unfair to reveal more details
about the plot. However, many older professorial readers
will find that John Felbridge, while not necessarily a
sympathetic character, is a man to whom they can readily
relate. And many faculty wives will take interest in the
portrait of John's wife, Alice, as she copes with the dis-
asters befalling her husband and her grown son and daughter.

532. Williams, Gordon Maclean (1934-). *The Siege of Trencher's Farm*. London: Secker and Warburg, 1969; New
York: William Morrow, 1969.

George Magruder takes his British-born wife and small
daughter from the University of Pennsylvania to a remote
Devon farmhouse for a year's sabbatical. A professor
of English, George hopes to finish his definitive study
of Brankshire, a late-eighteenth-century English diarist.
But Henry Niles, a mad child-murderer, escapes from a
nearby institution for the criminally insane and turns
up at the Magruder home-away-from-home, badly injured
after an automobile accident. The Magruders call for
the police to come and collect their unwanted guest,
but a blizzard is raging. The police are immobilized
in town. A band of drunken locals makes it through the
snow, however, with the aim of providing Henry Niles
with a lethal form of instant Devon justice. When George
refuses to turn Henry over to the vigilantes, they try
to take him by force. In the last half of the book,

great quantities of blood are spilled, a baseball bat
is put to good use, and George forgets completely about
his research.

Gordon Maclean Williams was born in Pauley, Scotland.
The Siege of Trencher's Farm was his fifth novel. The
book was adapted for film by David Zelag Goodman and
Sam Peckinpah. The especially gory motion picture,
titled *Straw Dogs*, was released in 1971 and starred Dustin Hoffman.

*533. Bernard, Robert [Martin, Robert Bernard (1918-)]. *Dead-
ly Meeting*. New York: W.W. Norton and Co., 1970.

The "deadly meeting" in the title of this novel is the
annual convention of the Modern Language Association.
In addition to the usual paper-giving, socializing, and
job-searching, the MLA agenda this particular year includes the death by poison of Professor Peter Jackson,
head of the English department at "Wilton University."
An autocratic and singularly unpopular chairman, Jackson obviously was done in by one of his faculty subor-
dinates. The puzzle for the reader is which one of
Jackson's departmental antagonists is guilty. The story
is told from the perspective of Bill Stratton, who becomes acting chairman after Jackson's death. Stratton
aides in solving the crime. But also in the book's
multi-person cast of sleuths are a sophisticated police
lieutenant named Moynahan and Dame Millicent Hetherege,
an aged, visiting medievalist from "St. Agatha's College," Oxford. Since Dame Millicent writes suspense
stories as an avocation, her mind is especially fine-
tuned for detection. Events at the MLA convention
occupy most of the first third of the intricate story.
and then the scene switches to the Wilton campus. The
descriptions of life at Wilton ring with academic ver-
isimilitude, and various Wilton English professors and
their spouses are etched in relentless detail.

An earlier mystery by Robert Bernard Martin, *Death
Takes a Sabbatical* (507), also is included in this bibliography.

534. Lait, Robert (1921-), *Switched Out*. London: McGibbon
and Kee, 1970.

"Strinager House," at Number Five West Road, is very
near Selwyn College of Cambridge University. It is a
small boarding house with five occupants. In flat number one is Miss Ballow, a forty-one-year-old, unmarried

assistant librarian at the University Library. In flat
number two is Brigadier Sheridan Johnson (retired) who
is writing a history of his regiment, The King's Own
Scottish Borderers. The occupant of flat number three
is Jonathan Simpson, a shy, bachelor bank clerk. And
in the basement are Pancho Jaego and his pregnant wife,
Meriel. Pancho is an undergraduate reading physics, and
he and Meriel serve as the building's caretakers in return for free lodging. A gifted inventor, Pancho creates a television system through which he can secretly
observe the upstairs tenants in their rooms. Television,
in Pancho's opinion, has never been better, since the
channels on his special machine offer him a rich selec-
tion of aberrant sexual programming not available on
the BBC or on ITV. But all good things must come to an
end. Brigadier Johnson discovers the apparatus and
leads Miss Ballow and Mr. Simpson in a plot to kill Pancho and Meriel. Like people's private behavior, the
climax of this novel is best left unbroadcast (at least
in this bibliography). But it will not be giving away
too much of the novel's plot to observe that there is
no detection in the book, that some of the tale is told
through flashbacks, and that Pancho's television set
does not survive to the end of the story.

Robert Lait was born in Salisbury, England. He holds
a diploma in social science from Liverpool University
and an M.A. from Cambridge. Lait's publishing credits
include mainstream novels, mysteries, and radio and
television scripts. At the time *Switched Out* was published, he was a lecturer in criminology and social science at University College of Swansea, University of
Wales.

*535.   Lockridge, Richard (1898-). *Twice Retired*. Philadel-
        phia: J.B. Lippincott, 1970; London: John Long, 1971.

Walker Brinkley, a retired professor of English from
New York City's Dyckman University, made his literary
debut in Richard and Frances Lockridge's *Accent on
Murder* (471). One of America's leading experts in regional accents, Brinkley's keen sense of verbal nuance
was of great help to State Police Captain Merton Heimrich, a Lockridge series-character detective, as Heimrich apprehended a murderer in posh Westchester County.
Brinkley also appeared, in a minor role, in *Murder Can't
Wait* (492). In *Twice Retired* Brinkley returns to the
pages of mystery fiction once again, this time as an
unofficial and somewhat-unwilling aide to Bernie Simmons,

a New York City assistant district attorney and another
Lockridge series-character sleuth. *Twice Retired* opens
with Brinkley driving from his suburban home to the
Dyckman Faculty Club in order to attend a publisher's
reception for his newest book. The Vietnam War is at
its height, and pickets and demonstrators roam the campus. When the reception ends Brinkley prepares to drive
home, only to find the dead body of General Philip Armstrong, U.S.A. (retired) in the backseat of the car.
Armstrong, the right-wing chairman of Dyckman's board
of trustees, has had the back of his skull bashed in
and, for good measure, has had a pig mask placed over
what remains of his head. Bernie Simmons, who happens
to be one of Brinkley's former students, handles the investigation, while the unnerved professor contents himself with offering occasional tidbits of sage advice.
Among Simmons' suspects is Carl Benson, a leftish-liberal
assistant professor of English whose employment at Dyckman is ending thanks to General Armstrong's orders.
Another person on Simmons' list of likely killers is
Lester Brownlee, a consultant on book design to the
Dyckman University Press. And still another suspect is
Robert Armstrong, the general's nephew. Robert is an
undergraduate at Dyckman, an R.O.T.C. cadet, and a dedicated American patriot who despises those of his fellow
students who find fault with America's foreign policy.

Twice Retired is the sixth Richard Lockridge novel included in this bibliography. Richard Lockridge wrote
the first four of these books--*Murder Is Served* (423),
Accent on Murder (471), *Murder Is Suggested* (476), and
The Drill Is Death (482)--in collaboration with his wife,
Frances Louise. The fifth Lockridge novel in the bibliography is *Murder Can't Wait* (492). Like *Twice Retired*,
Murder Can't Wait was written by Richard Lockridge after
his wife's death in 1963.

536. Maner, William. *Die of a Rose*. Garden City, New York:
Doubleday and Co., 1970.

Wilson Hartley, a young member of the English department at "Spotswood University," has an unpromising pu-
pil named Steve Zlados. Steve is a football star but
a dunce in the classroom. Moreover, Steve is something
of a bully. At one point, he threatens to reshape Hartley's face with a punch to his nose. One fine morning,
Steve is found dead with Hartley's scissors in his back.
A leading suspect, Hartley must now find Steve's killer

or face the prospect of arrest for a crime he only wishes he had committed. Before the end of the novel, Hartley becomes involved with rustic policemen, big-time
gamblers from Baltimore, local bookies, and a gaggle of
Spotswood faculty members and athletic department personnel. Barzun and Taylor, in *A Catalogue of Crime*
(see footnote 7, Introduction) call *Die of a Rose* "a
deplorable book." Still, although the story is exceedingly complex and the detection is implausible, professorial readers who have had their own difficulties
with Neanderthal-like football players may find that the
basic premise of the story constitutes a redeeming feature.

537. Melville, Jennie [Butler, Gwendoline (Williams) (1922-)].
     A New Kind of Killer, An Old Kind of Death. London:
     Hodder and Stoughton, 1970. Published in the United
     States as *A New Kind of Killer.* New York: David Mc-
     Kay/Ives Washburn, 1971.

The "University of Midport" is a new British university. It is so new, in fact, that it is about to in-
stall its very first vice-chancellor, and when radical
students stage a series of campus outrages there are
grave doubts that the young school can survive the up-
heavals. Then, when several murders occur within the
Midport community, things look very black indeed. It
is fortunate, therefore, that Charmian Daniels, a Jennie Melville/Gwendoline Butler series-character sleuth,
is at Midport taking courses in criminology. On leave
from her job as a detective with the "Deerham Hills"
police force, Charmian drops her studies to investigate
the killings, and, by the end of the story, Midport can
look forward to a bright future. The book offers many
descriptions of Midport under siege. And, as an added
bonus for college mystery fans, at one point in the
plot Charmian flies to Holland and does some field investigations among the radical students at the University of Amsterdam. During the course of her buswoman's
holiday, the married Charmian begins to develop a romantic relationship with Don Goldsworthy, an American
graduate student from Berkeley. As the story ends,
however, Charmian's husband returns unexpectedly from
a business trip to Hong Kong and reclaims his wife.
     A New Kind of Killer, An Old Kind of Death was Char-
mian Daniels' fifth published exploit. A non-Charmian
Daniels mystery by Gwendoline Butler, *Death Lives Next
Door* (477), appears earlier in this bibliography. It
was published under Gwendoline Butler's real name.

538. Ashe, Gordon [Creasey, John (1908-1973)]. *A Rabble of Rebels*. London: John Long, 1971; New York: Holt, Rinehart and Winston, 1972.

Radical students take over the campus of "Mid-Cal University" near San Francisco. "Gentle-faced" Dean Connell is imprisoned in his office, and two student bystanders are killed when they attempt to make an early exit from one of the radicals' more heated protest rallies. Meantime, in London, Deputy Assistant Police Commissioner Patrick Dawlish sees the Mid-Cal affair as the thin edge of a revolutionary wedge designed, ultimately, to destroy all Western universities. A Gordon Ashe/John Creasey series-character detective, Dawlish hops the next jet to California in order to investigate matters. His findings at Mid-Cal, and at a variety of other far-from-London locales which he visits only confirm his suspicions that all student uprisings are the product of an international conspiracy. *A Rabble of Rebels* was first published in 1971. Perhaps the best testimony to Dawlish's proficient sleuthing in this case is the fact that shortly after the book's appearance calm was restored, not only at Mid-Cal, but also at most non-fictional colleges and universities throughout the world.

John Creasey was born in Southfields, Surrey, Great Britain. He did not attend college and, hence, never had the advantage of formal academic training in creative writing. Nonetheless, Creasey published well over five hundred mystery and adventure novels, as well as assorted works of mainstream and historical fiction. Some of his books appeared under his own name, but he also used the pseudonyms Gordon Ashe, Norman Deane, Michael Halliday, Kyle Hunt, Peter Manton, J.J. Marrie, Richard Martin, Anthony Morton, Ken Ranger, William K. Reilly, Tex Riley, and Jeremy York.

*539. Candy, Edward [Neville, Barbara Alison Boodson (1925-)]. *Words for Murder Perhaps*. London: Victor Gollancz, 1971.

Words for Murder Perhaps is set at the extra-mural (evening adult extension) facility of the "University of Bantwich." Located in downtown Bantwich, a depressingly grim city in the British Midlands, the extra-mural division has a small permanent staff but draws most of its faculty on a part-time (extra pay) basis

from the nearby university itself. The story centers
on the murder of elderly Professor Arthur Hallam, an
Egyptologist, who dies after offering a guest lecture.
Seeking post-presentation refreshment, Hallam sips a
glass of water into which someone has dropped cyanide.
The leading suspect in the case is Mr. Roberts, a Bantwich lecturer in English who is teaching an extra-mural
course on the history of the detective novel. Roberts
is divorced and once tried to commit suicide. Furthermore, after finding Hallam's body, he makes the mistake
of picking up (and leaving his fingerprints on) the professor's glass of poison. Roberts is pinpointed by Inspector Hunt of the local police as a possible "nut
case." But there are many, many other suspects as well,
most of them extra-mural administrators, teachers and
students. Several of the important clues in the plot
are literary in nature. Although devotees of "serious"
mystery fiction will find that *Words for Murder Perhaps*
presents a significant whodunit challenge, the book can
also be read simply for its sly, witty commentaries on
academic life. For example, class attendance in Bantwich's extra-mural division (like class attendance in
almost every academic institution) declines precipitously as each term progresses. On the evening after
Professor Hallam's murder, however, the classes at the
facility are as full as they were on the term's first
night.

Barbara Alison Boodson Neville was born in London.
She received MB., B.S., and D.C.H. degrees from the
University of London. A mainstream novelist as well as
a mystery writer, she employs the pseudonym Edward Candy on all of her publications. *Words for Murder Perhaps*
was her third mystery.

540.   Fisher, David Elimelech (1932-). *Crisis*. Garden City,
       New York: Doubleday and Co., 1971.

This disturbing psychological novel is narrated by
Barney Ferber, a thirty-seven-year-old professor of
English at New York University. Barney, a karate expert, is having a breakdown, and in his less-lucid moments he attacks people with well-placed chops to their
bodies. The suspense in the story centers on the question of whom Barney will kill or maim before he is in-
stitutionalized. A patron in a Manhattan bar is the
first of his victims; a Harlem pimp becomes his second.
The climax of the book occurs when Barney barricades his
mistress, her small son, and himself in the woman's

apartment on Washington Square, and the police try to
rescue Barney's two captives before he can do them
harm. Part of the narrative is tortured flashback, in
which Barney reviews his student days at Harvard and
confuses his mistress, Laura, with his ex-wife, Catherine. And there is a riveting scene at N.Y.U., in which
Barney, who sees himself as more of a warrior king than
a professor, attends a department meeting and lets his
colleagues know in forceful terms what he thinks of
them.

David Elimelech Fisher received a B.S. from Trinity
College in Hartford, Connecticut, in 1952 and a Ph.D.
from the University of Florida in 1958. He was a professor of geophysics and cosmochemistry at the University of Miami when *Crisis*, his first novel, was published. A later novel by Fisher, *A Fearful Symmetry*
(561), also appears in this bibliography.

541. Graham, John Alexander (1941-). *The Involvement of*
      Arnold Wechsler. ·Boston: Atlantic Press/Little Brown,
      1971.

Arnold Wechsler is a wisecracking junior member of the
classics department at "Hewes University." His "involvement" begins when he is asked by Winthrop Dohrn, the
harrassed president of Hewes, to investigate the kidnapping of Dohrn's young granddaughter. Dohrn suspects
that David Wechsler, Arnold's younger, student-radical
brother is responsible, and he wants Arnold to look
into the matter. Arnold's sleuthing brings him into
closer-than-comfortable contact with Hewes' retinue of
anti-establishment undergraduates and also leads him to
a few skeletons in the Dohrn family closet. The book
is written in the first person, with the cynical Arnold
as narrator. This technique allows Arnold to offer a
great many jaundiced opinions of the Hewes scene. A
middling-status institution in eastern Massachusetts,
Hewes denies that its faculty must publish or perish.
However, as Arnold observes, all of the school's faculty
members seem to do one or the other. President Dohrn
is not long in a position to rectify this inconsistency
in his administration's policy. In the first chapter of
this partially inverted mystery, Dohrn is sundered into
bloody bits and pieces when a bomb, planted by parties
unknown, blows up his presidential mansion.

An earlier John Alexander Graham mystery novel, *Ar-*
thur (524), is included in this bibliography.

542. Hill, Reginald (1936-). *An Advancement of Learning*.
     London: William Collins Sons, 1971.

     Set at the "Holm Coultram College of Liberal Arts and
     Education" in the Yorkshire region of Great Britain, this
     wry, intricate mystery stars Reginald Hill series-char-
     acter detectives Superintendent Andrew Dalziel and Ser-
     geant Peter Pascoe. The two policemen come onto the
     Holm Coultram campus when human bones are unearthed in
     the staff garden. The bones, it turns out, belong to
     Alison Girling, a former principal of the school who
     was thought to have died in an automobile accident (and
     to have been buried) in Austria. Investigating the cir-
     cumstances surrounding the uncovered remains, Dalziel
     and Pascoe bring to light a whole series of potentially
     lethal romantic entanglements in the Holm Coultram com-
     munity. Professor San Fallowfield, for example, has
     apparently been falsifying grades in order to fail his
     former student-mistress, Anita Sewell. Franny Roote,
     a brilliant male student, has been carrying on with
     Marion Cargo, an art instructor. And Marion, whose
     sexual tastes include women as well as men, once had
     an affair with Alison Girling. Before the story con-
     cludes, Professor Fallowfield and Anita Sewell are both
     dead, and Superintendent Dalziel is thoroughly disgus-
     ted with academe. "So that's what I missed when I didn't
     get a college education," Dalziel muses as he and Pascoe
     drive away from Holm Coultram after concluding their
     inquiries.
       Reginald Hill was born in Hartlepool, Great Britain.
     He received a B.A. (honors) in English from St. Cath-
     erine's College, Oxford, in 1960. *An Advancement of
     Learning* was his third Dalziel-Pascoe mystery. At the
     time the book was published, Hill was a lecturer at
     the Doncaster College of Education in Yorkshire. Hill
     has employed the pseudonyms Patrick Ruell, Dick Morland,
     and Charles Underhill on some of his works of fiction.
     Death Takes the Low Road (569), an espionage thriller
     issued under Hill's Patrick Ruell alias, appears later
     in this bibliography.

543. Knight, David James. *Farquharson's Physique and What It
     Did to His Mind*. New York: Stein and Day, 1971; Lon-
     don: Hodder and Stoughton, 1971.

     This long (477-page) novel opens with the mysterious
     death by shooting of Henry John Farquharson. A thirty-
     seven-year-old British expatriate, Farquharson was a

professor of English at the University of Ibadan in Nigeria. The year is 1966. Nigeria is in the throes of a
bloody civil war, and Farquharson is killed at the Ibadan Airport as he, his wife, and his small son attempt
to flee the country on a plane bound for Rome. The rest
of the book is flashbacks, in which Farquharson's career
in Africa is reviewed and in which various characters
(including the professor's wife) are shown to have had
sufficient reasons for pulling the fateful trigger. At
the conclusion of the story, the shooting is described
in greater detail, and the culprit is revealed. Less
a conventional mystery than a character study of the
meretricious, womanizing Farquharson, the book includes
particularized accounts of the professor's sexual activities and also provides grim detail about the siege
atmosphere which pervades the University of Ibadan as
looting and pillaging take place nearby. Of special
note are the scenes in which Farquharson and other Ibadan faculty members mount armed guard inside the fence
which has been erected to keep the warring Nigerian
tribesmen from invading the campus.

544. Lynn, Jack (1927-). *The Professor*. New York: Dell
      Publishing Co., 1971; London: Allison and Busby, 1971.

      Joseph C. Pastore is a brilliant Italian-American pro-
fessor of psychology at New York University. However,
when he is passed over for the chairmanship of his department, he resigns from the school to become a tutor
to the teen-aged children of the Mafia. Joe has some
difficulties with his new pupils; some of them threaten
to kill him when he assigns them too much homework. But
eventually Joe proves equal to his tasks, and his Mafia
bosses respond by providing him with a lifestyle beyond
the fondest dreams of most academics. When a Congres-
sional Committee begins to investigate the Mafia, Joe
is called to testify. Always thoughtful and consider-
ate, his employers send a trio of thugs to demonstrate,
by means of a relatively light beating, what will happen to him and to his family if he talks to the Congress-
men. At the same time, of course, Joe's professorial
ethics prompt him to reveal all. Wishing that he had
never left NYU, Joe appears before the committee at the
end of the story, and not until the last moment does he
decide his course of action. Although there are only
a few on-the-NYU campus scenes in the book and even
though there is no detection, real-life professorial

proletarians may appreciate the several views of Joe as he
is being carried on his pedagogic rounds in a black chauf-
feur-driven, Cadillac limousine.
       The Professor was Jack Lynn's first novel. Lynn was
a television and motion picture producer when the book
was published.

545. Marin, A.C. [Coppel, Alfred (1921-)]. *A Storm of Spears*.
      New York: Harcourt Brace Jovanovich, 1971; London:
      Robert Hale, 1972.

      A veteran of the Vietnam War, Frank Charles enrolls as
      a graduate student at a university in California, hoping
      to leave violence behind him. But, alas, during this
      action-packed suspense saga, he is beaten senseless on
      several occasions, witnesses three separate kidnappings,
      is forced to burglarize a top-secret campus research
      institute, participates in bloody confrontation between
      radical students and the police, and is a party to an
      especially gory shooting. Why does a nice boy like
      Frank find himself in so many nasty situations? One
      reason is that he is being blackmailed into acting as a
      campus spy by agents from Red China. Frank has had the
      misfortune of being photographed during a torrid sex
      act with an undergraduate named Antonia. And since his
      warm-hearted wife Joanna is crippled and permanently con-
      fined to a wheelchair, poor Frank cannot risk damage to
      her psyche by having his affair with Antonia made pub-
      lic. *A Storm of Spears* contains many university scenes
      and offers an interesting portrait of Brock Fletcher,
      the university's dean of minority affairs. A sociolo-
      gist by training, Fletcher is one of very few black ad-
      ministrators to appear in college fiction.
          Alfred Coppel was born in Oakland, California, and
      attended Stanford University. A one-time reporter and
      critic for the *San Francisco Chronicle*, Coppel had pub-
      lished eight novels before writing *A Storm of Spears*.
      In addition to A.C. Marin, Coppel has employed the
      pseudonym Robert Cham Gilman on some of his works.

546. White, R(eginald) J(ames) (1905-1971). *A Second-Hand
      Tomb*. London: Macmillan, 1971; New York: Harper and
      Row, 1971.

      Maximilian Peck is a lecturer in history and archeo-
      logy at the "University of Halifax." As a sideline,
      Max conducts educational tours of ancient buildings in

Yorkshire. Pamela Peck, Max's wife, resents the attentions her husband pays to Iris Armstrong, the lady who
operates Holdernesse House, a stately mansion (now a
hotel) from which Max's tour groups journey forth in
search of cultural enrichment. When Pamela is found
dead in the Thimberling Tomb, a historical site near
her place of business, Max and Iris both come under suspicion of murder. But so, too, do several assistant
tour guides and many of Holdernesse House's other guests.
The sleuth in the story is Chief-Inspector Badgery, a man
who displays far more knowledge of medieval Yorkshire
architecture than does the average British policeman. A
thoroughly literate British mystery, *A Second-Hand Tomb*
includes many historical references, considerable wry
humor, and a liberal sprinkling of real and false clues.

Reginald James White was born in Norwich, Great Britain, and was educated at Dowling College, Cambridge.
A professor of history at Cambridge, White was best known
in professional circles for his many monographs about
various aspects of Georgian English history. *A Second-
Hand Tomb* was his third mystery novel.

547.   Ashford, Jeffrey [Jeffries, Roderic Greame (1926-)].
        A Man Will Be Kidnapped Tomorrow. London: John Long,
        1972; New York: Walker and Co., 1972.

Demonstrations at "Ruffbridge University" in Great
Britain lead to the arrest of five undergraduates. Some
miles away, at "Quetley University," four other students
decide to take it upon themselves to free the "Ruffbridge
Five." And so they kidnap Mrs. Stella Gould--a person
whom they seize by mistake--and announce that they will
release her alive only if the incarcerated Ruffbridgians
are quickly set free from their confinement. As it happens, the four kidnappers are male, and Stella Gould is
in her late twenties and attractive. Even while Detective Superintendent Abbott of the Special Section of
the Regional Crime Squad is running down every possible
clue, Mrs. Gould's captors quarrel among themselves over
the proper ways to entertain a nubile female hostage.
For her part, Stella Gould is not a happily married
lady--her husband is a worthless alcoholic--and she
begins to find that some of her abductors are more interesting company than others. The book contains several scenes on the Ruffbridge university campus, and
readers certainly learn a great deal about the four
Quetley University lads who appear in the story. The
Quetley students, in turn, discover to their sorrow one

of the cardinal rules of the kidnapping trade. Youthful male abductors should never walk into a lingerie shop and purchase peek-a-boo undies for their female victims.

Roderic Greame Jeffries was born in London. He studied for the law but practiced only briefly before undertaking a career as a writer. He has published over fifty mystery and suspense novels. In addition to Jeffrey Ashford, he has employed the pseudonyms Hastings Draper, Roderic Greame, and Graham Hastings on some of his works.

548. Davis, Dorothy Salisbury (1916-). *Shock Wave*. New York: Charles Scribner's Sons, 1972; London: Arthur Barker, 1974.

The protagonist of this story is Kate Osborn, a well-known writer for "Saturday Magazine." Kate travels to Venice, Illinois, to research a feature story on a local political kingpin. On the train to Venice she meets Professor Randall Forbes, a member of the physics department at "The State University of Venice." Shortly after her arrival in the southern Illinois town, Kate learns of the mysterious death of Professor Daniel Lowenthal, one of Professor Randall's colleagues, and she uses her prior contact with Randall to conduct some ad hoc investigative reporting about Lowenthal's demise. A large number of Venice faculty and administrators figure prominently in the plot of the novel. So, too, do assorted students, townspeople, and local policemen. By the end of the book Kate has gotten two stories, and a murderer has provided his own form of self-justice.

Enemy and Brother (504), an earlier novel by Dorothy Salisbury Davis, also appears in this bibliography.

549. James, P(hyllis) D(orothy) (1920-). *An Unsuitable Job for a Woman*. London: Faber and Faber, 1972; New York: Charles Scribner's Sons, 1973.

Set in and around Cambridge University, *An Unsuitable Job for a Woman* displays the sleuthing talents of Cordelia Gray, a novice private detective from London. On her first major case, Cordelia investigates the apparent suicide of Mark Callender, a Cambridge dropout. Although there are several on-campus scenes in this exceedingly well-written book, and even though assorted Cambridge students take part in the story, the novel is primarily concerned with non-academic matters. Mark, it seems,

had enemies within his own family, and the explanation
for his death hinges upon secret skeletons in the Callender family closet.
Phyllis Dorothy James was born in Oxford, Great Britain. Before launching her highly successful career as
a mystery writer, she served as a hospital administrator and as a civil servant in the Home Office, where
she worked in the criminal department. *An Unsuitable
Job for a Woman* was James' fifth mystery novel. The
book was adapted for film; the British-made motion picture, starring Pippa Guard as Cordelia Gray, was released in 1982.

550.   Millard, Oscar E. *A Missing Person*. New York: David
       McKay/Ives Washburn, 1972.

The protagonist of this cheerless suspense story is
Ann Benton, the twenty-six-year-old wife of Howard Benton. Husband Howard is a graduate student and an instructor of English at the University of California at
Los Angeles. Ann is abducted by Tony Wesley, a sadistic mental case with a high IQ, and is subjected to a
diverse assortment of sexual indignities during her
captivity. After a few days Tony tires of Anne and re-
leases her. Ann then returns home to tell Howard of
her experiences. Howard stops work on his thesis ("Aspects of Camelot and the Arthurian League") and sets
out to put an end to Tony's Marquis de Sade-like behavior. But wait! *A Missing Person* is not an orthodox
mild-mannered-academic-gets-revenge yarn. Howard is
properly mild-mannered, but Ann is not a conventional
rape victim. For the first time in her life, she has
felt real sexual fulfillment. Ann returns to Tony vol-
unarily and begs him for more of his special attentions.
What happens next is best left unrecorded in this bibliography, but it can be observed that only one of the
book's three major participants survives to the end of
the tale. There are several campus scenes in the novel.
And there is more than enough material to send feminists
into spasms of outrage.
Born in London, Oscar E. Milland was a motion-picture
and television writer when *A Missing Person* was published. *A Missing Person* was his first novel.

551.   Peters, Elizabeth [Mertz, Barbara Gross (1927-)]. *The
       Seventh Sinner*. New York: Dodd, Mead and Co., 1972;
       London: Coronet Books, 1975.

Seven graduate students in Rome (most of them Ameri-

can) band together for companionship. The four men and
three women of the group resist the efforts of Albert
Gebara to join their clique. Albert, a "flabbily obese"
Lebanese without "a single redeeming feature," is shortly thereafter found dead in a subterranean Roman temple,
his throat slashed from ear to ear. Who performed the
radical surgery? Jacqueline Kirby happens to be in Rome
and starting with the mysterious number seven which Albert managed to scrawl in the dust as he lay dying, she
sifts through a variety of obscure clues and identifies
the killer. Jacqueline, a middle-aged librarian at an
unidentified American college, is amazingly well-versed
in the niceties of Roman art and archeology. The novel
includes a few scenes at the "Institute" in Rome at
which the students are pursuing their studies, and, as
Jacqueline discovers, the motive which prompted Albert's
underground assassination was thoroughly academic in
nature.

Writing under the pseudonym Elizabeth Peters, Barbara
Gross Mertz created professorial series-character sleuth
Vicky Bliss (303-304). And another Jacqueline Kirby
story as Elizabeth Peters, *The Murders of Richard III*
(567), appears later in the bibliography. Mertz sometimes employs Barbara Michaels as a second alias. One
of her Barbara Michaels novels, *Someone in the House*
(627), also has an entry in the bibliography.

552. Hosegood, Lewis (1920-). *A Time-Torn Man*. London: Wil-
      liam Heinemann, 1973.

The "time-torn man" to whom the title of this melancholic tale of international intrigue refers is Wladys-
law Brunowicz, a visiting professor of history at "Westlands University" in Great Britain. "Bruno," as he is
known to his British friends, has come to Westlands from
St. Louis University in the United States. Before St.
Louis, he taught at Dartmouth College. And many years
before Dartmouth, back in the 1940s, he fought with the
Polish Resistance against Germany. Bruno is attempting
to escape the painful memories of his brutal activities
as a freedom fighter--some of his wartime escapades are
described in vivid flashbacks--and he is trying, too, to
forget that all of the members of his family died in
concentration camps. But Jerzy Olenski, a sinister
Polish diplomat who was one of Bruno's wartime colleagues, tries to get him to leave the West and return
to live in Poland. Bruno is now a famous name in academic circles and, presumably, he would lend respecta-

bility to the efforts underway behind the Iron Curtain to rewrite the history of World War II. There are no conventional murders in the story, although violent death is the central ingredient of several of the flashback scenes. Nor is there any detection. However, there is considerable tension as Bruno labors to resist both Olenski and his own conscience. The book includes many, many scenes on the idyllic Westlands University campus in the Cotswalds, and it also offers a collection of in-depth portraits of Westlands faculty members and their spouses.

At the time *A Time-Torn Man* was published, Lewis Hosegood was a teacher of English at a British secondary school. *A Time-Torn Man* was his second suspense novel.

553. Kemelman, Harry (1908-). *Tuesday the Rabbi Saw Red*. New York: Arthur Fields, 1973; London: Hutchinson and Co., 1974.

Rabbi David Small, whose natural habitat is the New England community of "Barnard's Crossing," is invited to offer a one-semester course in Jewish thought and philosophy at "Windemere College" in Boston. Windemere, charitably characterized by its regular faculty members as a "fallback school," is a classic example of an intellectually deprived institution. Most its students are featherbrains, and its instructors are tired and cynical after years of pedagogic frustrations. The mystery in the story centers on the murder of John Hendryx, an unpleasant, bachelor professor of English. Rabbi Small, Detective Sergeant Schroeder of the Boston police, Suffolk County District Attorney Matthew Rogers, and Barnard Crossing's Irish Catholic police chief, Hugh Lanigan, all share in the detection. It is Rabbi Small's perceptive logic, however, which finally puts Professor Hendrix's killer behind bars. The suspects in the case include Roger Fine (an assistant professor of English whose contract has not been renewed), Millicent Hanbury (Windemere's young and attractive dean of the faculty), and Betty Macomber (the twenty-five-year-old, unmarried daughter of Windemere's president). While the mystery element of the novel will satisfy even the most demanding votaries of detective fiction, the book also can be read exclusively for its commentaries on academe. Real-life American faculty members and administrators, especially those at non-elite institutions, will recognize themselves and many of their colleagues among the book's characters.

Tuesday the Rabbi Saw Red is the fifth work in Harry
Kemelman's Rabbi David Small series. Rabbi Small, a
man of wit, humanity, and immense learning, is one of
the most popular series-character sleuths in modern-
day literature. Kemelman was a member of the English
faculty at Boston State College when *Tuesday the Rabbi
Saw Red* was written. He is also the creator of Nicholas
Welt, a professorial sleuth whose story-length exploits
are collected in *The Nine Mile Walk* (292). Nicholas
Welt is described in the first section of this bibliography.

554.   Ludlum, Robert (1927-). *The Matlock Paper*. New York:
       Dial Press, 1973; St. Albans, Great Britain: Hart-
       Davis, 1973.

Who would ever think that "Carlyle University," an
elite institution in Connecticut, could be the secret
headquarters of an international crime-ring? The FBI
thinks so, and it recruits James B. Matlock II, a virile associate professor of English at Carlyle, as an
undercover investigatory agent. James finds that Carlyle is, indeed, a hub of drug-dealing, gambling, and
prostitution. Moreover, he learns that some of Carlyle's
more distinguished faculty members and administrators
are leading figures in the criminal activities. *The
Matlock Paper* is a fast-paced thriller with an abundance
of gore and a dearth of polysyllabic prose. A best
seller, it will never rate as one of the more intellectual works of college mystery fiction. However, real-
life academic fiscal officers may find that the book
suggests some cures for their schools' chronic budgetary
ills.
     Robert Ludlum was born in New York City. He received
a B.A. from Wesleyan University in Connecticut in 1951.
Before becoming one of America's most commercially successful writers of espionage and crime novels, he was
an actor and New York City theatrical producer. Some
of Ludlum's fiction has been published under the pseu-
doym Jonathan Ryder.

555.   Peden, William Harwood (1913-). *Twilight at Monticello*.
       Boston: Houghton Mifflin, 1973.

The "Jefferson Mafia," a group of academic scholars
passionately interested in the study of the United
States' third president, is holding a three-day meeting
in Charlottesville, Virginia. Various mysteries are in

the air. The University of Virginia is about to announce
a new appointment to the Jefferson Chair of History, and
several of the meeting's participants aspire to the post.
Armistead Davis, the grand old man of Jeffersonian biography, is rumored to be about to announce a new discovery about the relationship between Jefferson and his
slave, Sally Hemmings. And everyone wonders with whom
Dorsey Jack Morgan, the beautiful and notoriously las-
civious female archivist from Williamsburg, Virginia,
will spend her evenings. All of these issues fade into
secondary importance, however, after Armistead Davis
collapses and dies of poison while he is delivering a
speech at the group's final dinner. There is no classical sleuthing in the story, but all of the events are
observed and analyzed by Raymond Green, a professor of
history from the University of Missouri. Green's attractive wife, Margaret, a sometimes writer of mystery
yarns, is along to help her husband understand what is
happening. The book is must reading for those real-
life historians who enjoy fictional tales of murder
within their discipline. Non-historians who read the
work will, at the very least, come away from the experience with a greater knowledge of Thomas Jefferson's
life and times.

William Harwood Peden was born in New York City. He
received a B.S. in 1934, an M.A. in 1936, and a Ph.D.
in 1942 from the University of Virginia. He was a professor of English at the University of Missouri when
Twilight at Monticello was published. Many of Peden's
early professional publications dealt with Thomas Jefferson. His later professional works focus upon American literature. *Twilight at Monticello* was his first
novel.

556. Shaw, Robin (1936-). *Running*. New York: G.P. Putnam's
Sons, 1973; London: Victor Gollancz, 1974.

"Baxter College," in Seattle, Washington, is one of
America's newer and less-distinguished institutions of
higher learning. Craig Boyden, a young member of the
school's English department, is tired of academic life
He seeks new challenges and excitement. And so, in the
company of a seemingly friendly ex-convict, he hatches
a bomb-on-the-plane blackmail scheme through which Con-
solidated Airlines is forced to drop a bag containing
$250,000 onto a pre-arranged spot in Idaho's Sawtooth
Mountains. The story contains some detection, by the
FBI and by airline security agents, but the most ten-

sion-filled scenes take place as Craig and his partner
in crime trek in lonely splendor across high-altitude
wildernesses. The book is included in this bibliography
because it incorporates a few verisimilar on-campus
scenes and because readers are never allowed to forget
that Craig, despite his new avocation, is a Baxter College professor.

557. Stewart, Ramona (1922-). *The Apparition.* Boston, Little, Brown, 1973; London: Andre Deutsch, 1974.

Paul Timberly, a distinguished Harvard anthropologist,
goes to New York City to see his son. Chris Timberly,
a twenty-three-year-old maker of underground films and
an occasional political radical, has just returned from
Brazil. Chris is now living and filming in a derelict
mansion on Fifth Avenue, and when Professor Timberly
arrives he thinks he sees Vanessa King, a young lady
who supposedly died while participating in a well-pub-
licized bombing of a Cambridge computer center. Chris
swears that Vanessa really is dead--in fact, he claims
to have buried her after the explosion--but he, too,
admits to having experienced recent and disturbing visions of her presence. As the story continues, Professor Timberly becomes obsessed with Vanessa's whereabouts, and his usual cool rationality degenerates into
blurred perceptions of the people and events in Chris'
busy New York abode. Until the very end of the book,
The Apparition seems to be a well-written ghost yarn.
On the last page, however, the author provides an up-
to-date real-world explanation for most of the happenings in the tale. The novel contains no campus scenes,
but readers are accorded several glimpses of Professor
Timberly at his Waldon, Massachusetts, home. They can
learn that he is the author of the award-winning *Pre-
historic Man*, that he has a dog named Tule (who dies
suddenly during the story, and that he sometimes feels
guilty about the long-ago death of his wife, Sally.
    Ramona Stewart was born in San Francisco. She attend-
ed the University of Southern California. At one point
in her working life she served as a secretary for the
philosophy department at the University of California at Los Angeles. Stewart has written horror stories,
conventional mysteries, and mainstream novels. One of
her mainstream novels, *Professor Descending* (Garden City,
New York: Doubleday and Co., 1969), has as its protagonist Professor Benjamin F. Hilary, a fifty-year-old professor of philosophy at a provincial American University,
who comes to New York City with plans to commit suicide.

558. Taylor, Edith (1913-). *The Serpent Under It*. New York: W.W. Norton, 1973; London: Arthur Barker, 1973.

Set at "Hoyt College," in America's Berkshire Mountains, this intricate story centers on murderous behavior in the English department. Professor Archibald and the department's secretary are the victims. Numerous faculty members and graduate students are suspects. And Anne Redmond, the wife of a young instructor, is the sleuth. Some of the action takes place at the "Hoyt Memorial Gardens," a local beauty spot near the campus. Plagiarism is important to the plot, and the unique crucial clue is found deep in the department's dusty files. For readers who have difficulty keeping up with the super-energetic Anne, she stops her investigation at many junctures to offer long fact-filled summations of the-case-thus-far.
Edith Taylor was born in New York City. She received a B.A. from Swarthmore in 1935 and then did graduate work at Syracuse University. After five years in the English department of the University of Buffalo, she moved, in 1951, to Buffalo Seminary where she taught English and creative writing. In 1955 she became chairperson of the school's English department, and in 1970 she was appointed dean of studies. *The Serpent Under It* was her first novel.

*559. Barnard, Robert (1936-). *Death of an Old Goat*. London: William Collins Sons, 1974; New York: Walker and Co., 1977.

The "University of Drummondville" is a small, intellectual backwater in a remote part of Australia. Elderly Professor Belleville-Smith arrives from Oxford to deliver a series of lectures on Jane Austen. Something of a sham, Belleville-Smith has been giving the same presentations--word for word--for more than forty years. His first lecture thoroughly bores his audience, and the next morning he is found dead in his room in the "Yarumba Motel," his throat cut from ear to ear. Inspector Royle of the local police heads the inquiry. Royle is one of the least-appealing sleuths in detective fiction. Slow-witted, corrupt, and sour to the point of nastiness, he displays all of these negative qualities and more while attempting to discover the professor's killer. Many members of the Drummondville faculty enter into the proceedings, as do representatives of the town's sheep-growing squirearchy. Written with consi-

derable caustic humor, *Death of an Old Goat* adds some
inventive twists to the classic college mystery format.
It also provides a surprise ending. And it offers readers a lingering, richly satirical look at an undistin-
guished academic outpost in the Australian wilds.
Robert Barnard was born in Burnham, Great Britain.
Educated at Balliol College, Oxford, he spent six years
as a lecturer in English at the University of New England in Northern New South Wales. *Death of an Old Goat*
was Barnard's first novel. At the time the book was
published, Barnard was a senior lecturer in English at
the University of Bergen in Norway. Two later mysteries
by Barnard appear in this bibliography. They are *Posthumous Papers* (603) and *Death in a Cold Climate* (611).

560. Constantine, K.C. (pseud.). *The Blank Page*. New York:
      The Saturday Review Press/E.P. Dutton, 1974.

"Rocksburg Junior College" is a small emporium of edu-
cational mediocrity in western Pennsylvania. Only a
few of its faculty members have doctorates; its president, J. Hale Beverley, cares far more about his personal image than about his school's intellectual standards;
and plagiarism and drug-taking are the mainstays of
undergraduate life. When Janet Pistula, a slow-witted
Rocksburg coed, is found strangled with her own bras-
siere in a shabby rooming house, the killing is investigated by Mario Balzic, the local chief of police. A
K.C. Constantine series-character, Balzic is an earthy,
sometimes cynical, non-intellectual type who relies on
dogged detection. In the process of solving the case,
Balzic probes deeply into Rockburg J.C.'s academically
dismal milieu. He finds the killer, and his experiences
only reinforce his already-negative views about American
higher education.
K.C. Constantine is a pseudonym employed by a writer
whose real name has never been revealed to his or her
reading public. *The Blank Page* was the third book in
Constantine's Mario Balzic series.

561. Fisher, David Elimelech (1932-). *A Fearful Symmetry*.
      Garden City, New York: Doubleday and Co., 1974.

One day, toward the end of the semester, Henry Keller
is visited in his office by Becky Aaronson, a pretty
coed who asks for an A in Geology 103. Henry is a quiet
forty-seven-year-old professor at an American university.
He looks up Becky's record, finds that she is only an

indifferent student, and refuses her request. With Henry's stuffy response, Becky stands, doffs her clothes, and annouces that she is prepared to do anything to get the grade she wants. Becky's gracious offer jolts Henry out of his usual professorial stupor and propels him into a world comprised, in equal parts, of ecstacy and danger. Becky, it seems has an overprotective boyfriend, and not long after Henry begins to consort with his now-favorite student, the boyfriend concocts a series of diabolical schemes to end the affair. Although the book is not a novel of detection, its plot includes a violent death and more than enough suspense to keep most academic readers engrossed until the end.

An earlier novel by David Elimelech Fisher, *Crisis* (540), also appears in this bibliography.

562. Goldberg, Marshall. *The Anatomy Lesson*. New York: G.P. Putnam's Sons, 1974.

Set in Boston, this fast-moving novel deals with the adventures of Dan Lassiter, a medical student, after he begins to dissect his first cadaver. The body is that of a young man who apparently died from a blow to the head, and Dan sets out to discover the person's identity and the circumstances of his death. The institution at which Dan is a student is the Massachusetts State Medical College, and the school's leading professor of anatomy, Nathan Snider, plays a significant part in the story. So, too, does Lem Harper, a black militant with a heart of gold. And Kim Chatfield, the dead man's ex-girlfriend, helps Dan relieve the tensions he experiences from attempting to perform his self-appointed sleuthing tasks even as he tries to pass his anatomy course. The book is not a conventional mystery; the emphasis is on Dan's psychological adjustments as he juggles his several time-consuming activities. Nonetheless, Dan emerges as one of the more determined, if less-than-fully-successful amateur detectives in American fiction.

563. Goldman, William, (1931-). *The Marathon Man*. New York: Delacorte Press, 1974; London: Macmillan, 1975.

Thomas Babington ("Babe") Levy, the young protagonist of this slickly written story, would like to become both a Ph.D. and a champion marathon runner. A graduate student in history at Columbia University, Babe trains for his races by jogging from his room on

95th Street up to his classes on the Columbia campus.
And he studies for his doctorate under such demanding
Columbia faculty members as Professor Biesenthal. But
evil drives Babe away from his goals when international
spies, ex-Nazis, and diamond smugglers make him an unwilling victim of their emprises. Much of the novel
consists of off-campus chase scenes which culminate in
torture and/or killings. The early chapters, however,
deal in some length with Babe's academic experiences.
While Professor Biesenthal may not be as sadistic as
some of the archvillains who appear later in the narrative, he is nevertheless one of the more intimidating
academics in mystery fiction. Sarcastic, feisty, and
a man who says exactly what he thinks, Biesenthal walks
into Babe's seminar on the first day of the semester
and announces to the assembled students: "I hope you all
flunk."

William Goldman was born in Chicago and received a
B.A. in 1952 from Oberlin College and an M.A. in 1956
from Columbia University. Goldman is an extremely successful commercial novelist and screenwriter. *The Marathon Man* was transformed into a 1976 motion picture
starring Dustin Hoffman and Laurence Olivier.

564. Mann, Jessica. *The Sticking Place*. London: Macmillan,
      1974; New York: David McKay, 1974.

Angus Seton is a brilliant young historian at the
"University of Ferraby" in Great Britain. He also is a
television personality. When there is a major disaster
anywhere in the world, Angus appears on TV to inform
eager viewers of the tragedy's background. Thanks principally to his video fame, Angus is offered the direc-
torship of the Centre for Self-Determination, an organization devoted to the cause of Scottish nationalism.
Although the Centre's aim is to pursue the Scottish
cause by scholarly means, Angus decides that direct
action is more efficient and becomes involved in a series of violent attempts to end British rule. For the
most part, this taut, suspenseful story is told from
the viewpoint of Rachel, Angus' Jewish, long-suffering
wife. Rachel's interests in self-determination for
Scotland are nil, and the tension in the plot flows out
of her gradual discovery of her husband's violent, radical activities. Another of the book's major characters is Elizabeth, the Seton's teenaged daughter. Inclined more to her father's temperament than to that

of her mother, Elizabeth furnishes the book with a surprise ending.

Jessica Mann is the creator of Theodora Crawford (305-306), a professorial series-character sleuth described in the first section of this bibliography.

565. Masterson, Whit [Wade, Robert (1920-)]. *The Man with Two Clocks*. New York: Dodd, Mead and Co., 1974; London: Robert Hale, 1975.

Are America's defense secrets safe in the hands of the nation's academic scientists? After finishing *The Man with Two Clocks*, most readers probably will be ready to answer in the negative. Michael Grail is a young professor of nuclear physics at the California Institute of Technology. Emlyn Shade, an agent for the National Security Agency, suspects that Grail is selling classified weapons information to the Russians. Shade's suspicions grow when he discovers that Grail cannot account for his whereabouts during an entire summer vacation. A combination travelogue and tale of espionage, the book takes Grail and Shade on a series of enervating jaunts to such faraway locales as Antarctica before it reaches its unusual conclusion. It is included in this bibliography because Shade's investigatory tactics sometimes include classical modes of detection and because both protagonists, on occasion, perform in extended on-campus scenes.

Robert Wade was born in San Diego, California. He attended San Diego State College. After service in the Air Force during World War II, Wade joined forces with Robert Miller, a boyhood friend, to produce a lengthy series of mystery novels, screenplays, short stories, and radioscripts. Some of their novels were published under the pseudonym Whit Masterson. After Miller's death in 1961, Wade continued to employ the Whit Masterson pseudonym on some of his solo works. Another Whit Masterson novel by Robert Wade, *The Slow Gallows* (607), also is included in this bibliography.

*566. Parker, Robert B(rown) (1932-). *The Godwulf Manuscript*. Boston: Houghton Mifflin, 1974; London: Andre Deutsch, 1974.

This violent novel follows Spenser, Robert Parker's popular series-character private detective, as he investigates the theft of a rare fourteenth-century manuscript from one of Boston's less-prestigious universi-

ties. Operating in his rough, tough, and wisecracking
style (in the manner of the great private eyes in American fiction during the 1940s and 1950s), Spenser finds
that the case eventually involves him with radical students, with the collegiate drug scene, and with free-
loving coeds. Most of the action takes place on or near
the university's campus, and several faculty members
and administrators play key roles in the story. Professorial readers will appreciate the depiction of Bradford W. Forbes, the school's harassed president. Dr.
Forbes occupies an office which resembles "the front
parlor of a Victorian whorehouse" and is one of the few
university presidents in literature or in real life who
has the honesty to admit that his institution is "undis-
tinguished." The same professorial readers may not be so
enthralled, however, with the portrait of the principal
evildoer in the book. This individual is the only faculty villain in mystery fiction who wets his pants when
apprehended for his misdeeds.

Robert Brown Parker was born in Springfield, Massachusetts. He received a B.A. in 1954 from Colby College
in Maine and a Ph.D. from Boston University in 1970.
Parker's doctoral dissertation was a study of Dashiell
Hammett and Raymond Chandler. At the time of *The Godwulf Manuscript* was published, Parker was an associate
professor of English at Northeastern University in Boston. Although Spenser had appeared previously as the
protagonist of short stories, *The Godwulf Manuscript*
marked his debut in a novel-length publication. The
subsequent Spenser series, of course, has met with both
critical and commercial success.

567. Peters, Elizabeth [Mertz, Barbara Gross (1927-)]. *The
      Murders of Richard III*. New York: Dodd, Mead and Co,
      1974.

Did Richard III really murder his two young nephews
in the Tower of London? The members of the Riccardian
Society think not, and they gather, in medieval costumes, at the ancient Yorkshire mansion of Sir Richard
Weldon to celebrate the innocence of their hero. However, as the participants eat roast peacock and otherwise attempt to transport themselves back in time, someone begins playing deadly practical jokes which emulate
notorious fifteenth-century crimes. One of the guests
at the ill-fated gathering is Thomas Carter, a middle-
aged American professor of history who is spending a
year in Great Britain as a visiting lecturer at "one of

England's oldest universities." Thomas has taken the
liberty of asking Jacqueline Kirby, a sharp-tongued
American college librarian, to accompany him to the fes-
tivities. Jacqueline, a devotee of detective fiction,
puts her literary expertise to good use by assuming the
role of sleuth, and Carter acts as her foil and assistant. Although *The Murders of Richard III* does not
take place on a college or university campus, Professor
Carter plays an important part in the story, and Jacqueline Kirby, whose knowledge of arcane subjects is encyclopedic, displays so much academic-style acumen that
she almost qualifies as an honorary professorial detective.

The *Murders of Richard III* marked Jacqueline Kirby's
second appearance in a Barbara Gross Mertz/Elizabeth
Peters novel. The first Jacqueline Kirby story, *The
Seventh Sinner* (551), appears earlier in the biblio-
graphy. Writing under her Elizabeth Peters pseudonym,
Mertz also created professorial series-character sleuth
Vicky Bliss (303-304). And under the pseudonym Barbara
Michaels, Mertz wrote *Someone in the House* (627), a go-
thic mystery which is included in the bibliography.

568. Rennert, Maggie (1922-). *Circle of Death*. Englewood
Cliffs, New Jersey: Prentice-Hall, 1974.

"Elm Circle" is an elite residential cul-de-sac which
adjoins the campus of "Lambert University." The inhabitants of the exclusive enclave become uneasy when Lambert's Afro-American Association establishes its headquarters in one of the houses. Called in to assuage
the homeowners' fears is young, attractive Guy Silvestri, a detective lieutenant and a human relations spec-
ialist with the local police force. Silvestri, as it
happens, is also a part-time student at the university.
The lieutenant's efforts are not made easier when Hilary
Bridge, an associate professor of English and an Elm
Circle resident, is murdered in his garage. As the
story develops, Silvestri probes faculty politics, racial animosities, the Lambert homosexual scene, and the
school's drug culture before bringing the case to a surprise conclusion. Lambert University is an Ivy League
institution located in "Buxton," Massachusetts, "just
across the river from Boston," and a goodly number of
Lambert faculty members and administrators (most of
them unpleasant) cross Silvestri's path during the
course of his investigations.

Maggie Rennert was born in New York City. A poet,

editor, and teacher, she lived for many years in Cambridge, Massachusetts. Rennert was a resident of Israel
when *Circle of Death* was published. The book was her
first mystery novel. Her second mystery, *Operation
Alcestis* (577), also appearing in this bibliography,
describes the further efforts of Lieutenant Silvestri to
deal with the strange and often-nasty folk who make up
the Lambert University community.

569. Ruell, Patrick [Hill, Reginald (1936-)]. *Death Takes
      the Low Road*. London: Hutchinson Publishing Group,
      1974.

The protagonist of this cleverly fabricated mystery-
thriller is William Blake Hazlitt, the thirty-eight-
year-old deputy registrar at "Lincoln University" in
Great Britain. William, who inadvertently comes into
possession of some information about the activities of
Russian spies at Lincoln, tries to lose himself in
northern Scotland, but agents of various secret services
chase him from one rustic hiding place to another.
Joining in the hunt, too, is Caroline Nevis, a beautiful
American graduate student. Caroline, who has dated
William as part of her personal survey of British manners and morals, eventually locates the deputy registrar
but not before she is almost killed in the process.
Written in a sardonic style more than vaguely reminiscent of the novels of Michael Innes, *Death Takes the
Low Road* includes some singular characterizations. The
head of the British intelligence operatives in the story
is an implacable gentleman known as "The Old Etonian."
And William Hazlitt, who turns out to be the resourceful hero of the piece, is short, plump, and balding.
At the end of the story, The Old Etonian tries to recruit the deputy registrar for future counter-espionage
work. He compliments William by telling him that he
has fortitude, courage, ingenuity, and great powers of
survival. "But your main attaction," adds The Old Etonian, "is that to look at you, all of this would appear
completely out of the question."
    Reginald Hill is one of Great Britain's best-respec-
ted modern-day writers of mysteries and thrillers. Patrick Ruell is a pseudonym which Hill employs for his
espionage stories. *An Advancement of Learning* (542),
an on-campus detective story published by Hill under his
real name, appears earlier in this bibliography.

570. Westheimer, David (1917-). *The Avila Gold*. New York:
      G.P. Putnam's Sons, 1974; London: Michael Joseph,
      1975.

      Arthur McDowell, a pudgy, fortyish professor of his-
      tory at the University of California at Los Angeles,
      learns of the existence of a rich cache of Spanish gold
      coins hidden deep under the ground in downtown Los An-
      geles. With the help of Steve Sussman, a professor of
      engineering, Arthur begins a laborious, clandestine
      tunneling operation to gain access to the treasure. The
      scheme goes badly, however, when costs exceed Arthur's
      limited budget, when Arthur is distracted by an affair
      with Professor Sussman's mistress, and when it appears
      as though murder will be necessary in order to keep the
      digging a secret. Although the book contains generous
      helpings of mystery and suspense, it is in its essence
      a character study. Working with obsessive zeal to
      bring his task to a successful conclusion, Arthur is
      transformed from a soft, sluggish academic into a
      tough and alert man of action.
         Born in Houston, Texas, David Westheimer received a
      B.A. from Rice Institute in 1937. Before, in between,
      and after service in the United States Army Air Forces
      during World War II and the Korean War, Westheimer
      held a variety of editorial positions with newspapers
      and magazines in Texas and California. In the 1960s
      Westheimer turned his full attention to creative wri-
      ting. Among his major credits are the novelization of
      the screenplay for *Days of Wine and Roses* (New York:
      Bantam Books, 1963) and the novel *Von Ryan's Express*
      (New York: Doubleday and Co., 1964; London: Michael
      Joseph, 1964).

571. Davis, Mildred. *Tell Them What's-Her-Name Called*. New
      York: Random House, 1975; London: Robert Hale, 1976.

      A series of suspicious, fatal accidents occur at "White-
      field College," an exclusive school in the northeastern
      United States. One of the victims is Ruth Wehrmann, the
      wife of a Whitefield professor of English. The Wehrmann's
      daughter, Finley, takes it upon herself to investigate.
      Disturbed by Finley's sleuthing, the murderer tries to
      add our heroine to the book's long casualty list. But
      Finley carries on without much help or encouragement
      from the police, and in the last scene the elusive kil-
      ler is revealed. A few professors appear in the story,
      but the emphasis in the tale is upon Whitefield's under-

graduate culture.

A frequent contributor to the mystery-fiction genre,
Mildred Davis was a resident of Bedford, New York, when
Tell Them What's-Her-Name Called was published. The
book was her eleventh novel.

572. Dexter, (Norman) Colin (1930-). *Last Bus to Woodstock*.
      London: Macmillan, 1975; New York: St. Martin's,
      1976.

      After misreading one of those infernally reticular
      British timetables, two young women miss the last bus
      of the evening from Oxford to nearby Woodstock. They
      then decide to hitchhike. A few hours later one of
      them is found sexually assaulted and dead of a broken
      skull behind The Black Prince, a popular Woodstock pub.
      Detective Chief-Inspector Morse and his assistant, Ser-
      geant Lewis, are assigned the case. Figuring promin-
      ently in the police investigations are Bernard Crou-
      ther and his spouse, Margaret. Bernard is an Oxford
      don, a Milton expert, and a frequent patron of The Black
      Prince. Margaret, one of the least-appealing faculty
      wives in all college mystery fiction, has a part-time
      position at The School of Oriental Studies. A relent-
      lessly grim police procedural, *Last Bus to Woodstock*
      makes a few excursions behind the walls of Oxford's
      "Lonsdale College," a singularly somber academic insti-
      tution, and it offers its readers a painstaking look at
      the ways through poor Bernard compensates for an un-
      happy domestic sex life.
      Norman Colin Dexter was born in Stamford, Lincoln-
      shire, Great Britain. He received a B.A. and an M.A.
      from Cambridge. *Last Bus to Woodstock* was his first
      mystery novel. At the time the book was published, Dex-
      ter was a senior classics master at a British secondary
      school. A later Dexter mystery, *The Silent World of
      Nicholas Quinn* (586), also appears in this bibliography.

573. Gordon, Ethel Edison (1915-). *The Freebody Heiress*.
      New York: David McKay, 1975; London: Arthur Barker,
      1975.

      Ian Sexton, a thirtyish professor of English, leaves
      his post at Columbia University after his wife dies in
      a fire. Hoping to start his life anew, he joins the
      faculty of "Freebody College," a coed institution in
      Vermont. He is not at the Vermont school long before
      he falls in love with Iris Freebody, the shy, young

heiress to the Freebody fortune and a student in one of
his classes. Iris reciprocates Ian's love, but wicked
old Aunt Gladys tries to break up their romance. Aunt
Gladys wants Iris to marry Ralph, her stepson. Then
Aunt Gladys is killed in a fire. Is Ian a pyromaniac
and an academic fortune hunter? Or does Ralph (a Harvard student) have something to do with the affair?
What role does Nearing, the sinister caretaker of the
Freebody estate, have in the whole dark and brooding
business? And how about Sally Lukas, another of Ian's
students, who would like the handsome, mustachioed professor for herself? There are several campus scenes
early in this detectionless gothic novel, but as Ian
accelerates his quest for Iris, he understandably spends
most of his time at the Freebody mansion.

Ethel Edison Gordon was born in New York City and received a B.A. from New York University in 1936. A member of Phi Beta Kappa, the wife of a high-school principal, and the mother of two children, she is one of
America's best-respected writers of suspenseful gothic
mysteries.

574. Guild, Nicholas (1944-). *The Lost and Found Man*. New
York: Harper's Magazine Press, 1975; London: Robert
Hale, 1977.

During World War II, William Lukas was a United States
Army commando-assassin who worked behind the German lines.
William is now a professor of English at "Merton College," a two-year school in Los Angeles. Divorced and
unattached, William decides to take a vacation in London. But upon his arrival at Heathrow Airport, he is
met by an old commando colleague and blackmailed into
accepting a new lethal assignment. William's new task
takes him into Switzerland, where peril lurks at every
turn. It propels him into romance, too, when a beautiful young lady named Meg assists him in completing
his mission. Pure escapist literature, *The Lost and
Found Man* contains far more than its fair share of
action. Fortunately, William is prepared for his exploits because he is an expert in the arts of physical
combat. Indeed, his students at Merton College know
better than to complain about their grades. Early in
his teaching career, William broke the arm of a large,
loutish male who threatened to punch him after receiving a D in freshman English.

The Lost and Found Man was Nicholas Guild's first novel. In the late 1970s Guild created Raymond Guiness

(317-319), a professorial series-character sleuth who
bears a marked resemblance to William Lukas.

575. Lang, Brad. *Crockett on the Loose*. New York: Leisure
      Books, 1975.

The protagonist of this paperback action-saga is Fred
Crockett, a twenty-eight-year-old private detective who
operates in a city which very much resembles Ann Arbor,
Michigan. Long-haired, cynical, and impatient with
authority, Crockett is a former cop who holds an M.A.
in criminal science from the local state university.
The story focuses upon Crockett's search for Susan Sam-
uelson, the daughter of a wealthy Detroit businessman,
who has dropped out of the university and cut off all
contact with her family. There are several on-campus
scenes in the book, and a university security guard
named Jim Ford is murdered halfway through the story.
Before he locates Susan--working in a massage parlor--
Crockett runs afoul of sadistic policemen, drug dealers,
and representatives of organized crime. He also meets
and mates with Kathy Walker, a voluptuous coed who
earns her tuition by working as a topless dancer.

576. Lore, Phillips [Smith, Terrence Lore]. *Who Killed the
      Pie Man?* New York: Saturday Review Press/E.P. Dutton,
      1975.

The "Pie Man" in the title of this intricate mystery
is Dr. Albert Wren, a retired professor of history at
Northwestern University in Evanston, Illinois. Six-
foot-four-inches tall and well over three hundred pounds,
Dr. Wren acquired his nickname because of his fondness
for consuming a half-dozen or more pies at a single
sitting. The bachelor professor had other eccentricities as well. He drank exotic tea, smoked marijuana,
and had a passionate interest in rare coins. Dr. Wren
dies just before this story begins. He is shot dead
one night outside a coin collector's shop in Evanston,
and inside the store the police find the body of a
second victim, Jane Koenig, a wealthy Northwestern coed.
Although there is some modest police detection in the
book, the hardest-working sleuth is Leo Roi, a young
criminal lawyer who is hired to defend Billy Blue, the
leading suspect in the double murder. Billy, a black
civil rights activist, was Jane's live-in boyfriend.
Before the complicated opus ends, Leo Roi learns that
miscegenation is frowned upon in certain segments of

the Evanston community, that selected gold coins of the
Roman Empire can be worth more than $100,000, and that
some representatives of organized crime take their numismatics very seriously. He also finds that Northwestern is an excellent place "for girl and woman watching."
There are several scenes on the Northwestern campus (including one in a women's dormitory), and the cast of
characters includes one of very few professors of business administration to appear in a detective novel.
This individual, Dr. Oran Thompson, is tall, thin, and
egg-bald, and was Albert Wren's only friend.

Terrence Lore Smith attended Northwestern University.
Who Killed the Pie Man? was his third mystery novel.

577. Rennert, Maggie (1922-). *Operation Alcestis*. Englewood
      Cliffs, New Jersey: Prentice-Hall, 1975.

Professor Clarence Putnam, a biologist at "Lambert
University," is attacked and killed by three young
assailants as he works in the backyard of his home.
Putnam was a staunch conservative on campus political
issues, and everyone assumes that his killer came from
one of Lambert's radical student groups. These assump-
tions are soon given weight when Allie Tuttle, a beautiful radical coed, confesses to having been one of the
professor's murderers. But old Mrs. Roscoe, Professor
Putnam's housekeeper, swears that all three members of
the offending trio were male, so the authorities not
only doubt Allie's story but they begin to wonder about
her sanity as well. The sleuth in the saga is Detective Lieutenant Guy Silvestri, a young-but-wise officer
of the law for the town of Buxton, the Boston suburb in
which Ivy-League Lambert University is located. Digging
into various skeletons in academic closets, Silvestri
finds that Putnam's death was, in fact, part of an international espionage conspiracy and that the lovely
but strange Allie is indeed innocent. The story is
crowded with characters and sub-plots. In addition to
the late but generally unlamented Clarence Putnam, several professors enter the plot, as do a number of Lambert's large collection of dissident students. The novel is narrated by a New York drama critic named Herkimer, who once taught anthropology at Lambert and who
returns to the school to help defend Allie Tuttle, but
the text is interrupted at many points for excerpts (up
to eleven pages in length) from Lieutenant Silvestri's
"personal journal" of the affair. The last chapter provides readers with information about what happens to

several of the story's characters after the case of professor Putnam is closed. Herkimer returns to New York
to review Broadway shows. Lieutenant Silvestri is appointed an advisor on human relations to the governor
of Massachusetts. And, in an attempt to inject more
relevance into its administration, Lambert University
makes Allie Tuttle an assistant dean.
  An earlier novel by Maggie Rennert, *Circle of Death*
(568), also appears in the bibliography. Like *Operation
Alcestis, Circle of Death* is set at Lambert University,
and the sleuth in the story is Lieutenant Guy Silvestri.

578. Archer, Jeffrey Howard (1940-). *Not a Penny More, Not
      a Penny Less*. London: Jonathan Cape, 1976; Garden
      City, New York: Doubleday and Co., 1976.

  Four prominent people--an English lord, a doctor, an
art dealer, and an American professor spending a year at
Oxford--each lose vast amounts of money in a stock swindle. Stephen Bradley, a mathematician whose home base
is Harvard, leads the aggrieved quartet in a scheme to
gain revenge. Not a novel of detection, the book is instead a smoothly told tale of retribution. Most of the
action takes place in Great Britain, and there are several scenes at Oxford's Magdalen College. The ending,
though not entirely surprising, may nonetheless warm
the hearts of academic readers.
  Jeffrey Archer was educated at Brasenose College, Oxford. At the edge of twenty-six he was elected as a
Conservative to the Greater London Council. Then at the
age of twenty-nine, he was elected to Parliament. In
1973 he invested $1,000,000 in a Canadian company and,
a year later, found that his shares in the corporation
were worthless. Quoting from the book's dustjacket:
"Overnight Jeffrey Archer was penniless and was preven-
ted from seeking re-election. Instead he wrote *Not a
Penny More, Not a Penny Less*."

579. Ashe, Rosalind. *Moths*. London: Hutchinson Publishing
      Group, 1976; New York: Holt, Rinehart and Winston, 1976.

  Jim and Nemo Boyce live in Dower House, a stately residence near Oxford. Jim is a fellow in economics at the
university. Nemo is a manic-depressive housewife who
sometimes believes that her body has been invaded by the
spirit of Sarah Moore, a nineteenth-century actress and
one of Dower House's previous occupants. The lovely
Nemo is also a combination nymphomaniac and typhoid Mary.

She takes to bed various male Oxonians, many of whom, after enjoying her favors, meet mysterious deaths. *Moths* is narrated by "Harry" Harris, an English literature don. Harry falls for Nemo's charms and then almost perishes in a traffic accident after someone tampers with the brakes on his automobile. There is some modest detection in the book--by Inspector Blunt of the Oxford police--but the focus of the story is less upon traditional sleuthing than upon Harry's growing suspicions that Nemo's favorite sport is kiss and kill. Often poetic in tone and sometimes eerie, the book includes several university scenes, and at one point Harry gains a temporary respite from Nemo by serving as a visiting professor at Princeton.

Rosalind Ashe was born in Jamaica. Educated in Canada and Great Britain, she read English literature at Oxford. *Moths* was her first novel. According to publisher's publicity about the book, Ashe modeled the elegant but spooky Dower House after her own home--a Georgian rectory in Oxfordshire.

580. Clarke, Anna (1919-). *The Deathless and the Dead*. London: William Collins, 1976. Published in the United States as *This Downhill Path*. New York: David McKay/ Ives Washburn, 1976.

Emily Witherspoon was a minor Victorian poet. She died when still a young woman, apparently from a bicycling mishap, but her "tiny place" among the immortals of English literature is assured. Now, sixty years after Emily's demise, John Broome is researching her life. John, a graduate student at Oxford, meets and falls in love with Alice Heron, a young woman whose wealthy and aged aunt and uncle knew Emily before her untimely end. So John goes calling on Aunt Belle and Uncle Roderick at their home near Oxford, and his interviews suggest that Emily's death may well have been the result of foul play. Moreover, it appears to John that Emily's murderer may still be alive. As the story proceeds, Aunt Belle and Uncle Roderick lose both their female servant and their cat to an unknown assailant, and the mystery about Emily's last moments is unraveled. Samuel Woodward, a rather pompous Oxford professor, enters the plot at crucial junctures, and the book includes several scenes in and around the university. At the conclusion of the book, John decides that he cannot besmirch Emily Witherspoon's name by publishing his findings. By way of compensation, however, he is about to marry Alice, who has just inherited the vast Heron fortune.

Anna Clarke was born in Cape Town, South Africa. She received an external B.Sc. in economics from the University of London in 1945 and an M.A. from the University of Sussex in 1975. Early in her working life, Clarke held secretarial positions with the London publishing firms of Victor Gollancz and Eyre and Spottiswoode. Her first novel, *The Darkened Room* (London: John Long, 1968), was published when Clarke was forty-nine years old. *The Deathless and the Dead* was Clarke's seventh novel. All of her novels to date are mysteries, and most deal in one way or another with the world of literature.

581. Foote-Smith, Elizabeth (1913-). *Gentle Albatross*. New York: G.P. Putnam's Sons, 1976.

George Duddington Oldham is the president of "Barclay University," a school in the American Midwest. George drives a red jaguar, hides $300 in "lucky money" in his wallet, and (though his wife claims that "sex just isn't his thing") keeps a mistress. George also keeps a locked file which houses incriminating evidence about members of his faculty. He uses this information to blackmail professors into giving him money from grants which they receive. One day the loathsome Dr. Oldham disappears, and private detective Wilson Woodford is asked to investigate. Woodford joins forces with Mercy Newcastle, a nineteen-year-old graduate student whose M.A. dissertation is on "The Literary Evolution of the Crime Novel in France, England, and America," and the duo steps out in search of the missing prexy. When Woodford and Newcastle find the object of their hunt, strangled to death, their task is to discover which of the many likely suspects in the case can claim credit for the murder. Written, one must assume, with tongue-well-into-cheek *Gentle Albatross* is not the most puzzling of all college mysteries. Nevertheless, professorial president watchers may find that the book is among the more enjoyable novels in this bibliography.

Elizabeth Foote-Smith was born in Red Wing, Minnesota. After raising a family she returned to Northwestern University for a B.A. in 1964. In 1966 she was awarded an M.A. from the University of Chicago and then taught English at the University of Wisconsin at Whitewater until 1969. She was a full-time free-lance writer when *Gentle Albatross*, her first mystery novel, was published.

582. Holland, Isabelle (1920-). *Grenelle*. New York: Rawson
      Associates, 1976; London: William Collins, 1978.

This "had-I-but-known," gothic mystery is set at "Grenelle College," an Anglican-run institution in rural
Virginia. The heroine of the piece is Susan Grenelle,
the granddaughter of the school's major benefactor and
the daughter of its late but still-beloved president.
Thirtyish and unmarried, Susan returns after eleven
years in California to live alone in the large and eerie
family homestead on the Grenelle Campus. Shortly thereafter Samantha (the pre-teen daughter of Susan's recently deceased twin sister) also takes up residence in the
house. One of Samantha's playmates is murdered; Samantha is kidnapped; and some dastardly person or persons
steals the school's most prized possession, a splinter
which at least some of the Grenelle faculty believe came
from Christ's cross. Happily for Susan, an old boyfriend named Mark Czernick is now the local chief of
police. Susan and Mark not only detect together; they
rekindle their old romance as well. Unhappily for Susan, Mark cannot stay constantly by her side, and when
Mark is away sinister forces seem to lurk behind every
door of the dark and creaky Grenelle mansion. The faculty of Grenelle College is comprised largely of Anglican priests. A number of these worthies play prominent roels in the story, and some of them prove, by their
actions, that priest-professors can be as nasty as sec-
ular academics.
     The daughter of a United States Foreign Service offi-
cer, Isabelle Holland, was born in Basel, Switzerland.
She attended the University of Liverpool in Great Britain before receiving a B.A. from Tulane University in
1942. Before launching a successful career as a writer
of gothics and children's books, Holland served as publicity director for a number of major American publishing firms.

583. Lovesey, Peter (1936-). *Swing, Swing Together*. Lon-
      don: Macmillan, 1976; New York: Dodd, Mead and Co.,
      1976.

Swing, Swing Together is the seventh novel in Peter
Lovesey's often-whimsical and extremely popular series
of mysteries featuring Victorian-era detectives Sergeant Cribb and Constable Thackery of Scotland Yard.
Swing, Swing Together takes Lovesey's intrepid pair of
policemen to the "Elfrida College for the Training of
Female Elementary Teachers" and then to Merton College

at Oxford. Its inventive plot involves a nude, midnight
swim on the part of three young ladies from Elfrida College, the murder of an Oxford don, and a long boat ride
on the Thames in the manner of Jerome K. Jerome's *Three
Men in A Boat*. The story also takes Sergeant Cribb to
the Coldbath Fields House of Correction, one of Great
Britain's most cheerless prisons, where he receives the
information which allows him to resolve the mystery
which surrounds the don's death. As are all of the
books in the Cribb-Thackery series, *Swing, Swing Together* is thick with Victorian atmosphere, and the descriptions of Elfrida College and Oxford provide rich
(if somewhat fanciful) glimpses of two very different
British institutions of higher learning just before the
turn of the century.
    Peter Lovesey was born in Whitton, Middlesex, Great
Britain. After receiving a B.A. (honors) from the University of Reading in 1958, he served in the RAF as a
flying officer until 1961. From 1961 until 1969 he was
a member of the faculty at Thurrock Technical College in
Essex, and from 1969 until 1975 he was head of the general education department at the Hammersmith College
for Further Education. Lovesey published his first
Cribb-Thackery novel in 1970; by 1975 the success of the
series facilitated his leaving academe for full-time
creative writing. Lovesey has employed the pseudonym
Peter Lear on some of his mysteries which do not feature
Sergeant Cribb and Constable Thackery. One of his Peter
Lear works, *Spider Girl* (617), appears later in this
bibliography.

584. Rendell, Ruth (1930-). *A Demon in My View*. London:
      Hutchinson Publishing Group, 1976; Garden City, New
      York: Doubleday and Co., 1977.

          Anthony Johnson is a graduate student in criminology
      at the University of London. He resides in a seedy
      rooming house owned and managed by a resident landlord
      whose name, by coincidence, is Arthur Johnson. Anthony
      is writing a thesis titled "Some aspects of the Psy-
      chopathic Personality," and he finds Arthur ideal as
      case-study material. Arthur gets his sexual pleasures
      from strangling a female department-store mannikin
      which he keeps concealed in a coal shed. Unfortunately,
      the mannikin is destroyed in a fire, and Arthur must
      find his satisfactions elsewhere. As the neighborhood
      becomes cluttered with the bodies of brutally slain
      young women, student Anthony is a sometimes observer,

a sometimes amateur detective, and a sometimes suspect. In the end it is the fact that he and Arthur have the same last name which brings the real culprit to a bizarre form of justice. The novel has a few on-campus scenes, but most of the plot unfolds at the rooming house. Ruth Rendell is well known as a writer of taut psychological mysteries. A former journalist, she lived with her husband and son outside of London when *A Demon in My View* was published. The book won the British Crime Writers Association Golden Dagger Award for 1976.

585. Aird, Catherine [McIntosh, Kinn Hamilton (1930-).]
    Parting Breath. London: William Collins, 1977; Garden City, New York: Doubleday and Co., 1978.

One of Great Britain's older and more stately institutions of higher learning, the "University of Calleshire" has stood since the early Tudor times as a bastion of calm academic conservatism. However, the dismissal of a left-wing student agitator leads to the school's first sit-in; this is followed quickly by two murders. The first victim is an undergraduate; the second is Peter Pringle, the university's short, fàt librarian. Local Detective-Inspector C.D. Sloan, a Catherine Aird series-character, is the sleuth on the scene. Sloan finds a plethora of likely culprits among Calleshire's students and faculty members. Many of the faculty suspects are properly addled British academics who draw suspicion to themselves by various forms of unusual behavior. Real-life social scientists will be especially intrigued by the portrait of Roger Franklyn Hedden, a Calleshire lecturer in sociology. Hedden becomes a suspect because he stays on campus and works on a book during summer vacation. Detective-Inspector Sloan's attention to Hedden is prompted by a professor of ecology who remarks to the Inspector that "Hedden stayed on through the summer vacation when I did, [and] sociologists don't usually work as hard as scientists."
Kinn Hamilton McIntosh was born in Huddersfield, Great Britain. At the time *Parting Breath* was published, she lived in an East Kent village near Canterbury, where she served as a receptionist for her father, a medical doctor.

586. Dexter, (Norman) Colin (1930-). *The Silent World of Nicholas Quinn*. London: Macmillan, 1977; New York: St. Martin's, 1977.

Nicholas Quinn, a former teacher of English and history
at a grammar school in Yorkshire, joins the staff of the
Foreign Examinations Syndicate, an organization near Oxford which gives O- and A-level examinations to students
from third-world countries. Quinn, who is nearly deaf,
attends a party for visiting Arab oil potentates and is
able to lip-read secret conversations held by the participants at the gathering. Shortly thereafter, Quinn
is found dead of poison in his bachelor apartment. Detective Chief-Inspector Morse, a Colin Dexter series-
character sleuth, is assigned to the case. A man who
likes his beer, Morse spends considerable time in Oxford-area pubs during the course of this exploit, but
he eventually manages to unravel the mystery. Deadly
rivalries within the examining organization, a naughty
motion picture playing at an Oxford theatre, and a beautiful female employee of the Syndicate all prove central to his detection. Several Oxford University dons
appear in the story, both as unpaid members of the Syndicate's governing board and as members of the organization's various examining committees. And the book
offers many descriptive passages about various Oxford
street scenes.

An earlier Colin Dexter novel, *Last Bus to Woodstock*
(572), also appears in this bibliography. *Last Bus to
Woodstock*, Dexter's first mystery, introduced Chief-
Inspector Morse. At the time *Last Bus to Woodstock* was
published, Colin Dexter was a teacher in a British secondary school. By the time *The Silent World of Nicholas
Quinn* appeared, Dexter had become an assistant secretary
for the Oxford Local Examination Board.

587.   DiPego, Gerald Francis (1941-). *With a Vengeance*. New
        York: McGraw-Hill, 1977; London: Macmillan, 1978.

Twenty years after the death of Randal Nye during a
fraternity hazing, Stephen Nye--Randal's father--con-
tinues to seeth with anger. Stephen is a professor of
English at "Iverson Junior College," a school in the
American Midwest. One day Stephen suddenly resigns his
teaching post, withdraws his life savings from the bank,
and sets out to kill the college-age offspring of the
five boys-now-men who robbed him of his own son. Stephen's travels take him to the Universities of Wisconsin
and Missouri, to New York City, and to a variety of
other locales before his vengeful mission ends. There
is some sleuthing in the story--by Detective Dela of the
Chicago police--but the author of this exercise in par-

ental retribution devotes most of his attentions to
Stephen's determined pursuit of his victims.
Gerald Francis DiPego was born in Chicago. He received a B.S. from Northern Illinois University in 1963
and then did graduate work at the University of Missouri.
After a brief career as a newspaper reporter and as a
high school teacher of English, DiPego became a full-
time writer specializing in television dramas. His
works have been produced on all three major American
networks. *With a Vengeance* was his first novel.

588. Fitzgerald, Penelope (1916-). *The Golden Child*. London: Gerald Duckworth, 1977; New York: Charles Scribner's Sons, 1977.

A great London museum puts the ancient treasures of
Garamantia on display. The centerpiece of the collection is the gold-covered, mummified body of a child-
prince. School children and the general public flock
to the exhibition, but little do they know of the dark
happenings behind the scenes. Many members of the museum's staff suspect that the golden child carries a
curse, and their suppositions seem to have validity
when two prominent scientists die in the building as a
result of apparent accidents. Mummy mysteries do not
ordinarily qualify for inclusion in this bibliography,
but *The Golden Child* includes two non-mummified academic
characters who play important roles. One of them, Professor Rochegrosse-Bergson of the Sorbonne, emerges as
a murder suspect. The other, Professor Heinrich Untermensch from Heidelberg, assists Inspector Mace of the
Kings Cross Police Station with the book's sleuthing.
Untermensch is an internationally renowned Garamotolo-
gist and an expert decoder of hieroglyphics. Because
neither he nor Inspector Mace has much patience with
the idea of curses, the two doubting detectives trace
the evil in the museum to its human source.
Penelope Fitzgerald was born in Lincoln, Great Britain. Her father, E.V. Knox, was an editor of *Punch*.
She has written biographies of her father and of the
Victorian Pre-Raphaelite painter Edward Burne-Jones.
The Golden Child was her first novel.

589. Goodrum, Charles A(lvin) (1923-). *Dewey Decimated*.
New York: Crown Publishers, 1977.

The "Werner-Bok Library" is a vast, well-endowed re-
pository of written wisdom in Washington, D.C. Proud

of their world-famous collections, the members of the
Werner-Bok staff are shocked to learn that the library's
copy of the Gutenberg Bible may be a fake. They are
shocked to an even greater degree when Murchison DeVeer,
head of American manuscripts, is found deep in the institution's bowels with his skull bashed in. Betty Crighton
Jones, a young librarian, and Steve Carson, a Ph.D. candidate using the Werner-Bok's facilities for a dissertation on the American frontier, launch an amateur investigation. They are joined by Edward George, recently
retired as head librarian at Yale and a sometimes consultant to the Werner-Bok. In addition to Dr. George and
Steve Carson, a number of other academic characters
cross the pages of this book, most of them as patrons of
the library. Written with humor, with many references
to rare and not-so-rare books, and with copious detail
about the operation of a large, research library, *Dewey
Decimated* is required reading for those who enjoy inventive, highly literate mysteries.

Charles Alvin Goodrum was born in Pittsburg, Kansas.
He attended Princeton and the University of Witchita as
an undergraduate and received an M.A. from Columbia in
1949. He joined the staff of the Library of Congress
in 1949, and at the time *Dewey Decimated* was published
he was director of research. A later Goodrum mystery,
Carnage of the Realm (605), also appears in this bibliography. Also set at the Werner-Bok library, *Carnage of
the Realm* chronicles the further exploits of the Jones-
Carson-George trio of bibliophile-sleuths.

590.   Littlejohn, David (1937-). *The Man Who Killed Mick Jag-
       ger*. Boston: Little, Brown and Co., 1977; London:
       Corgi Books, 1979.

The Man Who Killed Mick Jagger is not a conventional
mystery. It is instead, the biography of a demented,
would-be killer named Ronald Harrington. Ronald is a
Ph.D. candidate in art history at the University of
California at Berkeley. Fat, unable to forge meaning-
ful sexual relationships, and an inveterate creator of
dark, self-torturing fantasies, Ronald finds that his
own inner torments are expressed in the music of The
Rolling Stones. No murders are depicted in the narrative. But at the end of the story, Ronald is perched
knife in hand, on a gantry above the stage of The Oakland Coliseum. The Rolling Stones are below, in concert. And for reasons which are rooted in his perverse
personality, Ronald is about to pounce on Mick Jagger.

Although there is no detection in the book--the only riddles are psychiatric in nature--academic readers may find fascination in a long scene in which Ronald breaks down during the oral examination for his doctorate. And they will understand just how far Ronald's mind has strayed from reality when they learn, midway through the volume, that young Mr. Harrington has chosen to become a professor because he aspires to the large salaries which he believes are paid to college teachers.

David Littlejohn was born in San Francisco. He received a B.A. from Harvard in 1959, an M.A. from Harvard in 1961, and a Ph.D. from that same institution in 1963. He was a professor of journalism and an assistant dean at the University of California at Berkeley when this book was published. Although *The Man Who Killed Mick Jagger* was Littlejohn's first novel, he had previously published many professional works on English, American, and French literature.

591. Litzinger, Boyd (1929-). *Watch It, Dr. Adrian*. New York: G.P. Putnam's Sons, 1977.

Matthew Adrian is a Harvard Ph.D. and an associate professor of English at "Thomas Jefferson University" in Washington, D.C. Hoping to lose himself in work after a divorce, Matthew flies off to Great Britain to spend a summer researching Victorian poets in the Bodleian Library and in the British Museum. Unbeknownst to Matthew, however, American intelligence has selected him to be the courier of microfilmed secret documents. When he arrives in London, he is mugged, given a false invitation to lecture to the Greater London Society for Literary Preservation, and otherwise abused by Russian, Arab, an British secret service operatives. Although Matthew is hardly the first American professor to be harassed by international spies, he does perambulate through more of the high and low spots of Oxford and London than do many of his predecessors. Furthermore, he comes into contact with some very intriguing British characters. Among those whom he meets in his travels are "Barb the Busty," a luscious young lady whose outstanding attributes are suggested by her nickname, and Mrs. Brock-Partington, an elegant, widowed author of Oxbridge mystery novels. Mrs. Brock-Partington, whose works do not appear in this bibliography, is the creator of John Douglas Bruce, an urbane, Oxbridge don who doubles as a professorial series-character sleuth.

Boyd Litzinger was born in Johnstown, Pennsylvania.

He received a B.S. from the University of South Carolina
in 1951, an M.A. from South Carolina in 1952, and a Ph.D.
from the University of Tennessee in 1956. At the time
of *Watch It, Dr. Adrian* was published, Litzinger was a
professor of English at St. Bonaventure University in
Olean, New York. *Watch It, Dr. Adrian* was his first
novel. Litzinger is best known in English literary circles for his many professional works about Robert Browning and other nineteenth-century British poets.

592. Ross, Robert. *A French Finish*. New York: G.P. Putnam's
      Sons, 1977.

What does a Harvard professor-emeritus of art history
do for amusement in his retirement? If he is Lewis
Tewkesbury, one-time winner of the Pulitzer Prize and a
member of the Federal Arts Commission, he concocts an
ingenious scheme to forge priceless antique French furniture. Then he gets a young, unemployed Harvard Ph.D.
and the Ph.D.'s libidinous girlfriend to join him, and
off they go on a romp through the artistic underworlds
and overworlds of Europe and America. *A French Finish*
contains little detection, but readers can certainly
learn a great deal about the bogus furniture business.
Moreover, in the first chapter, they are treated to a
lengthy excerpt from a Harvard commencement address.
Real-life professors will be heartened to learn that
graduation day oratory at Harvard would seem to be as
vacuous as that to which they have become accustomed at
their own institutions.

*593. Williams, David (1926-). *Treasure by Degrees*. London:
       William Collins, 1977; New York: St. Martin's, 1977.

The protagonist of this ultra-inventive exercise in
whimsical academic mystery is Mark Treasure, vice-
chairman of Greenwood, Phipps, and Co., a London merchant bank. Treasure, a David Williams series-character sleuth, represents the bank's interests as Mrs.
Amilia Hatch, a wealthy American widow, prepares to do-
nate her late husband's fortune to a rundown, rural British institution called "University College." But, as
Treasure and Mrs. Hatch discover to their dismay, there
are individuals at the school who do not want the money.
After attempting to discourage the donation by such tactics as bomb scares and the sending of a severed sheep's
head to Amilia's hotel room, one of the anti-Hatch forces takes the ultimate step of slitting the American

widow's throat. With some assistance from Inspector
Treet, an often-befuddled police official, Treasure
does his detection amidst thoroughly zany college students and even zanier University College teachers and
administrators. Moreover, the case is complicated by
the presence of a sinister Arab sheik who wants to provide University College with his own form of fiscal
assistance.

Born in New South Wales, David Williams read history
at Oxford before entering the advertising business.
Treasure by Degrees was his second Mark Treasure novel.
At the same time the book was published, Williams was
chairman of the advertising firm of David Williams and
Ketchum, Ltd.

594. Collins, Randall (1941-). *The Case of the Philosopher's
Ring*. New York: Crown Publishers, 1978; Brighton,
Great Britain: Harvester Press, 1980.

The Case of the Philosopher's Ring is a Sherlock Holmes
pastiche. The time is the summer of 1914. Holmes and
Dr. Watson journey to Trinity College, Cambridge, at the
request of none other than Bertrand Russell, in order to
investigate the bizarre behavior of philosopher Ludwig
Wittgenstein. Then an Indian mathematician is killed,
and Holmes and Watson are propelled into yet another
post-Arthur Conan Doyle adventure. Holmesian experts
will have to judge for themselves whether or not Randall
Collins' effort measures up to the standards set by
Doyle. But readers from the present-day academic world
will be fascinated by the portraits of Russell, Wittgenstein, Lytton Strachey, Virginia Woolf, John Maynard
Keynes, and the many other famous intellectuals who
appear in the story.

Randall Collins received a B.A. from Harvard in 1963,
an M.A. from Stanford in 1964, and a Ph.D. from the University of California at Berkeley in 1969. A prominent
American sociologist, Collins was a professor of sociology at the University of Virginia when *The Case of
the Philosopher's Ring* was published. The novel was
Collins' first work of fiction.

595. Gifford, Thomas Eugene (1937-). *The Glendower Legacy*.
New York: G.P. Putnam's Sons, 1978.

This inventive, if somewhat contrived thriller centers
on Colin Chandler, a forty-five-year-old professor of
history at Harvard. Thought to be in possession of

documents proving that George Washington delivered
Continental defense secrets to the British, even as the
American army starved at Valley Forge, Chandler is
chased through Boston and its environs by agents from
the Boston police, the KGB and the CIA. The interest
in Chandler and in the papers which everyone believes
are in his care is prompted in part by the murder of
Bill Davis, a Harvard undergraduate, and in part by the
desire of Maxim Petrov, the head of KGB, to embarrass
Arden Sanger, his CIA counterpart. Professorial readers
may only be modestly amused at the scene in which Petrov
and Sanger share hot dogs and spy gossip at a White Sox-
Red Sox baseball game in Fenway Park. But they are
likely to find escapist interest in Colin Chandler's
romantic exploits with Polly Bishop, a sexually generous
newswoman employed by a Boston television station. And
they will be positively enthralled by Bertram Prosser,
the aged chairperson of Harvard's history department.
A man of great wealth, Prosser is a staunch defender of
academic freedom who carries both a Dunhill pipe and a
"large" pistol in his professorial pockets.

Thomas Eugene Gifford was born in Dubuque, Iowa. He
received an A.B. from Harvard in 1959. Before becoming
a free-lance writer in 1975, he held a variety of positions with publishing houses and newspapers. From 1960
until 1968 he was a college textbook salesman for Houghton Mifflin. *The Glendower Legacy* was his fourth novel.

596. Hinkle, Vernon. *Music to Murder By*. New York: Tower
      Publications, 1978.

The sleuth in this breezy story is Martin Webb, the
head of one of Harvard's music libraries. In his late
thirties, Martin is short and wiry, a bachelor, and a
(though the fact is not central to the plot of the novel)
member of the Boston chapter of the Irish Republican
Army. Martin is also on friendly terms with Sergeant
Hollman, a Boston police detective. Although the precise history of their relationship is not made clear,
it appears that Martin has helped Hollman on previous
cases, and the sergeant considers him "a superior detective." In any event, the plot of this caper centers on
the apparent murder-suicide of Jerome and Doris Lamphear,
an estranged husband and wife of Martin's acquaintance,
who meet their deaths by gunshot in our hero's small
South Boston apartment. Martin, who discovers the blood-
splattered pair when he returns home one evening, sus-

pects that the outrage may in fact be a double murder
and sallies forth to investigate. Traveling to New York
City, where Jerome served as a scriptwriter for pornographic movies when not penning unpublished novels, Martin encounters a large collection of Gotham's more intellectually deprived citizens. Most prominent in this
multitude is a young lady known as "Chicken Coquette,"
a star of porno films. Chicken also doubles as a strip-
per at wakes and funerals. Librarian Webb resolves the
case in New York, but the book contains several scenes
on and near the Harvard campus. And an ancillary character is one Dr. Sterne, a Harvard professor of medieval
music, for whom Webb sometimes does research. Dr.
Sterne, whose encyclopedic knowledge of obscure composers is rivaled only by Webb's own familiarity with mus-
icological trivia, asks some probing questions about
the murders and, in general, offers proper, professorial
advice.

597. Jeavons, Marshall [Briet, William (1933-) and Kenneth
      G. Elzinga (1941-)]. *Murder at the Margin.* Glen
      Ridge, New Jersey: Thomas Horton and Daughters, 1978.

After calculating all of the costs and benefits, Henry Spearman, a professor of economics at Harvard, takes
his wife Pidge on a vacation to the Virgin Islands. The
Spearmans stay at a resort known as Cinnamon Bay Plantation and not long after their arrival two fellow
guests are murdered. The first to die is Hutson T.
Decker, a retired United States Army general. Decker
is poisoned. The second victim is Curtis Foote, a United States Supreme Court Justice who harbored ambitions
to be president. Foote is dispatched by an axe to the
skull. A local policeman, Inspector Franklin Vincent,
tries to solve the crimes, but he is out of his element.
Henry Spearman, on the other hand, proves to be a
sleuthing wizard. Utilizing economic theory (game ma-
trix theory in particular), Henry breaks both cases, and
Cinnamon Bay Plantation once again becomes a place where
visitors can enjoy crime-free fun in the sun.
   Marshall Jeavons is the joint pseudonym of William
Briet and Kenneth G. Elizinga, two economists at the
University of Virginia. Henry Spearman, the authors'
protagonist, is one of the more boorish sleuths in mystery fiction. He not only uses economic reasoning to
catch murderers; he also provides a ceaseless series of
mini-lectures about the economic motivations of human
behavior. There is a method behind this literary mad-

ness. Although *Murder at the Margin* can be read as a
conventional mystery, it is intended, too, for use in
college economics courses. Spearman's seemingly gratuitous explanations of economic phenomena are, in
reality, relatively painless lessons in "the dismal
science" for beginning undergraduates. Adopted as man-
datory reading in many economics curricula, *Murder at
the Margin* sold more than 50,000 copies in the first
two years after its publication.

*598. Langton, Jane (1922-). *The Memorial Hall Murder*. New
       York: Harper and Row, 1978.

Memorial Hall, the center for performing arts at Harvard, is rocked by a bomb explosion. Missing and pre-
sumed dead after the blast is Hamilton Dow, the rotund
conductor of Harvard's chorus. Homer Kelly, a Jane Langton series-character sleuth, happens to be in Cambridge
as a visiting professor of American literature, and by
the end of the book Homer has learned more than he cares
to know about the perfidious Harvard milieu. *The Memorial Hall Murder* is an extremely descriptive mystery.
It is enlivened by maps and sketches of various Harvard
scenes and contains vivid portraits of many Harvard
faculty members and administrators. Real-life professors will want to pay special attention to the depiction
of President James Cheever, a man whose forceful handling of campus political battles reveals true Ivy
League inventiveness. Overweight professors will also
want to take comfort in the book's overriding message.
Fat, so the author implies, can prove to be a significant component of one's academic survival kit.
    Jane Langton was born in Boston. She received a B.S.
and an M.A. from the University of Michigan and an M.A.
(in 1948) from Radcliffe. Best known as an author of
children's books, Langton has published three adult mystery novels. All of her mysteries have featured Homer
Kelly as detective. A Harvard graduate, a former policeman, and an attorney by profession, Kelly is an expert
on Herman Melville and on Thoreau. *The Memorial Hall
Murder* is the third Kelly novel and the only one in
which he deals with crime in an academic setting.

599.   MacDougall, James K. *Death and the Maiden*. Indiana-
       polis and New York: Bobbs-Merrill, 1978; London:
       Robert Hale, 1979.

The protagonist of this somber novel is David Stuart,

a James K. MacDougall series-character private detective.
David is asked to find the kidnapped, five-year-old
daughter of John Stanley, a member of the English department at an American state university. A wealthy man,
Stanley has acquired his bulging bank account not from
academic work but by marrying a wealthy woman. David's
initial efforts bear only bitter fruit. Thanks to some
apparent bungling on his part, John Stanley and his
daughter are both killed. But David perseveres, and the
singularly duplicitous villain in the story is eventually identified. Several members of the state university community emerge as suspects before the book's final
chapter. Not under suspicion, but certainly a nefarious
character, is Vincent Lightfoot, the university's dean
of undergraduate studies. A man who has made his accom-
modations to the dismal facts of modern academic life,
Dean Lightfoot dislikes John Stanley because the latter
shows no sympathy for students who plagiarize term papers. Such faculty members, in Lightfoot's view, do not
understand the problems faced by today's ill-prepared
students. By attempting to have classroom cheaters expelled, these individuals only succeed in "giving the
university a bad name."

Death and the Maiden is the second book in the David
Stuart series. At the time the novel was published,
James K. MacDougall was an associate professor of Eng-
lish at Ball State in Muncie, Indiana.

600. Roman, Eric (1926-). *A Year as a Lion*. New York: Stein
and Day, 1978.

A Year as a Lion is an international intrigue thriller with a professor as its protagonist. The central
character is Paul Brenner, a forty-three-year-old member of the history department at "Woodbridge University"
in Connecticut. A Jew, a survivor of the Holocaust, and
a man bored both with his academic existence and his
suburban family life, Brenner accepts an offer from
an unidentified intelligence agency to spend a year in
Europe (without wife and kiddies) doing unspecified espionage work. He flies off to Hungary (the nation of
his birth) under the guise of conducting document research in the Hungarian National Archives. Before the
story ends he is back in the United States masquerading
as Zvi Moshe, an East European Jewish poet. Written
with unusual sensitivity for a spy yarn, the book de-
emphasizes derring-do adventure in favor of a stress on
Paul Brenner's various mental puzzlements and awakenings.

There is an abundance of suspense, however, principally
because the author provides neither his characters nor
his readers with a scorecard through which they might
easily identify the nice people in the plot from the
nasty ones. Several scenes at Woodbridge University
are offered during the early portions of the book. Woodbridge is depicted as something less than an academically
excellent institution; thus Professor Brenner cannot
fail to notice Jean Cameron, an unusually attractive
and brainy coed in one of his classes. Jean turns out
to be a woman who specializes in identifying burnt-out
academics who might be willing to undertake exciting spy
missions. Real-life professors who toil in dreary
schools such as Woodridge and who harbor desires for new
and exhilarating experiences might want to be on the
look out for any Jean Camerons in their own lecture halls.

Eric Roman was born in Bekescsaba, Hungary. During
World War II he was an inmate of a Nazi concentration
camp. He became a United States citizen in 1959. Roman
received a B.A. from Hunter College and M.A. and Ph.D.
degrees from New York University. *A Year as a Lion* was
his third novel. At the time the book was published,
Roman was a professor of history and political science
at Western Connecticut State college in Danbury, Connecticut.

601. Sutton, Henry [Slavitt, David Rytman (1935-)]. *The
      Sacrifice*. New York: Grosset and Dunlap, 1978; Lon-
      don: Sphere Books, 1980.

The Sacrifice records the exploits of Roger Braithwaite, a middle-aged, widower professor of classics at
Yale. Roger attempts to discover the truth about a mysterious ancient Greek codex which has been donated to
the university. His interest in the matter arises when
Professor Don Trotter, a faculty colleague, suffers what
appears to be a total mental collapse as he tries to
translate the manuscript. The ingredients of the story
are part detective saga, part thriller, and part tale-
of-the-occult. Roger does considerable traveling during
his adventure, but much of his detection takes place in
and around New Haven. Indeed, there are several scenes
in Yale's Linsley-Chittenden Hall, an aging pile which
anyone who has ever spent time at Yale remembers as an
ideal site for a spooky mystery. The source of nastiness in the goings-on is not academic in nature, but
Roger Braithwaite nonetheless behaves in the finest traditions of the Yale professoriat. He provides several

women with sexual satisfaction. He skips three days of classes in order to fly (at his own expense) to Paris for a meeting with a dealer in rare literary treasures. And when he is captured by the villains and offered a gourmet meal in preparation for his appearance as the centerpiece for the ritual referred to in the title, Roger eats heartily and enjoys every morsel.

David Rytman Slavitt was born in White Plains, New York. He received an A.B. from Yale in 1956 and an M.A. from Columbia University in 1957. A poet and a writer of "serious" fiction under his real name, Slavitt writes highly commercial thrillers under the pseudonym Henry Sutton. *Cold Comfort* (620), a work issued under the name David R. Slavitt, appears later in this bibliography.

602. Banks, Carolyn. *Mr. Right*. New York: The Viking Press, 1979; London: Corgi Books, 1981.

The protagonist of this sexually explicit, psychological mystery is Lida, a thirty-five-year-old woman who teaches English at "Brady State College," Maryland. Although she is single, Lida is far from being a virgin. She attempts to add a novelist named Duvivier to the list of thirty men with whom she already has slept, but Duvivier's deviant in-bed preferences seem about to prevent her from accomplishing her mission. Moreover, the now rich-and-famous novelist was once a professor of theatre at a small college in New Hampshire, and those who remember him there are convinced that he is a homosexual sadist who once murdered a coed. Duvivier's suspicious past is uncovered by Diane, one of Lida's associates, when she travels to the New Hampshire school to give a lecture. The climax of the story comes when Paul Riley and Allan Dilworth, two of Duvivier's former New Hampshire colleagues, arrive in Washington, D.C., to help Diane prevent Lida from becoming the novelist's next victim. At this point, among the exhibits at the Smithsonian Air and Space Museum, the real villain is revealed. The story is cleverly constructed to create suspense. It includes several episodes at Brady State, a predominantly black institution (though all of the major characters are white), and it also offers a graphic, flashbacked description of the events leading to the murder on the New Hampshire campus.

Born in Pittsburgh, Pennsylvania, Carolyn Banks was a a member of the faculty at the University of Maryland when *Mr. Right* was published.

603. Barnard, Robert (1936-). *Posthumous Papers*. London:
      William Collins, 1979. Published in the United States
      as *Death of a Literary Widow*. New York: Charles Scrib-
      ner's Sons, 1979.

      Walter Machin, a British working-class novelist who
      died shortly after World War II, is being rediscovered
      by the arbiters of literary taste in Great Britain and
      America. Dwight Kronweiser, an ambitious assistant pro-
      fessor of English at the "University of East Louisiana,"
      travels to the North-of-England town of "Oswaldson" to
      study Machin's papers. Machin was twice married, and
      both of his ex-spouses live in the same Oswaldson house.
      As Kronweiser's work is concluding, the house burns
      down, and Hilda, Walter's first wife, dies in the con-
      flagration. Greg Hocking, who had befriended both women
      in the Spinner's Arms, a local pub, thinks the fire was
      suspicious and becomes an amateur detective. Greg's
      usual occupation is that of teacher of history at the
      "Oswaldson College of Further Education." With the
      help of Gerald Seymour-Strachey, a retired professor of
      English from the "University of Grimsby," Greg resolves
      matters without police intervention. Kronsweiser, mean-
      time, returns to America with his future as the world's
      leading Machin expert assured. Devilishly clever, and
      often very funny, *Posthumous Papers* is a spoof of clas-
      sic British mysteries, of the Anglo-American literary
      establishment, and of academe. Professor Seymour-Strachey,
      for example, is best remembered for his classic mono-
      graph "The Heterosexual Stain on Modern English Liter-
      ature." And Dwight Kronweiser, who spends much of his
      time in Oswaldston yearning for the back-home delights
      of Colonel Sanders' fried chicken, is the sort of career-
      oriented academic who knows "when to switch from express-
      ing genuine enthusiasm for Black Studies to expressing
      genuine enthusiasm for women's literature."
          Two other mysteries by Robert Barnard, *Death of An
      Old Goat* (559) and *Death in a Cold Climate* (611), also
      appear in this bibliography.

604. Goller, Nicholas. *Tomorrow's Silence*. London: Macmil-
      lan, 1979; New York: St. Martin's, 1980.

      The Gregdales, of "Banley University" in Great Bri-

tain, seem to constitute your average faculty family.
Mother Barbara is a schoolteacher with a fondness for
sailing along canals. Teenaged daughter Kathy likes
cats. And father Walter? Well, Walter is a senior lecturer in mathematics who yearns for a professorship,
worries about domestic finances, and feels obliged to
display "adequate hostility" toward visiting academics.
But if the Gregdales are pleasantly typical, the Banley
community is not. A murderer is on the loose. And not
just any murderer. This one strangles nubile young girls
by putting plastic bags over their heads; he then cuts
off their feet. Pressed for money, the Gregdales take
in a lodger, young Christopher Lodeman, an oh-so-nice
clerk with the local council. Christopher takes a liking to Kathy, and she reciprocates. Will Kathy survive
to the end of the novel? Since she narrates part of
the story, telling about "Mummy and Daddy" and how they
do such nice, average academic things, readers are
prompted to hope so. There is no detection in the book,
but those who like their mysteries grisly and gruesome
will have a jolly time doing their own psychological
sleuthing.

605. Goodrum, Charles A(lvin) (1923-). *Carnage of the Realm*.
    New York: Crown Publishers, 1979. Published in Great
    Britain as *Dead for a Penny*. London: Victor Gollancz,
    1980.

    Carnage of the Realm is the second Charles Goodrum
    mystery to be centered on the "Werner-Bok Library."
    The first work of the series, *Dewey Decimated* (589),
    introduced readers to a trio of amateur sleuths: Betty
    Crighton Jones, a librarian; Steve Carson, a Ph.D. stu-
    dent using the Library for research purposes; and Dr.
    Edward George, just retired as head librarian at Yale
    and now an occasional consultant to the Werner-Bok. As
    Carnage of the Realm begins, Steve's dissertation has
    been rejected, and Dr. Karl Vandermann, a professor of
    history at Georgetown, offers to help him with his re-
    visions. Shortly thereafter Vandermann, a collector of
    rare coins, is found dead in his home, and the Jones-
    Carson-George team of amateur detectives springs into
    action. Using all of the facilities of the Werner-Bok,
    including computerized information systems, the sleuths
    uncover the professor's murderer and, in the process,
    they become experts in priceless Richard III groats.
    They also learn how Vandermann, presumably dependent on
    his professorial salary, managed to live in a lavish
    French-style house in an ultra-expensive Washington sub-
    urb.

606. Holton, Leonard [Wibberley, Leonard (1915-)]. *The Mirror
      of Hell*. New York: Dodd, Mead and Co., 1979.

      Barbara Minardi, the sixteen-year-old daughter of a
      detective-lieutenant in the Los Angeles police force,
      attends summer classes at "Greenfield College." Green-
      field is a Baptist institution deep in the Mohave Desert.
      Barbara's roommate, Susan, is found dead one morning, her
      head bashed in by a baseball bat. Then the school's
      iconoclastic poet-in-residence drowns off Catalina Is-
      land after what appears to be a violent reaction to a
      drug overdose. When Lieutenant Minardi and his priest-
      detective sidekick, Father Breeder, look into the deaths,
      much of their sleuthing takes place on the stark, sun-
      drenched Greenfield campus. Before the two Leonard Hol-
      ton series characters break the case, they must deal with
      a drug ring, with a crooked cop, and with more than a
      few suspicious Greenfield students and faculty members.
        Leonard Wibberley was born in Dublin, Ireland. During
      his early working life he served as an overseas reporter
      for the *London Daily Mirror* and as an editor for news-
      papers in Singapore and Trinidad. Wibberley came to
      the United States in 1943. Although he has many detec-
      tive novels to his credit (all of them published under
      the pseudonym Leonard Holton), Wibberley is perhaps best
      known for his books for juveniles and for his whimsical
      non-mystery adult fiction. Two of Wibberley's non-mys-
      tery adult novels, *The Mouse That Roared* (Boston: Little,
      Brown, 1955. Published in Great Britain as *Wrath of
      Grapes*. London: Robert Hale, 1955.) and *The Mouse on
      the Moon* (New York: William Morrow, 1962; London: Fre-
      derick Muller, 1964) became popular motion pictures.

607. Masterson, Whit [Wade, Robert (1920-)]. *The Slow Gal-
      lows*. New York: Dodd, Mead and Co., 1979; London:
      Robert Hale, 1979.

      On a deserted island off the coast of California, Pro-
      fessor Theodoric Bronson and Penny Pennington, his gra-
      duate student assistant, are spending a week inventorying
      the wildlife. But midway through their stay, Rudy Tirk,
      a convicted murderer, arrives to spoil their scientific
      sojourn. Rudy has hijacked the small police plane
      carrying him to a northern California prison and has
      landed on the island's unused airstrip. Then he takes
      Bronson and Penny hostage. Meanwhile, back on the main-
      land, John Shu is mounting an airborne posse to appre-
      hend the flyaway convict. Shu, an investigator for

the San Diego County Attorney's Office, always gets his
man. He gets Tirk, after considerable trouble, but not
before Bronson and Penny suffer various physical and
emotional indignities. The ending of this story is
downbeat and will depress most professorial readers.
However, the early part of the book, before Tirk in-
flicts himself upon the scene, glows with academic virtue. Though the attractive, twenty-six-old Penny admits to Professor Bronson that she "likes older men,"
the two zealous scientists from the University of California at San Diego spend their days fully engrossed in
research. And at night, while the light from a million
stars illuminates their tropical paradise, Penny and
"Old Doc" Bronson play scrabble and listen to the radio.
   The Man with Two Clocks (565), an earlier Whit Masterson novel by Robert Wade, also appears in this bibliography.

608. Picano, Felice (1944-). *The Lure*. New York: Delacorte
      Press, 1979; London: New English Library, 1981.

      The protagonist of this long (406-page) crime novel is
Noel Cummings, a non-tenured member of the sociology department at New York University. One morning, while
bicycling along the West Side Highway, Noel witnesses the
murder of an undercover policeman. The head of the
undercover unit, a man known as "Fisherman," then asks
Noel to join his team as an unofficial agent. Fisherman hopes that the young sociologist, an attractive man
in fine physical shape, can help snare "Mr. X," a homicidal and homosexual gangland boss. Noel, in turn,
hopes that his decoy work for the police will provide
him with enough data for a monograph about New York's
gay subculture. Noel's plainclothes activities do, in
fact, yield him (and the book's readers) an abundance
of information about homosexual folkways and mores.
They also gain Noel a number of terror-filled nights in
Greenwich Village, some practical experience with the
sado-masochistic scene, and a lasting, romantic relationship with "Eric, the Red," one of the more endearing
of the story's boys in leather. A great number of unsavory characters appear in this very sober saga, but
from the academic viewpoint the worst of the bad lot is
Wilbur Boyle, Noel's department chairperson. Because he
needs best-selling books for a publishing firm with which
he is associated, Boyle threatens Noel with a negative tenure decision unless he produces a saleable manuscript for
his press. And, since Boyle knows that books about homo-
sexuals are hot commercial properties, he encourages

Fisherman to recruit Noel for perilous participation-
observation within the gay milieu.

Felice Picano was born in New York City and received
a B.A. in 1964 from the City University of New York.
Early in his career he served as a caseworker for the
New York City Department of Welfare and as an assistant
manager of several New York City bookstores. Picano became a full-time free-lance writer in 1974. In addition
to *The Lure*, his literary output includes several mainstream novels and books of poetry and many articles in
various small, specialty magazines.

609. Abrahams, Peter. *The Fury of Rachel Monette*. New York:
       Macmillan, 1980.

Rachel and Dan Monette live in Williamstown, Massachusetts. Dan, a junior member of the history department
at Williams College, has just published a treatise on the
shameful treatment of foreign Jews in France during World
War II. The book has attracted international attention
and Rachel, Dan, and the couple's five-year-old son, Adam,
are all basking in the glow of Dan's new fame. But just
as life seems to have reached a state of academic per-
fection, Dan is stabbed dead by an unknown assailant,
and Adam is kidnapped by a bogus rabbi. One of the
tougher and more resourceful faculty wives in fiction,
Rachel sets out in search of Adam, and her quest takes
her to Paris, to Israel, and to the sun-baked Sahara
Desert before she successfully concludes her mission.
Rachel is Jewish (though Dan was not), and in the course
of this action-filled story she learns that Adolph Hitler's disciples are still alive and well in remote cor-
ners of the world.

A Canadian, Peter Abrahams was a CBC radio producer
and a spear-fisherman in the Bahamas before turning his
hand to creative writing. *The Fury of Rachel Monette*
was his first novel.

610. Aswad, Betsy (1939-). *Winds of the Old Days*. New York:
       Dial Press, 1980.

Every Superbowl Sunday a group of Rosalind Chase's
friends and relatives gathers in her home to mourn the
death of her husband, Ben, on Superbowl V Sunday in
1970. Ben, a radical student at "Caliban College" in
Pennsylvania, was gunned down by an unknown assailant
and his frozen body was found in a forest near the Caliban campus. It is now Superbowl XII Sunday, in Janu-

ary of 1978, and though Rosalind is happily remarried
and a member of the Caliban department of English, neither she nor her houseguests can avoid rehashing the
mysterious circumstances which surrounded Ben's death.
As the discussion proceeds, even while the Dallas Cow-
boys are defeating the Denver Broncos by a score of 27-
10, the identity of Ben's killer is revealed. The book
does not contain any classical detection. However, it
does feature a host of suspects, many of whom take part
in the confabulation, and most of whom are faculty members and/or former students at Caliban. Told in part
through flashbacks, the unusually structured story includes graphic descriptions of Rosalind's active sex
life and also offers several classroom scenes.

Betsy Aswad was born in Binghamton, New York. She
attended Hood College and the State University of New
York at Binghamton. *Winds of the Old Days* was her
first novel. At the time the book was published, Aswad
was a member of the English department at the State University of New York at Binghamton.

611. Barnard, Robert (1936-). *Death in a Cold Climate*. London: William Collins, 1980; New York: Charles Scribner's Sons, 1981.

The naked body of a man is found frozen in the snow
outside of the Norwegian university town of Trumsoe.
The man, whose skull has been shattered by a heavy instrument, turns out to be Martin Forsyth, a British crew-
man from an oil exploration ship. The detective who
handles the case is Inspector Fagermo of the Trumsoe
police. During the course of his sleuthing, Fagermo
has cause to view several members of the University of
Trumsoe community as suspects. Among these are Steve
Cooling (an American graduate student in history), Dou-
gal Mackensie (a Scottish professor of geology), Professor Halvard Nicolaisen (of the university's department of language and literature), and Lise Nicolaisen
(Halvard's young, attractive wife). Written with Robert Barnard's customary blend of sardonic wit and
clever plotting, *Death in a Cold Climate* provides an
intensive if often unflattering look at the manners and
morals in a provincial Norwegian academic setting. The
book also offers some telling commentaries about overseas visitors to Norway's shores. American readers may
be especially interested in the brief but trenchant
depiction of Nan Bryson, a bilingual young lady from the

United States who works in the Trumsoe office of the
United States Information Agency. Nan sometimes adds
to her income by translating Norwegian works into English for clients at the university. Her patrons do not
complain about her talents as a translator. However,
they do find that her skills in English spelling and
punctuation are abysmal.

Two other Robert Barnard mysteries, *Death of an Old
Goat* (559) and *Posthumous Papers* (603), appear earlier
in this bibliography. At the time *Death in a Cold Climate* was written, Barnard was a professor of English
literature at the real University of Trumsoe, an institution which lies three degrees north of the Arctic Circle in Norway. In an author's note which precedes the
text of the novel, Barnard claims that while the "geo-
graphical facts" in the book are accurate, the characters in the story are entirely fictitious.

612.   Gloag, Julian (1930-). *Sleeping Dogs Lie*. London:
       Secker and Warburg, 1980; New York: Elsevier-Dutton,
       1980.

       Dr. Hugh Welchman is a British psychiatrist. He lives
       and works in Cambridge, his clients including students
       and faculty members from the university. One day he
       is visited by Alex Brinton, a first-year undergraduate
       at "Carol College." Alex, it seems, has a strange pho-
       bia against using a certain stone staircase in one of
       the college buildings. As Dr. Welchman probes Alex's
       curious malady, he begins to understand that his pa-
       tient's problem involves dark Brinton family secrets.
       Furthermore, as he delves even deeper into the matter,
       he comes to the startling realization that Alex Brin-
       ton's phobia has sinister meanings for the Welchman
       family as well. *Sleeping Dogs Lie* is a slick, well-
       written psychological mystery. It contains several
       scenes at the university, and many of the focal charac-
       ters have university connections. Those who read the
       book may not learn a great deal about the normal rou-
       tines of Cambridge University life. But they certainly
       will become acquainted with some of the malefic mental
       disorders which, if one chooses to take the story lit-
       erally, lurk behind the serene Cambridge University fa-
       cade.

       Julian Gloag was born in London. He received a B.A.
       in 1953 and an M.A. in 1958 from Magdalene College,
       Cambridge. Early in his career Gloag was an editor for
       Hawthorne Books in New York City. Now a resident of

Paris, Gloag has been a full-time creative writer since 1953. *Sleeping Dogs Lie* was his fifth novel.

613. Greenwald, Nancy. *Ladycat*. New York: Crown Publishers, 1980.

More a crime story than a novel of detection, this light and breezy tale centers on the escapades of Antonia Weiner, a graduate student in Russian history at the University of California at Berkeley. Separated from her husband and attempting to support herself and a small daughter without child support, Antonia solves her fiscal woes by burglarizing the homes and apartments of the wealthy. The sleuthing in the book is done by McQuade, a young private investigator. Considering Antonia's slim good looks and her liberated attitudes toward sex, it is little wonder that McQuade's dealings with his quarry eventually go beyond those found in the usual detective-criminal relationships.

At the time *Ladycat* was published, Nancy Greenwald was a Hollywood screen and television writer. Her credits include scripts for the long-running television series "The Waltons."

614. Haddad, C.A. (pseud.). *The Academic Factor*. New York: Harper and Row, 1980.

The protagonist of this semi-satirical thriller is Melissa Abrams, an associate professor of sociology at Ohio State University. While on a trip to present a paper on "The Male Israeli: Wither?," Melissa is plunged into murder and espionage. Then, as the fast-paced story moves into higher gear, she takes part in a series of frenetic, derring-do chases through Israel, Hungary, Bulgaria, and East and West Germany. Despite her enervating exploits, Melissa finds time to have a romantic fling with Shaul, a handsome Israeli secret service agent. Melissa survives her perilous exertions, but not because she shows any real aptitude for world-class spying. Rather, she is so aggressively naive that she inadvertently outfoxes her antagonists. Sociologists are seldom treated with kindness in fiction (see Kramer, "Images of Sociologists and Sociology in Fiction," footnote 3, Introduction), and *The Academic Factor* is not an exception to the rule. Rude and crude (her vocabulary centers around the words "fuck" and "schmuck"), Melissa even offends the consumers of her

own published scholarship. Notorious for her sociological monograph, *The Misfits: The American Jewish Community 1932-1967*, she receives "more hate mail than she
can possibly read." In retaliation, Melissa has recently burst forth with a sequel. This book is called
*Paranoia: The American Jewish Community 1932-1967 Comes
of Age.*

    The Academic Factor was C.A. Haddad's fourth work of
adventure fiction. His or her identity is a closely
guarded publishing secret.

615. Herzog, Arthur (1927-). *Aries Rising*. New York: Rich-
    ard Marek, 1980; London: William Heinemann, 1981.

    Recently separated from his wife, Philip Castle seeks
to lick his marital wounds by vacationing on the Caribbean Island of "St. Jean." Philip, a former United
States Air Force Pilot, is now a professor of psychology
at the University of Chicago. St. Jean, he discovers,
is not the quiet, contemplative place he had hoped it
would be. First of all, there's Marie-Celeste, a voluptuous woman of French and American ancestry, who
offers epicurean sexual delights. Then there are various smugglers, gamblers, and corrupt government officials
all of whom seek to involve Philip in their dangerous
pursuits. And, finally, there is a local fetish on
astrology, a topic for which Philip—an Aries—has little
patience. Written in slick, commercial prose, *Aries
Rising* is an escapist thriller. But lest professorial
readers seek to escape too deeply into its text, the
author has several of his characters offer bits of dialogue which will bring them back to reality. The gist
of these mini-speeches is that all academics—including
Philip—are dull and sexually repressed. Philip first
meets Marie-Celeste, for example, when she is sunbathing
nude on a beach. Noticing that he is staring at her
large, "pointed, firm, [and] ruby-nippled" breasts,
Marie-Celeste immediately accuses Philip of being a professor. The ending of the book may also prove disquieting to real-life faculty members. Having tasted and
survived heady macho adventure, Philip marries Marie-
Celeste, resigns from Chicago to start a small, island-
hopping airline in the Caribbean, and presumably never
enters a classroom again.

    Arthur Herzog was born in New York City. He received
a B.A. from Stanford in 1950 and an M.A. from Columbia
in 1956. Early in his career he served as an editor

for Fawcett Publications in Greenwich, Connecticut.
Since 1957 he has been a full-time free-lance writer
and has published mainstream novels, thrillers, social
satires, and several non-fiction works. Herzog's non-
fiction books have dealt with such diverse subjects as
politics, medicine, and religion.

616. Keech, (John) Scott (1936-). *Ciphered*. New York:
   Harper and Row, 1980.

   This elaborately plotted, on-campus mystery takes
place at "Thorpe University," a state-supported institution somewhere in the eastern part of the United
States. Ernest Feith and his wife are shot dead in
their home. Ernest, a professor of biochemistry and
director of the University Research Center, had many
faculty enemies. He was also a wealthy man, and his
two adult children stand to gain large legacies from
his death. The detective in the case is Inspector Jeff
Adams, a bachelor police officer and a part-time student
at the university. Jeff is ably assisted by Kate Shaw,
a young and beautiful member of the Thorpe history department. Complicating matters is the fact that Kate's
father, Mark Shaw, is a professor of theatre at Thorpe
and is himself a suspect. In addition to providing
Jeff with emotional support, Kate is able to decipher
a set of complex cryptograms found in Ernest Feith's
study. These suggest that espionage may figure, some-
how, in the affair. Kate's deciphering talents stem
from her professional work; she is writing a biography
of Ignatius Donnelly, the author of that "obscure master-
work," *The Great Cryptogram* (Chicago, New York, and London: R.S. Pearle, 1888). Meanwhile, even as Jeff hunts
down Feith's murderer, and as Kate's research on Ignatius Donnelly proceeds, student demonstrators attempt
to disrupt the secret work of the research center.

617. Lear, Peter [Lovesey, Peter (1936-)]. *The Spider Girl*.
   London: Cassell Ltd., 1980; New York: Viking Press,
   1980.

   Sarah Jordon is a graduate student in arachnology
(the study of spiders) at "Henry Hudson University" in
New York City. Thanks to her red-haired good looks,
Sarah is invited to host a television documentary about
her unusual field. She proves so effective on TV that
she is signed by NBC to host a series in which she dons

a sexy spider costume and performs in a giant web. Unbeknownst to NBC's programming executives, however, Sarah has some personality problems. As the book progresses, she begins to identify with spiders (female spiders
in particular), and her web becomes the site of some
murderous activity. There is no serious detection in
the tale, and most of the mysteries are of the psychiatric variety. But there are many scenes at Henry Hudson University, and Jerry Balin, a publicity-seeking
professor in the department of ecology, plays a significant role in the story.

Peter Lovesey is best known to mystery buffs as the
creator of the Sergeant Cribb mysteries. The books in
which Sergeant Cribb does his sleuthing are set in Victorian Great Britain. One of Lovesey's Sergeant Cribb
stories, *Swing, Swing Together* (583), appears earlier in
this bibliography.

618.   Lyall, Gavin Tudor (1932-). *The Secret Servant*. Lon-
       don: Hodder and Stoughton, 1980; New York: The Viking
       Press, 1980.

The Secret Servant is an action-packed espionage thriller with a mystery component. The espionage aspect of
the book concerns the KGB's infiltration of the British
defense establishment. The mystery revolves around the
suicide under suspicious circumstances of a highly
placed British government official. The detective on
the case is Major Harry Maxim of the British Army, but
just as crucial to the story is John Whyte Tylor, an
aging but energetic professor of international politics
at Cambridge. An expert on the political ramifications
of nuclear weaponry, Tylor serves as a Whitehall consultant and has access to Allied defense plans. He is also a womanizer, an egoist, and a man who must live with
a shameful secret from his past. Though the book takes
its readers to a number of far-flung locales, there are
several scenes at Cambridge. Perhaps of most interest
to academics will be the episode in which leftist students accuse cold-warrior Tylor of being a "Fascist
bastard" and then shout him down from his lecture plat-
form.

Gavin Tudor Lyall was born in Birminghall, Great Britain. He was educated at King Edward's School in Birmingham and at Pembroke College, Cambridge. After
military service from 1951 until 1953, during which he
served as a pilot in the RAF, Lyall became a journalist
with the *Picture Post* (London) and *The Sunday Times*.

In 1963 he left the newspaper world to become a free-
lance writer. In addition to *The Secret Servant*, his
literary credits include several other fast-paced thrillers as well as non-fiction books on aviation and military history.

619. Schwartz, Alan. *No Country for Old Men*. New York: New
American Library, 1980.

Can Eric Newman complete his biography of Harry Raven
in time to achieve tenure? Eric is a junior faculty
member at Columbia University, and Raven was a Depres-
sion-era, left-leaning American poet who presumably committed suicide in 1943. It looks as though Eric will
finish before the deadline given him by unctuous Professor Drake, his department chairperson. But, wait!
New documents which Eric unearths suggest that Raven is
still alive and well and living in Chili. And so off to
South America goes our professorial hero, only to find
himself caught up in international intrigue, romance,
and danger. In the end Eric does, indeed, obtain new
and startling information about Raven, but he does not
write the biography because no one would believe it.
Instead, he begins a "factional" account of his own adventures which, by some curious chance, starts with the
same lines as does *No Country for Old Men*. There are
several Columbia scenes in the novel and, in the course
of his research, Eric has the distinction of being the
only academic protagonist of a modern-day thriller to
be mugged near the University of Pennsylvania campus in
Philadephia.

No Country for Old Men was Alan Schwartz's first novel.
At the time the book was published, Schwartz was an as-
sociate professor of English at the City University of
New York.

620. Slavitt, David Rytman (1935-). *Cold Comfort*. New York:
Methuen, 1980.

A study in parental revenge, *Cold Comfort* follows the
machinations of Stanley Miller as he brings his own form
of justice to "Fargate College," a "less-competitive"
institution in the eastern United States. Stanley is
the widowed owner of a dry-cleaning shop. His son,
Howie, dies after guzzling an immense quantity of alcohol during a fraternity initiation. The college authorities hush the affair, and the local police conduct only
a cursory investigation. Knowing that only he can exact

proper retribution, Stanley begins to kill the people who were most directly involved in his boy's death and in its subsequent coverup. The first to die is Roger Chelmsford, the homosexual alumni president of good old Lambda Mu. Then Stanley dispatches selected members of Fargate's administration. By the end of the story Stanley's personal vendetta is over, but Fargate College is just beginning its search for a new dean of students and a new president. Although there is no significant detection in the book, there is tension aplenty as Stanley stalks his targets. And there is an abundance of academic malignity in the story as well. Not only are Dean Robinson and President Garside guilty of protecting the questionable reputation of their mediocre school; but Robinson is shown to have perfected sexual harassment into a high art, and Garside's behavior provides real-life faculty readers with insight into what college presidents really do in their lonely hotel rooms when away on out-of-town speaking trips.

The Sacrifice (601), an earlier novel by David Slavitt (published under the pseudonym Henry Sutton), also appears in this bibliography.

621. Cline, C. Terry, Jr. (1935-). *Missing Persons*. New York: Arbor House, 1981.

The protagonist of this slick commercial novel is Joanne Fleming, a thirty-six-year-old professor of criminology at Florida State University. Joanne moonlights as a paid consultant to local police forces, and as part of her extracurricular work she finds herself involved in the hunt for a psychopathic killer who abducts attractive young girls (some of them college coeds) and then beats them dead with a tire iron. Joanne's own teenaged daughter, Marcie, is stalked and then kidnapped by the killer. The result, at the book's conclusion, is a fevered attempt by Joanne and her police cronies to come to Marcie's rescue. The story incorporates several scenes on the Florida State campus, and Dr. Thaddeus Kreijewski, the head of the university's criminology department, appears in an interesting cameo role. Poor Dr. Kreijewski is worried that all of the negative publicity which Joanne is bringing to his department will make it difficult for him to build a top-flight criminology program at Florida State. As for Joanne, recently divorced from an unfeeling attorney named Ralph, Marcie's peril only adds to her already well-stocked bag of woes. Her self-esteem battered by Ralph, and with Dr. Kreijewski making her professional life something less than a bed of roses, Joanne is having

a difficult time maintaining a satisfactory sex life
with Ken Blackburn, her policeman boyfriend. Fortunately,
Joanne can find consolation in the fact that her second
book, *The Modality of Sex Crime*, (published by Tulane
University Press) already has sold 100,000 copies.

C. Terry Cline, Jr., was born in Birmingham, Alabama.
He attended Florida State University. A full-time pro-
fessional writer, Cline is best known for *Damon* (New
York: G.P. Putnam's Sons, 1975; London: Weidenfeld and
Nicholson, 1975), a chilling epic which features a sex-
crazed, four-year-old-boy in its leading role.

622. Danielle, Maria, *Fieldwork*. New York: Avon Books, 1981.

Fieldwork begins in the African nation of "Gobir,"
where Laurie Spencer is finishing a Ford Foundation-
sponsored study of native village women. A thirty-year-
old, beautiful anthropologist from the University of
Washington, Laurie is supplementing her research by serving as the mistress of Moussa Koulibaly, Gobir's president. But even the most enjoyable anthropological en-
terprises must end. Rebels suddenly seize control of
Gobir; President Koulibaly is imprisoned; and Laurie
is unceremoniously placed on the first airplane out of
the country. Unknown to the insurgents, however, Laurie carries with her a top-secret geological report
showing the location of rich Gobir uranium formations.
Various governments and multinational mining conglomer-
ates want the report, and even as Laurie tries to resume
her teaching chores at Washington, a small army of
agents in search of the document arrives in Seattle.
Some of the operatives murder a coed whom they mistake
for Laurie, and others kill Paul Chirot, a faculty colleague in whom Laurie has confided. Eventually, our
harassed heroine takes an unpaid leave of absence from
the university and returns to Gobir with a planeload of
well-armed mercenaries in an attempt to rescue President
Koulibaly. A fast-moving and sexually explicit thriller,
Fieldwork offers at least one insight into the dedication which some anthropologists bring to their professional endeavors. Always on the lookout for interesting
cultural data, Laurie begs President Koulibaly at the
beginning of the story to demonstrate "some of those
exotic African sexual positions." Reluctant to take
time from his important paperwork, the president obliges
only when Laurie seductively strips off her clothes in
his combination office-bedroom and when she tells him
that she wants to further African-American understanding

by incorporating materials about Gobir sexual practices
into her lectures.

623. Harrington, Alan (1919-). *The White Rainbow*. Boston:
      Little, Brown and Co., 1981.

      Todd Deming is a handsome, blonde, thirty-five-year-
      old, anthropologist at Harvard. Always on the lookout
      for new research material, Todd journeys to the hill
      country of Mexico to study a group of modern-day Aztec
      fundamentalists. Caught up in the Aztec's mind-numbing
      rituals and helped along by some drug-induced hallucin-
      ations, Todd finds himself becoming a member of the
      cult. But when he is commanded to cleanse his soul
      through a final act of lust with the fundamentalists'
      resident harlot (a woman who holds the dubious honor
      of being known as the "Goddess of Filth"), Todd reali-
      zes that he is being groomed as the principal figure in
      one of the sect's less pleasant customs—human sacri-
      fice. Meantime, back in Cambridge, Karen Deming, Todd's
      alcoholic wife, wants her husband to return to home and
      hearth. So, after failing in many attempts to have the
      United States Government extricate Todd from his new
      friends, Karen organizes a helicopter rescue effort.
      Much of the long (377-page) quasi-thriller takes place
      in Mexico, but there are several scenes on the Harvard
      campus. Deming, whose nickname among his faculty col-
      leagues is "Mr. Clairol," is portrayed as unpopular
      among his colleagues but a hero in his classrooms. Dur-
      ing his lectures students laugh uproariously at his
      jokes, applaud loudly when he criticizes the theories of
      other anthropologists, and cheer him with all the energy
      they can muster as he concludes each day's performance.
      Alan Harrington was born in Newton, Massachusetts.
      He received a B.A. from Harvard in 1939. A full-time
      writer, Harrington is a frequent contributor to popular
      American magazines. *The White Rainbow* was his fourth
      novel.

624. Law, Janice [Trecker, Janice Law (1941-)]. *Death Under
      Par*. Boston: Houghton Mifflin, 1981.

      This well-staged mystery is set in St. Andrews, Scot-
      land. Anna Peters, a Janet Law series-character detec-
      tive, and her new husband, Harry, visit the venerable
      old town on a combination honeymoon-business trip.
      Harry, a commercial artist, has been commissioned by
      Sports Illustrated to illustrate scenes from the Bri-

tish Golf Open which is being held on the St. Andrews
links. Anna, too, finds work during the sojourn. An
up-and-coming American golfer, Peter Bryce, receives
threatening notes, and the officials of the Open ask
Anna to investigate. Although the storyline of *Death
Under Par* centers on the more deadly aspects of golf, an
important character in the plot is Melvin Thornton, a
Duke University professor of linguistics. At St. Andrews University on a "Gruen Foundation" fellowship,
Professor Thornton is able to identify Anna's birth-
place--Hartford, Connecticut--merely by hearing her
say a few words. And on pleasant afternoons Thornton
wanders the streets of St. Andrews in buff-colored
leggings and a full-length black cape, masquerading as
"Wulf," a man from the fourteenth century. Some professorial readers may not appreciate the professor's
fate at the book's conclusion. But all academic grants-
people will want to take notes on the funded research
project in which Thornton and Wulf, his "alternate per-
sona," are engaged.

Janice Law Trecker was born in Sharon, Connecticut.
She received a B.A. from the University of Connecticut
in 1962 and an M.A. from the same institution in 1967.
Anna Peters, her series-character sleuth, is a Washing-
ton, D.C., private detective. *Death Under Par* was Anna
Peters' fifth novel-length adventure.

625. Lewin, Michael Z. (1943-). *Missing Woman*. New York:
Alfred A. Knopf, 1981.

Albert Samson, a cynical, down-on-his-luck Indianapolis private detective, is hired by a lady identifying herself as Elizabeth Staedtler, a Ph.D. in sociology. Elizabeth wants Albert to find Priscilla Pynne,
an old friend and classmate from her undergraduate days
at the University of Bridgeport. Before Albert finishes
the job, he encounters a murder and learns that a bogus
Ph.D. in sociology can provide a perfect cover for nefarious activities. Albert's search for Priscilla Pynne
takes him to Indiana University, to the Indiana Univer-
sity-Purdue campus in Indianapolis, and to Ball State
University in Muncie, Indiana. Except for the enigmatic
Dr. Staedtler, he meets no faculty members in the course
of his labors, but he does encounter a gun-toting dean
at Ball State. And at Indiana-Purdue he is treated
to a meeting with the dour, harassed secretary of the
sociology department.

Michael Z. Lewin was born in Springfield, Massachusetts, and received an undergraduate degree from Harvard

in 1964. A one-time New York City high-school teacher,
Lewin now lives in Great Britain. Albert Samson is a
Lewin series-character sleuth. *Missing Woman* was Lew-
in's seventh Albert Samson novel.

626. Mettler, George. *Down Home*. New York: Fawcett Gold
     Medal Books, 1981.

     The protagonist of this violence-and-sex-filled paper-
back is thirty-seven-year-old John Winters, an attorney
and an up-and-coming member of the criminology department at "Adelphi University" in "Adelphi" Georgia. When.
a black man murders a white family in its home, John
accepts an invitation from Georgia's governor to act as
special prosecutor in the case. John, who harbors ambitions to succeed Oliver Wendell Reed, the aging president of Adelphi, hopes that his job as special prosecutor will add yet another dimension to his image as a
promising young man. But the affair turns out to have
potential pitfalls. One member of the murdered family
was a prostitute, and her diary (which John uncovers
during his investigation) lists a great many Adelphi
personages along with their favorite perversions. As
John is trying to decide what to do with this fascinating material, the corrupt local sheriff arranges for
our hero to be photographed in a compromising sex scene
of his own, and the pictures are employed as encourage-
ment for John's continued silence. Is a college presidency worth such travails? Readers will have to make
their own ways to the end of the book to answer this
question. The story contains several scenes on the
Adelphi campus, and the cast of characters includes
Cecil Witcomb, the university's dean. Cecil is that
rarest of all fictional characters, a dean who realizes
that his administrative talents are limited. Cecil
wants only to be promoted to provost of the university,
and it is he who is John's principal sponsor for Adelphi's presidency.
     George Mettler was born in Tampa, Florida. He holds
a B.A. in journalism and a law degree. A former FBI
agent and college professor, Mettler now practices law
in Tampa.

627. Michaels, Barbara [Mertz, Barbara Gross (1927-)]. *Some-
     one in the House*. New York: Dodd, Mead and Co., 1981.

     The protagonist-narrator of this gothic suspense novel
is Annie, a nubile, red-haired instructor of English at

a liberal arts college in the eastern United States.
One of Annie's faculty colleagues is a wealthy bachelor
named Kevin Blacklock, and when Annie and Kevin decide
to co-author an English literature textbook, they repair for the summer to Kevin's ancestral home, an ancient English castle which has been re-erected, stone by
stone, in deepest Pennsylvania. Unfortunately for
aspiring textbook writers, there is little useful information in the story about how one might actually go
about creating best-selling classroom reading matter.
The emphasis, instead, is on squeaking doors, budding
romance, thunderstorms, and sinister secrets embedded
in the castle's crypt. But perceptive readers can
nevertheless gain some valuable "insight" into the psychology of lovely, bachelorette members of English de-
partments. Annie worries desperately about her professorial reputation, and even though she likes Agatha
Christie mysteries, she reads them only on the sly. And
in moments of stark terror, when danger seems to be her
only faithful companion, Annie composes herself by silently reciting all of *The Wasteland* and the entire
second act of *Hamlet*.

Barbara Gross Mertz is a prolific writer of romantic
mysteries. She employs the pseudonyms Barbara Michaels
and Elizabeth Peters. Under the Elizabeth Peters alias
she created professorial series-sleuth *Vicky Bliss* (303-
304) and wrote two novels, *The Seventh Sinner* (551) and
The Murders of Richard III (567), starring college-
librarian Jacqueline Kirby.

628. Murphy, Brian (1939-). *The Enigma Variations*. New
York: Charles Scribner's Sons, 1981.

Dora Pennington accuses Troyte Griffith of raping her.
Dora and Troyte are students at a midwestern American
university, and in the finest traditions of academe,
Dean Richard Arnold creates a special committee to investigate Dora's charges. The committee's chairperson
is Eliot Upton, a fifty-year-old professor of music.
Eliot does not need this time-consuming extracurricular
assignment. His book on composer Sir William Elgar is
far behind schedule. His marriage is falling apart.
And he has fallen in love with two women, one of them
a cool, beautiful publishing executive and the other a
marijuana-smoking, sexually rapacious member of the university's advisement staff. Then, just to add another
complication to Eliot's world, Troyte Griffith is shot
dead one dark night, and Captain Sinclair and Detective
Sergeant Baker of the local police arrest Dora for mur-

der. Eliot believes Dora to be innocent, and in between
torrid sex scenes with his several consorts, he tries
to identify Troyte's actual killer. Laced with musical
allusions and crowded with references to religious issues
(Eliot is a convert to Roman Catholicism), *The Enigma
Variations* is less an orthodox mystery than an exploration of Eliot Upton's frenzied efforts to cope with
the crescendo of crises in his personal life. The
book contains many scenes on the university campus, and
early in the story readers are treated to a lengthy vignette in which Eliot's investigatory panel attempts to
establish precisely how and why Dora Pennington lost her
virginity.

Brian Murphy received a Ph.D. from the University of
Detroit, an M.A. from Harvard, and a Ph.D. from the
University of London. *The Enigma Variations* was his
first novel. At the time the book was published, Murphy was a member of the department of English at Oakland University in Michigan.

629. Ogilvie, Elizabeth (May) (1917-). *The Silent Ones*.
      New York: McGraw-Hill, 1981.

Thirtyish, attractive, and single, Alison Barbour
leads a double literary life. As a member of the faculty at a small college in the New England town of "Hazle-
hurst," she writes erudite books about folklore. But
once a year she also produces (under the closely guarded pseudonym Marianna Grange) a "sexy thriller." Her
non-academic works have given Alison a bulging bank
account, and one summer she decides to spend some of
her royalties on the Isle of Lewis, a fog-bound bit of
land in the Outer Herbrides off the coast of Scotland.
Traveling first-class across the Atlantic on the Queen
Elizabeth 2, Alison leaves the penurious world of Hazle-
hurst far behind. Among her well-heeled shipmates she
meets a gaggle of suspicious characters, some of whom
turn up later in the story to cause her grief at her
island destination. At the center of Alison's troubles
is a long-lost and valuable seventeenth-century Celtic
manuscript which several treacherous book dealers are
trying to acquire. In the mode of most heroines of
gothic suspense sagas, the affluent Alison survives
her dangerous geneological sleuthing on Lewis, and by
the end of the book it appears as though she will become one of the island's small cadre of permanent residents. During the course of her adventure, she meets
and falls in love with a strong, well-educated, and

wealthy local squire named Ewen Chisholm. Ewen's source of income is something of a mystery to his fellow islanders, but as he and Alison discuss their future, the American academic learns that her husband-to-be conducts some clandestine literary endeavors of his own.

Elizabeth May Oglivie was born in Boston. A resident of Maine, she is a prolific writer of romantic mysteries and suspense stories, many of which have island or seacoast settings.

*630. Shaw, Howard. *Death of a Don*. London: Hodder and Stoughton, 1981; New York: Charles Scribner's Sons, 1981.

Death of a Don is a throwback to the droll Oxbridge mysteries of the 1930s, 1940s and 1950s. Set at Oxford's "Beaufort College," the book centers on the murders of two Beaufort fellows, David Ashe and Norman Duncan-Smith. Ashe, a young, leftist activist, had many enemies in the college. Duncan-Smith, a retired professor of music, was thoroughly innocuous, and no one can imagine who might possibly have wanted to kill him. The case is investigated by Chief Detective Barnaby, a tall, gaunt gentleman, who learns that the motives behind Oxford crimes need not be immediately comprehensible to the non-academic mind. While real-life professors from all disciplines will find *Death of a Don* rewarding reading, sociologists will want to make a close examination of the text for several items of special interest. The terrible David Ashe was a mathematician, but his colleagues feel that his anti-establishment (and anti-social) behavior was more in keeping with that of sociologists. At several junctures in the narrative, sociology is held up to ridicule, and Beaufort College (which also refuses to allow women to "live in") is determined never to create a sociological fellowship. After all, as one of the Beaufort dons puts it over coffee in the common room: "You've only got to count the sewers in Liverpool and you're on the way to a degree [in sociology], probably a doctorate."

Howard Shaw is a British schoolmaster. At the time *Death of a Don* appeared, he was teaching at Harrow. *Death of a Don* was his second mystery novel.

631. Stone, Robert (1937-). *A Flag for Sunrise*. New York: Alfred A. Knopf, 1981; London: Secker and Warburg, 1981.

A *Flag for Sunrise* is an international-intrigue thriller with a professor as its protagonist, and the plot of the story is not unlike the plots of many other professorial-thrillers which appear in this bibliography. Frank Holliwell, a chain-smoking, fortyish anthropologist at a university in Maryland, is a former CIA agent. On his way to deliver a lecture in the Central American nation of "Compostela," Frank is asked by an old CIA crony to look into the suspicious activities of an American priest and nun in the neighboring country of "Tecan." Reluctant at first to resume his work for the CIA, Frank nevertheless goes to Tecan, and there he encounters heinous local officials, incipient revolution, romance, and danger. But if the basic storyline of A *Flag for Sunrise* is not unique, the caliber of writing raises the book far above the usual professor-caught-up-in-espionage saga. Reminiscent of the brooding adventure tales of Joseph Conrad and Graham Greene, A *Flag for Sunrise* incorporates a host of multi-dimensional characters, most of whom are living in private worlds of inner pain. Furthermore, while there is considerable conventional suspense built into the narrative, the author also raises searching questions about the ultimate meanings of the central characters' lives. Devotees of pure blood-guts-and-sex epics may find that A *Flag for Sunrise* carries too much philosophical baggage. But every professorial reader will appreciate the scene in which Frank Holliwell delivers his lecture at Compostela's "Autonomous University." Frank has laboriously written his address in Spanish, but minutes before he is to talk his hosts ask him to speak in English. Well-fortified with alcohol in preparation for his appearance, Frank labors to effect an off-the-cuff translation of his script, fails miserably, and reels off the podium in disgrace.

Robert Stone was born in Brooklyn, New York. A well-respected novelist and filmwriter, Stone won the 1968 William Faulkner Foundation prize for his first novel, *Hall of Mirrors* (Boston: Houghton Mifflin, 1967; London: Bodley Head, 1968). A subsequent Stone novel, *Dog Soldiers* (Boston: Houghton Mifflin, 1975), won the 1975 National Book Award of the American Association of Publishers.

632. Valin, Jonathan (1948-). *Dead Letter*. New York: Dodd, Mead and Co., 1981.

Daryl Lovingwell, a sour, middle-aged professor of

physics at the University of Cincinnati, has a problem.
A top-secret nuclear power document has been stolen from
a safe in his home, and Lovingwell suspects that Sarah,
his Marxist-radical daughter, is the culprit. Lovingwell hires Harry Stoner, a series-character private eye,
to investigate, but shortly thereafter the professor is
murdered. Not a man to walk away from a case, even
when his employer is dead, Harry continues his sleuthing.
Some of Harry's detective work takes place on the University of Cincinnati campus, and in one especially
effective scene a departmental secretary tells him at
length about the frustrations associated with her job.
The woman also utters a pithy statement which will
simply be repeated in this annotation, without any editorial opinion. Lovingwell was once head of the Cincinnati physics department, and the secretary says:
"I haven't met a department chairman yet who wasn't a
secret fascist." In any event, Stoner resolves matters
by the end of the book, but not before several more
killings take place, and not before some long-hidden
jealousies among the physicists at Cincinnati come to
the surface.

Jonathan Valin was born in Cincinnati. He received
an M.A. from the University of Chicago in 1974. From
1974 until 1976 Valin was a lecturer in English at
the University of Cincinnati. *Dead Letter* was his third
Harry Stoner novel.

APPENDIX
Outstanding College Mystery Novels

Novels with Professorial Series-Character Sleuths

Murder in the Zoo (1932), 164
Harvard Has a Homicide (1936), 173
Don't Look Behind You! (1944), 234
The Cambridge Murders (1945), 237
Enrollment Cancelled (1952), 244
Death in the Quadrangle (1956), 259
Poetic Justice (1967), 281
Death in a Tenured Position (1981), 284
Death's Bright Dart (1967), 287
Captive Audience (1975), 306
Death Is Academic (1976), 312
By Frequent Anguish (1982), 323

Free-Standing College Mysteries

The Oxford Murders (1929), 343
The Dartmouth Murders (1931), 348
By the Watchman's Clock (1932), 356
Murder at the College (1932), 359
An Oxford Tragedy (1933), 360
The Mummy Case (1933), 361
Death and the Professors (1933), 363
Murder in the Stacks (1934), 365
Gaudy Night (1935), 372
Death at the President's Lodging (1936), 374
Candidate for Murder (1936), 375
The Case of the Seven of Calvary (1937), 377
Off with Her Head! (1938), 385
The Widening Stain (1942), 399

INDEX OF PROFESSORIAL
SERIES-CHARACTER SLEUTHS

Abrahams, Peter, 609
Aird, Catherine (pseud.),
  585
Alexander, Colin James, 516
Alington, Adrian Richard,
  388
Allen, (Charles) Grant
  (Blairfindie), 326
Allingham, Margery, 514
Ambler, Eric, 216-217
Angus, Douglas Ross, 485
Anthony, David (pseud.), 520
Archer, Jeffrey Howard, 578
Armstrong, Charlotte, 218-
  220, 446, 453, 486
Ashe, Gordon (pseud.), 538
Ashe, Rosalind, 579
Ashford, Jeffrey (pseud.),
  547
Asimov, Isaac, 465
Aswad, Betsy, 610

Banks, Carolyn, 602
Barnard, Robert, 559, 603,
  611
Bawden, Nina (pseud.), 448
Belloc, (Joseph) Hilaire,
  333
Berkeley, Anthony (pseud.),
  364
Bernard, Robert (pseud.),
  507, 533
Bishop, Morris Gilbert, 399
Blackstock, Charity (pseud.),
  521
Blair, Walter, 375
Blake, Nicholas (pseud.), 502

Bonnamy, Francis (pseud.),
  156-163
Bonnett, Emery (pseud.), 255-
  257
Bonnett, John (pseud.), 255-
  257
Bortner, Norman Stanley, 178-
  179
Boucher, Anthony (pseud.),
  377
Boyd, Marion (pseud.), 365
Brandt, Jane Lewis, 400, 406,
  437
Brebner, Percy James, 33-34
Briet, William, 597
Bristow, Gwen, 350, 351
Bronson, F(rancis) W(oolsey),
  425.
Broome, Adam (pseud.), 343
Brown, Frederic, 449
Brown, Zenith Jones, 356, 366
Butler, Gwendoline (Williams),
  477, 537

Cadell, (Violet) Elizabeth,
  503
Campbell, Mary Elizabeth, 404
Campbell, R.T. (pseud.), 245-
  251
Candy, Edward (pseud.), 539
Carey, Elizabeth, 407
Carr, John Dickson, 430, 466
Cassill, R(onald) V(erlin),
  447
Chapman, Raymond, 274-278
Chesbro, George C(lark), 314-
  316